T0337386

Social Security
in the
Global Village

International Social Security Series

In cooperation with the
International Social Security Association (ISSA)
Neil Gilbert, Series Editor

1. *Targeting Social Benefits:*
International Perspectives and Trends
Neil Gilbert, editor

2. *Social Security at the Dawn of the*
21st Century: Topical Issues and New Approaches
Dalmer D. Hoskins, Donate Dobbernack, and
Christiane Kuptsch, editors

3. *Activating the Unemployed: A Comparative*
Appraisal of Work-Oriented Policies
Neil Gilbert and Rebecca A. Van Voorhis, editors

4. *Recent Health Policy Innovations*
in Social Security
Aviva Ron and Xenia Scheil-Adlung, editors

5. *Who Returns to Work and Why: A Six-Country*
Study on Work Incapacity and Reintegration
Frank S. Bloch and Rienk Prins, editors

6. *Building Social Security:*
The Challenge of Privatization
Xenia Scheil-Adlung, editor

7. *Employability: From Theory to Practice*
Patricia Weinert, Michèle Baukens, Patrick Bollérot,
Marina Pineschi-Gapènne, and Ulrich Walwei, editors

8. *Social Security in the Global Village*
Roland Sigg and Christina Behrendt, editors

Roland Sigg
Christina Behrendt
editors

Social Security
in the
Global Village

International Social Security Series
Volume 8

Transaction Publishers
New Brunswick (U.S.A.) and London (U.K.)

Copyright © 2002 by Transaction Publishers, New Brunswick, New Jersey.

The International Social Security Association (ISSA) was founded in 1927. It is a nonprofit international organization bringing together institutions and administrative bodies from countries all over the world dealing with all forms of compulsory social protection. The objective of the ISSA is to cooperate at the international level, in the promotion and development of social security throughout the world, primarily by improving techniques and administration in order to advance people's social and economic conditions on the basis of social justice.

The responsibility for opinions expressed in signed articles, studies, and other contributions rests solely with their authors, and publication does not constitute an endorsement by the International Social Security Association of the opinions expressed by them.

All rights reserved under International and Pan-American Copyright Conventions. No part of this book may be reproduced or transmitted in any form or by any means, electronic or mechanical, including photocopy, recording, or any information storage and retrieval system, without prior permission in writing from the publisher. All inquiries should be addressed to Transaction Publishers, Rutgers—The State University, 35 Berrue Circle, Piscataway, New Jersey 08854-8042.

This book is printed on acid-free paper that meets the American National Standard for Permanence of Paper for Printed Library Materials.

Library of Congress Catalog Number: 2002017991
ISBN: 0-7658-0930-3
Printed in the United States of America

Library of Congress Cataloging-in-Publication Data

Social security in the global village / Roland Sigg and Christina Behrendt, editors.
    p. cm.—(International social security series ; v. 8)
  Includes bibliographical references and index.
  ISBN 0-7658-0930-3 (pbk. : alk. paper)
    1. Social security. 2. Globalization. I. Sigg, Roland. II. Behrendt, Christina. III. Series.

HD7091 .S6185 2002
362—dc21   2002017991

Contents

List of Tables   vii

List of Figures   xi

List of Boxes   xiii

List of Abbreviations   xv

Introduction
1. Social Security in the Global Village: Mapping the Issues   1
    Roland Sigg and Christina Behrendt

Part 1 Globalization and the Challenges for Social Security
2. Globalization and the Challenge for Social Security   17
    Bob Deacon
3. The Financing of Social Protection in the Context   31
    of Economic Globalization
    Alain Euzéby
4. Globalization and National Welfare Regimes: 47
    The East Asian Case
    Ian Gough
5. Southern European Welfare States Facing Globalization: 67
    Is There Social Dumping?
    Ana M. Guillén and Santiago Álvarez

Part 2 Global Pressures and Internal Adjustments
6. Globalization and the Welfare State: Constraints,   85
    Challenges, and Vulnerabilities
    Fritz W. Scharpf
7. The Impacts and Non-Impacts of Globalization on   117
    Social Policy: Social Insurance Quality, Institutions,
    Trade Exposure, and Deregulation in 18 OECD
    Countries, 1960-1995
    Eero Carroll

8. Globalization and Social Adjustment: The Case of the   141
    Small Developed Countries. A Comparative View of
    New Zealand, Sweden, and Switzerland
    François-Xavier Merrien
9. Income Distribution and Social Security in an   163
    OECD Perspective
    Koen Caminada and Kees P. Goudswaard

Part 3 Migration
10. Non-Discrimination, Free Movement, and Social   191
    Citizenship in Europe: Contrasting Provisions for
    EU Nationals and Asylum-Seekers
    Deborah Mabbett and Helen Bolderson
11. Migration and Social Security: Parochialism in the   211
    Global Village
    Simon Roberts

Part 4 Labor Markets and Social Security
12. Changing Rights and Obligations in Unemployment   227
    Insurance
    Jon Kvist
13. Combating Unemployment: What Can Be Learned   247
    from Whom?
    Karl Hinrichs
14. Is There a Trade-off between Employment and Social   273
    Protection in Europe's Economic and Monetary Union?
    Nadine Richez-Battesti and Audrey Koulinsky
15. Family Policy, Work Incentives, and the Employment of Mothers 297
    Katja Forssén and Mia Hakovirta

Part 5 Social Cohesion
16. The Welfare Pentagon and the Social Management of Risks   313
    Chris de Neubourg
17. Holes in the Safety Net? Social Security and the Alleviation 333
    of Poverty in a Comparative Perspective
    Christina Behrendt
18. Back to Basics: Safeguarding an Adequate Minimum   359
    Income in the Active Welfare State
    Bea Cantillon and Karel Van den Bosch

List of Contributors   377

Index   381

List of Tables

Table 2.1   The Complex Impact of Aspects of Globalization
            upon European Welfare States   19
Table 4.1   External and Internal Pressures Affecting
            Welfare Systems   49
Table 4.2   Components of the Extended Welfare Mix   52
Table 4.3   Welfare Regimes in East Asia: Summary Indicators   53
Table 4.4   The Social Impacts of the Crisis in East Asia   59
Table 5.1   Evolution of Expenditure on Social Protection (as a
            Percentage of GDP), 1970-1997   71
Table 5.2   Evolution of Per Capita Social Expenditure,
            1980 and 1997   71
Table 5.3   Tax Receipts as a Percentage of GDP, 1965-1997   73
Table 5.4   Specific Tax Receipts as a Percentage of Total   73
            Tax Receipts, 1985, 1990, 1994
Table 5.5   Social Protection and Competitiveness, 1997   74
Table 6.1   Taxes and Social Security Contributions as a
            Percentage of GDP, 1970-1997   105
Table 6.2   Taxes and Social Security Contributions as a
            Percentage of GDP, 1997   105
Table 6.3   Total and Sectoral Employment as a Percentage
            of the Population 15–64   106
Table 6.4   Selected Indicators of Welfare State Performance,
            1995-96   107
Table 7.1   Levels of Trade Exposure, Finance Market
            Regulation and Finance Market Openness in
            18 OECD Countries in the 1960s and the Mid-1990s   121
Table 7.2   Regulation and Social Transfer Expenditure as a
            Percentage of the GDP for 17 OECD Countries in
            the 1960s and the Mid-1990s (above and below
            contemporaneous averages)   125
Table 7.3   Country-specific Factors, Finance Market Regulation,
            and Insurance Institutions as Explanations of
            Unemployment Insurance Coverage, 1965-95
            (LSDV estimations, year dummies included in
            all analyses)   131
Table 7.4   Country-specific Factors, Finance Market Regulation,
            and Insurance Institutions as Explanations of
            Unemployment Insurance Replacement Rates,
            1965-95 (LSDV estimations, year dummies
            included in all analyses)   132

Table 8.1   Basic Information on Sweden, New Zealand, and
Switzerland, and Comparison with France, the
United Kingdom, and the United States   156

Table 9.1   Summary Measures of the Income Distribution   166

Table 9.2   Changes in Market and Disposable Income Inequality
during the 1980s   167

Table 9.3   Social Security Transfers as a Percentage of GDP   172

Table 9.4   Key Figures on Social Security in the Netherlands   177

Table 9.5   Decomposition of Inequality in Household Income:
Mean Log Deviation   181

Table 9.6   Comparative Database: Availability Data around 1979
and 1994   183

Table 9.7   Trends in Disposable Income Inequality, around 1979
and 1994   184

Table 9.8   Social Security Transfers as Percentage of GDP, around
1979 and 1994   184

Table 9.9   Gross Replacement Rates, around 1979 and 1994   185

Table 12.1   Specification of Empirical Indicators and the
Translation of Data into Fuzzy Membership Scores
and Verbal Labels   232

Table 12.2   Fuzzy Membership Scores in Accessibility (A) of
Unemployment Insurance, 1990-1998   233

Table 12.3   Fuzzy Membership Scores in Generosity (G) of
Unemployment Insurance, 1990-1998   234

Table 12.4   Fuzzy Membership Scores on Obligations (O) in
Unemployment Insurance, 1990-1998   235

Table 12.5   Models of Unemployment Insurance   239

Table 12.6   Fuzzy Membership Scores in Unemployment
Insurance Models, 1990-1998   241

Table 13.1   Increase in Unemployment Rates ("Commonly
Used Definitions") in Selected OECD Countries
(Difference in Percentage Points), Peak Level and
Figures for 2000   251

Table 13.2   Employment Rates in Selected OECD Countries,
Various Years between 1974 and 2000   252

Table 14.1   Change in Employment and Unemployment in
the Areas of the "Triad"   278

Table 14.2   Trade-off between Employment, Social Transfers and
Budgetary Capacity in the EU-14   288

Table 14.3   Trade-off between Employment, Social Transfers and
Budgetary Equilibrium in 14 Countries of the EU   289

Table 15.1   Family Policy Index in Various Countries in the 1990s   300

Table 15.2 Percentage of Single Mothers and Mothers with
            Partners Employed Full time and Part time,
            circa 1990   302
Table 15.3 Weekly Working Hours of Employed Mothers in
            Eleven Countries   304
Table 16.1 Risks and Their Effects   325
Table 16.2 Policy Options   329
Table 17.1 The Effectiveness of Welfare State Redistribution
            for Prime-Age Households, Early 1990s (household
            head under 55)   337
Table 18.1 Simulated Poverty Rates in the European Union
            in 2005 and 2010 under Various Assumptions of
            Income Growth, Using a Constant Poverty Line   372
Table 18.2 Simulated Poverty Rates in the European Union
            in 2005 and 2010 under the Assumption That
            Transfer Incomes Do Not Grow, Using a Constant
            Poverty Line   373

List of Figures

Figure 6.1	Average OECD-18 Employment Rates	90
Figure 6.2	Average OECD-18 Fiscal Performance	93
Figure 6.3	Tax Burden and Employment in Exposed Sectors (ISIC 1-5, 7, 8), 1997	96
Figure 6.4	Tax Burden and Public-Sector Employment, 1997	98
Figure 6.5	Tax Burden and Private-Sector Employment, 1997	98
Figure 6.6	Tax Burden and Employment in Private-Sector Services, 1997	99
Figure 6.7	Income Taxes and Employment in Private-Sector Services, 1997	100
Figure 6.8	Social Security plus Consumption Taxes and Employment in Private-Sector Services, 1997	100
Figure 6.9	D5/D1 Wage Differentiation (1994/95) and Employment in Private-Sector Services, 1997	102
Figure 6.10	OECD Employment Protection Legislation Ranks (1999) and Employment in Private-Sector Services (1997)	102
Figure 6.11	Functional Profiles of Different Types of Welfare States	104
Figure 7.1	Trade Dependence and Social Transfers in 17 OECD Countries, Early 1960s	126
Figure 7.2	Financial Market Openness and Social Transfers in 17 OECD Countries, Early 1960s	126
Figure 7.3	Trade Dependence and Social Transfers in 17 OECD Countries, Mid-1990s	127
Figure 7.4	Financial Openness and Social Transfers in 17 OECD Countries, Mid-1990s	127
Figure 9.1	Trends in Disposable Income Inequality 1979-1995: Average Percentage Change of Gini Coefficient per Year	168
Figure 9.2	Cross Country Changes in Social Security Transfers and Gini Index, 1979-1994	173
Figure 9.3	Gross Replacement Rates Unemployment Benefits in the OECD, 1985 and 1997	175
Figure 9.4	Changes in Gross Replacement Rates and Gini index, around 1979 and 1994	176
Figure 14.1	The Trilemma of the Welfare State	275
Figure 14.2	Correlation between Total Employment and Social Protection Expenditure	285
Figure 14.3	Correlation between Total Employment and Social Transfers	285

Figure 14.4 Correlation between Total Employment and
            Government Funding Capacity or Net
            Funding Requirement   286
Figure 14.5 Correlation between Government Funding
            Capacity or Net Funding Requirement and
            Social Transfers   287
Figure 15.1 Poverty Rates of Single-Parent Families by the
            Number of Earners, Early 1990s (%)   305
Figure 15.2 Poverty Rates of Two-Parent Families by the
            Number of Earners, Early 1990s (%)   306
Figure 16.1 The Simplistic Dyad   314
Figure 16.2 The Baseline Triangle   316
Figure 16.3 The Welfare Pentagon   317
Figure 17.1 Relative Poverty in Industrialized Countries   336
Figure 17.2 Welfare State Effort and the Alleviation of Poverty:
            Social Expenditure and Relative Poverty Rates
            for Prime-Age Households in OECD Countries
            (household head younger than 55 years)   339
Figure 17.3 Welfare State Effort and the Alleviation of Poverty:
            Social Expenditure and the Reduction of Poverty
            Rates through Transfers and Taxes for Prime-Age
            Households in OECD Countries (household
            head younger than 55 years)   341
Figure 17.4 Social Assistance Schemes and an Effective
            Alleviation of Poverty: A Simplified Model   345
Figure 17.5 Level of Social Assistance Entitlements in Percent
            of Median Income, Britain 1995   348
Figure 17.6 Level of Social Assistance Entitlements in Percent
            of Median Income, Germany, 1994   349
Figure 17.7 Level of Social Assistance Entitlements in Percent
            of Median Income, Sweden 1995   350
Figure 18.1 Poverty and Benefit Dependency among Households
            with Heads under the Age of 50, Flanders, 1976-1997 361
Figure 18.2 Proportion of Work-Poor and Work-Rich Households
            in Germany, France, Belgium and the UK, 1983-1994   363
Figure 18.3a Poverty and Unemployment in OECD Countries   364
Figure 18.3b Poverty and Employment in OECD Countries   364
Figure 18.4 Poverty and Low Wages in OECD Countries   365
Figure 18.5 Poverty among the Low-Paid and Non-Working
            Population in OECD Countries   366
Figure 18.6 Poverty and Social Expenditure in OECD Countries   369

List of Boxes

Box 14.1   Three Models for Building Social Europe   279

List of Abbreviations

ACP	Africa, Caribbean and Pacific
ALMP	Active Labor Market Policy
APW	Average Production Worker
ASEAN	Association of South East Asian Nations
ATTAC	Association for the Taxation of Financial Transactions for the Citizen's Help (*Association pour une taxation des transactions financières pour l'aide aux citoyens*)
CBS	Central Statistical Office, Netherlands (*Centraal Bureau voor de Statistiek*)
CEC	Commission of the European Communities
COMECON	Council for Mutual Economic Assistance
DLA	Disability Living Allowance (United Kingdom)
ECB	European Central Bank
ECJ	European Court of Justice
ECMSA	European Convention on Social and Medical Assistance
EEA	European Economic Area
EEC	European Economic Community
EFTA	European Free Trade Area
EMU	European Monetary Union
ESCR	Economic and Social Research Council
EU	European Union
FTE	Full-Time Equivalents
G7	Group of 7 (industrialized countires)
G77	Group of 77 (developing countries)
GATS	General Agreement on Trade and Services
GATT	General Agreement on Tariffs and Trade
GDP	Gross Domestic Product
IB	Incapacity Benefit (United Kingdom)
IBRD	International Bank for Reconstruction and Development
IFI	International Financial Institutions
ILO	International Labour Office
IMF	International Monetary Fund
INGO	International Non-Governmental Organization
ISIC	International Standard Industrial Classification
ISSA	International Social Security Association
LIS	Luxembourg Income Study
LO	Swedish Trade Union Confederation (*Landsorganisationen*)
LSDV	Least Squares Dummy Variables

MERCOSUR	Common Market of the South (South America; *Mercado Común del Sur*)
NAIRU	Non-Accelerating Inflation Rate of Unemployment
NGO	Non-Governmental Organization
OECD	Organization for Economic Co-operation and Development
PPP	Purchasing Power Parities
SUR	Seemingly Unrelated Regressions
UNCHR	United Nations Commission of Human Rights
UNDP	United Nations Development Programme
UNDPTCDC	UNDP Technical Cooperation among Developing Countries
UNESCO	United Nations Educational, Scientific and Cultural Organization
UNICEF	United Nations Children's Fund
UNRISD	The United Nations Research Institute for Social Development
WB	World Bank
WTO	World Trade Organization

1

Social Security in the Global Village: Mapping the Issues

Roland Sigg and Christina Behrendt

Social security has faced a number of new challenges over recent decades. The 1980s witnessed a falling off in the economic growth once enjoyed during the "golden years," changes in family patterns, and the transformation of the world of labor. In the 1990s, after the proclamation of the "crisis of the welfare state" by some observers and the rejuvenation of neo-liberal theories, social security programs throughout the industrial world were placed under greater pressure and often curtailed, while the ideas of targeting and stronger work incentives found strong support (ISSA, 1995). More recently, in a very short span of time, a number of new developments have been summarized in the catchword "globalization." This term has become unavoidable in discussions of political and economic issues in recent years. And, as is often the case for catchwords of this type, people give different meanings to the issues involved.

The effects of globalization processes on social security are often seen in three interlocking developments.[1] First, the internationalization of capital markets, the increased mobility of capital, and economic integration limit the fiscal capacity of national governments and therefore reduce their scope for action in social policies. Second, labor markets have undergone important changes, including processes of de-industrialization and the growth of the service sector, with strong demands for more employment flexibility, accompanied in some countries by high and persistent unemployment and an increase in low-wage employment. Third, social cohesion is threatened by growing income inequality and the socioeconomic marginalization of certain population groups, as well as problems in coping with increased international migration. These processes are taking place in a context of important sociodemographic changes, including the aging of the population and changing family and household structures.

These developments have created a dual challenge for social security. On the one hand, the scope for social policies is more constrained than before while, on the other hand, increased insecurity is enhancing the need for social security and putting greater strain on income transfer mechanism and social services (Hoskins et al., 2001). Pressing questions in this respect include the precise nature of the new strains and new demands on social security schemes and the manner in which social security can be maintained and modernized in a more globalized world.

Origin and Structure of This Volume

This book grew out of a selection of papers presented at the Third International Conference on Social Security Research, held in the fall of 2000 in Helsinki. From more than 100 papers presented at the Conference, the publication assembles a selection of seventeen contributions which have been thoroughly revised in the meantime. Limited space has forced us to leave out a large number of remarkable papers, including many rewarding single-country studies. Interested readers can find these papers at the ISSA website at http://www.issa.int/engl/publ/2conthelsinki.htm.

The scope of the book makes it necessary to focus on a number of specific issues, and perforce to neglect others. In particular, because these issues have recently been covered quite extensively in other publications, we have not included papers on the issues of demographic change and the sustainability of pension schemes (see, for example, special editions 1/2000 and 1/2002 of the *International Social Security Review*), disability (Bloch and Prins, 2001), health (Ron and Scheil-Adlung, 2001), and privatization (Scheil-Adlung, 2001). Furthermore, only papers with a general perspective or comparative outlook have been selected.

The book is divided into five sections. The first two sections deal with the broad issue of the interrelation between social security and globalization, while the last three sections focus on more specific policy issues. The first section of the book addresses the challenges to social security arising from globalization. The second part then takes a closer look at national adaptation processes and emphasizes the variety of national responses to these challenges. The last three sections of the book focus on three policy fields of particular relevance to these developments: migration and the social rights of migrants; the relationship between labor markets and social security; and social cohesion.

Globalization and the Challenges for Social Security

A number of studies have been devoted to the pressures on social security in a globalizing world.[2] If these studies agree on one point, it is that very complex procedures are in place that cannot easily be reduced to an un-equivocal causal relationship. In the rapidly growing body of literature, two main lines of argument can be discerned. One emphasizes the reduced scope for action by national governments due to economic and financial constraints. These constraints manifest themselves in particular in the shrinking capacity of governments to levy taxes because of the increased mobility of capital (Rodrik, 1997; Tanzi, 2000), resulting in the narrowing of leeway to promote social security policies. In contrast, a number of accounts argue that there is no close relationship between international economic integration and wel-fare state reforms, and that a downward spiral in tax policies cannot be de-tected (Garrett, 1995, 1998; Swank, 1998). There is, however, some evidence that governments face strong incentives to shift the burden of taxation on labor (Scharpf, 1991; Steinmo, 1993).

These common pressures stand at the center of the first part of the book. Four contributions discuss these issues from different angles.

Bob Deacon sets the stage for discussion in his account of the recent changes in the international social protection environment. He emphasizes the importance of paying attention to the discourse on social protection, rather than exclusively to policy changes. In particular, he discusses recent changes in the dominant discourse on social protection, with influential or-ganizations such as the International Monetary Fund (IMF) and the World Bank advocating a reduced role for the state. Deacon argues that a strategy of "socially responsible globalization" that promotes the targeting of public cash benefits and services on the poor, leaving the middle classes to rely increasingly on private solutions, has critical long-term effects for the future of social protection because it undermines the normative foundations of an equitable social policy in a globalized world.

Alain Euzéby reviews the growing constraints on the financing of social security in the context of an internationalized economy. Emphasizing the increasing insecurity in a globalized world, he defends social security as being more necessary than ever. In order to alleviate the negative social consequences of globalization on developing countries, he proposes the cre-ation of an "international social fund" that could be put under the auspices of an international organization, such as the ILO.

These two papers show that, far from being a remnant of the past and out of phase with the new constraints of a globalized world, a renewed—and possi-bly global—system of social security can address the challenges arising out of the new social and economic order, by reducing inequalities while provid-ing the labor market with the required flexibility. More broadly, it is sug-gested that, in parallel with the existing international financial institutions, a global social fund should be created with the primary objective of providing basic social security to the most deprived populations in the world. Some projects are under experimentation, the most recent being a study by the ILO to explore the feasibility of a Global Social Trust Fund. Based on the principle of global citizenship, it would foster worldwide social solidarity to address the problems of poverty and social exclusion in the developing world.

Discussion of the impact of globalization has often been associated with the expectation that countries with a less developed welfare state would use their lower social expenditure and lower labor costs as a strategic advantage to underbid more developed welfare states in the competition for foreign investment.[3] However, *Ana Guillén* and *Santiago Álvarez* show in their detailed analysis of recent policy changes in Southern European countries (Greece, Italy, Portugal, and Spain) that these countries have embarked on a process of catching up, rather than following a strategy of social dumping. Instead of deliberately using their lower social expenditure levels as a competitive advantage against their Northern neighbors in an increasingly integrated European market, the Southern European countries are aspiring to enhance their social security systems. This process has not precluded curtailing some programs, although such measures are deemed to improve the efficiency of the schemes, rather than following a strategy of overall retrenchment.

The chapter by *Ian Gough* comes to a similar conclusion in his analysis of the impact of globalization on East Asian countries and their development as welfare states. Emphasizing the role of national institutional structures and welfare state regimes, Gough's analysis of the impact of the Asian financial crisis on the Republic of Korea, Indonesia, Malaysia, the Philippines, and Thailand demonstrates that similar pressures have produced different policy responses in each of these countries. Rather than following a strategy of overall curtailment when confronted with the crisis, policy responses have been differentiated and innovative, in particular in Thailand and Indonesia. Gough also shows that the economic crisis has given rise to more critical attitudes with regard to the belief that economic growth alone is the best instrument for social development. Instead, there is growing awareness of the need for social protection as a part of a more balanced approach that reaffirms the belief that economic development and social protection complement and reinforce each other.

Global Pressures and Internal Adjustments

Among the rapidly growing literature on the new challenges of globalization, many observers agree that the global pressures involved are mediated by national institutional frameworks. The next section of the book is therefore devoted to national responses to global pressures, with emphasis on cross-national variations in adaptation strategies. Global pressures do not affect countries in the same way, but can have various positive and negative effects, depending on socioeconomic factors, and particularly on the structure of the labor market and institutional arrangements (Swank, 2001). It is also necessary to distinguish pressures that have their origin in the changing international environment from domestic changes, such as structural changes in the economy, the aging of the population or the transformation of household structures (Pierson, 2001c). The chapters in this section of the book assess the relationship between international and domestic factors in more detail.

Drawing on a large-scale study of recent developments in the welfare state (Scharpf and Schmidt, 2000), *Fritz W. Scharpf*'s contribution in this volume emphasizes the economic and financial constraints faced by OECD countries. These developments effectively limit the choice of policy instruments available to governments for social protection, especially in relation to employment effects. However, these effects are mediated by national structures, with the result that different types of welfare states are affected by these pressures in different ways. While Scandinavian and Anglo-Saxon welfare states are able to deal with structural constraints without radical reforms to their systems (although there may be political pressures to do so) because they can maintain high levels of employment in sheltered sectors of the economy, the Continental European welfare states are experiencing more fundamental distress. As employment in sheltered sectors is neither fostered to a sufficient degree by low tax and contribution rates and the payment of low wages (as in the Anglo-Saxon world), nor by publicly financed service employment (as in Scandinavia), it is particularly vulnerable to negative employment effects in an increasingly internationalized economy.

Eero Carroll's analysis takes a somewhat different approach. In his analysis of 18 OECD nations, he assesses the impact of globalization and of national institutional structures on the quality of social insurance in the field of unemployment benefits. While his observation that the two widely used measures of globalization processes employed here (the openness of the economy and the extent of financial market deregulation) offer divergent pictures of the effects of globalization is noteworthy in itself, his conclusions suggest that both measures only provide weak support for the hypothesis that globalization processes have a strong and unambiguous effect on national policies. In contrast, the results of this study lend support to the assumption that there is considerable leeway for political deliberation at the national level.

This conclusion is also supported by *François-Xavier Merrien*. In the tradition of comparative research on small open economies (Katzenstein, 1985), he analyzes recent policy changes in New Zealand, Sweden, and Switzerland as countries which are particularly exposed to external pressures in the international economy. Emphasizing the different adjustment strategies followed by these countries, he concludes that national economic, political, and institutional factors are decisive in mediating the effects of external forces and in translating them into actual policy developments.

The recent trend towards increased income inequality within and between countries has also been associated with the internationalization of the economy.[4] *Koen Caminada* and *Kees P. Goudswaard* assess these trends and reveal broad cross-national divergences in the development of income inequality. They argue that these developments are associated in some countries with a reduction in the generosity of the welfare system, particularly in the United Kingdom and the Netherlands. In a more detailed analysis of the latter case, they show that the reforms to Dutch social security schemes have contributed to the rise in income inequality.

The lessons in this respect are fairly encouraging. Several papers in this section show that some leeway, although it is not broad, exists for policy-makers at the national level. With some exceptions, there is good evidence that strong social transfer programs are not incompatible with globalization and do not necessarily hinder a country's capacity to be competitive on the world market. Indeed, such social transfers can make a difference and soften the impacts of globalization. Efficiency in managing these programs is, however, essential.

Challenges in Selected Policy Fields

Following this more general discussion, three sections of the book are devoted to challenges in selected policy fields. Three fields have been chosen because of their relevance to the debate and their relative neglect in the existing social security literature.

Migration and the Social Rights of Migrants

The issue of migration and the social rights of migrants is one of the major issues at stake, especially in the European Union (Bommes and Geddes, 2000). While the policies of some European countries towards migrants have largely concentrated on limiting further immigration, some formerly restrictive countries have recently started to seek actively highly qualified migrants because of shortages of skilled labor and concerns about the aging of the population. These processes will further increase the gap between groups of "appreciated" migrants with strong social rights, and the large groups of other migrants whose social rights are kept very weak so as not to attract further immigration.

The chapter by *Deborah Mabbett* and *Helen Bolderson* contrasts the social rights of migrants from other European Union countries with those of asylum-seekers from outside the European Union. In principle, the former enjoy similar social rights to the resident population, except for minimum income benefits, although these rights have had to be obtained through a long series of legal actions in the European Court of Justice. In contrast, the social rights of asylum-seekers are much weaker, and have been further reduced in many countries over recent years.

Simon Roberts addresses the social rights of third-country nationals in the European Union and gives a detailed account of the complex interaction of domestic rules and international social security agreements. Emphasizing the importance of immigration status in determining eligibility for social benefits, he argues that the social rights of migrants are seriously inhibited by the lack of agreements between major sending countries in the developing world and receiving countries within the European Union. This shortcoming is explained by the structural difficulty for sending countries with poor social security standards to establish agreements based on the principle of reciprocity. Rather than basing entitlement on reciprocity *between* countries, Roberts argues that reciprocity *within* countries should be the guiding principle for granting benefits to migrants, with social security rights being based on the contribution of migrants to the functioning of the economy, including their payment of direct and indirect taxes.

In view of the real challenge of demographic aging, its impact on the financing of pension schemes and the role that increased migration could play in resolving these issues (at least in part), it is urgent to reconsider the social rights of migrants on a regional and international basis. The precarious situation of most migrant workers, as indicated in the chapters in this section, calls for a radical change in policy: while bilateral and multilateral agreements will remain valuable, greater emphasis should be placed in the future on the recognition of full rights for migrants on the basis of their contributions and needs.

Labor Markets and Social Security

Globalization processes have placed major strains on the relationship between labor markets and social security. Many countries have experienced persistent unemployment and the exclusion of large parts of the population from the labor force, while others have been successful in increasing their employment ratios.

These developments have been associated with fundamental changes in the structure of labor markets and the nature of employment. While a large proportion of the population used to be able to rely on stable employment over a long period, for many people employment has become less secure, and increasing numbers of workers are finding themselves in precarious forms of employment or self-employment, if not unemployment. Although some countries have been successful in raising employment rates, the expansion of employment has largely taken place at the margins of the labor market. Many of these "new forms of work" are characterized by temporary and/or flexible contracts, often on a part-time basis, and the lack or inferiority of social rights compared to those derived from "regular" employment. The growing demand by employers for flexibility in employment tends to be accompanied by increased economic and social insecurity for employees.

At the same time, employment remains an important link for the acquisition of rights to social security in many countries. Employment is also becoming more important for the provision of occupational or other private social benefits, which are playing a more important role in supplementing public forms of social security around the world, either directly in the case of occupational benefits, or indirectly in the sense that any additional saving requires a relatively comfortable and stable standard of living.

In this context, the role of the labor market is changing as a social institution, as well as that of family structures and social policies. Growing wage inequality in many countries is contributing to the fact that many individuals and families are finding it more difficult to cope on their income from work; the "working poor" have become a well-known phenomenon. In addition, there are growing numbers of "workless households" with no formal attachment to the labor market.

Changes in the labor market are closely linked to processes of de-industrialization and the growth of the service economy in many countries. As the industrial sector provides steadily less employment, the service sector can partly compensate for these losses, although such changes are often related to substantial modifications in wage structures and employment stability and security. While the influential study by Iversen and Wren (1998) postulates that the three policy goals of equality, employment, and budgetary restraint will no longer be achieved simultaneously in modern service economies, *Nadine Richez-Battesti* and *Audrey Koulinsky* argue that this trilemma is reduced to a trade-off between employment and social protection in the context of the European Economic and Monetary Union. Their conclusion is based on an econometric analysis of 14 Member States of the European Union, and they show that there is indeed strong evidence for just such a trade-off in the European Union, although there are still some caveats to be resolved.

In spite of these grim prospects, recent years have seen a number of so-called "employment miracles," not only in the United States, but also in some European countries. These have attracted the interest of less successful countries seeking policy models and lessons to be taken on board. The chapter by *Karl Hinrichs* makes a critical assessment of these efforts and emphasizes the specificities of each country that hamper the transfer of employment policies from one country to another. He argues that "employment miracles," which have recently occurred in a number of countries, tend to be based on a complex constellation of different factors that cannot easily be replicated in other countries. Hinrichs calls for a more systematic analysis of actual employment performance and its institutional prerequisites in order to draw well-founded and balanced policy lessons.

In many countries, there has been a growing interest in recent years in "workfare" or "activation policies" (Lødemel and Trickey, 2001), which are considered to be more effective in reintegrating people into the labor market and avoiding unemployment traps. These reforms are closely connected to concerns to reduce the relative attractivity of social transfers, compared with participation in the labor market (OECD, 1996, 1999). In this context, the chapter by *Jon Kvist* assesses the changing relationship between rights and obligations in unemployment insurance in the Nordic countries, Germany, the Netherlands, and the United Kingdom. He uses "fuzzy-set" theory to map recent changes that have occurred in unemployment benefit schemes in terms of the balance between rights and obligations, as well as the generosity and accessibility of these schemes. This approach allows Kvist to detect whether a country's policies belong to a specific policy model or not, and his conclusions suggest that the stronger emphasis placed on obligations in a number of countries should be considered as constituting a major break with their earlier policies.

The question of work incentives and obligations is also the starting point for the chapter by *Katja Forssén* and *Mia Hakovirta*, who show that the labor market participation of mothers, especially single mothers, is closely associated with family policies, particularly in terms of the availability of child care arrangements. Linking the employment of mothers to the economic situation of their families, Forssén and Hakovirta show that employment constitutes effective protection from poverty, for both single-parent families and couples.

Once again, strong evidence is presented on the possible impact of social policies in improving the functioning of the labor market. It is important to recall that increasing the labor market participation rate is the best means of lowering the impact of demographic aging and increasing tax and contribution revenues. While the internal dynamic of the economy and a stable international financial environment are essential to foster economic growth, carefully drafted social policies can help to provide the required labor force: by providing the right incentives for the continued employment of older workers, developing the necessary family policies to allow women to integrate better into the labor market and making work resumption programs more successful. The evidence presented in these and other papers (Economic Policy Committee, 2000; Sigg, 2001) suggests that such labor market policies could, in fact, make a substantial contribution to resolving the aging crisis, while improving social cohesion, as seen in the next section.

Social Cohesion

The final section of the book is devoted to the question of how to guarantee social cohesion, in particular by providing better coverage for those most exposed to social risks. Especially in view of labor market changes and greater social and economic insecurity, a basic safety net is more necessary than ever to guarantee effective protection from poverty in the event that other income distribution mechanisms, either through the market or through taxes and other social security schemes, are unable to ensure adequate income.

The concept of social risks and social risk management has gained momentum in recent years, spurred by its discussion in a series of papers (Holzmann and Jørgensen, 2000) that fed into the World Bank's social protection sector strategy (World Bank, 2000). Re-framing the old discussion about the insurance character of social security, the social risk approach acknowledges the need for protection of the individual against a variety of risks and emphasizes the interlocking responsibilities of families, communities, non-governmental organizations (NGOs), market institutions, and the state. In similar vein, *Chris de Neubourg* presents a new conceptual approach to social risk management. His approach takes into consideration the fact that social security issues are closely intertwined with other policy fields, and overcomes the artificial analytical separation of social protection from other issues. He proposes a "welfare pentagon" that goes further than many existing models and includes markets, families, public authorities, social networks, and finally "membership institutions," such as firms or trade unions. Emphasizing the dynamic aspects of social risks, de Neubourg discusses different types of risks and possibilities of risk management within the welfare pentagon.

While the concept of protection against risk is at the very root of social security, and in particular of social insurance, minimum income schemes are recognized as playing an increasingly important role in terms of social protection (ILO, 1984). These schemes are the focus of the last two chapters of this volume. The chapter by *Christina Behrendt* reviews the available evidence on welfare state redistribution and the persistence of income poverty in Western Europe, and explores mechanisms of poverty alleviation through minimum income schemes as the basic safety net in the welfare state. This analysis reveals that the institutional design of social assistance schemes has a strong effect on the alleviation of poverty in the cases of Germany, Sweden, and the United Kingdom.

The question of how the alleviation of poverty in welfare states could be improved is also central to the chapter by *Bea Cantillon* and *Karel Van den Bosch*. They emphasize the importance of employment in the alleviation of poverty, with working households being exposed to a much lower risk of poverty than workless households. In some countries, however, there is a growing gap between working and non-working households, because increased employment has been concentrated on households that are already well-integrated into the labor market, while others have failed to gain access to the labor market. The authors, therefore, draw attention to the degree to which "activation policies" are able to increase the labor market attachment of previously workless households. In addition, they emphasize that minimum income schemes need to be improved to provide more effective protection from poverty for those left without a job, and call for a stronger role for the European Union in monitoring and evaluating national policies through a benchmarking system.

The Future of Social Security in the Global Village

The future of social security in the "global village" will depend on the capacity to combine good economic performance in an internationalized economy with viable protection against social risks. It is being increasingly widely recognized, even by former skeptics, that social security has a crucial role to play in a globalizing world. Careful reflection is therefore required on how social security schemes can be adapted to the coming challenges.

One of the most important factors is labor market performance. It is well known that social security and employment are linked through a dual mechanism: a rise in employment reduces social expenditure on unemployment, while at the same time expanding the financial base of the welfare state; in contrast, a decline in employment increases expenditure while constraining revenue. In the context of an aging population, this link will be even more crucial for the functioning of welfare states. The economic and social effects of the shrinkage in working-age cohorts and the growth in the population of pensioners require higher employment rates (McDonald and Kippen, 2001). Some countries have already started to restrict early retirement, raise the pensionable age, stimulate the employment participation of women and foster selective migration, while others are still more concerned to trim their high unemployment rates than to bring more people into the labor market. The challenges of an aging population will be difficult to manage in these latter countries in particular, in view of their structural problems on the labor market.

In addition, many countries face the challenge of improving social security coverage for the growing number of people in precarious or atypical forms of employment, especially if low-skilled employment in the service sector expands still further. They will also have to accommodate a growing number of migrants if they are to attempt to compensate some of the age-related decline in the working population through replacement migration. Social cohesion is at stake if the gap widens between the well-protected strata of the population and people with poor social rights.

These changes, together with the transformation of household structures and the aging of the population, require a "recalibration" (Pierson, 2001a) of the welfare state. If social security is to be adapted to the new challenges, it will be necessary to strike a new balance between work and caring responsibilities for both men and women, and to improve the effectiveness and adequacy of social security programs. This also involves ensuring that reliance on social security benefits, rather than undermining individual activity and independence, has the effect of improving the autonomy and social integration of the individual.

The future of social security will continue to be determined by financial austerity and a number of major problems that are still to be solved. Nevertheless, the contributions in this volume demonstrate that there is broad scope for political deliberation and country-specific paths in reaction to the global pressures of recent years, and that a variety of different strategies are possible. But all the available strategies will not necessarily be successful. It is therefore important to analyze the complex relationships between demographic, social, economic, and institutional factors even more thoroughly to shed further light on the prerequisites for a viable social security system in a rapidly changing world.

Notes

1. For an overview of recent debates of globalization processes, see, for example, M. F. Guillén (2001).
2. Prominent examples include the contributions in Scharpf and Schmidt (2000) and Pierson (2001b).
3. For a recent overview of this debate, see Alber and Standing (2000).
4. For a critical review of this debate, see Kapstein (2000).

References

Alber, J., and Standing, G. (2000). "Social Dumping, Catch-up or Convergence? Europe in a Comparative Global Context." *Journal of European Social Policy*, 10 (2), 99-119.

Bloch, F. S., and Prins, R. (eds.). (2001). *Who Returns to Work and Why? A Six-Country Study on Work Incapacity and Reintegration*. New Brunswick, N.J.: Transaction Publishers.

Bommes, M., and Geddes, A. (eds.). (2000). *Immigration and Welfare: Challenging the Borders of the Welfare State*. London: Routledge.

Economic Policy Committee. (2000). *Progress Report to the ECOFIN Council on the Impact of Ageing Populations on Public Pension Systems* (EPC/ECFIN/581/00). Brussels: European Commission.

Garrett, G. (1995). "Capital Mobility, Trade, and the Domestic Politics of Economic Policy in the Industrialized Democracies." *International Organization*, 49 (4), 657-687.

___. (1998). "Global Markets and National Politics: Collision Course or Virtuous Circle?" *International Organization*, 52 (4), 787-824.

Guillén, M. F. (2001). "Is Globalization Civilizing, Destructive or Feeble? A Critique of Five Key Debates in the Social Science Literature." *Annual Review of Sociology*, 27, 235-260.

Holzmann, R., and Jørgensen, S. L. (2000). "Social Risk Management: A New Conceptual Framework for Social Protection and Beyond." *Social Protection Discussion Paper Series*, No. 0006. Washington D.C.: World Bank.

Hoskins, D. D., Dobbernack, D., and Kuptsch, C. (eds.).(2001). *Social Security at the Dawn of the 21st Century*. New Brunswick, N.J.: Transaction Publishers.

ILO. (1984). *Into the Twenty-first Century: The Development of Social Security.* Geneva: ILO.

ISSA. (1995). *Social Security Tomorrow: Permanence and Change.* Studies and Research Series No. 36. Geneva: International Social Security Association.

Iversen, T., and Wren, A. (1998). "Equality, Employment, and Budgetary Restraint: the Trilemma of the Service Economy." *World Politics,* 50 (4), 507-546.

Kapstein, E. B. (2000). "Winners and Losers in the Global Economy." *International Organization,* 54 (2), 359-384.

Katzenstein, P. (1985). *Small States in World Markets: Industrial Policy in Europe.* Ithaca, N.Y.: Cornell University Press.

Lødemel, I., and Trickey, H. (eds.).(2001). *"An Offer You Can't Refuse": Workfare in International Perspective.* Bristol: The Policy Press.

McDonald, P., and Kippen, R. (2001). "Labour Supply Prospects in 16 Developed Countries, 2000-2050." *Population and Development Review,* 27 (1), 1-32.

OECD. (1996). *The OECD Jobs Strategy: Pushing Ahead with the Strategy.* Paris: OECD.

___. (1999). *Benefit Systems and Work Incentives: 1999 Edition.* Paris: OECD.

Pierson, P. (2001a). «Coping with Permanent Austerity: Welfare State Restructuring in Affluent Democracies.» In Pierson, P. (ed.), *The New Politics of the Welfare State.* Oxford: Oxford University Press.

___. (ed.).(2001b). *The New Politics of the Welfare State.* Oxford: Oxford University Press.

___. (2001c). "Post-industrial Pressures on Mature Welfare States." In Pierson, P. (ed.), *The New Politics of the Welfare State.* Oxford: Oxford University Press.

Rodrik, D. (1997). *Has Globalization Gone Too Far?* Washington D.C.: Institute for International Economics.

Ron, A., and Scheil-Adlung, X. (eds.).(2001). *Recent Health Policy Innovations in Social Security.* New Brunswick, N.J.: Transaction Publishers.

Scharpf, F. W. (1991). *Crisis and Choice in European Social Democracy.* Ithaca, N.Y.: Cornell University Press.

Scharpf, F. W., and Schmidt, V. A. (eds.).(2000). *Welfare and Work in the Open Economy,* 2 volumes. Oxford: Oxford University Press.

Scheil-Adlung, X. (ed.).(2001). *Building Social Security: The Challenge of Privatization.* New Brunswick, N.J.: Transaction Publishers.

Sigg, R. (2001). "Pension at Risk? Demographic Ageing, Labour Market and the Funding of Retirement." In Sarfati, H., and Bonoli. G. (eds.), *Labour Market and Social Protection. Reforms in International Perspective: Parallel or Converging Tracks?* Aldershot: Ashgate.

Steinmo, S. (1993). *Taxation and Democracy—Swedish, British, and American Approaches to Financing the Modern State.* New Haven, Conn.: Yale University Press.

Swank, D. (1998). "Funding the Welfare State and the Taxation of Business in Advanced Market Economies." *Political Studies,* 46 (4), 671-691.

___. (2001). "Political Institutions and Welfare State Restructuring: The Impact of Institutions on Social Policy Change in Developed Democracies." In Pierson, P. (ed.), *The New Politics of the Welfare State.* Oxford: Oxford University Press.

Tanzi, V. (2000). "Globalization and the Future of Social Protection." *IMF Working Paper,* No. 00/12. Washington D.C.: International Monetary Fund.

World Bank. (2000). *Social Protection Sector Strategy: From Safety Net to Springboard.* Washington D.C.: World Bank.

Part 1

Globalization and the Challenges for Social Security

2

Globalization and the Challenge for Social Security

Bob Deacon

Subsequent chapters in this volume address more directly the relationship between globalization and social security. Fritz Scharpf in chapter 6 examines the impact of globalization upon welfare states. Alain Euzéby in chapter 3 considers the issue of financing social protection in a global labor market. Part 5 of this volume examines the relationship between globalization and social cohesion and thus addresses the issue of responsibility for protecting against increased risks. This chapter sets these more detailed discussions in the context of what I call the global discourse of social policy. It is important to draw attention to globalization as a discourse and set of propositions rather than as a fait accompli. Too often globalization is regarded as a purely economic phenomenon that is driven by unstoppable forces to which we as policy-makers can only react. Globalization is also a product of political decisions made by governments and other actors. More importantly, the form that increased interconnectedness between nations takes is a matter of choice.

The choice in the 1980s was for a neo-liberal globalization that assumed, mistakenly, that global unregulated markets would maximize global welfare. It is possible to conceive of an alternative form of globalization. Just as neo-liberal globalization replicated at the international level the approach favored by some neo-liberal countries for their own economy so in principle the mechanisms adopted by social democratic governments could also be replicated at a global level. In this version of globalization global governance institutions would raise global revenues to facilitate global redistribution, oversee a set of global social regulations to ensure that economic activity served a social purpose, and empower "global" citizens to demand social rights that were inscribed in international agreements.

It is the contention of this chapter that the global political choice being made at the start of the twenty-first century by those who dominate the global social policy and social development discourse is neither for a fundamentalist neo-liberal globalization that characterized the last years of the twentieth century nor for a social democratic globalization just outlined but for a "socially responsible globalization" which, while it appears to be addressing the short comings of neo-liberal globalization, is actually, I argue, generating a fundamental threat to equitable social welfare provisioning. Such a trend poses major problems for existing social security institutions.

This chapter proceeds through four stages. First, a brief summary of how neo-liberal globalization has impacted upon welfare states in the north and social development prospects in the south is provided. Secondly, the emerging "socially responsible globalization" discourse is described. This is then critiqued from the standpoint of a concern with equity. Finally, the implications for social security are briefly addressed.

Neo-Liberal Globalization Challenges Northern Welfare States and Southern Social Development

I have argued elsewhere (Deacon, 1997, 2000a) that neo-liberal globalization:

- *Sets welfare states in competition with each other.* This generates the danger, but not the inevitability, of social dumping, deregulation, and a race to the welfare bottom. There are, however, political choices available within each welfare state. Does it indeed cut expenditures and loosen labor and other regulations and pursue the race to the welfare bottom? Does it spend on certain aspects of social welfare to increase productivity and political and social stability in order to attract investment? Does it steer a third course and maintain all welfare expenditures funded in ways that do least damage to competitiveness?
- *Raises issues of social redistribution, social regulation, and social empowerment to a regional and global level.* As a result new regional, international, supranational, and global actors enter the picture and complicate the politics of welfare. These include regional bodies such as the EU, MERCOSUR, ASEAN, Inter-governmental Organizations such as the Bretton Woods organizations, the U.N. family of agencies, the Organisation for Economic Co-operation and Development (OECD), etc., International Non-Governmental Organizations (INGO), Transnational Corporations, Global Social Movements, Transnational Policy Networks, Epistemic Communities, and Subcontracted Consultancy Companies. Policies of redistribution, social regulation and the articulation of social rights at both regional and global level are emerging.
- *Generates a global discourse within and between global actors on the future of national and supranational social policy.* In the emerging "com-

plex multi-lateralism" the future for social policy at both national and supranational levels is being shaped by a struggle between international organizations for the right to shape policy, and within and between international organizations for the content of social policy. Below we note, for example, how within this global discourse certain assumptions held by the International Monetary Fund (IMF) and the World Bank about desirable social policy have steered countries to an unnecessary convergence in the direction of the residualization and privatization of social protection.

- *Creates a global market in welfare providers.* The increased opportunity globalization generates for private providers of welfare services to become global and operate in many countries may contribute to the undermining of national social provision and national regulatory policies. It is clear that the international insurance market is waiting in the wings to sell its products to the less risky sections of the population in Europe if the pressures upon pay-roll taxes begin to create political alliances for reducing public pension commitments. Global markets in social care, health services, and other aspects of social welfare are expanding in the context of the General Agreement on Trade in Services (GATS).

In fact, empirical evidence suggests that developed European welfare states are differentially affected by globalization, some being more challenged, some in principle more sustainable in the face of globalization and others flowing with the tide of liberalizing globalization at the price of social equity (Deacon, 2000a). A summary of some of the considerations leading to this conclusion is set out below. Here globalization is unpacked into component elements. Capital flows and associated currency speculation is one element that has impacted on transition countries. Increased free trade is another that differentially affects countries. Embeddedness in the international produc-

Table 2.1

The Complex Impact of Aspects of Globalization upon European Welfare States

Type of welfare state	Impact of short term capital flows	Impact of lower trade barriers	Impact of embeddedness in international production	Impact of global financial actors
Former State socialist	Threatened	Short term benefit of low wages	Not yet embedded but challenges workplace welfare	Large push to liberal (residual) social policy
Bismarckian	Potential protection by Euro	Challenges labour market rigidities and payroll taxes	Positive history in high tech production	Little
Social democratic	Potential protection for some by Euro	Income and consumer tax based benefits resistant if political will	Positive history in high tech production	Little
Liberal Anglo-Saxon	Gamble upon being outside Euro	"Benefits" for jobs of flexibility and lower wages but at price of inequity and poverty	High tech production seen as threatened by some	Little

tion system is a third and here there are country differences. Finally, an element of globalization that is of particular relevance to the former state socialist countries is the role of the global financial institutions in shaping through loan conditionality a particular model of social protection (Deacon, 2000b).

The outcome of this review and analysis suggests that:

- Liberal social policy involving residualization, individualization, and privatization chimes with the phase of neo-liberal globalization but at the cost of inequity.
- Workplace based welfare systems of the former state socialist countries and the high payroll tax based Bismarckian insurance systems are vulnerable to global competitive pressures.
- Social Democratic citizenship based welfare systems funded out of consumption taxes are, given the political will, surprisingly sustainable and competitive in the face of global pressures.

In terms of developing countries and many emerging economies I have argued elsewhere (Deacon 1999) that there is a tendency for globalization to:

- *Generate severe indebtedness*. This has undermined the capacity of governments to secure education, health, and social protection so that in many countries it is now left to new Non-Governmental Organizations (NGO) and bottom-up credit initiatives to provide a partial network of coverage for some people.
- *Threaten assets and standards*. Globalization has encouraged the perfectly rational response of selling of country assets including those arising from low labor costs to attract capital at any price and with disregard for emerging global labor, environmental, and social standards. Tax havens for Transnational Corporations as part of this strategy further undermine the revenue raising capacity of such governments.
- *Segment social policy within many countries so that different population segments are living under very different internal welfare regimes.* Workers in Export Processing Zones may have limited access to workplace and citizenship rights. Some employees of transnational industries may be protected by company benefits that tap into global private provision. Some state employees in some countries may continue to access health and welfare benefits and pension schemes established either in post-colonial days or as part of the state social provision of former state socialist economies, but these, too, are withering.
- *Create zones of exclusion in Africa and elsewhere from the formal global economy*. These are zones within which the normal functions of the state such as taxation, regulation, and social spending are non-existent. Within such countries and areas a form of "adverse incorporation" is taking place whereby the poor without formal rights are obliged to engage in informal exchange and submit themselves to clientalist relationships to secure their practical survival needs. Within this con-

text the informal global economy of drugs, prostitution, arms dealing, and illegal trade flourishes.

The picture is bleak but not unremittingly so. The fears of a race to the bottom in the north have been partly allayed. There are some positive stories to tell in the south. In terms of the actual impact of economic globalization upon social policy north and south a new scholarly consensus is emerging that argues and demonstrates that:

- Globalization does not necessarily have to lead to the residualization (and privatization) of social provision. In the north, as is suggested in Table 2.1, there are arguments and experiences that show that redistributive social policy with high levels of income taxation and high levels of public health, education, and social security *are* sustainable in the face of global competition. In a comparative survey of Anglo-Saxon (e.g., UK), Conservative Corporatist (e.g., Germany), and Social Democratic (e.g., Sweden) welfare states both the neo-liberal and social democratic approaches remained competitive. The neo-liberal approach, of course, risked creating increased inequity that compensatory social policy such as tax credits seeks to minimize. The most challenged were work-based welfare states funded on the basis of labor taxes with locked-in inflexible labor contracts for industrial workers. So long as revenue for social provision was raised from citizens rather than capital and service jobs are high-quality public ones, high-level universal social provision is sustainable and does not undermine competitiveness and full employment (Scharpf, 2000, Sykes et al., 2001).
- At the same time the fears of social dumping in the south have been shown to be exaggerated (Alber and Standing, 2000). Moreover, evidence from a recent global survey of the impact of globalization upon economies has shown that some governments in the south have chosen to increase their social spending during liberalization (Taylor, 2000).
- Moreover, it is now recognized internationally that globalization and openness of economies generates the need for more not less attention to social protection measures (OECD, 1999).
- A response to globalization in some middle-income countries has indeed been to create universalistic forms of social policy. A good example is Korea (Kwon, 2001).
- Some of the social policy responses adopted in Latin America and elsewhere in the hey-day of the Washington neo-liberal consensus, such as the full privatization of pension schemes, are now being shown by comparative policy analysts to have questionable advantages in terms of net savings effects and other criteria (Mesa-Lago, 2000; Huber and Stephens, 2000). Mesa-Lago shows that neither old-fashioned state socialism (Cuba) nor new-fashioned neo-liberalism (Chile) but socially regulated capitalism (Costa Rica) does best economically and socially. (This echoes the seminal work of Doyal and Gough [1991] of some years ago.)

This is reassuring but despite this evidence I have argued (Deacon, 2000a) that certain tendencies in the globalization process and certain policy positions adopted by international organizations still give cause for concern. I examine these below.

Global Discourse of Social Policy and Social Development: Towards a "Socially Responsible Globalization"?

Earlier (Deacon, 1997) I argued that the IMF regarded welfare expenditure as a burden on the economy favoring a U.S. workfare style safety net approach to social policy and that the World Bank's focus on poverty alleviation led it, too, to favor a safety net approach. Within the International Labour Organization (ILO) and other U.N. agencies, on the other hand, supporters of the view that social expenditures were a means of securing social cohesion were found. The ILO in particular supported a conservative-corporatist Bismarckian type of social protection. The OECD favored the notion that certain state welfare expenditures should be regarded as a necessary investment. No international organization, save possibly the United Nations Children's Fund (UNICEF), could be said to defend the redistributive approach to social policy characteristic of the Scandinavian countries. In the study of the role played by such international organizations in shaping post communist social policy it was concluded (Deacon, 1997: 197) that the

> opportunity created by the collapse of communism for the global actors to shape the future of social policy has been grasped enthusiastically by the dominant social liberal tendency in the World Bank. In alliance with social development NGOs who are being given a part to play especially in zones of instability, a social safety net future is being constructed. This NGO support combined with the political support of many southern and some East European governments is challenging powerfully those defenders of universalist and social security based welfare states to be found in the European Union, the ILO and in smaller number in the World Bank.

These conclusions still broadly stand, although there continue to be interesting shifts of the position of particular players within this debate. The IMF has taken the social dimension of globalization more seriously, considering whether some degree of equity is beneficial to economic growth (IMF, 1998). The World Bank has articulated more clearly its risk management approach to social protection in the context of globalization (Holzmann and Jørgensen, 1999). The OECD now warns that globalization may lead to the need for more, not less social expenditure (OECD, 1999). The ILO has begun to show signs of making concessions to the World Bank's views on privatizing some part of social security (Gillion et al., 2000) while other moves within the ILO suggest an interest in a new universalism emerging from bottom-up movements in several countries (Standing, 2000). More recently, the role of the World Trade Organization (WTO) and its views on the desirability of fostering a global market in health and social service provision is assuming a prominence it did not have (Koivusalo, 1999). INGOs are more clearly now divided into those that are acting as substitutes for government and those that are more concerned to act as policy advocates for more greater government responsibility for welfare.

I have argued elsewhere (Deacon, 2000a) that within this discordant discourse can be discerned elements of what appear to be a new politics of "global social responsibility". Fundamentalist economic liberalism and inhumane structural adjustment appears to be giving way to a concern on the part of the World Bank and the IMF with social consequences of globalization. International development assistance is concerned to focus on social development. U.N. agencies are increasingly exercised by the negative social consequences of globalization. Among the shifts in policy thinking and concrete steps that are being taken, which herald this more "socially responsible globalization," are the following. The possible criticisms of these steps are also noted.

- The move from human rights to social rights and from declaration to implementation
  But moralizing about rights without resource transfers is counterproductive.
- The trend in international development cooperation towards setting goals/monitoring progress
  But attainable development targets may be a legitimating of residual social policy.
- The move to secure global minimum labor, social and health standards
  But core labor standards are a lowering of standards for some.
- The move to establish codes of practice for socially responsible investment and business
  But they may lead to dis-investment in the south.
- The calls for global social regulation of the global economy
  But the Principles of Good Practice in Social Policy are seen as new conditionality.
- The moves to extend constructive regionalism with a social dimension
  But regions are also social protectionist blocks?

Not all of these steps are given emphasize by the Bretton Woods organizations. The World Bank is reluctant to embrace the language of labor or social rights. Each of these steps is problematic in some ways, but taken together they do seem to suggest a shift away from a global politics of liberalism to a global politics of social concern. It is now the case that the emerging dominant intellectual strand within the epistemic communities within and around the World Bank and International Development community agrees that:

- global macro-economic management needs to address the social consequences of globalization;
- a set of social rights and entitlements to which global citizens might aspire can be fashioned;
- international development cooperation will focus aid on meeting basic social needs;
- debt relief should be speeded up so long as the funds are used to alleviate poverty;
- the globalization of trade generates the need for the globalization of labor and social standards;
- good governments are an essential ingredient in encouraging socially responsible development.

This is a long way from the situation, which prompted the writing of *Adjustment with a Human Face* (Cornia et al., 1987). One could almost be tempted to label the new era as globalization with a human face.

There are, however, a number of disagreements as to how to proceed with this new orientation:

- much of the south is understandably suspicious of even progressive social conditionality;
- how both world trade and world labor standards can co-exist without the standards being reduced to minimal core standards or being used for protectionist purposes is far from clear;
- initiatives to empower the U.N. with global revenue-raising powers are firmly resisted by some.

It could be said that the world is stumbling towards articulating a global social policy which embodies elements of international redistribution (but so far this is merely a call for countries to donate to global health and education funds), international social regulation (but north-south conflicts of interest restrain these moves), and international social rights (but declarations are not backed with resources).

The argument of this chapter is that even the positive aspects of this emerging globalization with a human face, this "socially responsible globalization," contain within them assumptions about desirable social policy within countries that are profoundly worrying from the standpoint of social solidarity and equity. It is to this argument that the chapter now turns.

"Socially Responsible Globalization": The Threat to Equity

My concern with the new consensus is that even if the disagreements could be overcome as to how the new global social agenda were to be implemented and funded this would still generate a situation that posed a fundamental threat to equitable social policy and equitable social development north and south. The history of the struggle to build welfare states teaches us that social equity and high levels of social provision accessible to all has only been secured and retained when the services of those welfare states are available to and used by the middle class. It is the sharp elbow of the middle class every bit as much as working-class pressure and/or concern for the poor that has ensured good quality social provision. The better-off will only be taxed if they also benefit.

The coexistence of four tendencies within the new global paradigm will undermine this essential precondition for equitable social progress just as the world enters a new millennium with the resources to fund such equitable development. These tendencies are:

- The World Bank's belief that governments should only provide minimal levels of social protection.
- The OECD Development Assistance Committee's concern to fund only basic education and health care.
- The International NGO's self interest in substituting for government services.
- The moves being made within the World Trade Organization to speed the global market in private health, social care, education, and insurance services.

Within the context of withering state provision the middle classes of developing and transition economies will be enticed into the purchase of private social security schemes, into the purchase for their children of private secondary and tertiary education, and into the purchase even at the expense of subsequent personal impoverishment of private hospital level medical care. The providers of such private services will be American or European enterprises. The potential to build on cross-class social contracts from the colonial era or to fashion new such contracts within the context of post-communism to build new welfare states will be undermined by the preexistence of the global market in private social provision. The conditions facing the emerging middle class of many countries in the context of globalization will be fundamentally different from the conditions that had faced earlier middle classes who helped fashion earlier welfare states. The result is predictable. We know that services for the poor are poor services. We know that those developed countries that do not have universal public health provision at all levels and public education provision at all levels are not only more unequal but also more unsafe and crime ridden.

While the global social development lobby are congratulating themselves on shifting the global agenda so that debt relief to reduce poverty and universal access to basic education are now the new orthodoxy, they are, for the most part, blind to the threat posed to social equity in both the south and the north by the pincer movement of the World Bank and WTO, fashioning a private future for welfare for the global middle class. To put it differently, "globalization is unraveling the social bond" (Devetak and Higgott, 1999) that ensured social justice within countries in the twentieth century.

The case for equity and for universalism in social provision has been seriously eroded within the global discourse about social policy in the past ten years. How did the idea of social policy geared to securing greater equity through processes of redistribution and universal social provision get so lost in the context of globalization? I have suggested (Deacon, 2001) that it was because:

- Globalization in terms of the form it took in the 1980s and 1990s was primarily a neo-liberal political project born at the height of the transatlantic Thatcher-Reagan alliance. This flavored the anti-public provision discourse about social policy within countries.
- The collapse of the communist project coinciding as it did with the height of neo-liberalism gave a further push to the rise of the myth of the marketplace.
- The perceived negative social consequences of globalization generated a new concern for the poor. In the name of meeting the needs of the poorest of the poor the "premature" or "partial" welfare states of Latin America, South Asia, and Africa were challenged as serving only the interests of a small privileged work force and elite state employees. A new alliance was to be struck between the Bank and the poor (see Graham, 1994; Deacon, 1997). The analysis of the privileged and exclusionary nature of these provisions was accurate. However, by destroying the public state services for this middle class in the name of the poor the politics of solidarity, which requires the middle class to have a self-interest in public provision which they fund, was made more difficult. The beneficiary index measures of the Bank showing how tertiary education spending, for example, benefited the elite contributed in no small measure to this development. The Bank technical expertise was ill-informed about the political economy of welfare state building.
- In the late 1980s and 1990s the self-confidence of defenders of the social democratic and other equitable approaches to social policy was temporarily lost. The critics of neo-liberal globalization came to believe their worst-case prognosis.

Counteracting this tendency will not be easy. Re-establishing the case for equity in social policy and social development will require major analytical and policy changes. A major shift is needed in the focus of development analysts from a focus on the global poor and their condition to the global rich and their private privileges. The mapping of the emerging global markets in social welfare and the inequity-generating impact they are having is an urgent necessity. There are, however, signs of a shift in the global discourse leading to a reassertion of the politics of social solidarity and universalism. There are a number of global initiatives that have the aim of re-establishing the case for and finding ways of implementing universal public provisioning as part of an equitable social policy in southern countries. Among them are:

- A new UNRISD research program on Social Policy in a Development Context under the leadership of Thandika Mkandawire, which has the stated objective to "move (thinking) away from social policy as a safety net…towards a conception of active social policy as a powerful instrument for development working in tandem with economic policy." This program held, with Swedish funding, its inaugural conference in October 2000, at which social policy scholars from most regions of the world were present. (See www.unrisd.org.)
- The rethinking presently being undertaken within the ILO concerning the sustainability of its traditional laborist approach to social protection is important. In particular is the Socio-Economic Security in Focus work program that is searching for new forms of universalistic social protection to complement the very limited coverage in the south of work based social security schemes. Good practices being revealed within this program could inform southern social policy-making (www.ilo.org/ses).
- The ongoing activities of several U.N. agencies support this more universal approach. Such activities include the U.N. Commission of Human Rights and its increased focus on the convention on Economic, Cultural, and Social Rights, the continuing work by UNICEF to work for Basic Services for All, the activities following on from the UNESCO conference on Education for All in 2000, the ongoing program of work leading to the high-level meeting on Finance for Development in 2002, and the new initiative of the UNDP Technical Cooperation among Developing Countries (UNDPTCDC) to set up a South-South Social Policy and Globalization Net (www.tcdcwide.net/SSPGnet).
- Also important is the follow-up work from Geneva 2000 by the U.N. Social Policy and Social Development Secretariat including the codification of U.N. social policy. The work program of the Commission for Social Development, which includes in 2000/01 a focus on social protection and in 2001/02 a focus on social and economic policy, is of especial relevance. Within this context the report of the U.N. Secretary-General: "Enhancing social protection and reducing vulnerability in a globalizing world" (www.un.org/esa/socdev/csd/csd39docs/csd39e2.pdf), prepared for the February 2001 Commission for Social Development, is an important milestone in an attempt to articulate U.N. social policy. Among the positive features of the report are the following: (a) It is the first comprehensive U.N. statement on social protection, (b) The thrust of its argument is that social protection measures serve both an equity-enhancing and an investment function and such measures need to be a high priority of governments and regions, (c) It

defines social protection broadly to include not only cash transfers but also health and housing protection, (d) It accepts that unregulated globalization is increasing inequity within and between countries, (e) It argues that social protection "should not (serve only) as a residual function of assuring the welfare of the poorest but as a foundation...for promoting social justice and social cohesion" (para 16), (f) It argues that if equity is the goal then "tax-funded social transfers are highly effective if the fiscal situation permits" (para 89 and 95k), (g) While being rather vague on the nature of a public-private welfare mix in provision it does point out that "insurance markets are difficult to operate effectively" (para 95c). It has to be said that discussion on even this paper became bogged down at the Commission. While the EU was supportive the G77 wished again to link it to issues of global financing and governance arrangements (Langmore, 2001).

So, from the standpoint of those concerned to see the case for universal provision to secure an equitable social policy at a national level being reasserted there is cautious room for optimism. The point should not be overstated, however, for two reasons. The Bank is still powerful and not convinced about redistributive politics and a north-south tension over social standards still complicates any global agreement on desirable social policy.

Rethinking Equity in Social Security

Globalization and the discourses associated with it therefore present a very real challenge to those who manage and defend social security institutions of the European kind within which a large role is often allocated to the state and provision for risk sharing across classes is provided for. The challenges may be summarized as:

- *The privatization threat.* Social security institutions are threatened by the push within the discourses of both neo-liberal globalization and the new so-called "socially responsible globalization" to privatize social security for all but the poor.
- *The fiscal base threat.* Global economic competition poses a threat to the payroll taxation base of public social security provision.
- *The legitimacy threat.* The narrow coverage of many social security schemes in developing countries undermines any claim such schemes have to serve the cause of equity.

This chapter does not end with detailed prescription. Other chapters in the book address these issues in more detail. It ends with a challenge. Those who would defend the principles of risk sharing and equitable social security need, in the context of globalization, to return to these principles and consider how they can be applied in a global era so that equitable socioeconomic security is truly available to all. If there is no such rethinking then the defenders of existing European-style social security schemes may be perceived from a global standpoint to be part of the problem and not a part of the solution as they will be accused of defending in a social protectionist way the privileged social security of the beneficiaries of the imperial epoch.

The challenge to the defenders and administrators of such schemes is to work with others who are concerned with universal social protection in a globalizing era to determine what part such schemes might play in a broader approach to the search for equitable social welfare. Because work-based social security schemes cover such a small constituency in many developing countries and because they are in any case threatened by global competition and because the individualization and privatization alternative preferred by the Bank also risks the social exclusion of many, interest has therefore developed in alternatives. Income tax or VAT-funded forms of social benefits payable to children or women or old people, either on the basis of citizenship or residency or on the basis of educational attendance in the case of children, has grown. These are measures that, in effect, act to support informal extended family forms of care. Experiments have taken place to extend formal social security entitlements to the informal sectors of the economy and to risks attached to means of livelihood other than formal work such as agricultural activity. New forms of mutuality and social insurance emerging among self-employed workers in several developing countries are also appearing. As part of a broader struggle to re-establish the case for equitable and universal social provision in countries at all levels of development social security may have a future in a globalized world.

References

Alber, J., and Standing, G. (2000). "Globalization and Social Dumping: An Overview." *Journal of European Social Policy*, 10 (2), 99-119.

Cornia, G. A., Jolly, R., and Stewart, F. (1987). *Adjustment with a Human Face*. Oxford: Clarendon Press.

Deacon, B. (1997). *Global Social Policy: International Organisations and the Future of Welfare*. London: Sage.

____. (2000a). *Globalization and Social Policy*. UNRISD Occasional Paper 5, Geneva: UNRISD.

____. (2000b). "Eastern European Welfare States: The Impact of the Politics of Globalisation." *Journal of European Social Policy*, 10 (2), 146-161.

____. (2001). Prospects for Equitable Social Provision in a Globalising World. Paper presented at the Social Policy Association Conference, Belfast, July.

Devetak, R., and Higgott, R. (1999). "Justice Unbound? Globalization, States and the Transformation of the Social Bond." *International Affairs*, 75 (3), 483-498.

Doyal, L., and Gough, I. (1991). *A Theory of Human Needs*. London: Macmillan.

Gillion, C., Turner, J., Bailey, C., and Latulippe, D. (eds.).(2000). *Social Security Pensions: Development and Reform*. Geneva: ILO.

Graham, C. (1994). *Safety Nets, Politics and the Poor*. Washington, D.C.: Brookings Institution.

Holzmann, R., and Jørgensen, S. L. (1999). *Social Protection: A Risk Management Approach*. Washington, D.C.: World Bank.

Huber, E., and Stephens, J. (2000). *The Political Economy of Pension Reform: Latin America in Comparative Perspective*. UNRISD Occasional paper No. 7, Geneva: UNRISD.

IMF. (1998). *Social Dimensions of the IMF's Policy Dialogue*. IMF Pamphlet No. 47. Washington, D.C.: IMF.

Koivusalo, M. (1999). *The World Trade Organisation and Trade Creep in Health and Social Policies*. GASPP Occasional Paper No. 4, Helsinki: STAKES.

Kwon, H.-j. (2001). "Globalisation, Unemployment and Policy Responses in Korea." *Global Social Policy*, 1 (2), 213-234.

Langmore, J. (2001). "The Commission for Social Development: Prospects for Global Political Evolution." *Global Social Policy*, 1 (3).

Mesa-Lago, C. (2000). *Market, Socialist and Mixed Economies: Comparative Policy and Performance-Chile, Cuba and Cost Rica*. Baltimore, Md.: Johns Hopkins University Press.

OECD. (1999). *A Caring World: New Social Policy Agenda*. Paris: OECD.

Scharpf, F. W. (2000). "The Viability of Advanced Welfare States in the International Economy." *Journal of European Public Policy*, 7 (2), 190-228.

Scharpf, F. W., and Schmidt, V. A. (eds.).(2000). *Welfare and Work in the Open Economy*. Oxford: Oxford University Press.

Standing. G. (2000). Towards a Charter on Economic Security. Paper presented at ILO In Focus Programe on Socio-Economic Security Seminar, Bellagio, 6-9 March.

Sykes, R., Palier, B., and Prior, P. (2001). *Globalization and the European Welfare States: Challenges and Change*. Basingstoke: Palgrave.

Taylor, L. (2000). *External Liberalization, Economic Performance and Social Policy*. New York: Oxford University Press.

3

The Financing of Social Protection in the Context of Economic Globalization

Alain Euzéby

Because it is financed largely out of compulsory levies (taxes and social security contributions), social protection is often regarded as a burden that supposedly weighs heavily on the economy and is an obstacle to employment. The levies involved vary considerably (from 20 to 35 percent of GDP in most countries of Western Europe, compared to less than 5 percent in most countries of sub-Saharan Africa), and in highly varied proportions are derived from contributions based on income from economic activity (in particular wages) and taxation (general taxation and/or designated taxes). The main problems raised by the financing of social protection are of two kinds:

- *Financial needs:* these are long term and universal. In developed countries expenditure on social protection tends to increase more rapidly than its revenue, probably as a result of demographic aging; in developing countries, which in many cases have only embryonic social protection systems, the extension and improvement of such systems face serious problems of financial means;
- *Modalities of financing:* these arise mainly in countries where social protection is largely financed by employer's contributions, which are accused of increasing manpower costs and cited as a factor affecting unemployment.

These two types of problems are quite old, but they become more acute under the pressure of economic globalization. While this process is not recent, it has increased considerably since the early 1980s with the major growth of international trade (under the combined influence of GATT [General Agreement on Tariffs and Trade] and progress in means of transport), the spectacular rise of multinational firms and foreign direct investment, and the explosion of international movements of capital made possible both by the liberalization of such movements and by the possibility now afforded to make instant transactions from one end of the world to the other, thanks to electronics and computer technology. It is important to stress that economic globalization in its present form is not the result of natural or spontaneous evolution. It is a *created phenomenon*, provoked for purely economic reasons. It is the outcome of decisions taken by most countries on earth, under pressure from the neo-liberal models advocated and disseminated by GATT, then the World Trade Organization (WTO), the International Monetary Fund (IMF), the World Bank and the Organisation for Economic Co-operation and Development (OECD). These models were developed in reaction to Keynesian analyses and increasing intervention by public authorities in economic and social issues. They offer an apology for free trade, competition and market mechanisms. They have served as justification for economic globalization, which, in turn, has become a powerful ideological tool in support of these neo-liberal analyses. Such analyses are based on the demands of constantly increasing international competition, and involve denouncing any public intervention thought excessive and advocating, in particular the reduction of social protection and substantial reductions in compulsory levies.[1] The combination of neo-liberal thinking and globalization hence poses a heavy threat for social protection, since it calls into question its very legitimacy.

Globalization will be seen, first, to make social protection both more difficult to finance and more necessary than ever; it will then be stressed that it lends weight to the criticism that the financing of social protection is an obstacle to employment; and finally, emphasis will be placed on the fact that social protection must stand up to the tyranny of international competition.

Social Protection is More Difficult to Finance, but More Necessary than Ever Before

Neo-liberal thinking, which now enjoys world dominance, only emphasizes the positive aspects of free trade and the free movement of capital. It stresses in particular the following arguments: each country has an interest in specializing in producing the goods for which it enjoys a relative advantage and in importing goods that are more expensive to produce locally;[2] international competition is an important factor in economic progress, since it encourages enterprises to be more dynamic, to innovate, reduce costs and prices, and adapt better to the desires of their clients; the free movement of capital is justified by the fact that it promotes the better allocation of resources worldwide.[3]

The trend towards free trade and the option taken by most countries in favor of their growing integration in the international economy are hence largely presented as being likely to make their enterprises more dynamic and to stimulate their economic growth.[4] However, the arguments in favor of trade liberalization and globalization are based on purely utilitarian reasoning, which only takes account of the generally positive effects of this process, without really accepting that where there are winners (individuals regarded as consumers, highly qualified people, owners of well-invested capital), there are also losers, of whom there are many: more than half the developing countries are virtually ignored by foreign investment; international competition and competition policy have exacerbated social inequality, poverty and exclusion in most countries worldwide (the UNDP's annual "World Development Reports").

If the liberalization of international trade is favorable to the growth of world production, then this ought to generate greater resources to finance social protection. Curiously, however, this link is very largely overlooked. The predominance of neo-liberal thinking and the intensification of international competition have, on the contrary, rather had the effect of reducing the availability of such resources. Since, moreover, international competition produces victims, globalization generates social costs that increase the need for social protection.

Reduced Resources

The liberalization of international trade at first considerably reduced fiscal income in many developing countries that derived a sizeable proportion of such income from customs duties. More generally, however, the reduction in the resources available to finance social protection is the outcome of both the pressures of fiscal and social competition and the demands of competitivity and profitability faced by enterprises.

Pressures of fiscal and social competition. With the major development of multinational firms and foreign direct investment, globalization has led to *competition between territories.* Countries have become regions of the world, and endeavor to attract and retain enterprises, investment, and foreign capital. *Tax havens* are an old and well-known issue, but the wide variety of practices to which they give rise are increasing exponentially. Simultaneously, *preferential fiscal schemes* are developing in a wide variety of forms. Emphasis should also be placed on the growing role of *export processing zones*, which are genuine enclaves established within the territory of certain countries, mostly in Asia and Latin America. These enclaves are totally or partially exempted from the fiscal and social legislation of the countries themselves. Multinational firms are encouraged to set up subsidiaries in such zones and to manufacture export goods there, in conditions that are particularly advantageous in terms of wages, social security contributions, and taxation. Fiscal and social competition can also be seen in the increased concern in various countries worldwide to ensure that fiscal and social security charges are not much higher, and if possible are lower, than those in neighboring countries or trading partners. Many countries are tempted to reduce the taxation and contributions payable by enterprises in the hope of deriving a competitive advantage. All these factors forcing the bids down bring increased difficulties for the financing of social security (OECD, 1998a; Tanzi, 1995, 1996; Zee, 1998).

The demands of competitivity and profitability faced by enterprise. Enterprises face demands of competitivity and profitability that often imply wage reductions and, in turn, have a negative impact on the social security contributions of employers and workers. These demands derive first from the constraints imposed by increased international competition, which leads enterprises to freeze and in some cases reduce wages so as to enable them to sell at a better price and increase profits, and hence to have greater capital available to finance their investments.[5] Technological progress and international competition are in effect forcing enterprises constantly to modernize their production techniques and to innovate by introducing procedures that require little manpower. There is also the growing influence, resulting from the free movement of capital, exerted by institutional investors (notably pension funds) on the management of the companies of which they are shareholders (a phenomenon termed *corporate governance*). Since the only demands that count in their eyes are the returns of their securities, they threaten to sell them if they do not perform well in this respect. They hence impose their demand for dividends and stock exchange performance and thereby exert pressure on employment and on workers' remuneration.

Public authorities are trying to attract and retain capital that is increasingly mobile, and this is leading them—especially in the United States and Western Europe—to make combating inflation the main objective of their economic policies. Not only does the slowing of wage increases promote the attainment of this goal, but also—where unemployment falls below a certain level (termed the *natural rate of unemployment*)—it can give rise to wage demands and cause inflation.[6] This is the reason why governments, and especially central banks, are not trying to reduce unemployment to its lowest possible level, but only as close as possible to its "natural" level! Any government taking measures deemed inappropriate by international financiers hence makes itself vulnerable to increasing difficulties in gaining access to capital markets, falls on the stock exchange, and a reduced rate of exchange for its currency. Hence the expression "dictatorship of financial markets" that is sometimes used to describe this form of influence exerted by financial globalization.[7] In any case, there is hardly any need to stress that all these elements—wage cuts or the lack of enthusiasm in tackling unemployment—have a harmful impact on the income available for social protection, whereas globalization makes it all the more necessary.

The Increasing Needs of Social Protection

Even if it has positive economic effects on the whole, economic globalization is accompanied by a considerable increase in inequality between countries and within them, while, at the same time, exacerbating the threat to individual security in society. Hence, while the world is becoming increasingly prosperous, many developing countries are unable to match international competition and are largely overlooked by foreign investment. Their exports, which are largely basic products, are highly vulnerable to the whims of international markets, and the structural adjustment plans that they have had to implement under pressure from the IMF and the World Bank have only brought greater suffering (unemployment, wage reductions, increased poverty) for large sectors of their populations (UNDP, 2000; World Bank, 2000).

Even in the wealthiest of developing countries economic globalization and heightened international competition have brought rivalry and even "economic war," leaving losers and victims in its wake. With the rise of free trade such countries are encouraged to concentrate on activities having a strong technological element and requiring highly skilled labor and to import products that require a large amount of unskilled labor from countries with low manpower costs. The unskilled workers in developed countries hence face competition from both machines and their counterparts in developing countries. In countries such as the United States this means reductions in already low wages and an alarming increase in the number of poor workers. In countries such as those of Western Europe, however, where the obstacles to reductions in manpower costs are greater, this has brought unemployment. The competitive demands of enterprises have also led to the development of various forms of precarious employment (interim and part-time work, short-term contracts) and to workers' accepting work part-time because they cannot find full-time jobs. Such arrangements enable companies to adapt their personnel structures or hours of work to variations in their activities and to manufacture on demand in "just-in-time" operations so as to avoid storage costs. They also meet the needs of manpower flexibility, which is increasingly regarded as essential and has led certain countries to relax legislation on dismissals.

More generally, globalization makes populations worldwide more vulnerable by increasing the many sources of economic insecurity, whether through the restructuring or delocalization of enterprises, the instability of financial markets and exchange rates, the risk of financial crises, fluctuations in commercial outlets and in the prices of exports, the decline in certain sectors of activity or the rapid obsolescence of certain professional skills.

The outcome is that poverty and exclusion have increased dramatically in many countries, even those in the wealthiest parts of the world, either as a result in particular of low hours of work or low wages, as in the United States, or of increased unemployment, as in the European Union.[8] In such circumstances social protection is increasingly necessary to compensate for some of the social costs of globalization by coming to the assistance of those "wounded" in the economic war and by international competition. A number of commentators have also noted in this respect the existence of a strong correlation between the degree of openness to international trade on the part of individual countries and the amount of their public expenditure as a percentage of GDP (Cameron, 1978; Katzenstein, 1985; Rodrik, 1996). Countries with a high degree of openness (the typical case being small countries such as Sweden and the Netherlands) are those in which intervention by public authorities, and particularly social security expenditure, are the most necessary in order to protect the population against the risks of such openness.

Globalization hence squeezes social protection on both sides, reducing its income and making its spending more necessary than ever. This contradiction could lend greater weight to the increasingly vocal and frequent criticism that it receives, which also implicates its financing as an obstacle to employment.

The Financing of Social Protection is Increasingly Singled Out as an Obstacle to Employment

Because social protection is a system based on collective solidarity, largely administered by public authorities or under their responsibility and financed for the most part out of compulsory levies, it has for a long time given rise to criticism, in particular by employers' organizations and liberal economists and politicians. However, with economic globalization such criticism has increased dramatically and been delivered to a growing audience. It is largely based on the notion that social protection is a heavy burden that increases compulsory levies, and that employers' contributions are allegedly a cause of unemployment.

Are Taxes and Social Security Contributions Too High?

After directly inspiring the economic policies of President Reagan in the United States and the Conservative party in the United Kingdom, neo-liberal American supply-side thinking (Meyer, 1981; Salin, 1986; Wanniski, 1978) permeated the work and recommendations of the main international economic organizations and the ideas of public authorities in many countries. The dominant ideas were henceforth geared to the demands of international competition and to the fiscal and social forms of competition to which it gives rise, meaning attacking taxes and social security contributions by presenting them solely as costs, burdens, and economic handicaps. In terms of social protection this has meant claims that it constitutes a burden on the economy that is difficult to bear and proposals to privatize the financing of certain types of benefit. The accusations made against compulsory levies are, however, exaggerated.

First, such taxes are traditionally accused of being excessive and therefore of reducing incentives to create jobs or save, discouraging the more dynamic elements of the population and damaging the competitivity of enterprises and contributing to unemployment.[9] What is striking, however, is that even with the best will in the world, the many and varied studies and countless calculations made cannot be regarded as having identified any significant negative impact of the level of compulsory levies on economic activity or the employment situation.[10]

Secondly, if one considers all the countries in the world as a whole, it can be noted that, with very few exceptions, there is a close match between the level of economic development and the levels of public expenditure, social protection, and compulsory levies. International comparisons also show very clearly that it is not the countries where compulsory levies are the highest—notably the Western European countries—that are showing the worst economic performance; similarly, those where compulsory levies and levels of social protection are the lowest—the least developed countries of Africa, Asia, and Latin America—are far from obtaining the best economic outcomes! Even among the EU countries alone, it is clear that it is not the countries with the highest taxes and contribution ratios[11] (Sweden, Denmark) that are the worst hit by unemployment.

Finally, and most significantly, the fact that compulsory levies return to circulate in the economy in the form of social security benefits, the remuneration of civil servants, and public investment, etc., is a factor that is often forgotten or deliberately hidden, but whose positive effects are undeniable.

It is true that compulsory levies are never a great pleasure to pay, and that much can certainly be said in many countries about their structure or the specific features of some of them. Nevertheless, the limits on their level and on any increases in them are chiefly psychological and political, and depend heavily on the quality of the management of public finances and of the agencies administering social protection, as well as the values that a society cultivates and which are advocated in political discussions and speeches.

Are Employers' Social Security Contributions a Source of Unemployment?

The problem is well known: because they are based on the gross wage and are paid in addition to it, contributions are often attacked as increasing labor costs and thereby damaging the competitivity of enterprises; of encouraging enterprises to replace workers by machines (the process of substituting capital for labor); of penalizing enterprises that use greater manpower than those that are comparatively highly mechanized; and of being an obstacle to the employment of unskilled workers, who are precisely the ones most affected by unemployment. These criticisms lead to a wide variety of proposals for the relaxation or reform of employers' contributions, but which are far from justified.

The question of labor costs. International comparisons show clearly that employers' contributions are not a determining factor in manpower costs. The latter are mainly linked to the level of economic development. It is hence normal for countries with high levels of productivity to have high manpower costs, since the remuneration of labor is a means of keeping production moving. In any case, if one considers countries with levels of development that are more or less comparable, such as the EU countries, for example, comparisons clearly show that in countries where employers' contributions are large, by contrast gross wages are relatively low. This is the case in France, Spain, and Sweden. Conversely, in countries such as Denmark and the Netherlands, where contributions are low, gross wages are high. This is explained by differences in the modalities of financing social protection. In Denmark it is financed largely out of taxation; gross wages are high, but heavily affected by income and purchase taxes. In the Netherlands gross wages are also very high, but workers' contributions are very high. International comparisons are often made of employers' contributions alone, but they are of little significance. As far as competitivity is concerned, it is manpower costs as a whole (gross wages plus employers' contributions) that should be taken into consideration.

Substituting capital for labor. Such substitution is certainly much less linked to the amount of employers' contributions based solely on wages than they are to technological progress and the demands of international competition, which increasingly forces enterprises to modernize so as to be more productive and competitive. If increases in productivity—which, especially in the most advanced countries, derive from the mechanization, computerization, and "robotization" of production—are actually to result in reductions in manpower needs, this should logically bring reductions in hours of work rather than layoffs and unemployment. However, international competition is often regarded as an obstacle to such measures.

Manpower-based enterprises. It is certain that employers' contributions constitute a heavier burden on enterprises using large amounts of manpower than for those which by contrast are highly mechanized. This lies at the root of various proposals to relax the financial burdens that derive solely from labor and to "make the machines pay" (by enlarging the contribution base to include all added value; introduction of contributions based on depreciation, fixed assets or net assets, etc; variations in the rate of contribution based on the degree of mechanization of the enterprise, etc.). However, it should first be observed that, whereas highly mechanized enterprises are in effect required to pay fewer social security contributions, by contrast they have greater costs linked to the use of machines (energy, maintenance, and replacement of parts). The real problem, however, is to determine whether or not employers' contributions are a *normal labor cost.* Here it is useful to make a distinction between the two major forms of solidarity realized by social security:[12] occupational and national solidarity. Where contributions, whether paid by employers or workers, are earmarked for the financing of social security benefits whose aim is not to compensate for loss of income from an occupation (the typical case being family benefits and medical care), and cover all or nearly all the population of the country, then it is advisable to replace them by financing out of taxation. As regards the distinction between workers' and employers' contributions, it seems clear that it is of no significance. Both are part of the workers' remuneration that they do not receive directly, but which are paid for their benefit to social protection agencies. This is, moreover, how they are regarded in national accounting systems. It would hence be more logical and more transparent to combine them into a single contribution representing their *indirect* or *deferred wage* (Euzéby and Euzéby, 1984; Van Langendonck, 2000).

Unemployment among unskilled workers. Such workers are admittedly generally the ones most affected by unemployment. However, the solution to this problem certainly lies more in the improvement of education and vocational training than in a reduction in employers' contributions, even where such reductions target low wages.[13]

Causes of unemployment. This is the subject of lively controversy, which we will not enter into here. It must, however, be recognized that, in the case of developing countries, the causes are largely to be found in the lack of productive activity and of solvent demand. In the developed countries the causes must not be dissociated from the demands of competitivity: under the pressure of international competition, the remuneration of wage earners is more often regarded as a cost to be contained or reduced than as incomes that make it possible to keep production moving, and enterprises are forced to adopt the most efficient production techniques. While it is a means of preventing unemployment from growing, the search for competitivity is hence not sufficient to bring it within acceptable limits (those represented by frictional unemployment linked to manpower mobility), since it implies increases in productivity enabling enterprises to produce more and more with less and less labor (Rifkin, 1995).

Various arguments put forward show that it is international competition, as practiced today—much more so than the financing of social security—that has a negative impact on employment. Yet it is this same competition that is invoked to justify freezing or cutting social protection.[14] Social protection must hence resist such threats, not only because it is unfairly accused, but also because it is increasingly necessary to repair the social costs of economic globalization and to help its victims.

Social Protection Must Resist the Tyranny of International Competition

Economic globalization and the exacerbation of international competition have led to *economism*, that is, economic logic pushed to the extreme, to a system of values in which the various spheres of human existence are subordinate to purely economic considerations, and in particular the demands of international competition. The mad race for market share and the competition to attract and retain foreign investment have meant that public authorities in many countries are tempted to resort to measures involving reducing the level or duration of payment of certain social security benefits so as to reduce the fiscal and social burden of enterprises on their territory. Hence, the risk of social protection falling in a downward spiral, since competitivity is a very relative notion. For it is always possible, even in countries that are relatively less developed in social terms, to invoke the "example" of other countries where wages are lower, working conditions are worse, and social protection is more rudimentary. Hence, it is absolutely essential to prevent social protection from being sacrificed, in the name of competitivity, on the altar of international competition. This means, first, that the values on which its financing is based must be affirmed and defended with vigor. On this basis, it is then important to emphasize that its financing stands the best chance of success and development worldwide if upheld by world social governance and promoted through the creation of an International Social Fund.

The Values of Social Financing

We know that it is the inadequacies of self-protection, charity, family solidarity, and private insurance that justified the creation and development of social protection (Barr, 1992; Euzéby, 1997). What differentiates it from mechanisms such as insurance is that it is financed largely by compulsory levies, and not on the basis of scales reflecting the probability of the risk covered. It lends itself well to the coverage of certain contingencies, such as unemployment, poverty, and family costs, but it can also be used so as to reject selective risk-taking and thereby give expression to genuine solidarity.[15] For these reasons social protection was recognized as a human right in the Universal Declaration of Human Rights of 1948 and can be regarded as one of the pillars of social justice.

Though often mentioned, the idea of social justice is still somewhat vague and subject to a wide variety of interpretations. Without going into detail on this point (Van Parijs, 1991; 1995), let us use the terms of the Declaration of Philadelphia, adopted in 1944 by the International Labour Organization, and take it that social justice is an ideal intended to ensure that all individuals in a society have the means "to pursue both their material well-being and their spiritual development in conditions of freedom and dignity, of economic security and equal opportunity." This concept, which also forms the basis of the definition of human development,[16] supposes that all individuals must be able to enjoy decent living conditions, to preserve their state of health and to live as long as possible. Because it fuels solidarity mechanisms based on income redistribution, the financing of social protection is a step in this direction. It hence embodies the values of solidarity, equity, social justice, and respect for the dignity of human life, which it is now more urgent than ever before to proclaim ceaselessly, and to define, to teach and to campaign for in the mass media so as to prevent them from being totally submerged by the hegemonic values inherent in neo-liberal thinking and economic globalization.

The Urgent Need for World Social Governance

The term *governance* refers to a set of rules, institutions, and practices that set limits on the behavior of individuals, organizations, and enterprises (UNDP, 1999: 34). Applied to the social field and approached at a world level, governance concerns the minimum and basic rules that States should apply and ensure respect for in relation to labor law and social protection. Such rules already exist in the form of the international standards defined in ILO (International Labour Organization) Conventions and Recommendations. However, Recommendations do not entail any obligation on the part of the Organization's member States, which are, moreover, free to decide whether or not to ratify a Convention. As regards supervision of the application of ratified Conventions, the procedures do not provide for any real sanctions in the event of failure to apply them (Bartolomei de la Cruz and Euzéby, 1997; Sengenberger and Campbell, 1994; Valticos, 1998). Hence the idea of giving much more force to certain standards by making their ratification and application more binding. This concern would be addressed by a *social clause.* Included in the agreements governing international trade, it would make it possible to take explicit account of its social dimension. For this purpose it might, for example, reserve the designation of most favored nation to countries that respect certain ILO standards, or it might draw on Article VI of the GATT to allow a country to levy "compensatory" customs duty on imports from countries that do not observe them.

In principle such a clause could be based on the Preamble to the ILO Constitution, which states, "the failure of any nation to adopt humane conditions of labor is an obstacle in the way of other nations which desire to improve the conditions in their own countries." Thus, what was already true in 1919 is even more so today! It is hence necessary not only to defend and promote fundamental social rights, but also to prevent social progress from being perceived as an obstacle to economic progress and to prevent the weakening of social protection and labor legislation from being turned into a means of reducing the obligations and constraints faced by enterprises simply in order to increase their competitivity. The rules embodied in a social clause would be instruments that genuinely regulated international competition. It is hence essential for discussions, both within the ILO and the WTO and between those two organizations, to achieve results rapidly.

The Need for an International Social Fund

Such a fund would serve the purpose of helping developing countries promote their social and human development, and in particular to extend and strengthen their social protection systems. In this way it would first further the promotion of economic, social and cultural human rights. But it would also promote the progressive reduction of the enormous differences in manpower costs and in social conditions that separate most developing countries from the developed countries and which penalize unskilled workers in the latter. The creation of such a fund would be justified by the provisions of several major international declarations, beginning with the Universal Declaration of Human Rights, Article 22 of which states that "Everyone, as a member of society, has the right to social security," and that international cooperation must contribute to the satisfaction of economic, social, and cultural rights. A similar provision is included in Article 2 of the International Covenant of 1966 concerning those rights. The Declaration of Philadelphia, which is annexed to the ILO Constitution, can also be mentioned here, since after recalling that "lasting peace can be established only if it is based on social justice," it includes social security among the programs that the ILO has the obligation "to further among the nations of the world."

Management of the fund could hence be assigned to the ILO whose mission is the promotion of social progress. Its role in world governance would thereby be extended and strengthened. The ILO would provide assistance to countries on the basis of clearly defined objectives, and would supervise the use to which such assistance was put. Determining the resources for the fund should not pose any major problems in view of the vast wealth produced worldwide and the dimensions of the profits achieved by the main beneficiaries of economic globalization. Hence, it depends essentially on the political will of the international community to promote social development. The best solution would certainly be to institute world taxes. There is no shortage of possibilities: a "Tobin tax" on international movements of capital, which are already several dozen times larger than the trade in goods and services, and which often have very destabilizing effects on national economies and exchange rates (Ul Hacq et al., 1996; Chesnais, 1999); a tax on foreign direct investment (Wachtel, 1998), which would make it possible to thwart the evasion of fiscal and social security costs by enterprises that globalization makes possible, the rate of which tax could take account of the extent of respect for workers' fundamental rights in the host country; world taxes on energy and on polluting activities; taxes on "bytes," that is, the volume of data transmitted by Internet; and a world tax on international airline travel, etc. (UNDP, 1994, 1998).

In view of the negative social effects of exacerbated world competition and the risk of losing its legitimacy that it increasingly faces, the financing of social security must be defended. Its specific role must not be interpreted as an anomaly or an economic handicap, but as a set of financial means serving the cause of social protection that is regarded as a human right and consequently an end in itself. Unemployment in the developed countries is due more to the excesses of globalization than the excesses of social protection. As a factor in economic progress, international competition should be favorable to social progress. However, for this to happen, genuine global social governance must set up a system of checks to prevent it from becoming excessive, that is, from becoming a dominating, destructive and untamed force. If it does not, then the demands of competitivity that it implies could mean that social considerations will be subordinated to economic considerations, and means treated as ends, and vice versa.

Notes

1. The main initiators of neo-liberal currents of thought include F. A. Hayek, M. Friedman, J. Buchanan, G. Tullock, E. Borcherding and A. Laffer.
2. This recommendation is based on the neoclassical theory of international trade which is a continuation and development of the famous "law of comparative costs," formulated at the beginning of the nineteenth century by D. Ricardo and which provided justification for free trade. At the heart of this theory lies the Heckscher-Ohlin-Samuelson theorem. However, such analyses are based on hypotheses that now have little to do with the current economic context, since they suppose that production factors do not move from one country to another, which means ultimately that they completely overlook the transfer of technology, capital movements, and foreign direct investment, and in particular the delocalization of enterprises.
3. For the advantages offered and the problems raised by the liberalization of international capital movements, see, for example, Obstfeld and Rogoff (1996) and Obstfeld (1998).
4. Many theoretical and empirical studies stress the existence of a positive relation between openness to international trade and economic growth. For a review of literature on this issue, see WTO (1998: chap. IV). Similarly, the World Bank (1995) considered that application of the Uruguay Round (1994) would result in annual increases of $100 to 200 billion worldwide. In 1995 world GDP totaled $28,800 billion.
5. However, this does not mean that the additional profits are fully utilized for self-financing. They are also largely earmarked for distribution as dividends to shareholders and for financial investments.
6. The concept of "natural rate of unemployment" is related to the NAIRU (Non-accelerating inflation rate of unemployment). This is the rate of unemployment below which inflation may accelerate.
7. Economic literature on this issue is increasing in volume. See, for example, Block (1996), Garrett (1996), or, in French, ATTAC (Association pour une taxation des transactions financières pour l'aide aux citoyens) (1999).
8. Even the World Bank recognizes that international trade "brings hardship for unskilled workers in the industrialized countries." On this issue, see, in particular, its

World Bank (1995: chap. 8). On inequality, unemployment, and poverty caused by international trade, see, among countless references, Burtless (1995) and Giraud (1996).

9. For a presentation of these issues and discussion, see, in particular, Euzéby (1994).

10. Thus, even though it has followed this issue for more than thirty years, the OECD regrets, in a recent study, "In addition to their sensitivity to the modeling methods used, such calculations crucially depend on the elasticity of supply and demand, and particularly the elasticity of manpower in relation to supply. Unfortunately, there is no consensus on the empirical value of these essential parameters." (OECD, 1998b: 180).

11. The rate of compulsory deductions is the amount of taxes and social security contributions as a proportion of GDP.

12. This is an old idea put forward more than twenty-five years ago by J. J. Dupeyroux (1976) and was later also presented in subsequent editions of the reference work by this expert (Dupeyroux and Ruellan, 1998) and widely taken up by other writers. See, in particular, ILO (1983) and Euzéby (1995).

13. On the reduction of employers' contributions for lower wages, see, in particular, for the French case, Euzéby (2000).

14. A good illustration of this type of reasoning is provided in the study carried out by Kopits (1997). The author of that study stresses that "globalization will impose the hardest constraint on further payroll tax rate increases." He deduces from this that the EU countries should take action to reduce their expenditure on social protection, which should include some degree of privatization of retirement pensions and health care.

15. Nevertheless, this does not prevent the financing of social security from being the subject of discussion on ways of making it more equitable or from giving rise to extensive reflection on the structure of fiscal systems and methods of calculating contributions (ceilings, proportional or progressive contributions, etc.).

16. It was the UNDP that, in its first Human Development Report (1990), offered the definition of "the process that enlarges the scope of possibilities available to individuals: to live long and in good health, to be educated and to have resources that make possible an appropriate standard of living are fundamental demands; to these can be added political freedom, the enjoyment of human rights and self-respect."

References

ATTAC (Association pour une taxation des transactions financières pour l'aide aux citoyens). (1999). *Contre la dictature des marchés financiers*. Paris: éditions La Dispute.

Barr, N. (1992). "Economic Theory and the Welfare State: A Survey and Interpretation." *Journal of Economic Literature*, XXX (June), 741-803.

Bartolomei de la Cruz, H., and A. Euzéby. (1997). *L'Organisation internationale du Travail (OIT)*, Collection Que sais-je?, n° 836. Paris: Presses universitaires de France.

Block, F. (1996). *The Vampire State and Other Stories*. New York: New Press.

Burtless, G. (1995). "International Trade and the Rise of Inequality." *Journal of Economic Literature*, XXXIII (June), 800-816.

Cameron, D. (1978). "The Expansion of the Public Economy: A Comparative Analysis." *American Political Science Review*, 72 (4), 1243-1261.

Chesnais, F. (1999). *Tobin or not Tobin. Une taxe internationale sur le capital*. Paris: L'Esprit frappeur.

Dupeyroux, J. J. (1976). "Sécurité sociale: adapter la nature des ressources à celle des dépenses." *Le Monde*, 21 September 1976.

Dupeyroux, J. J., and Ruellan, R. (1998). *Droit de la sécurité sociale*. Paris: Dalloz.

Euzéby, A. (1994). "Les prélèvements obligatoires sont-ils excessifs?" *Droit social*, (4), 319-326.

___. (1995). "Reduce or Rationalize Social Security Contributions to Reduce Unemployment?" *International Labour Review*, 134 (2), 227-242.

___. (1997). "Social Security: Indispensable Solidarity." *International Social Security Review*, 50 (3), 3-15

___. (2000). "L'allégement des cotisations sociales patronales: quels espoirs pour l'emploi?" *Droit Social*, (4), 368-374.

Euzéby, A., and Euzéby, C. (1984). "The Incidence of Employers' Social Security Contributions: The Factors at Stake." *International Social Security Review*, 42 (2), 139-149.

Garrett, G. (1995). "Capital Mobility, Trade and Domestic Politics of Economics." *International Organization*, 49 (4), 657-687.

Giraud, P. N. (1996). *L'inégalité du monde. Economie du monde contemporain*. Paris: Gallimard.

ILO. (1983). *Financing Social Security: The Options: An International Analysis*. Geneva: ILO.

Katzenstein, P. (1985). *Small States in the World Markets: Industrial Policy in Europe*. Ithaca, N.Y.: Cornell University Press.

Kopits, G. (1997). *Are Europe's Social Security Finances Compatible with EMU?* Papers on Policy Analysis and Assessments PPAA/97/3. Washington: IMF.

Meyer, L. H. (ed.). (1981). *The Supply Side Effect of Economic Policy*. Proceedings of the 1980 Economic Policy Conference. St. Louis, MO.: Federal Reserve Bank of St. Louis.

Obstfeld, M. (1998). "The Global Capital Market: Benefactor or Menace?" *Journal of Economic Perspectives*, 12 (4), 9-30.

Obstfeld, M., and Rogoff, K. (1996). *Foundations of International Macroeconomics*. Cambridge, Mass.: MIT Press.

OECD. (1998a). *Harmful Tax Competition: An Emerging Global Issue*. Paris: OECD.

___. (1998b). *Economic Outlook June 1998*. Paris: OECD.

Rifkin, J. (1995). *The End of Work: The Decline of the Global Labor Force and the Dawn of the Post-Market Era*. New York: Tarcher/Putnam.

Rodrik, D. (1996). *Why Do More Open Economies Have Bigger Governments?* NBER Working Paper, no 5537. Washington, D.C.: National Bureau of Economic Research.

Salin, P. (1986). *L'arbitraire fiscal*. Paris: R. Laffont.

Sengenberger, W., and Campbell, D. (1994). *International Labour Standards and Economic Interdependence*. Geneva: International Institute for Labour Studies.

Tanzi, V. (1995). *Taxation in an Integrating World*. Washington, D.C.: The Brookings Institution.

___. (1996). *Globalization, Tax Competition and the Future of Tax Systems*. IMF Working Paper, no. 96/141, Washington, D.C.: IMF.

Ul Hacq, M., Kaul, I., and Grunberg, J. (1996). *The Tobin Tax: Coping with Financial Volatility*. Oxford: Oxford University Press.

UNDP. (1990). *World Development Report 1990*. New York: UNDP.

___. (1994). *World Development Report 1994*. New York: UNDP.

___. (1999). *World Development Report 1999*. New York: UNDP.

Valticos, N. (1998). "International Labour Standards and Human Rights: Approaching the year 2000." *International Labour Review*, 137 (2), 151-164.

Van Langendonck, J. (2000). "La cotisation patronale et l'évolution des formes du travail." *Revue belge de sécurité sociale*, 42 (1), 5-18.

Van Parijs, P. (1991). *Qu'est-ce qu'une société juste? Introduction à la pratique de la philosophie politique*. Paris: Seuil.

___. (1995). *Real Freedom for All. What (if Anything) Can Justify Capitalism?* Oxford: Oxford University Press.

Wachtel, H. M. (1998). "Trois taxes globales pour maîtriser le capital." *Le Monde diplomatique*, October.

Wannisky, J. (1978). Taxes, Revenues and the Laffer curve. *Public Interest*, 50 (Winter): 3-16.

World Bank. (1995). *World Development Report 1995*. Washington, D. C.: World Bank.

___. (2000). *Can Africa Claim the 21st Century?* Washington D.C.: World Bank.

WTO. (1998). *Annual Report 1998*. Geneva: WTO.

Zee, H. (1998). "Taxation of Financial Capital in a Globalized Environment: The Role of Withholding Taxes." *National Tax Journal*, 51 (September): 587-599.

4

Globalization and National Welfare Regimes:
The East Asian Case*

Ian Gough

"Globalization" is frequently alleged to constrain and undermine national welfare states where they exist, to stall their development elsewhere, to encourage "social dumping" and to generate a "race to the bottom." The effects are claimed to operate via lower tax levels, labor standards, social expenditure ratios, coverage of social programs, and income redistribution. Yet evidence to back this up is remarkable by its absence, judging by a sample of recent empirical work.

It is not unusual for a taken-for-granted truth to lack evidential support. The lack here suggests problems in defining and operationalizing one or more of the following: the independent variable, the dependent variable, the causal links between the two, the relevant time period, and the impact of other factors in the policy environment. To sketch each in turn:

"*Globalization*" is a protean term. A recent survey ranges over increasing global connectedness in governance, trade, finance, production, migration, communication, culture, and the environment (Held et al., 1999). The focus of this chapter is *economic* globalization, but even then we must at least distinguish between trade, direct investment, the international integration of production, and the globalization of financial markets. Each has different potential impacts on the "welfare state," suggested in Table 4.1. The period from the mid-1980s has witnessed accelerating global integration on all fronts, with further tariff reductions, an escalation of foreign direct investment, and a notable integration of financial markets.

One feature of the present period is the enhanced power of capital compared with that of nation states and other actors in civil society such as trade unions. Kevin Farnsworth and I argue that this reflects its greater *structural* power—the ability of business and finance to influence policy without applying direct pressure on government through their agents. This is based on "exit" rather than "voice," though in practice the two are intertwined (Gough and Farnsworth, 2000). Greater economic openness has enhanced the exit options of capital invested in many fields of activity, and, *ceteris paribus*, has made governments, unions and other actors more responsive to capital's demands. However, there are two important caveats. First, this is not something new. In a capitalist society, the owners of the means of production always exert structural power of a qualitatively different kind to other actors by virtue of their majority control over investment and thus future prosperity. Second, this structural power is a variable, not a constant. It varies according to national (and supra-national) institutions and ideologies. Thus, among the G7 countries, we find that the structural power of capital grew most in the 1980s and 1990s in Britain, where restrictions on capital mobility were decisively removed, investment was privatized, and labor was unemployed, deregulated, and then recommodified. Yet this was not the case—at all or to the same extent—in the other G7 countries. The influence of Britain's institutions and its place in the world economy, and of the neo-liberal ideology of the Thatcher government were also decisive.

Globalization, as defined here, excludes global economic *governance*. The ideas and leverage of the U.S. Treasury, the Federal Reserve, the International Monetary Fund (IMF), the World Bank (WB), and now the World Trade Organization (WTO) are of immense importance throughout the developing and transitional world and indeed the Organization for Economic Co-operation and Development (OECD) world. High U.S. interest rates from 1980 onwards and the subsequent injunctions and impositions of the IMF and other international financial institutions (IFIs) on the developing world clearly had a deleterious and often catastrophic impact on many countries during the "lost decade" of the 1980s, and on the transition process of countries like Russia in the 1990s. If this is "economic globalization" then its impact on the social fabric of much of the world has been powerful and negative (Wade, 2001). But my focus here is on the automatic, non-intentional effects of the processes of economic globalization on the social capacities and outcomes of different nation states.

Second, "*social policy*," "social welfare" and the "welfare state" are also slippery terms. Extensive social policies may harm social welfare (as in Apartheid South Africa), high spending ratios may signal anti-welfare states (when spent on the military and elites), welfare states may not be a necessary or sufficient condition for improved social welfare. This makes it difficult to track "improvements" and "retrenchments." Not all social programs contribute to meeting basic human needs and other desirable outcomes. The welfare state remains contradictory.

Third, the causal *link* between globalization and welfare systems is difficult to establish. The positive correlation between social expenditure ratios and openness to trade appears to be stronger now than when first identified by Cameron (Rodrik, 1998). A recent study of four world regions found practically no evidence of trends towards social dumping in Southern Europe, Central Europe, East Asia, and the southern cone of Latin America (Alber and Standing, 2000). Others claim the picture is different when specific measures of social programs or indicators of welfare outcomes are used, but then the causal links are more tenuous and the measurement problems are greater. Fourth, the issue of *time periods* and lags may rescue the pessimistic analysis: it is possible that the full impact of economic globalization is yet to be witnessed, let alone measured. This is especially true of "strategic retrenchment" when measures are put in place to systematically slow down or reduce social measures over the medium to long term (Pierson, 1994). These dynamic effects on welfare-concerned political coalitions are of great concern.

Lastly, the wider *environment* may counteract any globalization influences there are. Pierson (1998) has documented the major domestic shifts which are profoundly modifying the social policy environments in the OECD world (see the lower half of Table 4.1). As Pierson points out, few of these have any links with globalization. Indeed, the moves towards a post-industrial service economy directly undermine the globalization thesis, implying a shift towards more non-tradables and location-specific production. Lastly, national social policies are continually driven by domestic conflicts and

Table 4.1
External and Internal Pressures Affecting Welfare Systems

Source	Pressure	Consequences for Advanced Countries (Examples)
External: 'globalisation'	Trade competition	Deindustrialisation; loss of unskilled jobs
	Capital mobility and integrated production	Tax competition; "social dumping"; reduced bargaining power of states and labour
	Internationalised financial markets	Decline of states' macro-economic policy autonomy
Internal: 'post-industrialisation'	Slow growing service sector productivity	The "trilemma" of employment, equity and budget stability
	Aging	Growing pension and health expenditure
	Transformation of households	Smaller household sizes, more single parent households, more women working
	Maturing of social entitlements	Automatic growth of social expenditure

policy feedbacks operating within nationally specific institutional forms and constellations of actors. These decisively mediate pressures of globalization.

The (perhaps obvious) conclusion is that globalization pressures are always mediated by domestic and international institutions, interests, and ideas. This argument has been developed in relation to the advanced capitalist countries of the North, most notably by Scharpf (2000), but is rarely applied to the South (Lee, 1999 is one exception). This chapter considers social policies and globalization pressures within the framework of comparative welfare regimes in the South.

Welfare Regimes North and South

In the classic formulation of Esping-Andersen (1990), welfare regimes are ways of conceptualizing the welfare programs, outcomes, and effects of those capitalist societies that have been transformed into welfare states. The concept of welfare regime embraces at least the following features:

1. the pattern of state social policies and programs, usually distinguishing social assistance, social insurance, and universal citizenship modes of distributing benefits in cash and in kind;
2. the wider pattern of welfare provisioning in society, usually in terms of the division of responsibility between the state, the market, and the household;
3. the welfare outcomes of these institutions, in terms of the degree of "decommodification" achieved—the extent to which a household's standard of living is insulated against their position in the labor market;
4. the stratification outcomes of these institutions: how and to what extent the welfare system in turn shapes inequalities, interests, and power in society and in this way reproduces the welfare regime through time.

The first two components are sometimes referred to as the "welfare mix." Thus in a nutshell:

welfare regime = welfare mix + welfare outcomes + stratification effects

This all takes place within a constellation of forces and power shaped by the dominant "political settlement" in that society. Such settlements usually emerge following periods of crisis, such as the post-Second World War period in Western Europe. The political settlement between classes and other crucial power groups then shapes inequalities, interests, and power which reproduce the welfare regime through time—until the next crisis. This does not mean that welfare regimes cannot adjust to pressures for reform, but it does mean that social policy reforms are heavily regime-dependent.

Within the OECD world, Esping-Andersen distinguishes three welfare regimes—the liberal (exemplar countries: the U.S. and the UK), conservative (exemplar countries: Germany, Italy), and social-democratic (the Nordic countries). One intent is to develop a middle range theorization of welfare systems which avoids, on the one hand, teleological or functionalist approaches emphasizing commonalities and convergence and, on the other hand, post-modern perspectives emphasizing national and sub-national uniqueness. In particular, by demonstrating the way welfare regimes shape interests, ideas, and power constellations in different societies, he claims to show that, once established, they follow different paths of development.

Can this paradigm be adapted to analyze social policy in the South? There are numerous differences which may invalidate such a conceptual transfer. Our work at Bath proposes that the original model needs drastic modification to take the following differences on board (Wood, 2000, Gough, 1999). First, there are a series of international constraints. A history of colonialism, settler societies or externally constrained development has contributed to economic dependency in the international economy (e.g., greater levels of indebtedness and capital inflows, sectoral imbalances) and political dependency in the international polity. Second, developing countries of course differ fundamentally in their socioeconomic environment: lower levels of marketization, industrialization and income, different forms of peasantry, land ownership, kin structures, household forms and gendered relationships.

Based on these, patterns of group formation based more on ascriptive, status-based identities are more common than the class-based movements assumed in welfare regime theory. Third, this generates more particularistic patterns of political mobilization, with regional, patrimonial, and clientelistic forms, resulting in the "adverse incorporation" of weaker groups. State institutions are less autonomous, democratic practices less embedded, or absent, state infrastructural (though not necessarily repressive) capacities are weaker.

The resulting range and form of social policies are different. The range of functional alternatives to Western-style social protection is wider, both beyond the state (religious, enterprise-based, Non-Governmental Organization (NGO), foreign aid, local/communal, clan and household provision) and within the state (e.g., consumption subsidies, agricultural support, work programs, micro-credit schemes). The traditional boundaries of social policy need extending still further to include improving governance and voice. Lastly, almost by definition, levels of welfare outcomes are lower, except among the rich. De-commodification is less relevant or irrelevant as an index of welfare outcomes: alternative and more direct measures are required.

This huge range of contrasts urges caution in applying welfare regime analysis to the South. On the other hand, these dimensions offer a rich matrix for understanding differences within the developing, transitional—and declining—worlds of the South. The welfare regime approach has much to offer if appropriately reformulated. First, the welfare regime approach is precisely concerned with the broader "welfare mix": the interactions of public sector, private sector, and households in producing livelihoods and distributing welfare: a fruitful theme in the development literature. Second, it is a "political economy" approach which embeds welfare institutions in the "deep structures" of social reproduction: it forces researchers to analyze social policy not merely in technical but in power terms, and this has much to offer. Third, it enables one to identify clusters of countries with welfare features in common; it holds out the promise of distinguishing between groups of developing countries according to their trajectory or paths of development. With this approach we can avoid the ludicrous situation where common and universal remedies are proposed for Malawi, Malaysia, Mexico, and Moldova. It accords mutual respect to global pressures and regime-specific features within the "South" as well as the North.

In order to enjoy these benefits without imposing inappropriate frameworks, we propose to extend the welfare mix, or the "institutional responsibility matrix" (Wood, 2000), to include the eight components in Table 4.2. The task of developing an appropriate social politics in underdeveloped, developing, and transitional countries entails at least this degree of conceptual innovation.

The remainder of this chapter describes, analyzes, and conceptualizes the welfare regime(s) in East Asia. East Asia typically refers to the "long strip of coastal capitalist states stretching down from South Korea to the eastern edge of the Indian Ocean" (Anderson, 1998: 300). Of these, I concentrate on five: Indonesia, Korea, Malaysia, the Philippines, and Thailand. These countries are of interest for several reasons. They have all been participants in the "East Asian miracle" and beneficiaries of the alleged benefits of economic openness and market-friendly policies (World Bank, 1993). They have in common a very restricted range of social protection measures combined with relatively good welfare outcomes, and they were all notable victims of the Asian financial crisis of 1997-99, and thus provide a good test case of the risks of globalization.

Table 4.2
Components of the Extended Welfare Mix

	Domestic	Supra-national
State	Domestic governance	International organizations, national donors
Market	Domestic markets	Global markets, multinational corporations
Community	Civil society, NGOs	International NGOs
Household	Households	International household strategies

Welfare Regimes in East Asia

Notwithstanding these similarities, the five countries differ in many respects, including level of development. Korea is an upper income group country, and now a member of the OECD. Its income per capita is double that of the next richest, Malaysia, which, in turn, is roughly double that of Thailand, which, in turn, has roughly double the per capita income of the Philippines and Indonesia. These are wide divergences, though, when calculated at purchasing power parity, the overall gap between Korea and Indonesia falls to 4.4:1 (see Table 4.3). The focus in this chapter is thus on four major countries of Southeast Asia plus Korea. As we shall see, Korea is an outlier, a representative of Northeast Asian welfare capitalism, and thus provides a useful pole of contrast with which to compare the Southeast Asian countries. In addition, the Philippines is a partial exception in Southeast Asia. This section describes the welfare mix and welfare outcomes of these countries.[1]

Institutional Programs: The Welfare Mix

State social policies. Public social expenditures in East Asia are very low on a world scale. Total spending on education, health, and social security varies with level of development, ranging from 3 percent of GDP in Indonesia, 6 percent in the Philippines and Thailand to 8 percent in Malaysia and 11 percent in Korea. The share of total government spending devoted to social services is less than one half, varying between around one quarter in

Table 4.3
Welfare Regimes in East Asia: Summary Indicators

		Korea	Malaysia	Thailand	Philippines	Indonesia	Average
State	Social spending/ GDP	11.0	8.2	5.9	6.0	3.1	6.8
Market	Share of private finance in health and education	54	36	53	66	58	53
Household	Private transfers: percent of income of receiving household	4	11	..	12*	10	9
Welfare outcomes	Human Development Index	.85	.77	.75	.74	.68	.76
	Poverty rate: <$2 p.p. a day	..	22	24	63	50	40
	Gini index of inequality	.36	.48	.46	.43	.37	.42
Basic data	*Population (m)*	*46*	*22*	*61*	*75*	*204*	*408*
	Income pc (ppp) $000	*12.3*	*7.0*	*5.8*	*3.5*	*2.8*	*6.2*

* Remittances from abroad amount to 10 percent of Gross Domestic Product (GDP), and a higher share of household incomes, so are not fully reflected in this figure.

Source: Gough (2000).

the Philippines to just over one half in Korea. There is a generalized hostility to Western ideals of the "welfare state" except paradoxically for employees of the state—social provision for civil servants, the military and police, teachers, etc. is everywhere extensive and generous.

East Asian governments have consistently emphasized the central role of *education* in economic development, though this is not matched by a higher than average expenditure for middle-income countries. But with fast economic growth real spending has climbed rapidly (except in the Philippines) and the general verdict is that the allocation of resources is more rationally targeted on basic education than in other developing countries (World Bank, 1993: 192-203). All five countries have achieved near-universal primary education. Secondary school enrollment is rising but the countries are at different stages on this path: the Philippines and Korea had enrolled over one half of children in the 1970s and Malaysia in the 1980s, whereas Thailand and Indonesia still remain below this level.

Health expenditure is low in East Asia compared with other middle-income countries and actually fell as a share of GDP in the 1990s in all countries except Thailand (Ramesh, 2000: Table 4.5). Since private spending accounts for about one half of the total, public health expenditure is remarkably low—between 0.7 percent GDP in Indonesia and 2.3 percent in Korea. Not surprisingly, all health inputs (doctors, nurses, hospital beds) are very scarce on a world scale. Yet all countries provide reasonable access to basic and preventive health care, with Korea and Malaysia as the best performers. "The widespread availability of public health care in Southeast Asia suggests that most sick people have some access to health care" (Ramesh, 2000: 113). Beyond this, there are significant inequities. The dominant medical system in the region is "public provision—private finance." In all countries civil servants and state employees have their own superior systems of insurance and provision, private provision is rising until interrupted by the financial crisis, and different measures to decentralize or "corporatize" public hospitals, or to contract-out key services are being tried out. The rich have the further option of treatment abroad. A general hierarchy can be observed in medical treatment: overseas > private > public > self-medication and traditional medicine—though the latter has a high status in Thailand (EIU, 1999).

All countries have some form of public health insurance, apart from Malaysia which is closer to a national health service. The Philippines has a long-established health insurance system, but with low coverage and erratic provision of services. The 1995 National Health Insurance Act plans to provide universal health care by 2010. In the space of a little over a decade Korea has moved to a fully-fledged National Health Insurance System—universal and integrated but with high co-payments and not yet redistributive. Thailand and Indonesia have both introduced health insurance for limited sections of the population backed up by medical assistance schemes. Malaysia has a more British-style National Health Service, backed up by personal medical accounts within the Employee Provident Fund.

Public spending on social protection, including *pensions*, is remarkably low in comparative perspective, whatever the comparator (Asher, 1998; Asian Development Bank, 1998). Again, pensions for civil servants, the military and some other public sector employees are the exception. For the rest of the population, the national pension systems divide into two main types: social insurance in the Philippines, Korea, and Thailand, and provident funds in Malaysia and Indonesia. The Filipino scheme is more than forty years old and continues to expand its coverage, including voluntary membership even for Filipinos working overseas. Replacement rates are high at around 60 percent, but the employer compliance rate is low, with up to two-thirds of the paper members not contributing at any one time (Ramesh, 2000: 71). From a late start in 1988, the National Pension Scheme in Korea is extending its coverage and building up a transitory fund over a twenty-year period—full pensions will not start until 2008. Thailand, in January 1999, added an old age pension element to the Social Security Act of 1990. This is a defined benefit pay-as-you-go scheme but will not pay out full pensions until 2014. Non-compliance or evasion is estimated to be high.

The Malaysian Employee Provident Fund (EPF), the first in the world and now in its fiftieth year, is a developed, expensive, and savings-effective fund. Since 1994, members have been able to opt for an annuity instead of a lump sum. Reforms have established separate accounts for education and health and have encouraged more flexible individual investment. However, the EPF provides weak protection against poverty in old age, offers insecure returns and, through tax exemptions and other features, is perversely redistributive. Despite an almost equally long history the *Jamsostek* fund of Indonesia has a small coverage, uneven record keeping, tiny reserves, and poor governance.

Formal safety nets can be defined as public programs targeted to the poor with the objective of raising living standards to a specified social minimum. They can take the form of cash transfers, public works employment, and subsidies for important need satisfiers, such as food and housing. They are limited in scale, coverage, and cost throughout the region, but they have been expanded in response to the crisis. As a share of GDP they are most extensive and expensive in Korea (2 percent of GDP in 1999) and Indonesia (planned 1.25 percent of GDP in 1999-2000), but are tiny in Malaysia and Thailand (World Bank, 1999: Table 3). The extensive Korean public works programs were a short-term response to mass unemployment and have since almost disappeared to be replaced by the more significant public assistance reform of 1999.

Market. Access to the labor market is a major resource in East Asia, as in the OECD, and the expansion of wage labor in the region has been remarkable. Over the last two decades until 1997 the labor force grew by 2 percent per year. The regional participation rate is high: ranging from 89 percent in Thailand to 66 percent in Malaysia. This labor force is becoming feminized but, with the exception of Thailand where it is higher, the overall share of women at about 40 percent is roughly the world average. Until the economic crisis of 1997-98, unemployment rates were consistently low, except in the Philippines, until the crisis of 1997-98 (World Bank, 1999: 14). Despite remarkably extensive labor protection legislation, the practice is poor due to weak government agencies, bribery of officials and weak trade unions (Deery and Mitchell, 1993; Rigg, 1997: 223-227). Nevertheless, growing access to the formal labor market—commodification—has been a critical feature of East Asian welfare regimes.

The private market for *social services* is substantial and fast-growing. One half of all education spending and almost two-thirds of all health spending is privately financed. Much of this is reactive and unorganized, comprising out-of-pocket expenditures, book purchases, self-medication, etc. The dominant pattern is of "mainly private finance and mixed provision"—unlike OECD countries, where public finance plus mixed provision is more typical. For example, Korean households spend 10 percent of their income on education and 5 percent on health, compared to 1.4 percent and 1.3 percent in the UK (Shin, 2000). Government regulation of private providers is typically weak. There is as yet little development of private life insurance or pensions.

Community, civil society, and NGOs. Non-profit and non-governmental organizations active in the field of human development and welfare are a very recent phenomenon in East Asia, where in the past they have been discouraged by authoritarian regimes (Yamamoto, 1995). The one exception is the Philippines where they have a longer history due to the American and Catholic legacy. Community development is now a burgeoning part of social policy, and includes such innovations as community health financing in Thailand. However, the total amount of such funds is small relative to Thailand's total health expenditure. Moreover, all NGOs remain heavily dependent on external sources for funds, notably official overseas aid organizations, U.S. philanthropic funds and Japanese corporate funds.

Households and the family. Throughout East Asia, the extended family persists as a provider, saver, and redistributor, despite rapid economic development and urbanization. The level of savings is extremely high in East Asia, the Philippines excepted, which should permit more families to mitigate risk by "self-insuring": saving in good times and dis-saving in bad times (World Bank, 2000a: chapter 5). However, despite the substantial development of micro-finance and credit schemes, the unequal distribution of incomes undermines this in Southeast Asia. On the other hand, calculations of private transfers show high levels in the Philippines, Indonesia, and Malaysia, adding between 9 and 20 percent to the average incomes of recipient house-holds. These outweigh public transfers by several orders of magnitude. In the 1980s, the majority of people over sixty years of age were receiving income from family members and an even higher proportion lived with children or family—between three-fourths and over 90 percent in the Philippines and Thailand. These remarkably high proportions are now falling in Korea, from 78 percent in 1984 to 49 percent in 1994.

International components of the welfare mix. Official development assis-tance by the OECD countries fell throughout the 1990s as a share of donors' GNP, recipients' GNP and in dollars per head. Before the Asian financial crisis, Korea and Malaysia received no official development assistance, but it remains of some significance—between 0.4-0.8 percent GNP—in the other three countries. Short-term crisis aid to countries such as Indonesia since 1997 has raised this share but it remains a marginal contributor to the East Asian welfare mix.

In contrast, international firms see the region as a growing market for a variety of health products, ranging from drugs to health maintenance organi-zations. This is mainly the result of gaps in public provision, but is increas-ingly being sponsored by governments. For example, Indonesia permitted for-profit hospitals in 1988, extended this to foreign investment in large hospitals in 1994 and, in 2003, will permit unrestricted foreign investment in all health care (EIU, 1999: 115). There is also a growing market for overseas health treatment of the rich, notably in regional centers such as Singapore, Hong Kong, and Australia.

The dominant international household strategy is labor migration and remittances of money, especially in the Philippines. By 1995, 1.5 million Filipinos lived abroad as permanent immigrants and a further 2 million at least worked temporarily abroad or at sea (Woodiwiss, 1998: 101). The remit-tances they send home amount to 6.4 percent of Filipino GNP, and 10 percent if unrecorded cash and goods brought home by workers are included (ILO, 2000: Tables 2, 4). These flows, together with the household flows within the country discussed above, constitute a significant element of the Filipino welfare regime.

In summary, the *welfare mix* in the region is one of relatively low public responsibility (in terms of expenditure, provision. and regulation), extensive family provision and redistribution, and growing private markets and com-munity-based organizations. Until the 1997 financial crisis, the countries had been curtailing their dependence on aid, but they have increased their openness to commercial penetration from abroad. Within the public sector priority is given to social investment in health and education, nota-bly basic health care and primary education, with very little attention to social protection. In all countries, state personnel are supported most gener-ously.

Welfare Outcomes

The region (apart from the Philippines) has witnessed an impressive reduction in poverty rates from above 40 percent in the 1970s to around 10 percent or less in the 1990s. However, inequality is high and rising (Manuelyan Atinc and Walton, 1998: 10). Furthermore, income distribution data typically excludes capital gains, which escalated before the crisis. At the other extreme are groups suffering from significant and quasi-permanent social exclusion, including "hill peoples," migrant workers, street children, orphans, and refugees (Rigg, 1997: ch.4; World Bank, 1999: 6). "De-commodification" has less meaning in societies with significant agricultural and informal labor and is not systematically measured in East Asia, but we may be confident that it is low. Labor in Southeast Asia is either pre-commodified, working in subsistence agriculture, or it is commodified—reliant on the labor market with few statutory protections or substitutes. Indeed, opportunities to participate in the labor market are a key feature of the East Asian welfare regime. In other aspects of welfare outcomes, the region achieves relatively high scores in health and education, but with persistent and worrying gaps and inequalities, especially in less well-monitored areas such as morbidity, school drop-out rates, working conditions, and social exclusion. Yet until the crisis, East Asia achieved something akin to the liberal alchemists' dream: fast-improving welfare outcomes at very low cost in terms of public social expenditure.

East Asian Welfare Regimes

It is beyond the scope of this chapter to analyze the stratification effects and political economy of these systems, and thus to typify their welfare *regimes*. Holliday (2000) proposes that (North) East Asia comprises a fourth welfare regime of *productivist welfare capitalism*, in which social policy is subordinated to economic policy.[2] In particular the social ministries are subordinated to the Economic Planning Board and its goals, which permit state spending only on productive social investments, notably education (Shin, 2000). Though the form of capitalism differs between Northeast and Southeast Asia, all the states in the region have considerable autonomy from business and other social interests, and have prioritized economic over social policy. In my view, all the countries (with the partial exception of the Philippines) can be described as *productivist social development regimes*. What social policy there has been has concentrated on basic education and health as part of a strategy of nation-building, legitimation, and productive investment. The combination of social investment, low taxes, and favorable economic conditions has fostered the rapid development of formal and informal employment without thus far seriously weakening family support systems. The outcome was rapid social development combined with absent formal social protection and high vulnerability to external shocks (Gough, 2001: 177-181).

Within this basic regime type we can identify national variations. *Korea*, by far the richest economy, has higher standards of educational and other social outcomes. Now it is embarking on a rapid and thorough-going expansion of social insurance. The *Philippines* enjoys much lower growth, a long-established, segmented and partial social insurance tradition, high levels of unemployment, poverty, and inequality, yet good access to education. The outcome has been labor emigration and high remittances which augment the role of the family. *Malaysia* has a different policy profile with its Provident Fund alongside a British-influenced national health system and relatively low levels of private finance. *Thailand* is less institutionally developed, though the recent Social Security law has the potential to expand as a social protection system. *Indonesia*, despite rapid economic transformation (until 1997) exhibits the most rudimentary social protection regime.

Welfare Regimes and the East Asian Crisis

These, then, were the welfare regimes suddenly overwhelmed by the East Asian crisis in 1997. The main social effects of the crisis came through the following mechanisms: collapsing currency values, which generated higher import prices and extensive internal price changes, including falling asset values; a drastic fall in output and thus in demand for labor; and falling state revenues and a squeeze on public spending. The upshot was a Keynesian-style collapse in demand (see Table 4.4). Moreover, at the same time the Philippines, Indonesia, and Thailand suffered a severe drought.

Table 4.4
The Social Impacts of the Crisis in East Asia

	Korea	Malaysia	Thailand	Philippines	Indonesia	Average
Change in proportion of private consumption 1997-8, percent	-10.2	-12.6	-15.1	1.3	-4.7	-8.3
Inflation 1997-8, percent	7.5	5.3	8.1	9.7	57.6	17.6
Poverty increase 1996-98, percentage points	9.6	..	1.5	..	5.4	5.4
Unemployment 1998, %	6.8	3.2	4.5	10.1	5.5	6.0
Public education expenditure1997-98, percentage points	-5.8	-13.7	-1.3	+3.8	-27.7	-12.1
Public health expenditure 1997-98, percentage points	-3.2	-9.7	-10.7	-7.8	-12.2	-8.7

Source: Manuelyan Atinc (2000: Table 6.1).

It is beyond the scope of this chapter to analyze the causes of this crisis. Standard explanations distinguish external and internal factors. External factors include the instability of financial markets, prone to over-reaction and a "herd mentality," an instability compounded by the combined rapid expansion and liberalization of international capital markets in the 1990s. The internal factors stress either macro-economic mismanagement—not commonly advanced apropos East Asia—or structural and regulatory problems. The latter, which have tended to be advanced by the IMF and World Bank, refer to "crony capitalism," corruption, moral hazard, and suchlike. This distinction between external and internal is hard to justify, when IFIs have played such important roles in shaping government policies in the South. In particular, the very liberalization of capital accounts has expanded the ability of politically connected groups to profit from their contacts: liberalization created new avenues for cronyism (Pincus and Ramli, 1998; Wade, 2001). The important conclusion from my point of view is that the very openness of the East Asian economies, one source of their previous success, was deeply implicated in the crisis that afflicted them in 1997.

The social impact of the crisis has been portrayed and analyzed by Manuelyan Atinc and Walton (1998) and Manuelyan Atinc (2000). Poverty rates rose in all countries as did the depth of poverty. The demand for labor and the share of wages declined everywhere, bringing about a collapse of private consumption, yet inequality did not rise notably, partly due to the collapse of asset prices hurting the rich and middle classes. Undoubtedly, many poor households coped by cutting back on nutrition, postponing health care, taking some children out of school, and other painful adjustments. It bottomed out in 1998 and recovery began in 1999. Moreover, the impact differed: it was acute in Indonesia, severe in Thailand, Malaysia, and Korea, and mild in the Philippines, where the preceding boom had been least. This, together with different inherited welfare regimes, resulted in different policy impacts (Asian Development Bank and World Bank, 2000).

In Korea, labor demand fell sharply and, though real wages fell, the major impact was on unemployment, especially among women. As a developed industrial economy, Korean households had fewer rural resources to fall back on. At this time, Korea had already begun a restructuring of trade, economic, and social policy, under pressure from the U.S. and the Uruguay Round, to liberalize its economic structure, and internal demonstrations by trades unions and social movements. The first wave of reforms introduced by the Rho Tae-woo government in 1988 included Medical Insurance, the National Pension Programme, the Minimum Wage, and new labor laws. Following the crisis, a second wave of reforms in 1998-99 followed, coinciding with the election of Kim Dae-jung as president. The economy was significantly liberalized and the close links between the state and the *chaebol* loosened. This was coupled with moves towards a more Western welfare system. Expenditure on unemployment insurance, wage subsidies and public works programs escalated, to a remarkable 4 percent of GDP in 1999. In addition, the National Health System was restructured and expanded, pension entitlements were liberalized and an expanded Labour Standard Law introduced. A "Labour-Management-Government" Committee was established which moved away, at least in name, from state-business symbiosis to a tripartite corporatism. In brief, greater exposure to the global economy and the subsequent crisis has undermined the influence and the social provisions of the *chaebol* and required the state to develop a more autonomous Western-style social policy. The unintended consequence of globalization and liberalization has been to *expand* the Korean welfare state (Shin, 2000).

In Malaysia and the Philippines the policy impact has been less, for related but opposite reasons. The Philippines is an outlier from the East Asian model: over the last two decades it has recorded lower growth rates (and thus less reliance on labor market income growth) coupled with chronically high poverty and unemployment rates. On the other hand, for a combination of largely fortuitous reasons, it suffered less in the 1997 crisis. It has for long relied on officially encouraged emigration as a safety valve and income source: the 1995 Migrant Workers and Overseas Filipinos Act and the Philippine Overseas Employment Administration both facilitate emigration and offer some degree of assistance to emigrants. Since most Filipino emigrants are not working in crisis-affected countries, their remittances (amounting to some 10 percent of GNP) have cushioned the impact of the crisis and resulted in little policy innovation.

Malaysia, by contrast, has managed to cushion the domestic impact of a severe crisis by offloading its impact onto immigrant workers, which account for some 7-10 percent of the labor force (Oberndörfer and Berndt, 2000). Early on the Malaysian government announced plans to repatriate large numbers of these workers: up to 200,000 laid off in the construction industry and another 700,000 whose permits would be denied renewal after expiry. Despite some opposition from employers, at least 200,000 illegal foreign workers, and probably many more, had left the country by August 1998 (Haggard, 2000: 208-209). As a result the official unemployment rate in Malaysia barely rose from 2.5 percent in 1996 to 3.2 percent in 1998. In both the Philippines and Malaysia, but for opposite reasons, labor migration has reduced the direct crisis impact and forestalled significant social policy innovation.

Thailand and Indonesia represent a different response. Both have strong rural hinterlands, where extensive smallholder agriculture acted as a shock absorber, and where escalating food prices helped real incomes. The crisis led to a drastic fall in formal sector wages (by 34 percent in Indonesia in real terms) and a shift from the formal sector back to the informal and agricultural sectors. Poor people without this fallback suffered doubly from unemployment and the mushrooming costs of food. High inflation in Indonesia also contributed to a sharp fall in real public spending on education and health, which Thailand protected more successfully. The response of both governments, with inducements from the IMF, World Bank, and Asian Development Bank, was to instigate decentralized safety nets, expand community-based programs, and emphasize credit and savings groups.

By mid-1998, the government of Thailand had secured social loans from the Asian Development Bank and World Bank to expand existing safety net programs and instigate new ones. The former included scholarship and educational loan programs, fee waivers and free provision of uniforms to keep pupils in school, plus an expanded school lunch program. The low-income health card program was also increased. In addition new public works and a Social Investment Program were introduced with funding from the World Bank. These, more open to patronage and "leakage," attracted growing criticism and were soon cut back (Haggard, 2000).

Indonesia followed a similar course with donor-funded safety net programs. The OPK subsidized rice scheme launched in July 1998 provided 20 kg of low quality rice per household per month at a subsidized price, allocated according to an official list of poor households. A scholarship program provided scholarships and school grants to schools in poor areas and poor households within them. A previous health card program was expanded to fund clinics and midwives in poor districts. All suffered from leakage but were adjudged relatively successful. By contrast, community social funds and public works programs were sources of patronage and corruption (Ananta and Siregar, 1999). Concerns over leakage and corruption led the World Bank to pull out of many programs and it is unclear at present to what extent the government of Indonesia will supplement their funding. In any case spending on all SSNs is tiny in amount, accounting for 0.25 percent GNP (Asian Development Bank, 2000; World Bank, 2000b; Irawan et al., 2001).

Thus, a common crisis, indubitably a result of the increased economic openness of this dynamic region of the world, has generated different policy responses in interaction with varying welfare regimes. The separate, distinctive regimes in Malaysia and the Philippines have been little affected, due to the cushion of immigrant labor in the former and emigrant labor in the latter. Indonesia and Thailand have relied primarily on the cushion provided by more closely integrated rural-urban households and families, but are encouraging community-based social safety nets in a limited way. Korea, more industrialized, urbanized and, in recent years, more democratic, has been propelled by the crisis towards a fully-fledged social insurance state.

Conclusions

"Economic globalization" is changing the environment of welfare systems North and South, East and West. However, its impact is mediated by, first, forms of global economic and social governance (not discussed here), and second, by national and regional welfare regimes. The latter comprise the institutional bases of provision of livelihoods and security, the welfare outcomes resulting, and the patterns of stratification, interests and power which generate this matrix and contribute to its reproduction. This chapter goes on to apply this framework to five countries in East Asia, interesting as examples of emerging market economies with woefully inadequate social protection systems, all of which were engulfed by the East Asian crisis of 1997-99. Their welfare regimes have been described and analyzed and the impact of the crisis has been then assessed. The conclusion is that a common crisis has engendered very different outcomes, with Korea moving swiftly to a developed social insurance state, Thailand and Indonesia developing a "third way" based on community and local innovations, and Malaysia and the Philippines exhibiting less policy innovation.

However, in all countries the crisis has sparked interest in social policy as a newly relevant domain of state policy. The older confidence in economic growth as *the* social policy is eroding. On the one hand, there is more awareness of the growing domestic pressures for social policies stemming from population aging, shifts towards more technologically based economies, urbanization, and nucleating households. The dangers of a further financial crisis are not insignificant and thus there is growing debate about the need for formal social protection systems. On the other hand, there remains a deep distrust among elites in the region about welfare states and the "European model." Internal and external pressures will continue to be refracted through domestic regimes. It is unlikely that the other countries will follow Korea in its move towards extensive public provision. It is possible that the Malaysian EPF will provide a regional model for pension provision. It remains to be seen whether education and health services succumb to the current fads about privatization or will build on the successful elements of universal public provision. One thing we can be certain of: "globalization" will not call forth uniform policy responses in the region, let alone across the developing world.

Notes

*   This chapter is a revised version of the author's contribution to the Third International Conference on Social Security Research in Helsinki. A different version has been published in *Global Social Policy* 1 (2). The research on which this chapter is based was made possible by the UK Department for International Development which funded the research program Social Policy in Development Contexts at the University of Bath, 1999-2001. Thanks to my doctoral students, Shin Dong-myeon and Kim Jin-wook, and colleagues in the Bath research group for valuable comments on an earlier draft.
1.   Cf. Rodrik (1998), Garrett (1998), Scharpf (2000), Bonoli et al. (2000), and Alber and Standing (2000).

2.   There is by now a considerable literature on Northeast Asia; see Kwon (1998), Goodman et al. (1998), Jacobs (1998) for some recent surveys. That on Southeast Asia is much less developed, though Ramesh (2000) provides a first synthesis.

References

Alber, J., and Standing, G. (2000). "Social Dumping, Catch-up or Convergence? Europe in a Comparative Global Context." *Journal of European Social Policy,* 10 (2), 99-119.

Ananta, A., and Siregar, R. (1999). "Social Safety Net Policies in Indonesia." *ASEAN Economic Bulletin,* 16 (3), 344-59.

Anderson, B. (1998). *The Spectre of Comparisons: Nationalism, Southeast Asia and The World.* London: Verso.

Asher, M. (1998). "The Future of Retirement Protection in Southeast Asia." *International Social Security Review,* 51 (1), 3-30.

Asian Development Bank. (1998). *Pension Systems and Policy in the APEC Economies.* 3 Volumes. Prepared by D. Stanton and P. Whiteford. Manila: Asian Development Bank.

___. (2000). *Assessment of Poverty in Indonesia.* Manila: Asian Development Bank.

Asian Development Bank and World Bank. (2000). *The New Social Policy Agenda in Asia.* Proceedings of the Manila Social Forum. Manila: Asian Development Bank.

Bonoli, G., George, V., and Taylor-Gooby, P. (2000). *European Welfare Futures: Towards a Theory of Retrenchment.* Cambridge: Polity Press.

Deery, S., and Mitchell, R. (1993). "Introduction." In Deery, S., and Mitchell, R. (eds.), *Labour Law and Industrial Relations in Asia.* Melbourne: Longman Cheshire PTY Ltd.

EIU. (1999). *Healthcare Global Outlook.* 2000 Edition, edited by J. Haresnape. London: Economist Intelligence Unit.

Esping-Andersen, G. (1990). *The Three Worlds of Welfare Capitalism.* Cambridge: Polity Press.

Garrett, G. (1998). *Partisan Politics in the Global Economy.* Cambridge: Cambridge University Press.

Goodman, R., White, G: and Kwon, H.-j. (eds). (1998). *The East Asian Welfare Model: Welfare Orientalism and the State.* London: Routledge.

Gough, I. (1999). "Welfare Regimes: On Adapting the Framework to Developing Countries." *Discourse: A Journal of Policy Studies,* 3 (1), 1-18.

___. (2000). *Welfare Regimes in East Asia.* SPDC Paper No. 4, University of Bath: http://www.bath.ac.uk/Faculties/HumSocSci/IFIPA/GSP.

___. (2001). "Globalization and Regional Welfare Regimes: The East Asian Case." *Global Social Policy* 1 (2), 163-189.

Gough, I., and Farnsworth, K. (2000). "The Enhanced Structural Power of Capital: A Review and Assessment." In Gough, I., *Global Capital, Human Needs and Social Policies: Selected Essays 1994-99.* Basingstoke: Palgrave.

Haggard, S. (2000). *The Political Economy of the Asian Financial Crisis.* Washington DC: Institute for International Economics.

Held, D., McGrew, A., Goldblatt, D., and Perraton, J. (eds.). (1999). *Global Transformations.* Cambridge: Polity Press.

Holliday, I. (2000). "Productivist Welfare Capitalism: Social Policy in East Asia." *Political Studies,* 48 (4), 706-723.

ILO. (2000). "Migrant Worker Remittances, Micro-finance and the Informal Economy: Prospects and Issues." *Social Finance Unit Working Paper 21.* Geneva: ILO www.ilo.org/public/english/employment/ent/papers/wpap21.htm.

Irawan, P., Rahman, E., Romdiati, H., and Suhaimi, U. (2001). Social Safety Nets Analysis and Recommendations: Prospects in Indonesia. Paper presented at Regional Seminar on Strengthening Safety Nets, Bangkok, May.

Jacobs, D. (1998). *Social Welfare Systems in East Asia*. CASE Paper No.10, London: LSE Centre for the Analysis of Social Exclusion.

Kwon, Huck-ju. (1998). "Democracy and the Politics of Social Welfare: A Comparative Analysis of Welfare Systems in East Asia." In Goodman, R., White, G., and Kwon, H.-j. (eds.), *The East Asian Welfare Model: Welfare Orientalism and the State*. London: Routledge.

Lee, H. K. (1999). "Globalization and the Emerging Welfare State: The Experience of South Korea." *International Journal of Social Welfare,* 8 (1), 23-39.

Manuelyan Atinc, T., and Walton, M. (1998). *Social Consequences of the East Asian Financial Crisis*. Washington, D. C.: World Bank.

Manuelyan Atinc, T. (2000). Coping with Crises: Social Policy and the Poor. Paper presented to World Bank seminar "Lessons Towards the New Social Policy Agenda in East Asia," Paris, 27 June.

Oberndörfer, D., and Berndt, U. (2000). The 1997-99 East Asian Crisis: Implications for Policies Affecting Migrants. Paper presented to ASEM-World Bank Workshop, October.

Pierson, P. (1994). *Dismantling the Welfare State? Reagan, Thatcher and the Politics of Retrenchment*. Cambridge: Cambridge University Press.

___. (1998). "Irresistible Forces, Immovable Objects: Post-Industrial Welfare States Confront Permanent Austerity." *Journal of European Public Policy,* 5 (4), 539-560.

Pincus, J., and Ramli, R. (1998). "Indonesia: From Showcase to Basket Case." *Cambridge Journal of Economics,* 22, 723-734.

Ramesh, M., with M. Asher. (2000). *Welfare Capitalism in Southeast Asia*. London: Macmillan.

Rigg, J. (1997). *Southeast Asia: The Human Landscape of Modernization and Development*. London: Routledge.

Rodrik, D. (1998). "Why Do More Open Economies Have Bigger Governments?" *Journal of Political Economy* 106 (5), 997-1032.

Scharpf, F. W. (2000). "The Viability of Advanced Welfare States in the International Economy: Vulnerabilities and Options." *Journal of European Public Policy* 7 (2), 190-228.

Shin, D.-m. (2000). "Financial Crisis and Social Security: The Paradox of South Korea." *International Social Security Review* 53 (3), 83-107.

Wade, R. (2001). "The US Role in the Long Asian Crisis of 1990-2000." In Lukauskas, A. J., and Rivera-Batiz, F. (eds.), *Tigers in Distress: The Political Economy of the East Asian Crisis and its Aftermath*. London: Edward Elgar.

Wood, G. (2000). "Prisoners and Escapees: Improving the Institutional Responsibility Square in Bangladesh." *Public Administration and Development* 20, 221-237.

Woodiwiss, A. (1998). *Globalization, Human Rights and Labour Law in Pacific Asia*. Cambridge: Cambridge University Press.

World Bank. (1993). *The East Asian Miracle: Economic Growth and Public Policy*. Oxford: Oxford University Press.

___. (1999). *Towards an East Asian Social Protection Strategy*. Human Development Unit, East Asia and Pacific Region. IBRD. Draft. September. Washington, D. C.: World Bank.

___. (2000a). *World Development Report 2000/1: Attacking Poverty*. Consultation Draft, January. Washington, D. C.: World Bank.

___. (2000b). *Poverty Reduction in Indonesia: Constructing a New Strategy*. Draft Report, October. Washington, D. C.: World Bank.

Yamamoto, T. (1995). "Integrative Report." In Yamamoto, T. (ed.), *Emerging Civil Society in the Asia Pacific Community*. Singapore: Institute of Southeast Asian Studies and Tokyo: Japan Center for International Exchange.

5

Southern European Welfare States Facing Globalization: Is There Social Dumping?

Ana M. Guillén and Santiago Álvarez

Up to the mid-1970s, Southern European welfare states almost failed to be taken into account because of their low level of social expenditure: other pioneering or paradigmatic countries monopolized the analytical efforts of social experts. However, attention on Southern welfare states has been mounting for a few years already, because of the growing importance of their social expenditure, their peculiar political histories (long periods of authoritarian rule), and their cultural traditions, among other reasons. Seemingly, and so far, Southern welfare states have not withstood comparative analysis very successfully for they have enjoyed the privilege of being considered as special and different, but rarely on a positive qualification. Thus, they have been labeled as "rudimentary" (Leibfried, 1993), forming part of a "catholic family" (Castles, 1994), and "clientelistic" (Ferrera, 1996).

Another aspect of this growing interest in Southern welfare states is "social dumping." Social dumping may be understood as those intentional practices enhancing competitiveness on the part of national economies by means of reducing or preventing growth of social and employment protection, because of the impact that such actions have on the reduction of labor costs. In older established welfare states there is much concern about national competitiveness in international markets and the threat from the adoption of a social dumping policy in newly emerging competitor nations, especially on the part of countries that also happen to be members of the European common market. Moreover, the more developed welfare states fear that social dumping strategies will be conducive to a "rush to the bottom," a convergence or harmonization of social policy at the minimum level within the European Union (EU).

This chapter examines to what extent social policies in Southern European countries were motivated by the notion of social dumping rather than the concept of catching up (i.e., ameliorating and expanding social protection) in recent years. In other words, the study analyses whether Southern countries have followed the American model of the market economy rather than the European model of the welfare state. Reference is also made occasionally to Ireland, for it is also one of the economically less-developed countries in the EU.

The chapter is divided into three sections. The first section consists of an examination of the concept of social dumping. Then, the study goes on to consider a quantitative approach to social dumping behaviors in section two. This section is devoted to ascertain whether the evolution of public social expenditure and financing mechanisms reflect the adoption of a social dumping strategy in Southern European countries. The search for competitiveness (through the lowering of the social contribution components of labor costs) may have had an impact on reduced or stagnant levels of social expenditure and financing. This would be a sign indicating a potential presence of social dumping. Other quantitative indicators are also analyzed in the second section. In particular, the evolution of labor costs themselves is assessed. Finally, section two pays attention to the fluxes coming from the European Cohesion and Structural Funds. EU members benefiting substantially from Communitarian economic transfers may be able to reduce their national effort on social protection thanks to EU subsidies.

But quantitative indicators are not enough. Even when public social expenditure and public financing are growing and labor costs are high (thus contravening the presence of a social dumping strategy), social programs may be reshaped in a more restrictive way or may be redesigned so that they leave part of the population unprotected. This is why the third section evaluates program specific changes qualitatively, that is, it deals with the most important extensions and cutbacks of welfare state schemes. It also includes an analysis of the factors shaping recent policy patterns.

What is Social Dumping?

The social dumping argument is probably as old as the European Economic Community (EEC). The idea that competition among the economies of the member states would be distorted unless a harmonization of social standards and working conditions was achieved within the Community has proved long lasting. The Treaty of Rome reflected in part this worry in Article 117, which stated the need to "promote improved working conditions and an improved standard of living for workers, so as to make possible their harmonization while the improvement is being maintained," that is, the principle of "upward harmonisation."[1]

However, during the 1960s and 1970s, harmonization of social policies did not take place as a prerequisite for the liberalization of trade inside the Community. As Sapir (1995) notes, two elements were crucial in diminishing pressures in favor of harmonization in that period. First, the six original members of the Community enjoyed similar economic and social conditions. Second, such conditions underwent a rapid amelioration throughout the Community up to the oil shocks in the1970s. With the coming of the Single Market, the social dumping debate has gained momentum. Again, the social dumping argument is phrased in terms of competitiveness among the economies of the European partners.

The contradiction between economic integration and social protection diversity—or at least its perception on the part of policy-makers—has been deepened ever since Southern European countries became members of the Community because of the increase in differences regarding social and wage costs. In such an environment of disparity of levels of social protection among the well-developed European welfare states and the developing Southern counterparts, the social dumping argument defends that fair competition within the European Union requires upward harmonization of social protection standards. Those member states with lower levels of protection offer a competitive advantage to companies producing in those countries (Dearden, 1995). The process of social dumping, with the relocation of firms to exploit these cost advantages, is most likely to take place in the less advanced EU economies, that is, the Southern countries and Ireland. It can be easily deduced from the above, that social dumping is related primarily with economic competitiveness.

We will take competitiveness as the capacity of an economy (a firm) to offer products at a price and quality level that demand can identify and compare with those of other national or foreign firms. These two factors of competitiveness—price and quality—depend on a high number of variables that may be classified as factors affecting all the firms in one country (social provisions, industrial relations, training and educational conditions) and those affecting single firms or group of firms, such as technological capacities, access in favorable conditions to natural resources, or competitive costs of transport and energy. The latter are very difficult to measure for comparative purposes among countries, but they are likely to be higher in less developed economies.

In sum, social dumping is generally understood as those intentional practices enhancing competitiveness on the part of national economies by means of reducing or preventing growth of social and employment protection, because of the impact that such actions have on the reduction of labor costs.[2] From this point of view, competitiveness is tightly related to the level of social protection enjoyed by the citizens of a country. However, effects of the level of social protection may be twofold. In the first place, the financing of social protection is part of the labor costs of firms, and it may reduce firms' competitiveness if they are obliged to raise prices or reduce benefits. However, it should also be pointed out that firms could also charge workers with social contributions by diminishing real salaries. In the second place, expenditure on social policy may be conducive to an increase in competitiveness, for it may ameliorate the quality of workers and of the production process.

Finally, as noted earlier, there is another less orthodox way of considering social dumping. One may argue that social dumping, that is, a diminished effort in social protection, is also possible in the less-developed economies of the EU because of the transfers received in such countries from the EU itself (and having an origin in the wealthier EU economies). The following section will analyze the evolution of social expenditure, financing mechanisms, and labor costs in Southern European countries as compared with those of other EU member states, as well as EU economic transfers.

Assessing the Welfare Effort in Comparative Perspective

Evolution of Expenditure on Social Protection

Expenditure on social protection grew significantly in all European member states during the 1950s, 1960s, and 1970s, and then stabilized during the following two decades. While in 1970 the European average of expenditure on social protection represented 19 percent of Gross Domestic Product (GDP), in 1985, this proportion reached 26 percent. From 1985 onwards, stagnation or even a slight decrease took place: 25.4 percent of GDP in 1990, so that despite the positive cycle of the economy, expenditure on social protection increased to a lesser extent than GDP. In the early 1990s, and in the presence of economic crisis, the tendency was inverted so that expenditure reached 28.2 percent in 1997. As Table 5.1 shows, the level of expenditure on social protection as a percentage of GDP is very different among EU member states, although differences have been reduced gradually.

Despite the comparative low levels of social expenditure in Southern countries, they are, together with the United Kingdom, the member states having experienced a larger growth of social protection in purchasing power parities during the period 1980-1997, as Table 5.2 indicates.

If we take into account the wealth of the country and the part of it that is dedicated to social protection, a high correlation can be stated, with the exception of the Netherlands and Denmark, which spend more on social protection than other wealthier countries, and Italy, where the opposite occurs. Southern European countries other than Italy are the least well off and also those spending less in absolute terms (see Table 5.5).

Table 5.1
Evolution of Expenditure on Social Protection
(as a Percentage of GDP), 1970-1997

Country	1970	1980	1985	1990	1995	1997
Belgium	18.7	28.0	29.3	26.7	28.4	28.5
Denmark	19.6	28.7	27.8	29.7	33.4	31.4
Germany	21.5	28.8	28.4	25.4	29.6	29.9
Greece		9.7	15.4	23.2	22.6	23.6
Spain		18.1	19.9	19.9	22.1	21.4
France	19.2	25.4	28.8	27.7	30.7	30.8
Ireland	13.2	20.6	23.6	19.1	19.6	17.5
Italy	17.4	19.4	22.6	24.1	25.0	25.9
Luxembourg	15.9	26.5	23.1	22.6	24.9	24.8
Netherlands	20.8	30.1	31.7	32.5	31.5	30.3
Portugal		12.8	14.1	15.6	20.8	22.5
United Kingdom	15.9	21.5	24.3	23.2	27.7	26.8
Average	19.0	24.3	26.0	25.4	28.7	28.2

Source: Eurostat (1997, 2000).

Table 5.2
Evolution of Per Capita Social Expenditure, 1980 and 1997

Country	Purchasing power parities		% variation	Percentage over EU average	
	1980	1997	1997/1980	1980	1997
Belgium	2,124	6,144	289.3	126.6	115.2
Denmark	2,149	6,796	316.2	128.1	127.4
Germany	2,419	6,230	257.6	144.2	116.8
Greece	436	2,912	668.5	26.0	54.6
Spain	915	3,297	360.4	54.5	61.8
France	2,052	6,082	296.4	122.3	114.0
Ireland	884	3,339	377.8	52.7	62.6
Italy	1,415	5,200	367.6	84.3	97.5
Luxembourg	2,174	8,837	406.4	129.6	165.7
Netherlands	2,296	6,257	272.5	136.8	117.3
Portugal	524	2,868	547.3	31.2	53.8
United Kingdom	1,465	4,982	340.0	87.3	93.4
Average	1,678	5,334	317.9		

Source: Eurostat (1997, 2000).

All the above contradicts the presence of a social dumping strategy in Southern European countries.

Evolution of Financing Structures

If we can talk about a dramatic and unprecedented rate of growth of social expenditure until the late 1970s, followed by subsequent stagnation, this trend is even more marked in the case of public social revenues. During the 1960s and 1970s, high economic growth rates and low unemployment rates allowed high returns of personal taxes on income that were articulated by high taxation rates although tax bases became increasingly limited by tax breaks and deductions. Increases in real salaries, coupled with inflation, made the financing of the welfare state possible in the most developed countries in Europe.

A second period ranging from 1975 to 1985 was marked by mushrooming increases of unemployment and inflation. Most governments did not dare to introduce reforms in their fiscal systems and the dynamic of growth of public revenues went on eased by the simultaneous presence of high inflation rates and an upward trend of nominal wages. From 1985 onwards, fiscal systems began to be restructured. This change was fostered by the upsurge of a theoretical paradigm assigning greater importance to the achievement of economic efficiency—mainly to the contribution of tax policies to the reduction of unemployment—than to the use of taxes as an instrument to gain a more equitable distribution of income. These reforms led to reductions of tax on income that were generally compensated by an increase in indirect imposition, as it can be ascertained in Tables 5.3 and 5.4.

Following the example of the USA, Great Britain pioneered the reform of the structure of taxes on income within Europe. Germany and the Netherlands followed suit, and then the experience was generalized to other European countries. Southern countries were the last to adopt changes conducive to a stronger reliance on indirect taxation (for example, Spain did not produce such a change until 1997). Re-formulation of fiscal policies in Southern Europe was fostered by the perception that increased freedom in the movement of capitals within Europe, coupled with the existence of stronger international financial markets in countries like Great Britain, Germany, and Belgium, could result in re-localization of capital towards these countries.

The reform of tax systems is far from having been completed. Thus, some Northern countries and Austria have recently adopted significant reforms, and complementary measures are being considered in Sweden. Moreover, economists who have always shown strong worries about the need to preserve equity (as, for example, Atkinson, 1996) are in favor of the shift towards a stronger reliance on indirect taxation, despite the decrease on redistributive capacity it may entail.

Table 5.3
Tax Receipts as a Percentage of GDP, 1965-1997

Country	1965	1975	1985	1995	1997
Belgium	31.2	41.8	47.7	45.4	46.0
Denmark	29.9	41.4	49.0	49.4	49.5
Germany	31.6	36.0	38.1	38.5	37.2
Greece	22.0	25.5	29.0	32.1	33.7
Spain	14.7	19.5	28.8	32.8	33.7
France	34.5	36.9	44.5	44.0	45.1
Ireland	25.9	31.3	36.4	33.1	32.8
Italy	25.5	26.2	34.5	41.2	44.4
Luxembourg	30.6	42.8	46.7	44.4	46.5
Netherlands	32.7	42.9	44.1	42.0	41.9
Portugal	16.2	21.7	27.8	33.3	34.2
United Kingdom	30.4	35.5	37.9	35.2	35.4
Unweighted Average	28.3	34.8	40.3	40.5	41.5

Source: Messere (1997, 2000).

Table 5.4
Specific Tax Receipts as a Percentage of Total Tax Receipts, 1985, 1990, 1994

Country	Income Tax			Corporate Tax			Social Security			VAT and Sales			Exercises		
	1985	1990	1994	1985	1990	1994	1985	1990	1994	1985	1990	1994	1985	1990	1994
Belgium	35	32	31	5	5	6	32	34	34	15	16	16	8	8	9
Denmark	50	53	54	5	3	4	4	3	3	20	21	19	13	11	11
Germany	29	28	26	6	5	3	36	37	39	16	17	18	9	9	9
Greece	14	14	10	3	5	6	36	31	35	17	26	22	21	15	17
Spain	20	22	23	5	9	5	41	35	39	15	16	15	13	10	10
France	13	12	14	4	5	4	43	44	43	20	19	17	9	8	9
Ireland	31	32	31	3	5	9	15	15	14	21	21	20	22	20	17
Italy	27	26	25	9	10	9	35	33	31	14	15	15	9	11	11
Luxembourg	26	23	21	18	16	17	26	27	27	12	14	13	11	11	13
Netherlands	19	25	20	7	7	7	44	37	42	16	16	15	7	7	9
Portugal		16	19		8	7	26	27	26	13	20	23	29	23	21
United Kingdom	27	28	28	12	11	8	18	17	18	15	17	20	14	13	14

Source: Messere (1997).

The reliance on indirect taxes was maintained during the early 1990s, owing mainly to the influence of the Maastricht Treaty and that of the agreements regarding the European Monetary Union (EMU). These obliged the member states to reduce their budgetary deficits substantially (Greece was an exception, for it did not comply with any of the requisites of convergence) and to moderate fiscal pressure in order to avoid international re-localization of capital. On the whole, as Tables 5.3 and 5.4 show, Southern European countries that departed from lower levels of fiscal pressure have experienced a more intense growth during the last decades, which has resulted in a leveling off of differences with the rest of the European members. This is evidence that competitiveness of firms has not been enhanced in Southern Europe by means of reducing the fiscal burden, but rather the opposite has taken place.

In the period 1965-1997, in all Southern European countries (with the exception of Greece) fiscal pressure has grown above the European average, especially in the cases of Spain and Portugal. In particular, the period ranging from 1985 to 1997 has been characterized by moderate increases of fiscal pressure (1.2 percent of GDP), while Greece, Spain, Portugal, and Italy have significantly departed from the general tendency (see Table 5.4).

Evolution of Unit Labor Costs

Effects of social protection on competitiveness—increase of labor costs and increase of productivity—have opposite consequences. Both influences may be measured by unit labor costs, defined as labor costs per worker divided by labor productivity. Even though absolute labor costs may show significant differences among countries, these differences tend to be compensated by differences in productivity, which has the effect of homogenizing unit labor costs across the EU (see Table 5.5).

The analysis of unit labor costs shows that there is no direct relation between the level of social protection and competitiveness, for those countries enjoying a high level of social protection are also competitive in interna-

Table 5.5
Social Protection and Competitiveness, 1997

Country	Social expenditure % GDP	Per capita GDP EU=100	Real Unit Labor Costs 1991 =100
Belgium	28.5	110.9	96.5
Denmark	31.4	117.1	95.2
Germany	29.9	108.8	97.6
Greece	23.6	68.2	97.8
Spain	21.4	79.9	94.0
France	30.8	103.6	96.1
Ireland	17.5	103.9	89.1
Italy	25.9	101.9	91.7
Luxembourg	24.8	170.9	
Netherlands	30.3	105.4	96.9
Portugal	22.5	70.9	94.3
United Kingdom	26.8	99.7	94.2
EU	28.2	100.0	95.3

Source: Eurostat (2000) and European Economy (1999a, 1999b).

tional markets. Southern European countries show an evolution that is leading them to converge towards the European average (see Table 5.5).

European Union Economic Transfers

Finally, it could also be considered that transfers from the EU help the less-developed member states gain higher levels of competitiveness than those of their richer counterparts. Net fluxes from the EU amount to very low proportions of GDP when compared to those dedicated to social protection by Southern countries. For example, in Spain, which is the country most favored by EU transfers, structural actions undertaken have not overcome 0.7 percent of GDP in yearly average during the last few years (Carrasco, 2000: 235). Besides, it should be taken into account that EU transfers are in a way a compensation for industrial and productive capacity cutbacks in those sectors that are not competitive any longer, a process that entails an increase of expenditure on social protection because of pre-retirement policies and other social measures that have to be financed by each country.

In sum, neither the consideration of the evolution of social expenditure and its financing nor of unit labor costs renders any positive result leading to a suspicion of the existence of social dumping in Southern Europe. Let us turn now to assess qualitative change of social provision in Southern Europe, as well as considering the factors that have shaped the chosen strategies for the reformulation of social policy.

Recent Policy Patterns in Southern Europe: Social Dumping or Catching-up?

This section refers to the latest social reforms only as a general overview of those aspects more closely related to the potential existence of social dumping. As Alber (1998) points out, increases in aggregate spending levels may occur at the same time as particular welfare state programs are rendered less generous and/or public provisions are replaced by private ones. We can also add that such a phenomenon is also possible not only when expenditure grows, but even when fiscal pressure (be it through general taxation or social contributions) is increasing and unit labor costs are becoming similar.

To start with, it should be pointed out that the reference model, the welfare state(s) most admired by Southern European countries has never been the American model of the market economy. Contrarily, Southern countries, although departing from an occupational model of Bismarckian tradition, have turned their eyes in the last decades to those European welfare states they thought the most developed, i.e., those of the Scandinavian countries. In Spain, since the early 1970s (that is, even before the dictatorship had come to an end), a general wish was felt among all the social and political actors of trying to emulate the Scandinavian models. In later years, as it also happened in other Southern countries (Portugal, Greece), the presence of social democratic parties in office allowed for the maintenance of such an ideal (Maravall, 1995). In Italy, the only Southern European country enjoying a democracy since the end of the Second World War, such aspirations were also present. In general, an acute conscience of backwardness was shared (and still is) by South European countries in social protection matters, to which the Italian case has hardly been an exception.

In fact, a significant share of the efforts made for the reform of social policy during the last fifteen years has yielded important results in the direction of the adoption of universalist policies. This has been the case above all in what regards the health care and the education systems. In the first case, national health services have been adopted in all Southern European countries, starting with their formal inception in Italy (1978), followed suit by Portugal (1979), and later by Greece (1984) and Spain (1986).

However, differences in the level of implementation of these reforms among the Southern European countries are notorious (Guillén, 1999). Portugal and Greece have encountered a great many difficulties in implementing their reforms; in Portugal the share of private expenditure has been growing dramatically (Pinto, 1997; Guibentif, 1997). In Italy and Spain, the reforms so far have been much more successful, although also presenting differentiating characteristics. While Italy put into practice its sweeping reform straightforward and rapidly during the 1980s, Spain lagged some years behind, so that universal coverage in Spain, for example, was not attained until the late 1980s and some 200,000 people (0.3 percent of the population) belonging to the highest income bracket still remain out of the public system. Italy also passed a reform in 1998 regarding the financing of health care services out of state and regional revenues. Spain finances health care services out of taxes (100 percent in 1999) and user co-payments only exist for pharmaceuticals. Patient co-payments are also low in Greece (Venieris, 1997). Cost-sharing for health services were introduced in Italy in 1983 and more decidedly in 1992, and are also of considerable importance in the Portuguese case. Still, if compared with the level of other European countries, user co-payments do not seem particularly high in Southern Europe (Guillén, 1999; Guillén & Cabiedes, 1997).

In general, and in the health care domain, maybe with the partial exception of Portugal, where privatization of previously public schemes has taken place, it is difficult to see a clear attack on the core of Southern welfare states in recent rearrangements of public provision. This has also been the case with pensions. However, in this latter domain, whereas no decided privatization trends may be observed, cost control measures have been adopted in all Southern European countries. Increased public incentives for private pension plans have been introduced in all of them in the late 1980s or early 1990s, but private plans have not come to constitute an opting-out possibility and, so far, small proportions of citizens have engaged in them.

In general, income guarantee policies in Southern Europe have remained occupational and have suffered a good number of both expansionary and retrenchment measures, which have acted as a pendulum in the past two decades. Pensions were indexed to inflation in the 1980s, while such indexing was corrected in the 1990s to expected, rather than to past, inflation rates or even discontinued, as has been the case in Greece. After several unsuccessful attempts undertaken in the 1980s at the face of dramatic fiscal deficits, pensions have also been linked much more strictly to individual social contributions in Italy since the Amato reform in 1992, and more intensely since the Dini reform in 1995 (Ferrera, 1997). Something akin, although probably less intense, has happened in Spain since the Toledo Pact was signed in 1995 among parties represented in parliament. The law on the reform of the pension system was approved in 1997. Both in Italy and Spain, a drastic reduction of the replacement rate of pensions has taken place: around 35 percent for Spain (adding up the results of the 1985 and 1997 reforms that will be totally in force in the year 2002). In Greece several laws were passed at the beginning of the 1990s, targeted at reducing the public debt and social security measures (Petmesidou, 1996). In Portugal restrictive reforms of the pension system have been proposed only recently and are being debated currently (Romao, 1998). However, it should be recalled that replacement rates are the highest of the whole EU in Southern countries (Ferrera, 1996), so that these reforms bring the pension systems of Southern Europe in line with the rest of the EU members.

Conversely, expansionary measures of different kinds have taken place in order to complete (or try to) the safety net in the domain of income guarantee. The introduction of such measures has been more intense in Spain, Italy, and recently in Portugal, and has consisted most of the time in the introduction of means-tested programs aimed at particular social groups, such as the long-term unemployed and poor elders. These programs are of a limited scope when compared with the provisions of other European welfare states and they show two distinctive traits: first, broad inequalities between benefits linked to previous participation in the labor market and those covering non-participants; and second, inequalities among the levels of protection of the elders and people within active ages (Ferrera, 1996; Gough, 1997). Nonetheless, such inequalities have been somewhat diminished in recent years by the restrictive reforms of the contributory pension systems on the one side, and the amelioration of non-contributive benefits on the other.

Labor market policies have also undergone some changes, so that passive protection of the unemployed has been reduced. This reduction has been compensated for, at least partially, by the intensification of active labor market policies, which have doubled their percentages over GDP between 1985 and 1995 (OECD, 1997: 43). Private employment agencies have been timidly introduced in Spain, Italy, and Greece in recent years, although with negative results in this latter case (Petmesidou, 1996).

In sum, qualitative assessment of policy reform in Southern European countries does not lead to suspect that a social dumping strategy is taking place in the domains of health care, income maintenance, and labor market protection policies. Expansion has been much larger than retrenchment. Moreover, changes in social policy and cutbacks have not been produced by the intentional search of disloyal economic competition, but rather by searching to endow the system with more efficiency. Given that the present analysis is accurate, it should be concluded that even though both catching-up and retrenchment moves have been present in Southern welfare states in recent years, the former have been both quantitatively and qualitatively more intense than the latter, as happens to be the case in all EU welfare states. Now, how to explain this?

Interpreting the Evolution of Policy Reform

In this section, we will consider some interpretative arguments and also reconsider some other explanations that have been already advanced in order to assess both expansionary and retrenchment tendencies in Southern Europe. The aim is to explain why expansionary tendencies have outmoded restrictive ones. None of the arguments presented here claims to constitute a definitive explanation but only to contribute to the existing debate on the recent development of Southern welfare states.

In the first place, growth in social policy financing and expenditure and the adoption of expansionary measures were related in Southern European countries to legitimization needs of governments in the process of transition to democracy, which Portugal, Spain, and Greece underwent from the mid-1970s onward. It should be recalled that governments not only needed to stabilize the countries politically but also to respond to new and pressing social needs that were brought about by the coincidence of political transitions to democracy and economic crises (Castles, 1995; Guillén, 1992). Moreover, the establishment of democratic regimes allowed interest groups to exercise pressure and to participate in the decision-making process.

Secondly, the permanence of left-wing parties in office for substantial periods of time during the last two decades could also be forwarded as a reason for the expansion of social policies (Maravall, 1995). Moreover, and in general, public preferences and pressure groups were also clearly in favor of the "attainment of European standards" in welfare policies. Unions were able in many occasions to press decidedly for the introduction of expansive reforms and to block restrictive ones or, at least, to postpone or make them hard to approve.

Thirdly, a deep decentralization process has taken place in Spain and Italy, especially in the domains of welfare services such as health care, education, and personal social services. This devolution process has led to a clear increase in expenditure and also to competitive behaviors on the part of the regions as to which of them was and is able to offer better welfare services to their citizens. Innovation has also been fostered by decentralization, so that regions have forced the central state in many cases to renew or complete obsolete legislation on social policy. However, some evidence exists that inequalities among citizens are also mounting at the national level because of increasing differences in the provision of services at the regional level.

Another line of argument could take into account the influence of EU recommendations and demonstration effects. In fact, in our view, EU membership and integration processes have had a twofold crucial influence on the evolution of social policy among the Mediterranean countries. On the one side, joining the EU has had the effect of fostering the expansion of social policies in order to close the existing gap with other European welfare states. On the other side, pressures for economic convergence and the reduction of the public deficit have acted in the opposite direction of facilitating short-cuts. Retrenchment policies have been presented by governments very frequently as unavoidable and necessary if the country was to join the EMU, providing in this way a very convenient excuse for governments to dilute their responsibility and escape negative electoral consequences, that is, by facilitating the use of blame avoidance strategies.

Many experts on social policy in Southern Europe have pointed to the existence of a weak civil society and to the reliance on the family as a social services provider. These are considered factors hindering the expansion of social policy, because of the absence of demands and pressure on public authorities that this circumstance entails. This may be partially true as far as the generation of demands is concerned. However, it is also in contradiction with the ability that pressure groups have shown for blocking restrictive reforms in a good number of cases in the last decades.

Distinctiveness of Southern welfare regimes is sometimes related to the persistence of a Catholic ideology (Van Kersbergen, 1995) that has consequences for the behavior of families and the gendered division of labor and for the formulation of social policy. One could start by asking whether this could apply also to Orthodox Greece or to Muslim Turkey, a country that is sometimes considered to be part of the Southern European family (as for example in Gough, 1997). So far, and in our view, the issue of cultural and ideological determinants of welfare provision has not as yet been studied enough for a clear-cut conclusion to be reached. The division of labor as regards household tasks has changed very little in the whole of Europe, not only in the South. Whether the role played by the family in Southern countries is due to the influence of religious ideology, or other ideological traditions, or to the fact that the need still exists for the family to complement public welfare provision is still a matter for investigation. Lastly, differences in the incorporation of women into the labor market may be due to the existence of a traditional view on women's roles, or equally possible, as Castles (1994) defends, to the evolution of labor market opportunities and employment structures. In fact, the participation of women in the labor market has increased dramatically over the last decades in Southern Europe, even if strong institutional barriers for new entrances of young workers (both for men and women) have persisted.

Retrenchment and/or rationalization reforms have been closely related to external pressures stemming from the process of European integration and the Maastricht conditions for economic convergence. A second reason has been that of re-addressing the unbalances of the traditional welfare systems in order to reach a more equitable situation, that is, reducing the privileges of those profiting most from the welfare system and increasing those of the population left aside, mainly non-core labor market participants. So far, intentional retrenchment of social provisions in order to gain economic competitiveness has not been detected, either from a quantitative or a qualitative point of view.

Notes

1. Cited in European Industrial Relations Review (1993: 17).
2. Although employers tend to stress in the negative consequences of social charges for their competitiveness in external markets, it should not be forgotten, as Herce (1996) highlights, that the most adequate measure of the degree of competitiveness of an economy is the effective rate of exchange, that fluctuates much more rapidly than changes in social contributions. Moreover, as it absorbs variations in the relative levels of prices, it tends to compensate relative changes in unitary labor costs in the long run. We are not taking this aspect into account, for potential fluctuation of exchange rates are very narrow at present in the EU and will become non-existent for those countries adopting the Euro.

References

Alber, J. (1998). "Welfare Spending and Welfare Reforms in the European Union." Rapporti Mondadori Lecture, 3 April, Florence.
Atkinson, A. B. (1996). *Public Economics in Action.* Clarendon Press, Oxford.
Ayala Cañón, L. (1994). "Los sistemas generales de rentas mínimas en Europa: logros, límites y alternativas." *Documentación Social*, 96 (July-September): 223-277.
Carrasco, E. (2000). *La cohesión Económica y Social en la Unión Europea.* Madrid: Consejo Económico y Social.
Castles, F. G. (1994). "On Religion and Public Policy: Does Catholicism Make a Difference?" *European Journal of Political Research*, 25 (1), 19-40.
____. (1995). "Welfare State Development in Southern Europe." *West European Politics*, 18 (2), 291-313.

Dearden, S. J. H. (1995). "European Union Social Policy and Flexible Production." *International Journal of Manpower*, 16 (10), 3-13.

European Economy. (1999a). 1999 Broad Economic Policy Guidelines.

___. (1999b). The EU Economy: 1999 Review.

European Industrial Relations Review. (1993). International Section: The Hoover Affair and Social Dumping, 230 (March), 14-20.

Eurostat. (1997). Data Base *Eudor-Stat, No. 2/1997* (CD Edition), Luxembourg: Eurostat.

___. (2000). *Social Protection Expenditures and Receipts 1980-1997*. Luxembourg: European Communities.

Ferrera, M. (1996). "The 'Southern Model' of Welfare in Social Europe." *Journal of European Social Policy*, 6 (1), 17-37.

___.(1997). "The Uncertain Future of the Italian Welfare State." *West European Politics*, 20 (1), 231-249.

Gough, I. (1997). "La asistencia social en el sur de Europa." In Moreno, L. (ed.), *Unión Europea y Estado del Bienestar*. Madrid: Consejo Superior de Investigaciones Científicas, 405-429.

Guibentif, P. (1997). "The Transformation of the Portuguese Social Security System." In Rhodes, M. (ed.), *Southern European Welfare States. Between Crisis and Reform*. London: Frank Cass.

Guillén, A. M. (1992). "Social Policy in Spain: From Dictatorship to Democracy." In Ferge, Z. and Kolberg, J. E. (eds.), *Social Policy in a Changing Europe*. Boulder, Colo.: Campus/Westview.

___. (1999). "Improving Efficiency and Containing Costs: Health Care Reform in Southern Europe." *European University Working Papers*, No. 16. Florence: European University Institute.

Guillén, A. M., and Cabiedes, L. (1997). "Towards a National Health Service in Spain: The Search for Equity and Efficiency." *Journal of European Social Policy*, 7 (4), 319-336.

Herce, J. A. (1996). *Protección social y competitividad: el caso español*. Working Paper. Bilbao: Fundación BBV.

Leibfried, S. (1993). "Towards a European Welfare State?" In Jones, C. (ed.), *New Perspectives on the Welfare State in Europe*. London: Routledge.

Maravall, J. M. (1995). *Los resultados de la democracia*. Madrid: Alianza.

Messere, K. (1997). "OECD Tax Developments in the 1990s." *Bulletin of the International Bureau of Fiscal Documentation*, July, 298-314.

___. (2000). "20th Century Taxes and Their Future." *Bulletin of the International Bureau of Fiscal Documentation*, January, 2-29.

Ministerio de Trabajo y Seguridad Social. (1996). *Proyecto de presupuestos de la Seguridad Social. Ejercicio 1996*. Madrid: Ministerio de Trabajo y Seguridad Social.

OECD. (1997). *Labour Market Policies: New Challenges. Policies for Low-Paid Workers and Unskilled Job Seekers*. Meeting of the Employment, Labour and Social Affairs Committee at Ministerial Level, held at the Château de la Muette, Paris, 14-15 October. OECD/GD (97) 160. Paris: OECD.

Petmesidou, M. (1996). "Social Protection in Greece: A Brief Glimpse of a Welfare State." *Social Policy and Administration*, 30 (4), 324-347.

Pinto, C. G. (1997). "Health Care Systems, Equity and Social Welfare." In *Comparing Social Welfare Systems in Southern Europe*. Volume 3. Paris: MIRE, 141-154.

Romao, J. (1998). Segurança Social. Nao há crise. *Vida Mundial*, 2 (March), 44-53.

Sapir, A. (1995). "The Interaction Between Labour Standards and International Trade Policy." *World Economy*, 18 (November): 791-803.

Van Kersbergen, K. (1995). *Social Capitalism*. London: Routledge and Kegan Paul.
Venieris, D. N. (1997). "Dimensions of Social Policy in Greece." In Rhodes, M. (ed.), *Southern European Welfare States. Between Crisis and Reform*. London: Frank Cass.

Part 2

Global Pressures and Internal Adjustments

6

Globalization and the Welfare State: Constraints, Challenges, and Vulnerabilities

Fritz W. Scharpf

The advanced capitalist welfare states developed their characteristic aspirations, policy patterns, sources of finance, and institutional structures in the decades following World War II under conditions in which the nation state was able to exercise a historically exceptional degree of control over its own economic boundaries. As governments were able to regulate capital movements, to determine exchange rates, and to adjust tariffs on imports, external economic factors had little or no influence on domestic policy choices. Thus, if there are commonalities among "families" of national welfare states and industrial-relations systems (Esping-Andersen, 1990), they were primarily due to shared ideological world views and aspirations among dominant political parties. Politics, in other words, did matter very much in the postwar decades.

These cozy conditions changed after the early 1970s, when the viability of advanced capitalist economies was severely tested by the stagflation crisis following the first oil price shock. As it turned out, countries differed greatly in their capacity to cope with the new international turbulence that was exacerbated by the destruction of the Bretton Woods regime of fixed but adjustable exchange rates. Countries that failed to find effective responses found themselves confronted by rising mass unemployment and/or runaway inflation and, in any case, high public-sector deficits at the onset of the second oil price crisis in the early 1980s which added a dramatic rise of real interest rates in international capital markets to the external challenges they had to meet.

In the present chapter, I will omit the analysis of successful and failed responses to the international macro-economic challenges of the 1970s and early 1980s, and will focus exclusively on the adjustment of employment and welfare systems to challenges arising from the international (global and European) integration of product and capital markets that had slowly increased after the 1960s, but reached new levels of intensity in the late 1980s and 1990s. In doing so, I am quite aware of the fact that international economic changes are not the only ones with which welfare states had to cope during this period, and that changing gender roles and family structures, rapidly aging populations, and the rising costs of health care would have challenged golden-age welfare states even in the absence of "globalization" and the European Monetary Union (EMU). Nevertheless, in the absence of new international constraints on policy choices, these endogenous challenges would be much easier to deal with.

The New Constraints

In the comparative political economy literature, there is considerable dispute over the question of whether economic globalization does, or does not affect welfare-state policy at the national level. While some of this literature is alarmist in tone, predicting a race to the bottom in standards of social protection as a consequence of international regulatory and tax competition (Rodrik, 1997; Steinmo, 1994; Strange, 1991; 1996; Tanzi, 1995), others find no statistical evidence for the predicted convergence but, rather, a continuation of national differences determined by partisan preferences (Garrett, 1995; 1998; Quinn, 1997; Rhodes, 1996; Swank, 1997). If this dispute seems to have generated more heat than light, the reason may be a lack of clarity over two basic distinctions—between binding constraints and price effects on the one hand, and between effects on policy instruments and policy outcomes on the other hand.

Thus, the dramatic rise of real interest rates in the international capital markets in the early 1980s did not prevent countries from running high fiscal deficits—but it surely did raise the costs of the debt service. Similarly, more intense competition in internationalized product markets does not rule out aggressive real wage strategies by national unions, but it raises their costs in terms of job losses. Moreover, where international integration does, in fact, impose legally binding constraints, as it does for the monetary and exchange-rate policies of member states of the European Monetary Union, these constraints rule out the choice of specific policy instruments, rather than policy outcomes. Hence, even if devaluation and deficit spending are no longer an option, social benefits or public-sector employment may still be increased if they are paid for through higher taxes or the reduction of other expenditures. In short, price effects do not strictly determine the choice of policy instruments, and even binding constraints on policy instruments need not lead to convergent policy outcomes.

Logically, therefore, empirical findings showing persistent national differences of policy outcomes achieved, or policy instruments employed, could not falsify the claim that advanced welfare states are severely challenged by the global or European integration of product and capital markets. Instead, it seems more instructive to consider first the differences between the international (legal and economic) policy environment of the late 1990s and conditions at the end of the "golden age" in the late 1960s, and then to relate these differences to the employment and social-policy aspirations of advanced welfare states.

In the early postwar period of "embedded liberalism" (Ruggie, 1982), national economies had been only weakly coupled to their international environment and national governments were still able to control capital transfers, exchange rates, and the conditions under which goods and services could be imported and exported—which allowed them considerable freedom in shaping national systems of employment, taxation, regulation, and welfare provision. More specifically, even in the 1970s and early 1980s, when the international economic environment lost its benign character, governments were still able to resort to a wide range of policy options that are no longer available today. To list a few:

- Britain, Sweden, Italy, Australia, New Zealand and other countries frequently attempted to restore international competitiveness through politically determined devaluations of the currency;
- in the 1970s, a majority of countries still relied on exchange controls to prevent capital outflows;
- during the first oil price crisis, most advanced industrial economies attempted to stimulate productive investments through monetary policies ensuring very low, and often negative, real interest rates;
- during the first oil price crisis, most advanced industrial countries tried to stabilize aggregate demand through spending and investment programs financed by massive fiscal deficits;
- Australia and New Zealand supported full employment by promoting import-substituting industrialization that was protected by extremely high tariff barriers and quantitative restrictions on imports;
- Italy, France, and other European countries frequently imposed special tariffs and quantitative restrictions to protect specific branches that were threatened by import competition;
- Sweden and some other countries had highly regulated credit markets that allowed them to channel consumer demand and investment funds to specific sectors, regions or firms;
- Austria, France, Germany and other countries used their influence on state-owned banks for the same purpose;
- Austria, France, and Italy did use a large range of nationalized industries as an employment buffer in the first oil price crisis, and Sweden nationalized its crisis-ridden shipbuilding and steel industries in order

to ease the transition to new employment opportunities in other branches;

- practically all countries did subsidize declining industries in order to reduce job losses;
- in all countries, service-public functions in telecommunications, transport, energy supply, etc. were protected not only against international but also against national market competition;
- practically all countries protected national producers by requiring importers to comply with nationally specific product regulations;
- Austria, Germany, Switzerland and other countries did exclude foreign workers in order to reduce open unemployment in the first oil price crisis.

It should be understood that I am not suggesting that the use of these policy options was then, or would now be, generally desirable. The fact is, nevertheless, that less than two decades ago, many countries found them useful under certain circumstances, and that they would no longer be available today. In Europe, they are ruled out by Treaty obligations, enforced as the supreme law of the land, that ensure the free movement of goods, services, capital and labor among the member states of the Community. Moreover, European rules have replaced national product standards or required their mutual recognition; they have required the liberalization, deregulation and in effect, privatization of service-public utilities in communications, transport, and energy supply; European competition law has drastically limited the range of permissible subsidies; the Maastricht criteria for joining the Monetary Union have practically eliminated deficit spending as a policy tool; and the realization of the Monetary Union has completely removed monetary policy and exchange rate policy from the control of its member states.

For countries outside of the European Union, legal constraints are not as tight, but even there the Uruguay Round of GATT (General Agreement on Tariffs and Trade) negotiations has considerably extended existing obligations to free trade in services and in agricultural markets, and the creation of the World Trade Organization (WTO) has increased the legal effectiveness of these obligations. Moreover, countries that became dependent on World Bank and International Monetary Fund (IMF) support faced strong external pressures to implement fiscal consolidation, hard-currency policies, and unrestricted capital exchange; and even in the absence of explicit IMF pressures, policies adopted by Australia and New Zealand after the late 1980s are fully compliant with prescriptions of the "Washington consensus." In Europe, the same is true of Sweden, Denmark, and the United Kingdom, that did not choose to join the Monetary Union, but whose fiscal and monetary policies were nevertheless fully compatible with the Maastricht criteria of EMU membership.

Instead it seems that legal pressures are reinforced, and may be even be replaced by economic pressures once the de facto openness of economies has passed a certain threshold. The constraints on macro-economic policy and the pressure to liberalize capital-exchange policies were particularly severe in countries that depend on capital imports to finance large budget deficits or persistent current-account deficits. But as capital became more mobile, and as the relative importance of international competition in the markets for goods and services increased, economic constraints were felt in a whole range of other policy areas as well. At the most abstract level, these may be described as follows:

- Since consumers have a free choice among domestic and imported products, market shares will be lost if national taxes, regulations, and collective-bargaining agreements increase the relative price of domestically produced goods and services;
- since firms have a free choice among production locations, jobs will be lost if national taxes, regulations and collective-bargaining agreements increase the relative costs of domestic production;
- since capital has become internationally mobile, productive investment will decline if national taxes, regulations and collective-bargaining agreements reduce relative post-tax profits; and
- since capital has become internationally mobile, high relative tax burdens on capital incomes will reduce revenues.

As a consequence, countries are forced into tax competition, regulatory competition and wage competition to defend or improve their shares in the world markets for goods and services, their attractiveness as a location for productive investments, and their ability to collect revenue from mobile tax bases. This much is generally accepted. The question is whether and how these conditions will affect the employment and social-policy goals of advanced welfare states as they had been defined at the end of the postwar golden age.

General Challenges

In discussing this question, it is useful to distinguish between general challenges that affect all countries, and the specific vulnerabilities of particular countries or groups of countries. The general challenges will be discussed with regard to their effects on employment and on the financial viability of advanced welfare states.

Employment Effects

Beginning with the effects on employment, it is noteworthy that in the Organization for Economic Co-operation and Development (OECD) average, total employment rates (employment as percent of population 15-64) in 1998 were at 66.5 percent, almost exactly as high as they had been in 1970. There are of course interesting differences between countries to which I will return later. What matters here is that this seeming stability appears as the result of two divergent processes if we distinguish between employment in the sectors that are exposed to, or sheltered against, international competition (Figure 6.1).

In the exposed sector (which under the conditions of the 1990s includes not only agriculture and industry but also construction, energy supply, trans-

Figure 6.1
Average OECD-18 Employment Rates

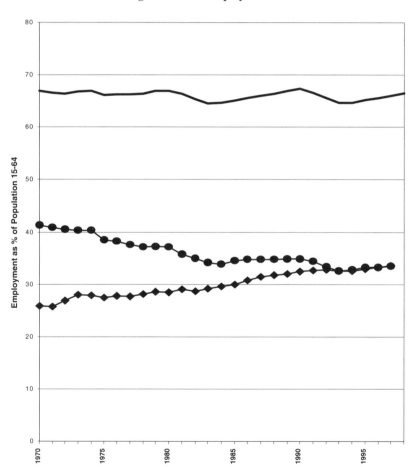

port, communications, financial services and business services—i.e., International Standard Industrial Classification (ISIC) 1-5, 7 and 8), average OECD-18 employment rates declined by almost eight percentage points, from 41.3 percent in 1970 to 33.5 percent in 1997. While there are interesting differences between countries, to be discussed later, the trend is the same: Employment declined steeply in the deep recessions of the mid-1970s and early 1980s. It never returned to its previous volume, even though international trade continued to rise more rapidly than Gross Domestic Product (GDP). But as trade increased and national boundaries lost their economic effectiveness, competition in the exposed sectors—including competition from producers in low-cost countries—also became more intense. As a consequence, firms in countries with high labor costs were forced to either move upmarket to less price-sensitive quality products, or to use all available organizational and technical options to cut production costs through labor-saving rationalization. In either case, skill requirements would rise, and the total volume of employment would decline.

Losses in industry, it is true, were in part compensated by the expansion of production-related services and increases in the final consumption of communications and financial services (which are also included in our definition of the exposed sector). Here again, some countries have done better than others. But these services are now also affected by the rapid advance of information and communications technology and, in any case, their rise is not enough to fully compensate the loss of production jobs. If, nevertheless, total employment rates recovered after each recession and, on average, are now as high as they were in 1970, the effect is entirely due to the continuous rise of employment in the sheltered sector—also by almost eight percentage points, from 25.9 percent in 1970 to 33.6 percent in 1997.

Our definition of the sheltered sectors comprises jobs in "wholesale and retail trade, hotels and restaurants" (ISIC 6) as well as in "community, social and personal services" (ISIC 9)—among which education and health care constitute the largest blocks. Obviously, the category comprises very heterogeneous activities, united merely by the fact that they are more or less immune to international competition because services are locally provided and locally consumed by the ultimate beneficiaries. Beyond that, differences abound: Trade and gastronomical services are generally provided and financed in the private economy, whereas primary education is publicly financed and provided in most countries; in health care, privately provided services may be publicly financed on a fee-for-service basis, or publicly provided services may be privately co-financed through user charges. Moreover, some of these services (surgery, for instance) have extremely high skill requirements, whereas others (house cleaning, for instance) may require little specific training. Often, however, high- and low-skill jobs exist in symbiotic interdependence.

As is to be expected, differences among countries matter even more in this heterogeneous sector. What can be said generally is that the more or less inevitable decline of exposed-sector employment could be compensated or even overcompensated only in countries in which conditions were favorable for the expansion of either publicly financed or privately financed local services. But even though sheltered sector employment was not itself exposed to international competition, the conditions that facilitated its expansion were largely shaped by differences in the structures of welfare states which, in turn, were directly affected by the impact of economic integration on their financial viability.

Fiscal Effects

In a nutshell, the story of tightening fiscal constraints is contained in Figure 6.2, representing average GDP shares of total government outlays, of total revenues from taxes and social security contributions, and of net public-sector borrowing. At the end of the postwar golden age, budgets in most countries were in balance or in surplus. With the beginning of the first oil price crisis, total government outlays increased steeply as countries responded to the threat, or the actual rise, of mass unemployment with deficit-financed investment and spending programs, and in most cases with rapidly increasing social expenditures. As a consequence, average deficits jumped from zero to 2.6 percent of GDP in 1975 and continued at about the same level until the end of the decade. By contrast, revenues from taxes and social security contributions increased more steadily, and continued to do so beyond the end of the decade.

The second oil price crisis, which began to be felt in the 1980s, caused another steep rise of total government outlays to which the initial response was another rise of average public-sector deficits. But now conditions had changed: the monetarist switch of the U.S. Federal Reserve had driven up real interest rates in the international dollar markets from -2 percent in 1980 to +8.1 percent in 1984. Hence the debt service implied by high budget deficits became prohibitively expensive, and fiscal consolidation, which had not been an issue in the cheap-money environment of the 1970s, became a high political priority. Average deficits declined from a peak of 4.4 percent in 1982 to 1 percent at the end of the decade, and the conservative governments, that had come into office in the 1980s, also tried to reverse the seemingly inexorable rise of welfare spending. Nevertheless, total tax revenue continued to rise until 1988. In most countries, in other words, the reduction of public borrowing was at least in part achieved through further increases in taxation.

When the recession of the early 1990s resulted in another and even steeper increase of total government outlays, the pattern changed once more. Now, average tax revenues did not rise at all—in fact, they even declined slightly

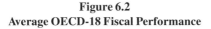

Figure 6.2
Average OECD-18 Fiscal Performance

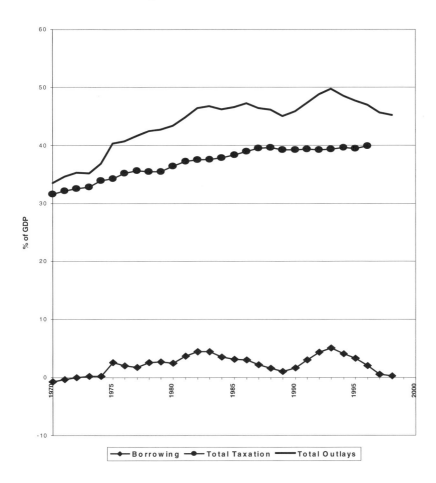

from their peak in 1988. By default, therefore, public-sector borrowing rose more steeply after 1989 than in any period before—but then it declined just as steeply from its 1993 peak to levels unheard of since the early 1970s. At the same time, total government outlays also declined more steeply than ever before after 1993, even though average unemployment rates remained at record levels, and even though the balance of political power was shifting from conservative to social democratic governments in the course of the 1990s. The reasons for this implausible coincidence provide the key to an understanding of the present fiscal constraints facing advanced welfare states. I will discuss them separately for borrowing and for taxation.

Borrowing

For European countries aspiring to membership in the European Monetary Union, the need for rapid fiscal consolidation derived directly from the very restrictive criteria on gross public debt and on public-sector borrowing that were defined in the Maastricht Treaty of 1992 and the subsequent Stability Pact. In order to meet these legal requirements of membership, most countries had to cut expenditures, and if they were unable to raise taxes, they often had to rely on proceeds from privatization to reduce borrowing. For my general argument, however, it is more important to note that fiscal consolidation was equally or even more effective in countries like Sweden, Denmark, the United Kingdom, Australia, and New Zealand that had not aspired to membership in the Monetary Union.

The reason is that in the course of the 1980s all these countries had abandoned capital-exchange controls, so that their currencies were now fully exposed to the volatility of global financial markets and the recurrent waves of currency speculation—whose destructive force (combined with the government's efforts to resist it) had driven Sweden into the deepest crisis experienced by any industrial country in the last three decades. This lesson, which was reinforced by lesser disruptions in New Zealand, Australia, and Britain as well as by the Southeast Asian crisis a few years later, has not been lost: Under conditions of complete and instant capital mobility, governments have come to realize that a reputation for "unsound" fiscal policies will not only affect their credit rating and the interest rates they must pay, but will also make their currencies vulnerable to speculative attacks with potentially catastrophic economic consequences. In short, and even in the absence of Maastricht criteria and IMF pressures, it has become much preferable for governments to be net lenders, rather than net borrowers, in international capital markets.

Taxation of Mobile Tax Bases

What needs more of an explanation is the fact that, in contrast to earlier recessions, the average GDP-share of tax revenues did not rise at all as total government outlays shot up once again in the early 1990s. Unlike borrowing, after all, taxation was not legally constrained by Maastricht-type obligations in any of countries. Even more remarkably, the flattening of the revenue curves cannot be understood as a "growth-to-limits" phenomenon, since it occurred in low-tax as well as in high-tax countries, and since the difference between countries with the lowest and the highest total tax burdens has remained almost constant from 1970 to the end of the 1990s (see Table 6 1). In other words, while all countries seem to be constrained on the revenue side, there is no evidence of a race to the bottom or, for that matter, of a convergence toward the mean.

Ganghof (2000a; 2000b) explains this pattern as a result of cross pressures: On the one hand, international tax competition in an environment of highly mobile capital and mobile firms would push governments to reduce the tax burden on mobile tax bases. On the other hand, governments are unable to move very far in this direction because they are simultaneously pushed to reduce budget deficits and confronted by political resistance against measures of welfare-state retrenchment that would have to go beyond the cutbacks that conservative governments had already imposed in the 1980s.

In the literature, the causal effectiveness of international tax competition is in dispute (Swank, 1997; Garrett, 1998). There can be no question, however, that the removal of all barriers to capital mobility has not only provided new opportunities for tax evasion and tax avoidance, but has also created incentives for countries to increase the relative attractiveness of their tax systems for mobile capital. Taxes on interest incomes of non-residents are often reduced to zero in the hope that additional revenue and jobs will be generated by the expansion of financial services. But even in the absence of outright discrimination in favor of non-residents, lower rates may pay off for small countries that will gain more revenue from a larger tax base than they will lose by lowering taxes for residents. That logic also applies to the taxation of corporate profits since companies are free to move their legal residence, or the residence of their financing subsidiaries, to low-tax jurisdictions without having to relocate production facilities as well. As a consequence, all countries have been under pressure to reduce nominal tax rates on incomes from capital interest and on corporate profits, but small countries have been more successful than large countries in maintaining the level of revenue (Ganghof, 2000a).

Taxation of Immobile Tax Bases

Obviously, tax competition is not only about revenue but also about productive investments, and hence about production and employment—all of which presumably depend on expected post-tax profits. Paradoxically, however, here the negative impact of high corporate income taxes is mitigated if firms are, in fact, able to choose the jurisdiction where profits will be taxed regardless of the location of production. But of course these options are not available to all firms. In all firms, however, pre-tax profits must be earned before their tax treatment can be optimized—which shifts competitive concerns to the quality and price of labor and other local factors of production. In this context, taxes on labor are thought to play a major role. If they raise the costs of production above the level of competing locations, they should produce disinvestment and job losses.

Impact on Employment in the Exposed Sectors

Without more evidence, however, the argument is not economically convincing. Why should profits be affected by differences in national factor costs, or even by nationally uniform tax increases (or wage increases, for that matter) except in the very short term? In the exposed sectors, these costs will determine the price, in national currency, of nationally produced goods and services which, in functioning international currency markets, should be reflected in exchange rates with no adverse effects on consumer demand, profits, and employment. Even though currency markets are far from perfect, it should thus not really come as a surprise that the bivariate statistical association between employment rates in the exposed sectors and the total tax burden of OECD-18 countries was extremely weak ($r^2 = 0.13$) at the end of the 1990s (Figure 6.3). In fact, Denmark and Sweden as extreme high-tax coun-

Figure 6.3
Tax Burden and Employment in Exposed Sectors (ISIC 1-5, 7, 8), 1997

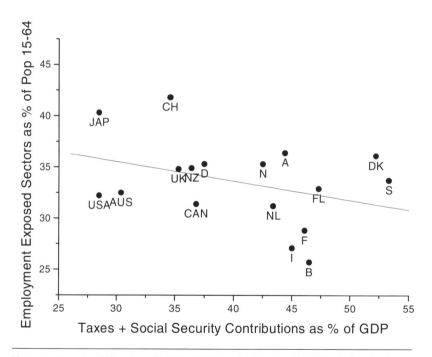

Note: A = Austria, AUS = Australia, B = Belgium, CAN = Canada, CH = Switzerland, D = Germany, DK = Denmark, F = France, FL = Finland, JAP = Japan, I = Italy, N = Norway, NL = Netherlands, NZ = New Zealand, S = Sweden, UK = United Kingdom, USA = United States.

tries have relatively more jobs in the internationally exposed branches than the United States as an extreme low-tax country.

For members of the European Monetary Union, however, these data cannot provide much comfort since they do not yet reflect the fact that among them the exchange-rate buffer has been eliminated. For the time being, it is true, even large differences between national levels of taxation should not have an effect on exposed-sector employment if the exchange rates at which national currencies were converted to the Euro were chosen appropriately. But from now on, all changes in factor costs will affect intra-EMU competitiveness. National tax increases (or wage increases, for that matter) that raise relative unit costs of production will produce job losses, and member states will be tempted to cut taxes on labor and other factors of production as a competitive strategy. As in the taxation of incomes from mobile capital, therefore, there is now also a possibility of ruinous competition on social security contributions and "green taxes." It is here, then, that coordination at the European level would be most useful. But these are challenges to be faced in the coming years that are not yet reflected in current practices.

Impact on Employment in the Sheltered Sectors

If this is true in the exposed sectors, what then is the effect of different levels of taxation on employment in the sheltered sectors? Since a part of these jobs (in education and in health care) is publicly financed in all countries, the overall answer must be ambivalent: There is a moderately positive association ($r^2 = 0.38$) of tax levels with public-sector employment (Figure 6.4), and there is an much stronger ($r^2 = 0.62$) negative association with private-sector employment (Figure 6.5) which—since exposed-sector jobs are only weakly affected—must be primarily due to a negative impact of high tax burdens on private services in the sheltered branches. For these, we have to take employment rates in ISIC-6 as a proxy, since services in wholesale and retail trade, restaurants and hotels are privately provided and privately financed in all countries, whereas ISIC-9 employment may be public or private. Here, the impact of taxation is indeed strongly ($r^2 = 0.59$) negative (Figure 6.6). In other words: Countries with high levels of taxation may have high employment rates in the public sector, but they generally pay for this by having fewer jobs in private-sector services.

Why this should be so is, again, not obvious from the perspective of economic theory. In the consumer-oriented services included in ISIC-6, there is no reason to think that private suppliers would be crowded out by public services. Moreover, since foreign competitors play no role here, nationally uniform taxes and other cost factors should merely raise the prices of private services that national consumers have to pay. But precisely that is the problem: Since many of the services included here are characterized by relatively

Figures 6.4
Tax Burden and Public-Sector Employment, 1997

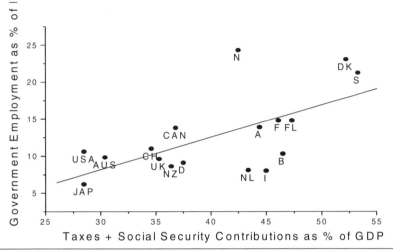

Note: For the country codes, see Figure 6.3.
Source: OECD.

Figure 6.5
Tax Burden and Private-Sector Employment, 1997

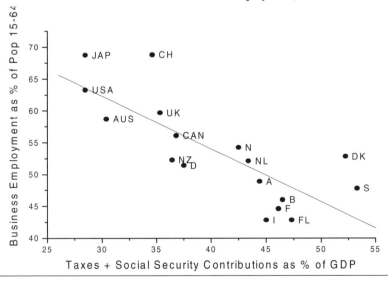

Note: For the country codes, see Figure 6.3.
Source: OECD.

Figure 6.6
Tax Burden and Employment in Private-Sector Services, 1997

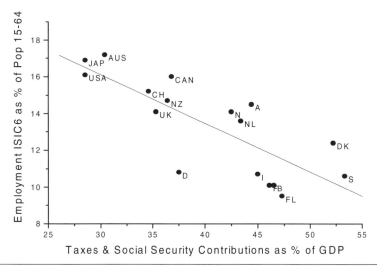

Note: For the country codes, see Figure 6.3.
Source: OECD.

low productivity and qualification requirements, consumers often have the option of resorting to self-service, do-it-yourself solutions, and of course to services provided tax-free in the "unoffical economy" (Gershuny, 1978). In other words, demand is likely to be price elastic, and the less productive services may be priced out of the private market if production costs are increased through taxes and social security contributions—or, for that matter, through cost-increasing employment regulations and high minimum wages.

There is also statistical evidence supporting these explanations. For one thing, different types of taxes differ in their impact on the price of the less productive private services. Progressive income taxes, for instance, fall more heavily on medium and high-wage jobs than on low-wage services, and they are not collected on incomes below a basic tax exemption (so that wages from low-paid and part-time jobs may not be taxed at all). As a consequence, the statistical association between income taxes and ISIC-6 employment is practically zero (Figure 6.7). By contrast, consumption taxes will directly increase the price of services, and social security contributions are generally (except in the Netherlands and in Britain) collected as a proportional tax and without an exemption for very low wages. Unlike income taxes, therefore, they may add a very large tax wedge to the wage costs of services whose market-clearing wages may not be far above rock-bottom reservation wages that are defined by social-assistance benefits. Taking both together, it is not

Figure 6.7
Income Taxes and Employment in Private-Sector Services, 1997

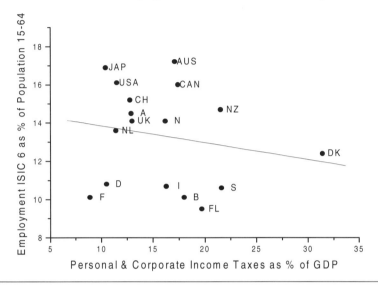

Note: For the country codes, see Figure 6.3.
Source: OECD

Figure 6.8
Social Security Plus Consumption Taxes and Employment in
Private-Sector Service, 1997

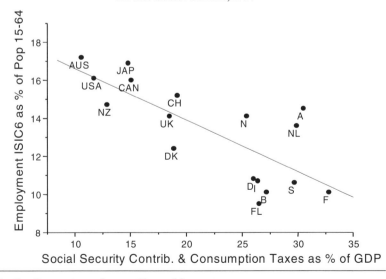

Note: For the country codes, see Figure 6.3.

surprising to see a fairly strong negative ($r^2 = 0.51$) association between ISIC-6 employment and the aggregate GDP share of consumption taxes and social security contributions (Figure 6.8). But these tax effects do not yet tell the whole story.

Other Influences

Taxes are not the only way in which the welfare state affects employment in the sheltered sector. It is of course positively influenced by a Scandinavian-type expansion of publicly financed social services. In the private sector, however, the expansion of service employment may be impeded by egalitarian or protective welfare-state regulations. More specifically, the price of less productive services may be raised above market-clearing levels by the effect which generous social assistance and unemployment benefits may have on the net reservation wages of economically rational job seekers, or by high statutory minimum wages, or by the solidaristic wage policy of unions (Iversen and Wren, 1998). These effects are reflected in available statistics on wage dispersion. Taking the ratio of incomes in the median and the bottom decile (D5/D1) of the wage distribution as the most appropriate measure, the bivariate association with ISIC-6 employment rates is relatively weak ($r^2 = 0.29$), but the influence is clearly in the expected direction (Figure 6.9).

Similar impediments may be created by regulations increasing the security of present job holders. By raising the anticipated cost of dismissals, rigid rules of employment protection are likely to create disincentives to hiring that will be most significant for small firms and start-ups in service branches where future demand is highly unpredictable. Using an OECD ranking of countries according to the strictness of their employment protection legislation, we find that there is indeed a negative and moderately strong ($r^2 = 0.38$) association of Employment Protection Legislation (EPL) ranks with ISIC-6 employment rates (Figure 6.10).

Summary

In an international environment of open product and capital markets, countries are constrained in the use of many policy instruments which they had employed in past decades, and they are facing new challenges to their employment goals and to the fiscal viability of the welfare state.

In the exposed sectors of the economy, employment rates are stagnant or declining as firms respond to the pressures of more intense international competition and to the more rapid diffusion of labor-saving organizational and technical solutions. Where overall employment gains are being achieved, these are due to an above-average expansion of service branches that are not exposed to international competition.

Figure 6.9
D5/D1 Wage Differentiation (1994/95) and Employment in
Private-Sector Services, 1997

Note: For the country codes, see Figure 6.3.

Figure 6.10
OECD Employment Protection Legislation Ranks (1999)
and Employment in Private-Services (1997)

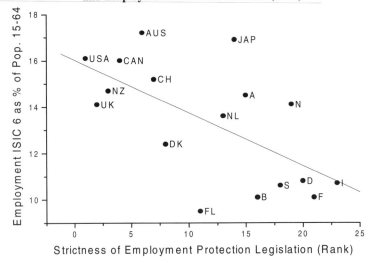

Note: For the country codes, see Figure 6.3.

At the same time, advanced welfare states are now operating under tighter fiscal constraints that have reduced their capacity to resort to deficit financing and to tax incomes from mobile capital and business profits. European countries, moreover, must now also hesitate to increase taxes on less mobile factors of production which will have a direct impact on competitiveness within the Monetary Union, and hence on employment in the exposed sectors of the economy. In addition, countries should also take account of the fact that service employment in the sheltered sectors is negatively affected by high payroll and consumption taxes. As a consequence, average GDP shares of total taxation have stagnated after the late 1980s, and total government outlays have sharply declined after the mid- 1990s, even though average unemployment rates were still at a postwar high.

These fiscal constraints have reduced the scope for a further expansion of employment in the public sector, and they have created pressures to reduce the generosity of welfare-state benefits. At the same time, welfare-state regulations and collective-bargaining agreements ensuring high levels of employment protection and egalitarian minimum-wage policies are also under pressure because of their negative impacts on sheltered-sector service employment. In short, there is indeed reason to think that the postwar aspirations and achievements of welfare states committed to full employment, social security, and social equality are seriously challenged by the new constraints on national policy choices that are imposed by the international and European integration of capital and product markets.

Differing Vulnerabilities

But if these were the common challenges that confronted all advanced welfare states in the open economies of the 1990s, they had to be faced by countries differing greatly in their structures of employment, taxation, and welfare-state benefits. Among the twelve countries covered in our project, not even two are highly similar with regard to all important characteristics. Nevertheless, in describing the most important of these differences, we found it useful to refer to Esping-Andersen's (1990) distinction between Anglo-Saxon, Continental, and Scandinavian welfare states—which, in the postwar decades have been largely influenced by "liberal," "christian-democratic," and "social-democratic" political parties and social philosophies.

The most important difference among these groups of countries concerns the dividing line between the welfare functions assumed by the state and those which families and individuals are expected to provide for themselves or through the market. Leaving aside primary and secondary education and health care, the most fundamental differences can be described as follows (Figure 6.11):

Figure 6.11
Functional Profiles of Different Types of Welfare States

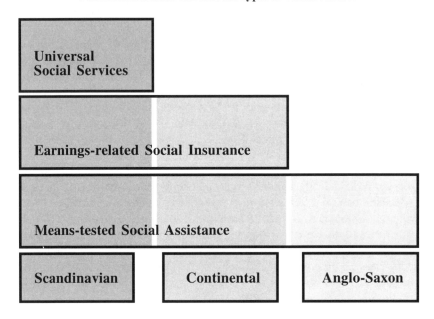

In all three groups of countries, the state is providing social assistance as a safety net assuring a basic livelihood for individuals and families without other sources of income. Even though there is growing support in the literature for an unconditional "basic income" (van Parijs, 1995; Jordan, 1998), existing programs are everywhere means-tested, and able-bodied beneficiaries are generally expected to accept work offers.

- In the Anglo-Saxon welfare states, that is essentially the limit of welfare-state benefits as means-testing has been introduced in what were originally "Beveridgean" programs providing flat-rate unemployment benefits and public pensions. In other words, all except the very poor are expected to make private provisions for periods of unemployment and retirement.
- By contrast, Scandinavian and Continental welfare states have gone further in protecting the income status of wage earners by providing earnings-related unemployment benefits and retirement pensions as a public function.
- Finally, the Scandinavian welfare states also assume public responsibility for providing universal social services for all families with small children, for the sick, the handicapped, and for the old. In Continental and Anglo-Saxon countries, such services also exist, but they are only available in the context of social assistance for the needy.

Table 6.1

Taxes and Social Security Contributions as a Percentage of GDP, 1970-1997

	1970	1980	1985	1990	1997
United States	27.4	26.9	26.0	26.7	28.5
Australia	24.2	28.4	30.0	30.6	30.4
New Zealand	27.4	33.0	33.6	38.0	36.4
United Kingdom	37.0	35.2	37.5	36.6	35.3
Switzerland	22.5	29.1	30.8	30.9	34.6
Austria	34.9	40.3	42.4	41.0	44.4
Belgium	35.7	43.7	46.9	44.0	46.5
Germany	32.9	38.2	38.1	36.7	37.5
France	35.1	41.7	44.5	43.7	46.1
Italy	26.1	30.4	34.5	39.2	45.0
Netherlands	37.1	45.2	44.1	44.6	43.4
Denmark	40.4	45.5	49.0	48.7	52.2
Sweden	39.8	48.8	50.0	55.6	53.3
OECD 18	31.8	36.6	38.4	39.3	39.8

Source: OECD Revenue Statistics 1999, Statistical Compendium.

Table 6.2

Taxes and Social Security Contributions as a Percentage of GDP, 1997

	Total taxation as % of GDP	Social security contributions as % of GDP	Taxes on goods and services as % of GDP	Personal and corporate income tax as % of GDP
United States	28.5	6.8	4.9	11.5
Australia	30.4	2.0	8.6	17.1
New Zealand	36.4	0.3	12.6	21.5
United Kingdom	35.3	6.0	12.5	13.0
Switzerland	34.6	13.1	6.1	12.8
Austria	44.4	18.0	12.5	12.9
Belgium	46.5	14.8	12.4	18.0
Germany	37.5	15.6	10.4	10.5
France	46.1	20.2	12.6	8.9
Italy	45.0	15.2	11.2	16.3
Netherlands	43.4	17.7	12.2	11.4
Denmark	52.2	1.8	17.1	31.4
Sweden	53.3	17.7	12.0	21.6
OECD 18	39.8	10.9	11.2	15.7

Source: OECD Revenue Statistics 1999, Statistical Compendium.

As countries differ in the functions assumed by the welfare state, they also differ in the share of resources claimed. As was pointed out above, the distance between low-tax and high-tax countries did not narrow over the last three decades; between Sweden and Australia it now amounts to more than 20 percentage points of GDP (Table 6.1). As one should expect, the total tax burden is generally highest in the multi-function Scandinavian welfare states, lowest in the lean Anglo-Saxon welfare states and in Switzerland, and intermediate in the Continental countries (Table 6.2). What is more interesting, in light of the analyses just presented, is that Anglo-Saxon countries and Denmark collect very little revenue from social security contributions, and depend very heavily on income taxes, while in the typical Continental country this relationship is reversed. There is less of clear pattern with respect to consumption taxes.

Differences in employment levels and structures are equally substantial (Table 6.3), with a gap of almost thirty percentage points separating the total employment rate in Switzerland from that in neighboring Italy. In general, total employment is very high or high in Scandinavian and Anglo-Saxon welfare states (with the exception of New Zealand), and relatively low or very

Table 6.3
Total and Sectoral Employment as a Percentage of the Population 15–64

	Total employ-ment as % of pop. 15-64	Government employ-ment as % of pop. 15-64	Business employ-ment as % of pop. 15-64	Industrial employ-ment as % of pop. 15-64	Employment in ISIC 6 as % of pop. 15-64
United States	73.9	10.6	63.3	11.8	16.1
Australia	68.5	10.4	58.3	9.8	17.2
New Zealand	60.9	9.0	53.8	12.0	14.7
United Kingdom	70.3	9.6	59.7	13.2	13.7
Switzerland	79.8	11.1	68.8	15.7	15.2
Austria	62.8	14.3	49.1	14.5	14.4
Belgium	56.3	10.4	44.9	10.4	10.1
Germany	60.5	9.1	51.4	16.4	11.0
France	59.4	14.6	44.2	11.3	9.9
Italy	50.8	8.0	42.8	12.1	10.9
Netherlands	61.8	8.1	52.1	10.2	13.4
Denmark	75.8	22.6	52.0	14.4	12.1
Sweden	69.6	21.2	47.8	13.5	10.6
OECD 18	66.5	12.6	52.7	13.0	13.0

Sources: Columns 1-3: OECD Economic Outlook; Columns 4-5: OECD Labour Force Statistics.

low in Continental countries. If we compare public and private-sector employment rates, it is clear that the exceptional employment performance of the Scandinavian welfare states is directly related to their functional profile: Providing universal social services in the public sector, their government employment rates are about twice as high as those of other countries. Since most of the jobs provided in services for families and the aged are filled by women, and since women are freed from caring duties in the home by the availability of these services, it is also no surprise that participation rates of women in the labor market are highest in the Scandinavian countries (Table 6.4). Rates of business employment, by contrast, are somewhat below the OECD average. By the same token, the generally lean Anglo-Saxon welfare states and Switzerland have low public-sector employment rates, but they also have the highest rates of business employment.

Continental countries, however, seem to have the worst of both worlds: employment rates in the public sector (with the exception of Austria and France) are as low as or lower than those in Anglo-Saxon countries, and employment rates in the private sector are as low as or lower than those in the

Table 6.4
Selected Indicators of Welfare State Performance, 1995-96

	Labor force partici-pation of women (%)	Labor force partici-pation of older men (55-64, %)	Total social expendi-ture as % of GDP	Services for families, the handi-capped and the aged as % of GDP	UE-benefit replacement low-income families[a] (%)	Earnings dispersion (D5/D1) both genders
United States	72.0	67.6	15.8	0.36	n.a.	2.09
Australia	64.4	59.6	15.7	0.56	82	1.64
New Zealand	68.0	69.3	18.8	0.15	77	1.73
United Kingdom	68.4	63.6	22.5	1.16	80	1.78
Switzerland	68.9	81.9	21	0.47	88	1.58
Austria	62.4	40.7	26.2	0.85	77	2.01
Belgium	52.3	33.9	27.1	0.28	76	1.43
Germany	61.0	54.6	28	1.36	76	1.44
France	60.7	42	30.1	1.14	87	1.65
Italy	42.9	55.9	23.7	0.30	46	1.75
Netherlands	60.4	44.2	27.8	1.03	86	1.56
Denmark	74.0	63.8	32.1	5.14	95	1.38
Sweden	77.9	71.3	33	5.10	85	1.34
OECD 18	61.2	n.a	24.0	1.63	n.a.	1.65

[a] Single-earner couple with two children; wages at two thirds of average production wage; including unemployment benefits, family and housing benefits; first month of benefit receipt.
All sources OECD.

Scandinavian countries. Here, low government employment rates are explained by low levels of expenditures on social services (Table 6.4), but the low rates of business employment need more attention. They cannot generally be ascribed to a lack of competitiveness in the industrial sector, since at least Germany and Austria, along with Switzerland, have much higher employment rates in industry than all of the Anglo-Saxon countries, including the United States. As these same countries are also doing quite well in the exposed sectors as a whole (Figure 6.3), the low level of business employment must be located in sheltered-sector services, for which we again take the ISIC-6 branches as a proxy. There, employment rates are indeed lower in Sweden and in Continental countries (except for Austria and the Netherlands) than they are in all Anglo-Saxon welfare states and in Denmark—which corresponds well with the fact that Continental welfare states and Sweden also have the highest GDP shares of wage-based social security contributions (Table 6.2).

With these structural differences in mind, we can finally discuss the characteristic vulnerabilities of advanced welfare states to the challenges of internationally integrated capital and product markets that became fully manifest in the 1990s.

Scandinavian Countries

In the Scandinavian countries, the range of functions assumed, and the share of societal resources claimed by the welfare state are the most extensive. It would be plausible to expect, therefore, that they would also be most affected by the fiscal constraints of international capital mobility and tax competition. In fact, however, social spending continued to rise in Denmark during the 1990s, and while in Sweden it had again fallen below the 1993 peak, it still was higher than in any other OECD country. Moreover, both countries were running budget surpluses by 1998, and revenue from personal and corporate income taxes (which supposedly should be most vulnerable to international tax competition) were also the highest among OECD countries and did actually rise after the mid-1990s. The explanation of this remarkable fiscal performance is clearest in Sweden, which has switched to a "dual income tax" by which all incomes from capital are taxed at a uniform low rate, while personal incomes from work continue to be subject to a steeply progressive tax with very high top rates. In Denmark, the same result is achieved by a more complex pattern of rules and exceptions that reflect the fact capital in the Danish economy with its large share of family-owned small firms is less mobile than it is in Sweden (Ganghof, 2000a). In other words, the present revenue bases of the Scandinavian welfare state are no longer vulnerable to international capital mobility—but they might be politically vulnerable to tax resistance.

On the employment side, there is no question that the exceptional performance of Denmark and Sweden is primarily owed to extremely high rates of public-sector employment which are due to a rapid expansion of social services from the 1960s to the mid-1980s. Considering only services for families, for the disabled and for the aged, expenditures in Denmark and Sweden exceed those in all other countries by at least four percentage points of GDP—which also suggests that total social expenditures for other purposes are entirely within the normal range of Continental European countries (Table 6.4).

Business employment is somewhat below the OECD average (and in Sweden it is still affected by the deep recession of the early 1990s). But it is noteworthy that in spite of extremely high total tax burdens, employment rates in industry and in the exposed sectors as a whole are also as high or higher than the OECD-18 average. If there is reason for concern, therefore, it must focus on below-average employment rates in private-sector services in the sheltered sector, for which we again take ISIC-6 as a proxy (Table 6.3). Here, Denmark and even more so Sweden are indeed below the OECD average. One reason is that generous social benefits and strong unions committed to an egalitarian distribution of primary incomes have achieved the lowest rates of D5/D1 wage dispersion in the OECD (Table 6.4 and Figure 6.9). The remaining difference between Sweden and Denmark is in part explained by the fact that the GDP share of combined revenues from social contributions and consumption taxes is significantly higher in Sweden than it is in Denmark (Figure 6.8). It should also play a role, finally, that employment protection in Sweden is very rigid, whereas dismissal rules in Denmark are almost as "liberal" as they are in the Anglo-Saxon countries (Figure 6.10).

As a consequence, the continuing viability of the Scandinavian model of work and welfare depends critically on high levels of public-sector employment. From what was said above, it follows that these are not challenged by international tax competition or by international competition in product and investment markets, but they might be challenged by political tax resistance. So far, however, there is no evidence of that in the revenue statistics or in political practice. Even though public opinion polls suggest that dissatisfaction with the tax system is high and may be increasing in Sweden (Edlund, 2000), nevertheless, the Social Democrats were able to return to office in 1994 with a campaign promise of higher taxes on incomes. In Denmark, opinion surveys even suggest that more than two-thirds of the Danes are content with the existing level of taxation (Schmidt, 2000). It appears, therefore, that the universal benefits ensured by the Scandinavian welfare state, and in particular the universal social services and the jobs which they provide, have also created the political constituencies among middle-income groups that defend it against demands for retrenchment (Svallfors, 1999). As long as this political support holds up, there is no reason to think that the Scandinavian model cannot be maintained in the open economy.

Anglo-Saxon Countries

In the Anglo-Saxon countries, by contrast, middle-income individuals and families have long had to rely on private provision for a wide range of insurance and service functions that are performed by the state in Scandinavian countries. Thus, welfare state spending had traditionally been very low in Australia and New Zealand, where full employment policies and wage regulation had constituted an "informal welfare state" instead (Schwartz, 2000). In the United Kingdom, the tax-financed National Health Service had pushed up the GDP share of social spending, but the level was still below that of Continental, let alone Scandinavian welfare states. At the same time, overall tax burdens remained low, and while the share of corporate and personal income taxes is comparatively high, their impact on international tax competition was largely neutralized through tax reforms in the 1980s that combined reductions of nominal rates with base broadening (Ganghof, 2000a).

As a consequence of the lean welfare state, public sector employment had always been very low in Australia and New Zealand; in the United Kingdom, where it had risen until 1979, it was subsequently reduced to similarly low levels. Thus, the generally high rates of total employment are achieved in the private sector. Industry, however, had not been internationally competitive in the postwar decades, and had declined dramatically in the 1970s. In all three countries, moreover, the monetarist and neo-liberal turnaround of the 1980s resulted in further massive job losses that only bottomed out in the 1990s. On balance, the losses in industry could not be compensated by gains in other branches of the exposed-sector, even though financial and business services did benefit from the radical liberalization and deregulation of capital and product markets. In any case, these gains did almost exclusively benefit high-skill and high-wage groups among the work force, rather than workers whose jobs in industry were being destroyed.

If Anglo-Saxon welfare states, nevertheless, have relatively high total rates of business employment, their success is mainly due to above-average employment rates in private-sector local services (Table 6.3)—which are also reflected in above-average participation rates of women (Table 6.4). In these less productive service branches, expansion is structurally facilitated by very low levels of social security contributions (Table 6.2), by low levels of employment protection (Figure 6.10), and by extremely decentralized or even individualized processes of wage determination. The downside of highly flexible wages and employment conditions is, however, a growing population of "working poor" whose market-determined wages are at or below subsistence levels.

For Anglo-Saxon societies (whose commitment to their specific postwar welfare goals is not necessarily weaker than it is on the Continent or in Scandinavia), this rise of poverty constitutes a moral, and at the same time a practical problem: Even though they are "lean" in terms of the overall functions assumed by the state, and generally "mean" in terms of benefit levels (Rhodes, 2000), social assistance as a last resort is similar to Scandinavian and Continental programs, and, in fact, quite generous for low-income families with small children (Table 6.4). For low-skilled workers, therefore, these benefits are likely to be higher than the wages they could earn in less productive service jobs. Under these conditions, the fact that social assistance benefits are means-tested may impose a prohibitive tax on earned incomes. The resulting unemployment traps would then not only frustrate efforts to reduce social expenditures, but would also increase the number of children growing up in poverty and socialized in "workless families."

In coping with these severe risks of the Anglo-Saxon welfare state, all three countries are generally turning to "workfare" solutions which replace unemployment benefits with training and "job-seeker allowances" for single workers, and which allow the combination of wage incomes with "in-work" welfare benefits for families. If fully developed, such combinations of flexible and unprotected low-wage labor markets with benefit programs applying the logic of the negative income tax may indeed allow high levels of total employment to be realized in the private sector without a dramatic increase in inequality and poverty. However, as the expansion of the Earned Income Tax Credit in the United States has demonstrated, if they are to be effective in their own terms, such programs cannot be cheap.

As is true of the Scandinavian model, therefore, the viability of Anglo-Saxon welfare states that attempt to remain true to their Beveridgean aspirations is not challenged by the international economy or by tax competition. If there is a challenge, it is again political. But here, conditions differ. In the Scandinavian welfare states, the majority of middle-class voters are defending universal social insurance benefits, universal social services and the associated jobs when they resist proposals for welfare-state retrenchment. In Anglo-Saxon countries, by contrast, middle-class voters—who do not expect to become dependent on social assistance, and who are bearing the costs of private provisions for expected contingencies—have no self-interested motive to pay higher taxes in order to improve purely redistributive welfare programs. In other words, and perhaps paradoxically, the political discourses defending the generous Scandinavian model may succeed by appeals to enlightened self-interest; in Anglo-Saxon countries, by contrast, any extension of the lean and mean welfare state must depend on appeals to solidaristic morality.

Continental Countries

With regard to international challenges, however, the comprehensive Scandinavian welfare states and the lean Anglo-Saxon welfare states appear to be equally viable. Moreover, both models are compatible with high levels of employment in sheltered-sector services that are able to compensate for stagnation or decline in the exposed sectors. Neither of these statements would generally apply to the Continental welfare states.

By and large, it is true, personal and corporate income taxes, which are potentially most vulnerable to international tax competition, play a comparatively minor role in the revenue structure of Continental countries (Table 6.2). Nevertheless, nominal rates may still be high since these taxes are often collected from a very narrow base. Where that is true, demands for tax cuts tend to be stronger than political support for base broadening or for a dual income tax—with the result that "tax reforms" responding to perceived international competition may further reduce already low revenues from income taxes—as was true of Germany, the Netherlands, and Belgium after the mid-1980s.

By contrast, revenues from social security contributions, which are not directly vulnerable to international tax competition, are generally high or very high in Continental welfare states, and they were further increased in the 1990s in Austria, Germany, and Italy (and in Sweden). As I pointed out above, however, such changes will have a major impact on competitiveness in product markets once the exchange-rate buffer is removed. Since all Continental welfare states covered by our project are now members of the European Monetary Union, their financial dependence on social security contributions has turned into a massive fiscal constraint: If it is disregarded, employment in the exposed sectors will suffer; if it is respected, social spending will need to be contained, and may have to be reduced if competitor countries choose to cut their own contribution rates. In other words, Continental welfare states will in the near future become very much vulnerable to international tax competition, even though these effects cannot yet be observed in empirical studies.

For the time being, the main problems of Continental welfare states are generally low rates of total employment (Table 6.3) that are no longer sufficient for providing jobs for all those who need or want them—which includes core workers who lost their jobs in the overall decline of industrial employment as well as outsiders, in particular women and in some countries young job-seekers, who are unable to enter the labor market. These problems are closely related to the characteristics of Continental welfare states that emphasize the protection of existing jobs of the core workforce as well as relatively attractive social insurance benefits for core workers who lose their jobs. Thus, the effects of industrial decline were mitigated by the exit options of disability and early-retirement pensions (Ebbinghaus, 2000), whereas active measures that would have improved employment opportunities and incentives for women were generally low on the agenda of governments and unions (Daly, 2000). As a consequence, Continental countries have the lowest employment rates of older workers as well as the lowest participation rates of women (Table 6.4).

It needs to be emphasized, however, that the characteristics of Continental welfare states do not necessarily undermine international competitiveness. Continental employment rates in industry (Table 6.3) and in the exposed sectors as a whole (Figure 6.3) vary considerably, but in both regards, Austria and Germany, together with Switzerland and Denmark, are among the high performers—and in any case doing better than the United States. On the other hand, exposed-sector employment is particularly low in Belgium, Italy, and France, which suggests that factors unrelated to the structure of welfare states must be decisive here—among them the historical legacies of industrial specialization and past industrial policies, and perhaps also of confrontational industrial relations. By contrast, the general weakness of Continental countries in sheltered-sector employment is indeed explained by the characteristic structures of their welfare states.

With the exception of France and Austria, government employment in Continental countries is as low or lower than it is in Anglo-Saxon countries and, in any case, far below the Scandinavian level. The main reason is that in the Continental tradition, caring services for the young, the handicapped and the old are not generally treated as a welfare-state function, but are primarily performed by mothers, wives, and daughters in the family. Hence, public expenditures on these social services are much lower than they are in Scandinavian countries (Table 6.4). In contrast to the Anglo-Saxon countries, moreover, service employment in the private sector was also constrained by the structures of Continental welfare states.

With the exception of Austria and the Netherlands, ISIC-6 employment rates in all of them are well below the OECD-18 average. After what has been said above, the reasons are fairly clear: In all countries, the tax wedge of high social security contributions increases the costs and reduces the private market for price-elastic consumer and personal services (Table 6.3). In addition, employment protection legislation is generally very strict in Continental countries (Figure 6.10), and in some countries union wage policies or government minimum-wage legislation have reduced D5/D1 wage differentials to almost the Scandinavian level (Table 6.4). This composite explanation is not contradicted by the two exceptional countries: In Austria, wage differentials are unusually high, and the Netherlands have not only somewhat more liberal employment-protection rules, but have also integrated social security contributions into the income tax schedule—with the effect that the basic tax exemption reduces the cost burden on part-time and low-wage jobs.

Conclusion

This overview of the findings of an extremely complex comparative project could only highlight very basic patterns. Nevertheless, even at this level of simplification, the basic message seems worth telling: In the 1990s, the international and European integration of capital and product markets has replaced the postwar regime of "embedded liberalism." As a consequence, nation states are no longer able to use a wide range of policy instruments that had depended on control over their own economic boundaries. These constraints are particularly tight for member states of the European Union and of the European Monetary Union. Countries must now defend or regain the competitiveness of their exposed sectors in highly contested international product markets; they must maintain or restore the attractiveness of national locations for profit-seeking investments; and they must cope with the impact of high capital mobility on their revenue bases. As a consequence, all welfare states are operating under tighter fiscal constraints, and all have to cope with stagnant or declining rates of employment in the exposed sectors of their economies. If the level of total employment is to be maintained or increased, that can only be achieved through an expansion of public or private-sector services in the sheltered sectors.

In all countries, the defense of economic viability in an environment of internationally integrated product and capital markets did and does require difficult and painful policy adjustments. The question is whether these must endanger political legitimacy by violating the values embedded in postwar commitments to full employment, social security, and social equality. The answers are necessarily contingent on the success or failure of policy learning and policy discourses in each country. Nevertheless, our analysis of characteristic vulnerabilities suggests that the difficulties differ considerably among groups of countries.

From the analyses presented here it would follow that Scandinavian and Anglo-Saxon welfare states, though being extremely different, have a chance to achieve these adjustments within the basic normative and institutional frameworks of their postwar models. They should be able to maintain economic viability and political legitimacy without reengineering the basic structures of their policy legacies. For Continental countries, by contrast, the challenges are more difficult to meet.

Under conditions of the Monetary Union, their traditional revenue base will become vulnerable to new competitive pressures, while a shift to—economically feasible—higher income taxes would violate the Zeitgeist of current tax reforms. Moreover, it is more difficult for them to compensate employment losses in the exposed sectors by an expansion of sheltered-sector services. There are no strong political demands for "Scandinavian" levels of publicly financed social services, and if there were, it would be hard to accommodate them under present fiscal constraints. At the same time, there is strong political opposition against an "Anglo-Saxon" deregulation of private-sector services, even if incomes from low-wage jobs were publicly supplemented. As a consequence, overall employment rates and female participation rates remain lowest in the Continental group of countries. It is at least uncertain, however, whether this state of affairs can remain economically viable and politically legitimate in societies which are rapidly aging and where the acceptance of traditional gender roles is rapidly eroding.

References

Alber, J. (2000). "Recent Developments of the German Welfare State: Basic Continuity or a Shift of Paradigms?" Konstanz: University of Konstanz.

Bonoli, G., and Mach, A. (2000). "Switzerland. Adjustment Politics within Institutional Constraints." In Scharpf, F. W., and Schmidt, V. A. (eds.), *Welfare and Work in the Open Economy. Vol. II. Diverse Responses to Common Challenges*. Oxford: Oxford University Press.

Daly, M. (2000). A Fine Balance. Women's Labor Market Participation in International Comparison. In Scharpf, F. W., and Schmidt, V. A. (eds.), *Welfare and Work in the Open Economy. Vol. II. Diverse Responses to Common Challenges*. Oxford: Oxford University Press.

Ebbinghaus, B. (2000). "Any Way Out of 'Exit from Work'? Reversing the Entrenched Pathways of Early Retirement." In Scharpf, F. W., and Schmidt, V. A. (eds.), *Welfare and Work in the Open Economy. Vol. II. Diverse Responses to Common Challenges*. Oxford: Oxford University Press.

Edlund, J. (2000). "Public Attitudes towards Taxation: Sweden 1981-1997." *Scandinavian Political Studies*, 23 (4), 37-66.

Ganghof, S. (2000a). "Adjusting National Tax Policy to Economic Internationalization. Strategies and Outcomes." In Scharpf, F. W., and Schmidt, V. A. (eds.), *Welfare and Work in the Open Economy. Vol. II. Diverse Responses to Common Challenges*. Oxford: Oxford University Press.

___. (2000b). Corporate Tax Competition, Budget Constraints, and the New Trade-Offs in Domestic Policy: Germany and Italy in Comparative Perspective. Paper prepared for the 2000 Annual Meeting of the American Political Science Association, Washington D.C., 31 August-3 September 2000.

Garrett, G. (1995). "Capital Mobility, Trade, and the Domestic Politics of Economic Policy." *International Organization,* 49 (4), 657-687.

___. (1998). *Partisan Politics in the Global Economy*. Cambridge: Cambridge University Press.

Genschel, P. (2000). Der Wohlfahrtsstaat im Steuerwettbewerb. MPIfG Working Paper 00/5. Cologne: Max Planck Institute for the Study of Societies (http://www.mpifg.de).

Gerschuny, J. I. (1978). *After Industrial Society? The Emerging Self-Service Economy*. London: Macmillan.

Iversen, T., and Wren, A. (1998). "Equality, Employment, and Budgetary Restraint: The Trilema of the Service Economy." *World Politics,* 50 (4), 507-546.

Jordan, B. (1998). *The New Politics of Welfare. Social Justice in a Global Context*. London: Sage.

Quinn, D. (1997). "The Correlates of Change in International Financial Regulation." *American Political Science Review,* 91 (Sept.), 531-551.

Rhodes, M. (1996). "Globalization and West European Welfare States: A Critical Review of Recent Debates." *Journal of European Social Policy,* 6 (4), 305-327.

___. (2000). "Restructuring the British Welfare State. Between Domestic Constraints and Global Imperatives." In Scharpf, F. W., and Schmidt, V. A. (eds.), *Welfare and Work in the Open Economy. Vol. II. Diverse Responses to Common Challenges.* Oxford: Oxford University Press.

Rodrik, D. (1997). *Has Globalization Gone Too Far?* Washington, D.C.: Institute on International Economics.

Ruggie, J. G. (1982). "International Regimes, Transactions, and Change: Embedded Liberalism in the Postwar Economic Order." *International Organization*, 36, 379-415.

Schmidt, V. A. (2000). "Values and Discourse in the Politics of Adjustment." In Scharpf, F. W., and Schmidt, V. A. (eds.), *Welfare and Work in the Open Economy. Vol. II. Diverse Responses to Common Challenges.* Oxford: Oxford University Press.

Schwartz, H. (2000). "Internationalization and Two Liberal Welfare States. Australia and New Zealand." In Scharpf, F. W., and Schmidt, V. A. (eds.), *Welfare and Work in the Open Economy. Vol. II. Diverse Responses to Common Challenges.* Oxford: Oxford University Press.

Steinmo, S. (1994). "The End of Redistribution? International Pressures and Domestic Policy Choices." *Challenge*, November-December.

Strange, S. (1991" Casino Capitalism." In Stiles, K. W. (ed.), *International Political Economy: A Reader.* New York: Harper Collins.

___. (1996). *The Retreat of the State. Diffusion of Power in the World Economy.* Cambridge: Cambridge University Press.

Svallfors, S. (1999). "The Middle Class and Welfare State Retrenchment: Attitudes to Swedish Welfare Policies." In Svallfors, S., and Taylor-Gooby, P. (eds.), *The End of the Welfare State? Public Responses to State Retrenchment.* London: Routledge.

Swank, D. (1997). "Funding the Welfare State: Globalization and the Taxation of Business in Advanced Market Economies." *Political Studies*, 46 (4), 671-692.

Tanzi, V. (1995). *Taxation in an Integrating World.* Washington, D.C.: Brookings Institution.

Van Parijs, P. (1995). *Real Freedom for All. What (If Anything) Can Justify Capitalism.* Oxford: Clarendon Press.

7

The Impacts and Non-Impacts of Globalization on Social Policy: Social Insurance Quality, Institutions, Trade Exposure, and Deregulation in 18 OECD Countries, 1960-1995[*]

Eero Carroll

Where is the welfare state headed in an age heralded as that of unprecedented globalization? One of the two questions implicit here is descriptive, one of them (potentially) causal. Firstly, is it actually the case that current levels of globalization are unprecedented? Secondly, if so, what difference can this be expected to make for social welfare programs? In a world economy which has long been impacted by globalization, and where arguments on tax pressure and international migration as threats to the viability of welfare programs have been used ever since the eighteenth century (see Rieger and Leibfried, 1995), it is imperative to get some perspective on these issues with empirical data. Otherwise, causal inferences become premature and misleading at best.

The goal of this chapter is to provide preliminary answers to the following two questions: (1) To what extent has the phenomenon of economic globalization been given a precise conceptual definition in studies on its impact on social policy, and how do choices of conceptualization affect conclusions on the extent of globalization? (2) Is economic globalization an inhibiting or stimulating factor for welfare state development?

I begin to address these questions by reviewing some representative social science work, both on globalization processes' extent and policy impacts. I then review some of the empirical indicators in this work, addressing the descriptive question of how far globalization has actually gone. Some overall cross-national tabular comparisons are also made to relate globalization levels to social transfer expenditure volume.

Secondly, I address the potential causal question of globalization's connection to social policy with the help of multivariate methods. I combine both time and spatial dimensions in pooled time series analysis, by the so-called LSDV method (least squares dummy variables; see Sayrs, 1989). Comparisons are made of statistical connections between finance market regulation or social policy institutions on one hand and, on the other, unemployment benefit development in 18 Organisation for Economic Cooperation and Development (OECD) countries from 1965 to 1995. I conclude with a discussion of the results and of fronts for further research advance.

Investigations Previously Pursued: Theory, Claims, and Evidence[1]

Debates pursued on globalization and its policy impacts have dealt both with the question of what has happened to the world economy since the early 1970s (or earlier), and with the question of what difference this is likely to make for the integrity of the nation-state and of national welfare programs. Regarding the descriptive question, one group of researchers has seen current trends towards increased integration of the world polity and economy as virtually unprecedented, and entirely indisputable (see e.g. Castells, 1998). Other researchers have been more critical of the proposition that current levels of global finance market integration would be historically unprecedented, pointing out that volumes of international financial trade from the 1970s on are comparable to those attained already at the turn of the last century (see e.g. Hirst and Thompson, 1992). It appears that, even on the descriptive question, conclusions reached are often affected both by what measures are used and by what time perspective is employed—a reflection to be pursued at greater length below.

Competing hypotheses are also possible to formulate on the second-order question on globalization's policy impacts. At least two points of view may be discerned, which can in abbreviated fashion be termed "the optimistic view" and the "pessimistic view." Here Scharpf's (1991) analysis is to be viewed as more pessimistic, in the sense that globalization is seen as generally inhibitory for pursuit of expansionary economic policies and social policy. It has been argued that the second oil shock of 1979 marked the transition to an era of declining opportunities for successful Keynesian policies for full employment and low inflation, since the financial markets of the world were assumed to have become more globalized than ever before. On the basis of such facts, Scharpf draws the conclusion that there no longer exists a credible Keynesian policy alternative which could simultaneously deliver full employment, higher real wages, higher levels of social transfer payments, and improvement in social services (Scharpf, 1991).

If Scharpf's arguments hold, we might expect that states will generally try to decrease social insurance quality (both in the course of recent and upcoming years), probably through cutbacks in social insurance systems. Such predictions obtain certain support in research by Stephens et al. (1999), who discern the trend that social policy's emphasis since the 1980s in the industrialized world changed character in focusing on maintenance, or even cutbacks, of social programs rather than around their expansion.

There is, however, a basis in recent literature also for drawing other conclusions about the impact of globalization on social policy. When globalization is measured and defined as countries' degree of exposure to international trade, or (alternatively) the mobility of capital, Garrett and Mitchell (1996a) find that increased degrees of globalization seem to be associated with lower levels of cash child benefits, but actually with higher levels of pension and unemployment benefits.

The explanation which the authors have for their results take their point of departure in the assumption that globalization leads to higher degrees of domestic uncertainty regarding future income security, which increases demands for state income transfers. Such social maintenance systems also contribute to social stability, and thereby to a more attractive investment climate. Similar arguments have been invoked in other literature (Kosonen, 1995; Garrett and Lange, 1991), with recent work by political scientists also finding "no support for the proposition that financial liberalization erodes the corporate tax base" (Quinn, 1997: 541). All in all, it thus seems that economic openness, with decreasing state interventionism in regulating economic transactions, may be perfectly reconcilable with increasing interventionism through social transfer systems and other welfare programs. These findings are fully in accordance with a long-standing tradition also of prior work, wherein market interventionism is seen as a modal strategy of small states to deal with their high levels of economic openness to the world system (Katzenstein, 1985; Cameron, 1978; Stephens, 1979; Montanari, 1995).[2]

Why could it be that global economic forces run into persisting obstacles in transforming welfare provision, especially in a consistently more restrictive direction? On the basis of various kinds of institutionalist theory (see e.g., North, 1990), it seems that there are potentially powerful alternative determinants to be sought to welfare provision—on the more proximate level of existing national structures of power, coordination and domination, not least those of the nation-state. For purposes pursued in the upcoming analysis, institutions can be defined as "… the formal or informal procedures, routines, norms and conventions embedded in the organizational structure of the polity or the political economy" (Hall and Taylor, 1996: 938). More specifically, the rules and conventions to be studied here are those constituting nation- or regime-specific forms of social insurance program governance (classifiable as voluntary, targeted or variously compulsory)—with the constituting legal rules together specifying which domestic groups are included in or excluded from provision, and on what terms. Though international actors may have their own views of which of these groups should be—with the International Monetary Fund (IMF), for example, often advocating increased targeting—the force of historically established national welfare regimes makes for persistence of rules applied that have an impact of their own on how inclusive and/or generous social policy may be.

The conclusion of this review of some central sources thus indicates that the effects of globalization on the economic policy and social policy of nation-states is an area of continuing disagreement for social researchers. What, more exactly, does this disagreement depend on? One crucial source thereof, as already indicated, may lie in differing operationalization of what basic concepts like those of globalization, and of the welfare state, are taken to mean, which indicates the need for comparing and contrasting the various definitions available. I pursue such an agenda by reviewing some of the empirical evidence heretofore on how far globalization has advanced, here with a time perspective beginning in the early 1960s.

What Happened, Anyway? Three Measures on the Extent of Globalization

One major distinction in the classes of globalization definitions used by social scientists goes between globalization as import/export dependence (see e.g., Cameron, 1978), or alternatively as the deregulation of international financial transactions (see e.g., Garrett and Mitchell, 1996a). Varying ways of measurement are also used among those focusing on the dismantlement of regulations. Some researchers are interested not only in assessing the presence or absence of formal legislative codes regarding global economic activity but also on the degree to which these codes are implemented, and complemented by the use of taxation instruments and treaties (see Quinn, 1997).

Taking this multiplicity of definitions seriously is advisable, in that all of these aspects of global and domestic international activity may be interrelated. The development of globalization by three major classes of indicators is assessed for 18 OECD countries at two points in time, the 1960s and the mid-1990s, in Table 7.1.[3]

Beginning with trade exposure, here defined as the percentual share of imports' and exports' value as a share of Gross Domestic Product (GDP), it appears as if levels of trade exposure indeed have generally increased from 1960 to 1994. From having comprised less than half of the studied OECD countries' GDP on average, imports and exports have come to include approximately two-thirds thereof by the mid-1990s. However, rates of increase have been quite modest for some countries which already previously have

Table 7.1

Levels of Trade Exposure, Finance Market Regulation, and Finance Market Openness in 18 OECD Countries in the 1960s and the Mid-1990s

Country	Imports and exports as a share of GDP		Presence or absence of regulations on international financial transactions[a]		Finance market openness[b]	
(Year:)	1960	1994	1967	1994	1965	1993
Australia	30.6	39.0	C	——	8.5	11.5
Austria	49.3	74.1	C, B2	——	9.0	12.5
Belgium	77.7	137.2	B1, B2	——	10.5	14.0
Canada	35.6	66.4	——	——	13.0	14.0
Denmark	65.6	64.0	C, B1, B2	——	7.5	14.0
Finland	45.7	65.4	C, B1, B2	——	6.5	12.0
France	26.9	43.4	——	——	11.0	13.5
Germany	33.1	44.8	——	——	14.0	14.0
Ireland	66.5	130.4	C	——	7.5	14.0
Italy	26.5	46.7	C	——	10.5	14.0
Japan	20.9	16.8	C, D	——	6.5	11.0
Netherlands	90.9	97.3	C, B2	——	10.5	14.0
New Zealand	46.2	60.4	C	——	5.0	13.0
Norway	76.9	71.0	C, B2	C	6.0	13.5
Sweden	46.0	69.0	C, B2	——	10.0	12.5
Switzerland	58.9	67.7	——	——	10.5	13.0
United Kingdom	43.2	53.6	C	——	6.5	14.0
United States	9.6	22.9	——	——	13.0	14.0
Avg., 18 countries	47.2	65.0	1.28	0.06	9.22	13.25

[a]) The presence of regulations is indexed by letters, depending on the kind of transaction or activity in question: capital transactions, bilateral payments arrangements for IMF member countries (B1) and/or for non-member countries (B2), and/or deposit restrictions. The eighteen-country average is based on an additive index, with the scale varying from 0 (no regulations) to 4 (all four kinds of regulations present).

[b]) This measure varies on a scale of 0 to 16, based on codings reflecting increasingly strict regulation, rules implementation and taxation regarding a number of different transactions involving both current and capital accounts. Exchange rates regime strictness and international treaty adherence is also factored in.

Sources: OECD (various years, a) (columns 1-2), Garrett and Mitchell (1996a), IMF (various years, a), (columns 3-4), Quinn (1997) (columns 5-6).

been highly integrated into the international economy—trade dependence has even decreased slightly for Denmark, Norway, and Japan. In addition, as implied above, values are sometimes difficult to interpret, particularly for those small and trade-dependent states (such as Ireland and the Benelux countries) where the volume of goods-in-transition contributes to import/ export shares actually approximating, or even exceeding GDP.

By the second measure assessed, indexing the simple presence or absence of national regulations on international financial transfers, conclusions on the extent of globalization appear to be less qualified. In the 1960s, a majority of the OECD countries had regulative restrictions in force on at least one class of international financial movements, with capital account restrictions (indexed by C) being the most commonly used. By the mid-1990s, not least as the result of implementation of European treaties, these restrictions have virtually disappeared. Only Norway retains some restrictions on international capital transfers in its national legislation.

In compiling the third measure assessed, researchers have gone more deeply into how the regulations are actually used (see Quinn, 1997; Quinn and Toyoda, 1997). Here, content analysis techniques are applied to the "thick descriptions" assembled by the IMF in the same report (various years, a) whose annual codified reviews constitute the basis for the dichotomous indicators reviewed above. Whether laws actually on the books are used or not may vary in strictness—ranging from straight-out prohibition to procedures for prior transfer approval (more or less frequently granted) to total freedom of transfers. In this broader-ranging indicator, differentially heavy taxation of transactions and international exchange rate regimes of differential strictness are also taken into account.

The resulting measure of openness as used here varies over a much broader range of values than does the discrete indicator reviewed first. Arguably, it is thus also a more sophisticated measure of ongoing financial market globalization. What such measurement tools gain in sophistication is, however, inevitably lost in transparency and interpretability. Interestingly enough, substantial increases in the extent of globalization are most clearly evident at the national level for this indicator, not least for countries which in the 1960s had relatively insular economies. The extent of liberalization on financial transfers has approximately doubled for economies which previously appear to have been relatively insular by this measure, such as Denmark, Finland, Ireland, Japan, New Zealand, Norway, and even the UK. Just as for the more delimited deregulation trends assessed by the second measure, no reversals are to be noted here, and the extent of globalization which can be seen to have taken place is thus more extensive and definitive than for trade. As noticeable, however, is also the great number of countries where financial market openness has increased only marginally, or remains at already previously high levels.

Despite the diversity of definitions already considered, it should be evident that many alternative conceptualizations of globalization remain. For purposes of understanding the upcoming analysis, it should thus also be noted what the globalization indicators reviewed here do *not* cover—processes as diverse as foreign direct investment (see OECD, various years, b; IMF, various years, b), volumes of cross-border capital flow, the activity of international financial institutions like the IMF and the OECD, and technological developments in, for example, the communications industry and in electronic data transfer (on the significance of technology, see not least Castells, 1998). The emergence of regional economic areas and integrated markets is a development of its own to account for. Though not in themselves coterminous with the global economy, they entail pressures of their own for national welfare states which are important to consider in their own right—and which, in particular, may differ very much in their potential relevance for international trade and for regional capital markets integration. Such aspects of regional economic integration as European Monetary Union (EMU) convergence criteria may impact underlying aspects of welfare state financing and market regulation, if not the "superstructure" of state transfer programs themselves (see Krugman, 1994a).

Further, it must be emphasized that globalization is not only a matter of the economy but of ideology. Here, the emergence of so-called "epistemic communities" of economists, trade lobbyists and policy consultants constitutes an area of its own, central to the concept. Members of these communities, both individually and through networks to decision-makers, advocate not only a praxis, but an ideology and discourse of globalism and globalization. This means that globalization, even while not posing non-negotiable objective constraints on what decisions can be made, means that decision-makers experience increasing subjectively felt difficulties in defending national welfare states against increasingly global advocacy of neo-liberal economic thinking.[4] This remaining plurality of concepts has implications for research beyond that which can be pursued here, and which there is occasion to return to for purposes of later discussion.

What kind of difference could the globalization trends which *are* covered here potentially make for welfare state programs? Answers here naturally depend not only on how globalization is defined, but also on what the welfare state itself, or those welfare programs assumed to be affected by globalization, can be taken to mean. Focusing only on social expenditure would here be risky, insofar as broad trends and level differences in highly aggregated social transfer expenditures say little about underlying differences in welfare state effort (see Palme, 1990; Carroll, 1999). Disaggregating expenditures by kind of social transfer program is one avenue of advance—so is the use of replacement rate and coverage indicators more directly assessing program outputs than what expenditure series do, also explored in the analyses to be pursued here.

Again, it should be noted what such indicators will *not* cover. Welfare state development could otherwise be operationalized not only as the development of social transfers but also of social service expenditure and quality, including expenditures on active labor market policies (for data, see OECD, various years, c). Besides being an important dimension of welfare state effort in its own right, social services are also the object of increasing efforts at international regulation and intense speculative efforts by market actors interested in privatization. World Trade Organization (WTO) negotiators' efforts to bring about GATS (the General Agreement on Trade in Services) is one example of ongoing international efforts here. Many national variants of or equivalents to active labor market policies are also potentially strongly affected by international competition directives. This is reflected also in, for example, Norwegian resistance to European Union membership, which was seen as endangering many statist regional industry subsidies of a kind which the European Commission sees as distorting competition. However, active labor market policies on the more market-conforming lines pursued in Sweden are also the object of increasing positive international interest, insofar as the emphasis of these policies on re-employment rather than on benefit recipiency is seen to fit in well with internationally espoused policy objectives of increasing employment rates (see OECD, 1994).

Given, then, more restricted definitions, what can be said about the impact of globalization trends reviewed on welfare state development? Both further descriptive data and multiple regression can be applied to sort out the potential answers, which I turn to in the section that follows.

So What Difference Does It Make? Preliminary Tabular and Regression Results on Globalization, Social Transfer Expenditure, and Unemployment Insurance Quality

What overall cross-national connections can be made evident between globalization trends and welfare state development? The overall review pursued above has focused, by means of diachronic comparisons, on the endpoints of trends over time. If, however, predictions obtain that pressure is exercised on countries to engage in "social dumping," these might well hold true in strictly cross-national perspective as well. Insofar as they do so at all, countries do not compete with each others' pasts or long-term statistical averages. In a given competitive situation obtaining at a given time, if one is to believe the "negative view" of globalization's welfare effects, a higher degree of global market integration could be expected to increase the pressure to keep welfare states lean, cheap, and as non-interventionist as possible. We could thus expect that countries with high levels of global market integration at a given point in time would have relatively low-cost welfare states. Correspondingly, we could expect that countries with low levels of global market integration could afford relatively higher-cost welfare states.

A very rough assessment of whether this is true is made with the help of tabular comparisons and scatterplots. For deregulation (see Table 7.2), coun-

Table 7.2

Regulation and Social Transfer Expenditure as a Percentage of the GDP for 17 OECD Countries in the 1960s and the Mid-1990s (above and below contemporaneous averages)[5]

1960 / 1967	Regulated (at least one set of transactions)	Unregulated
Transfer expenditure, below average (8.5% of GDP)	Australia, Denmark, Finland, Ireland, Japan, Norway, Sweden, UK	Canada, Switzerland, USA
Transfer expenditure, above average	Austria, Belgium, Italy, Netherlands	France, Germany
1994		
Transfer expenditure, below average (19% of GDP)	——	Australia, Canada, Germany, Ireland, Japan, Switzerland, UK, USA
Transfer expenditure, above average	Norway	Austria, Belgium, Denmark, Finland, France, Italy, Netherlands, Sweden

tries are cross-classified above and below contemporaneous averages (or a dichotomous threshold) on regulation and the level of social transfer expenditure as a share of the GDP. For trade dependence and financial market openness, both are plotted against social transfer expenditure levels, both for the 1960s and the 1990s (see Figures 7.1 to 7.4).

The "negative view" does not come out very well in this preliminary assessment (though the "positive view" can certainly not be regarded as confirmed either). For trade dependence in the 1990s (see Figure 7.3), there are even weak indications of a positive effect. A number of larger G7 countries relatively less dependent on imports and exports in the 1990s have relatively low-cost welfare states, having to some extent already had them. At the same time, small trade-dependent countries are overrepresented among those countries with high-cost welfare states.

It thus appears that "negative" hypotheses on the constraining effect of globalization on welfare states are not confirmed by cross-sectional data. Countries at high contemporaneous levels of global market integration have not tended to have contemporaneously low-cost welfare states either in the 1960s or the 1990s—regardless of whether such integration is measured with respect to trade dependence, regulation of international financial transactions, or relative openness of financial markets.[6]

Figure 7.1
Trade Dependence and Social Transfers in
17 OECD Countries, Early 1960s

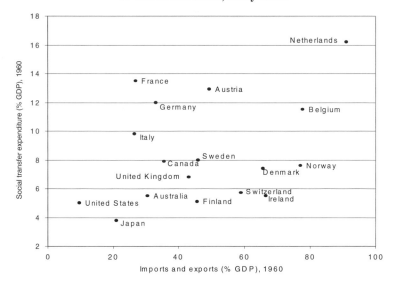

Figure 7.2
Financial Market Openness and Social Transfers in
17 OECD Countries, Early 1960s

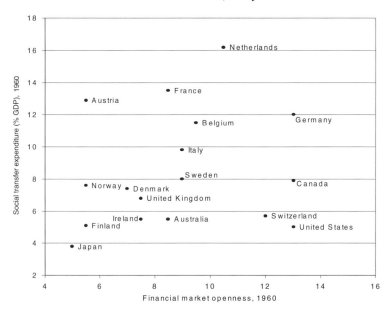

Figure 7.3
Trade Dependence and Social Transfers in
17 OECD Countries, Mid-1990s

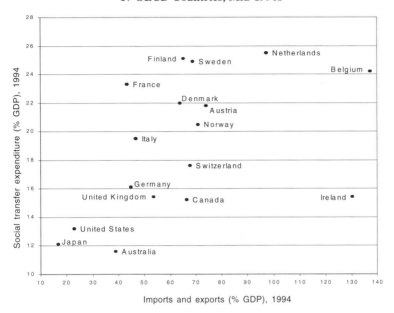

Imports and exports (% GDP), 1994

Figure 7.4
Financial Openness and Social Transfers in
17 OECD Countries, Mid-1990s

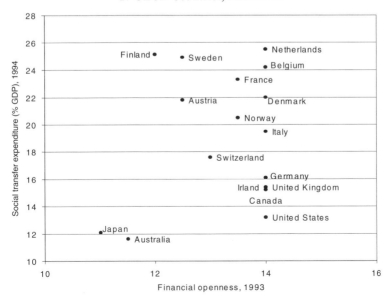

Financial openness, 1993

What results can be obtained by analyses taking both the time dimension and the cross-national dimension into account? I will here attempt to compare the significance of institutional design and globalization (by various definitions of the term) for explaining social insurance quality development in the OECD countries since 1965. More specifically, as discussed above, social insurance inclusivity and generosity at the domestic level will be related, alternatively, to finance market deregulation, as well as to the presence or absence of given traditions of national insurance program governance. In accordance with prior work (Carroll, 1999), I here focus on unemployment insurance, a transfer program that has been viewed as particularly inimical to facilitating macro- and micro-economic adjustment (see Bean, 1994). I also take a step away from expenditure data to indicators more directly assessing both welfare state scope and generosity. These are respectively indexed by unemployment insurance coverage as a share of all employees, and as unemployment net benefit replacement rates.[7]

To test the impact of more proximate institutional influences, dummy variables have been constructed for each country year indexing (in each year) a nation's adherence to one of four institutionalized traditions of benefit provision and governance.[8] The first type of program is based on *targeted benefits,* providing minimum benefits to those unemployed with prior incomes or means below a given standard. The second kind of program is constituted by *voluntary state-subsidized insurance,* providing first flat-rate and (later) income-related benefits to members of funds. A third kind of program, *corporatist compulsory insurance,* provides income-related benefits within occupational benefit regimes under bi- or tripartite governance. Finally, *comprehensive compulsory insurance* can be distinguished, providing flat-rate and/or income-related benefits to all of the qualified unemployed, within a single unified state benefit regime. As can be noted, underlying principles of benefit entitlement and payment are united here in various ways that can be viewed as syndromes of legal compulsion, segregation, and (though much less systematically) the extent of benefit income-relatedness, of potential relevance for the structure of program outputs.

In brief, it can be hypothesized that voluntary and corporatist forms of program governance are likely to elevate benefit rates while decreasing coverage, in accordance with the historical orientation of these programs to covering relatively well-organized core workers. By contrast, it is assumed that comprehensive, statist programs oriented to (in principle) all wage earners provide better institutional conditions for extending formal coverage to all employees. However, comprehensive unemployment insurance can be expected to restrict generosity of benefits to the greater amount of beneficiaries it covers. Similar tendencies could be expected for means-tested programs, where program constituencies are potentially socially marginalized and politically isolated.

One major problem should be mentioned with this institutional indicator, which indicates some of the limits of the present analysis. Institutional structures of policy governance are in themselves problematic to view as determinants of policy, insofar as the structures involved are not in themselves actors, but rather can be seen as systematic constraints on the ability of social actors, both within the polity and the global economy, to change these policies as they please. The variables indexing such institutional traditions are used, in turn, to assess (in concordance with current social scientific debate) whether it is state institutions themselves, or (indirectly) their openness to the global economy surrounding them, which appear to constrain policy action more. The potential of more directly actor-oriented analysis is naturally not hereby obviated, and the trends impacted may not be adequately assessed with any kind of volume indicators (either of trade or of social policy generosity) in a situation where the entire structure of both the world economy and the state system is under transformation—these issues are addressed in the concluding discussion.

Pooled time series analyses by the LSDV method are here used (see Sayrs, 1989)—with the two different kinds of independent variables included in models serially, one kind at a time (see Table 7.3 and Table 7.4). The tables are separated by the kind of dependent variable used, since policy-maker choices of institutional design for social policy will have different likely consequences for different dimensions of policy development. *Program scope* as a share of those potentially entitled, measured in the analyses for Table 7.3 by unemployment insurance coverage, here needs to be separated from *program generosity* to those actually entitled, measured by benefit replacement rates in the analyses for Table 7.4.

For each series of analyses, the least squares dummy variables method is used so as to effectively contrast the significance of deregulation and of national social policy institutions with one another. By this method, so-called "dummy variables" are constructed so as to index (in turn) the presence or absence of unspecified factors operating only in one given country and/or year at a time, of deregulation, or of specific unemployment insurance policy regimes. The "dummy variables" for a given country or year take on the value of 1 for the country or year in question, and zero otherwise. Similarly, the deregulation and policy regime variables are also measured dichotomously. If a country, in a given year, applies at least one form of regulations on international financial transactions, the deregulation variable takes on the value of 1 for that country and year. The absence of a developed body of regulations in that country or year makes for a value of zero on the deregulation variable. The presence or absence of a given unemployment insurance policy regime is analogously operationalized, with the difference that a "reference category" here must be specified by leaving the dummy variable for a given policy regime out of each set of analyses.

In each set of analyses, the globalization indicator is tested first, in model 2 (in Column 2 of each table). The institutional dummy variables are included instead, and the globalization indicator taken out, in Model 3 (in Column 3 of each table). In replacing the country-specific dummy variables included in the reference alternative model (1), where only country and year effects are accounted for, I assess whether including the degree of financial market regulation improves model performance over a model where variation in benefit provision is accounted for only with reference to unspecified, idiosyncratic, nation- and time-specific factors (O'Connell, 1994). The degree of model improvement is similarly assessed for the inclusion of institutional effects.

A comparison of model performance realized in accounting for unemployment insurance coverage (see Table 7.3) indicates that replacing substantively meaningless country dummies with the level of finance market regulation (albeit by a crude indicator) actually causes model performance to deteriorate. This is reflected by all overall measures of model performance on the first five table rows for the respective models in Columns 1 and 2. The first model, with country and year dummy variables only (coefficient values excluded), realizes higher levels of explained variance, a higher overall goodness of fit (F), and lower levels of unexplained residual variance and standard errors than Model 2.[9] Strangely enough, examining the coefficient for the regulation factor itself further down in Column 2 indicates that the direct impact of having legal restrictions in force on at least one major class of international financial transfers has a weak negative connection with levels of unemployment insurance coverage realized. However, the impact is far enough from standard significance levels to be, in all likelihood, plain spurious.

By comparison, the more proximate impact of institutional factors in Model 3 (as indicated by coefficient values on the two last rows in Column 3) is strong and significant, as expected. Corporatist and comprehensive variants of insurance program design elevate coverage levels over reference levels under voluntary arrangements (here country years for targeted programs have been selected out of the database entirely, since coverage is not codeable under these conditions). Overall model performance declines by most measures though, if not as much as upon the inclusion of the globalization factor. This indicates that highly parsimonious models such as those compared here may be under- or even misspecified, which calls for investigation of fuller models in later work. This particular set of results is also influenced by the fact that unemployment insurance coverage ratios have tended to be rather stable over time, and have changed little in any of the OECD countries after the mid-1970s when many compulsory programs reached comprehensive levels of coverage among employees.

In assessing model performance in accounting for more variable policy trends, that is replacement rate development (see Table 7.4), the coefficient value in Column 2 now indicates that the finance market regulation factor

Table 7.3
Country-specific Factors, Finance Market Regulation, and Insurance
Institutions as Explanations of Unemployment Insurance Coverage, 1965-95
(LSDV estimations, year dummies included in all analyses)

	Model 1: Country-specific dummy variables	Model 2: Regulation	Model 3: Insurance institutions
SS Reg.	2.161	0.705	1.671
SS Resid.	1.220	2.676	1.710
Adj. R^2	0.544	0.155	0.494
Std. Err. Est.	0.1171	0.1612	0.1295
F	7.509	3.876	12.461
Finance market regulation (t-statistic)	———	-0.003 (0.034) -0.093	———
Institution DV, corporatist # (t-statistic)	———	———	0.014 (0.032) 4.312***
Institution DV, comprehensive # (t-statistic)	———	———	0.255 0.034 7.558***

Sources: Garrett and Mitchell (1996a), IMF (various years, a), Social Citizenship Indicators Project (forthcoming).
Institutional dummy for voluntary insurance excluded as reference category.
*** = $p < 0.01$, ** = $p < 0.05$, * = $p < 0.10$, ^ = $p < 0.20$. Standard errors within parentheses.

has a less counter-intuitive positive impact on upholding replacement rates. This is not in disaccordance with the "negative view" of globalization as entailing potential risks for welfare state generosity. However, the impact is once again substantively minor, and far from significant. As for coverage, overall model performance again declines (though here by considerably more) in relation to the (admittedly vacuous) model with country- and year-specific dummy variables only in Column 1. Insurance institutional effects once again appear to be stronger here and provide a better overall explanation of developments than does finance market globalization—even though model performance again deteriorates by almost all measures and though the effect of institutionalized corporatist benefit arrangements here is more ambiguous.

Here, datapoints for those countries with targeted regimes of provision in given years are possible to include, with benefit rates being codeable under such conditions in a way in which rights to coverage are not. In accordance with what we might have expected, targeted institutional arrangements (as reflected by the strong negative coefficient on the first institutional factor row in Column 3 of the table) make for significantly lower benefit rates than

Table 7.4

Country-specific Factors, Finance Market Regulation, and Insurance
Institutions as Explanations of Unemployment Insurance Replacement Rates,
1965-95 (LSDV estimations, year dummies included in all analyses)

Variable|Model statistics	Model 1: Country-Specific Dummy Variables	Model 2: Regulation	Model 3: Insurance institutions
SS Reg.	1.763	0.287	1.094
SS Resid.	0.971	2.447	1.640
Adj. R^2	0.565	0.105	0.354
Std. Err. Est.	0.0098	0.1440	0.1189
F	8.051	1.976	8.603
Finance market	——	0.028	——
Regulation		(0.029)	
(t-statistic)		0.957	
Institution DV,	——	——	-0.242
targeted #			(0.039)
(t-statistic)			-6.187***
Institution DV,	——	——	-0.022
corporatist #			(0.030)
(t-statistic)			-0.742
Institution DV,	——	——	-0.135
comprehensive #			(0.031)
(t-statistic)			-4.371***

Sources: Garrett and Mitchell (1996a), IMF (various years, a), Social Citizenship Indicators Project.
Institutional dummy for voluntary insurance excluded as reference category.
*** = $p < 0.01$, ** = $p < 0.05$, * = $p < 0.10$, ^ = $p < 0.20$. Standard errors within parentheses.

those obtaining under reference levels within a voluntary institutional regime. It appears that institutions segregating the less well-off, insurance-entitled unemployed from the better-off in practice makes for worse benefits, regardless of what the pressures from the world economy may be.

What are the preliminary conclusions that can be drawn from these results? I will conclude by offering some interpretations on the overall patterns of results, as well as sketching out some directions for continued research in this area.

Discussion and Conclusions

Starting with the empirical issues, matters appear at first to be rather settled. Levels of globalization indeed appear to have increased, no matter what indicator is used. Trade dependence and financial market openness are up by the mid-1990s as compared to the heyday of the "golden age." Major instruments of financial market regulation have been as good as removed from use, fully in accordance with triumphalist calls for progressive abolition issued by such institutions as the OECD (1990). This is reflected in the fact that both deregulation and financial market openness have increased by much more than trade, and do not seem to have decreased by the 1990s anywhere in the industrialized world.

Nonetheless, there are some complications in the description that give pause for more thought. As reflected also in diachronic comparisons, countries which are highly integrated in the global economy by one measure are not necessarily so by others—and in many cases, their levels of integration appear far from unprecedented in all hitherto existing history. While many large G7 countries have also historically combined an absence of financial market regulations with low levels of trade exposure, partly the opposite appears to be true for a number of small nations at high levels of trade dependence, and with a historical commitment to capital market regulation (only recently abandoned in many cases). This indicates, as discussed only briefly until now, that high trade exposure may itself reflect whether states are large or small, and thus whether they have domestic markets of sufficient extension so as to obviate both the need and opportunity for extensive foreign trade. The impact of state size should itself probably be controlled for in future analyses, with the help of such indicators as territorial and population sizes (see United Nations, 2000).

In longer-term historical perspective, such as that employed by Hirst and Thompson (1992), it is fully possible to find precedents also for the current era of disappearing regulations—the possibility of future re-regulation also cannot be excluded a priori, though then most likely at national, international as well as supranational levels of jurisdiction. As far as future empirical work is concerned, the partial incommensurability of the various indicators of globalization used here speaks for the possibility of further developing multi-component indicators, and more systematically assessing the degree to which globalization trends along various dimensions of economic activity actually intercorrelate.

Regarding potentially causal issues, there appear to be no strong reasons whatsoever (again, at least, in shorter-term historical perspective) for claiming that economic openness must with necessity lead to social dumping and the shrinking of the welfare state. Overall diachronic comparisons give the impression that contemporaneous competitive demands on national economies leave room for all possible combinations of social transfer expenditure levels and globalization. Indeed, there are strong theoretical reasons for why we might expect trade and welfare state activism to go hand in hand, besides the arguments on social policy's stabilizing impact noted previously. States are crucial actors for upholding international trade, which could hardly take place without state arbitration of contracts and policing of international borders. Further, political negotiation on trade (both in organizations like the WTO and bilaterally) is even constitutive of trade activity—here states are in a number of respects more central actors than are either companies or NGOs (see Helliwell, 1998; Leibfried, 2000).

Similarly problematic results for the "negative view" of globalization's impact on the welfare state are also derived from more systematic multivariate analysis. The effects of finance market regulation on unemployment insurance quality, albeit assessed with a crudely defined independent variable, are found to be weak to nonexistent. The impact of more proximate national-level institutional effects on the scope and generosity of welfare benefits (in this case to the unemployed) are considerably more determinate. By these indices, it appears that we have occasion to comment on current affairs in the spirit of Mark Twain: the news of the nation-state's death in a global economy appears to be highly exaggerated.

For purposes of future research, it can be argued that questions on the relative importance of domestic and international factors in impacting social policies are profitably illuminated from a theoretical and methodological perspective emphasizing multiple determinism, and in models including both political and institutional factors—as advocated by, for example, Garrett and Lange (1991). Globalization can impact national decision-making differently under differing institutional and political conditions, and its significance can thus best be estimated with the help of multi-factor explanations subject to multivariate statistical testing and through the use of a comparative and long-term historical perspective. Globalization should in all likelihood not be used to explain macro-economic and political decision-making as long as the contemporaneous impacts of other factors are not controlled for at the same time: these include not least changed distributions of political power and priorities, and other macro-economic trends.

Continued study in this area would also do well to assess robustness of results with different operationalizations both of independent and dependent variables. As discussed above, none of the multifarious processes often included in globalization which do not deal with trade or deregulation, ranging from direct investment to international financial institutions' strategizing, have been covered by the relatively more restricted definitions of globalization used for the purposes of this study. As discussed previously, the question also remains open here on *which* welfare state dynamics are potentially most affected by globalization, as variously defined. Thus, further research could aim to confirm what combination of positive and negative impacts globalization could be having on social services in employment subsidization, child care, and health—as well as on employment rates generally, particularily for women (see Garrett and Mitchell, 1996b).

On an even broader scale, the whole tenor of the analysis as here advanced has been to consider changes in volume, both of globalization and of policy interventionism, rather than changes in the entire structure of both the global economy and of welfare states. Entirely different classes of policy reform indicators, and the need for more qualitative and historical analysis, is hereby indicated. Within national welfare states, outcomes to be more extensively assessed may need to include restructuring of overall budget priorities, systemic reforms such as the internationally advocated transformation of pension systems from "defined benefit" to "defined contribution" principles, and the consolidation of so-called social pacts on overall macro-economic policy (see Regini, 2000). Within the global economy, future attention should be similarly directed not only to the volume but to the structure of foreign trade and international capital markets. Also the trade exposure levels discussed above, particularly for small countries like the Benelux nations, are crucially impacted by the increasing importance of intra-firm trade (also across national borders), as well as the increasing prevalence of trade in financial instruments over trade in real goods and services.

Finally and most crucially, analyses of states in global markets need to be reoriented from structural connections, as focused upon in this essay, to the activities of concrete sets of social actors. The various component processes of globalization may be less important in themselves than the changes (sometimes disproportionate) which these processes bring about for the opportunity structures and action alternatives (perceived and real) of governments, political parties, multinational companies, social movements, and elites within academia and the media. With company assets becoming increasingly liquid, and company action strategies such as labor force rationalization and defensive firings perhaps again becoming more usual than in the past, understanding how firm decision-making takes place on global markets is crucial. State elites often appear to be trying to act the same way, rationalizing social policies in the name of "national competitiveness"—a concept as incoherent as its underpinning notion that all nations could somehow simultaneously become more competitive with each other (see Brittan, 2001; Krugman, 1994a, 1994b; Willmore, 1998).

Globalization cannot be seen as a purely exogenous, compelling force which by definition excludes the possibility of alternative courses of action for national elites. The impact of such forces can either be made milder or strengthened by national traditions, by conscious political action, and by institutional developments which were put into place well before current trends towards increasing globalization ever got underway.

Data Appendix

In the multivariate assessments for 1965-95, a number of compromises had to be made in data commensurability over one and the same year. The financial deregulation indicator has been derived from the IMF (various years, a), coded in a database provided by Geoffrey Garrett. The first values of the indicator pertain to 1967 rather than 1965, as noted in Table 7.1. Further, values of this indicator for New Zealand were assumed equal to those for Australia for the years 1965-1985—direct data from the IMF reports (various years, a) were obtained for 1990 and 1995. In the financial openness indicator made available to me by Dennis Quinn, values for the 1995 cross-section of the pooled dataset constructed actually pertain to 1993 (as also noted in Table 7.1).

The unemployment insurance quality indicators are included in the Social Citizenship Indicators Project database, still under revision at this writing. Insurance coverage in 1995 has been set equal to that of 1990 for Canada, Denmark, Norway, and the UK. Net half-year replacement rates for 1995, as defined in footnote 4, are estimated on the basis of deflators computed from change in net whole-year replacement rates between 1990 and 1995. The measure used for the deflators is computed as the share of net unemployment benefits in total net income over one year, with unemployment having lasted for half of this time (average for the single and for the familied worker).

Imports/exports and social transfer expenditures as shares of GDP have been obtained from the OECD report Historical Statistics (various years, a). Combined shares for 1965 were linearly interpolated between 1960 and 1970. In Figure 7.1, 1994 expenditure levels were set equal to those of 1991 for Norway, and the levels of 1960 to those of 1968 for the Netherlands (the substitute years are the closest adjacent years to those surveyed for which comparable national data was available in published reports).

Notes

*   Work on this chapter has been made possible as part of a long-term interdisciplinary research project, "Welfare State at the Crossroads" (VIB), led by Anders

Berge, Walter Korpi, Joakim Palme, Sten-Åke Stenberg, and Klas Åmark at the Swedish Institute for Social Research, Stockholm University. Long-term project financing from the Bank of Sweden Tercentenary Fund is gratefully acknowledged. Special thanks go to the participants of the Year 2000 International Research Conference on Social Security in Helsinki in September of 2000, as well as VIB project group conference participants, for very useful comments. Special thanks also to Dennis Quinn, Geoffrey Garrett, and Deborah Mitchell for generously providing access to their data, which the VIB project group has the ambition to reciprocate, as well as to Helena Höög for important bibliographical assistance.

1. In its present form, this section builds closely on previous reviews by Carroll (1999), by Ferrarini and Nelson (1999), and Obsie et al. (2000). For more far-reaching reviews, see e.g., Rieger and Liebfried (1995), as well as Rhodes and van Apeldoorn (1998).

2. Crucially, it should be noted that Cameron's study does not even use globalization as a term or concept to capture import/export volumes as a share of GDP, but instead that of "trade openness."

3. The group of countries constitutes the entire population of highly industrialized or (earlier in historical time) industrializing states with democratic rule consolidating by, and lasting throughout, the postwar period. The nations hereby included are Australia, Austria, Belgium, Canada, Denmark, Finland, France, (West) Germany, Ireland, Italy, Japan, the Netherlands, New Zealand, Norway, Sweden, Switzerland, the UK, and the United States. Countries with populations of under 1 million (specifically Iceland and Luxembourg) have been excluded due to their much lower degree of autonomy as states from the international environment.

4. For a critical study, arguing that the abolition of national capital controls reflected the increasing economic and political costs of applying such controls rather than ideological persuasion from "epistemic communities," see Goodman and Pauly (1993).

5. New Zealand has been excluded for reasons of transfer statistics incommensurability.

6. The use of different average cutoffs here might have changed the results. Also, the tabular comparisons should be identified as less meaningful for the deregulation measure, where the average has decreased very substantially by the 1990s, with the vast majority of the countries included finding themselves below it.

7. The *coverage ratio* is measured as the percentual share of all dependent employees in a given country and year who are formally entitled to benefits. *Replacement rates* of benefits are assessed on a post-tax, post-benefit basis (including child benefits and any housing benefits provided specifically to the unemployed as such.) These are averaged over four typical household situations: (a) single-person household, over a one-week spell of unemployment, (b) family with a dependent spouse and two children of pre-school age, again over a one-week spell, (c) single-person household as under (a) but over a half-year spell of unemployment, with net benefits over the course of this half-year being assessed as a share of the preceding half-year's net wage, and (d) family as under (b), and over a half-year spell as under (c). See Carroll (1999), and the Data Appendix, for more detail.

8. It should be noted that these institutional classifications are, in practice, completely exogenous to the trends which they are to explain. Institutional classification of a country's insurance regime is not changed by increasing benefits, given that the classification is determined by a combination of the principles on which benefits are paid, the ways in which they are administered, and of how given groups are covered.

9. It should also be noted that the model comparisons performed here are in some respects unfair. Unit and time point dummy variables will always absorb disproportionate shares of the variation to be explained—it would be as good as impossible to estimate models with substantive factors included with a lower proportion of unexplained variance.

References

Bean, C. R. (1994). "European Unemployment: A Survey." *Journal of Economic Literature* XXXII (June), 573-619.

Brittan, S. (2001). Freedom and Economic Policy. http://www.samuelbrittan.co.uk/inter2_p.html, login date July 15, 2001.

Cameron, D. (1978). "The Expansion of the Public Economy: A Comparative Analysis." *American Political Science Review* 72 (4), 1243-1261.

Carroll, E. (1999). *Emergence and Structuring of Social Insurance Institutions: Comparative Studies on Social Policy and Unemployment Insurance.* Stockholm: Akademitryck AB.

Castells, M. (1998). *End of Millennium.* Oxford: Blackwell Publishers.

Ferrarini, T., and Nelson, K. (1999). The Role of Capital in Internationalization Processes. Working Paper. Stockholm: Swedish Institute for Social Research.

Garrett, G., and Lange, P. (1991). "Political Responses to Interdependence: What's Left for the Left." *International Organization* 45 (4), 539-564.

Garrett G., and Mitchell, D. (1996a). Globalization and the Welfare State: Income Transfers in the Industrialized Democracies, 1966-1990. Paper presented at the Annual Meeting of the American Political Science Association, San Francisco.

____. (1996b). "Women and the Welfare State in the Era of Global Markets." *Social Politics,* 3 (2-3), 185-94.

Goodman, J. B., and Pauly, L. W. (1993). "The Obsolence of Capital Controls? Economic Management in an Age of Global Markets." *World Politics* 46 (1), 50-82.

Hall, P. A., and Taylor, R. C. R. (1996). "Political Science and the Three New Institutionalisms." *Political Studies* 44 (5), 936-57.

Helliwell, J. (1998). *How Much Do National Borders Matter?* Washington: Brookings Institution Press.

Hirst, P., and Thompson, G. (1992). *Globalization in Question.* Cambridge, Mass.: Polity Press.

IMF. (various years, a). *Annual Report on Exchange Arrangements and Exchange Restrictions* (previously *Annual Report on Exchange Restrictions, 1950-78*). Washington, DC: IMF.

____. (various years, b). *Balance of Payments Statistics* (previously *Balance of Payments Statistics Yearbook,* 1950-80). Washington, DC: IMF.

Katzenstein, P. (1985). *Small States in World Markets: Industrial Policy in Europe.* Ithaca, N.Y.: Cornell University Press.

Krugman, P. (1994a). *Peddling Prosperity: Economic Sense and Nonsense in an Age of Diminished Expectations.* New York: Norton.

Krugman, P. (1994b). "Competitiveness: A Dangerous Obsession" *Foreign Affairs* 73 (2), 28-44.

Kosonen, P. (1995). Competitiveness, Welfare Systems and the Debate on Social Competition. Contributed paper at the conference Comparative Research on Welfare State Reforms, International Sociological Association (Research Committee 19), Pavia, Italy, 14-17 September.

Leibfried, S. (2000). The Compensatory Role of Welfare States in Open Economies. Paper presented at the COST A15 Conference European Welfare States: Domestic and International Challenges, Cologne, 6-8 October.

Montanari, I. (1995). "Harmonization of Social Policies and Social Regulation in the European Community." *European Journal of Political Research* 27 (1), 21-45.

North, D. C. (1990). *Institutions, Institutional Change and Economic Performance.* Cambridge: Cambridge University Press.

Obsie, A., Sterba, J., and Henningson, M. (2000). Globalization: A Conceptual Review. Examination Paper. Department of Sociology: Stockholm University.

O'Connell, P. J. (1994). "National Variation in the Fortunes of Labor: A Pooled and Cross-Sectional Analysis of the Impact of Economic Crisis in the Advanced Capitalist Nations." In Janoski, T., and Hicks, A. M. (eds.), *The Comparative Political Economy of the Welfare State.* Cambridge: Cambridge University Press.

OECD. (1994). *The OECD Jobs Study.* Paris: OECD.

___. (1990). *Liberalisation of Capital Movements and Financial Services in the OECD Area.* Paris: OECD.

___. (various years, a). *Historical Statistics.* Paris: OECD.

___. (various years, b). *International Direct Investment Statistics Yearbook.* Paris: OECD.

___. (various years, c). *OECD Employment Outlook.* Paris: OECD.

Palme, J. (1990). *Pension Rights in Welfare Capitalism.* Stockholm: Akademitryck AB.

Quinn, D. (1997). "The Correlates of Change in International Financial Regulation." *American Political Science Review* 91 (3), 531-551.

Quinn, D., and Toyoda, A. M. (1997). *Measuring International Financial Regulation.* Typescript. Washington, D.C.: Georgetown University.

Regini, M. (2000). "Between Deregulation and Social Pacts: The Response of European Economies to Globalization." *Politics and Society* 28 (1), 5-33.

Rhodes, M., and van Apeldoorn, B. (1998). Globalization, Employment and Social Policy: Report for DGV. Florence: Robert Schuman Centre, EUI.

Rieger, E., and Leibfried, S. (1995). *Globalization and the Western Welfare State: An Annotated Bibliography.* Mannheim: Centre for European Research.

Sayrs, L. W. (1989). *Pooled Time Series Analysis.* Newbury Park, Calif.: Sage.

Scharpf, F. W. (1991). *Crisis and Choice in European Social Democracy.* Ithaca, N.Y.: Cornell University Press.

Social Citizenship Indicators Project (forthcoming). *Social Citizenship Indicators Project Machine-readable Database.* Swedish Institute for Social Research, Stockholm: Stockholm University.

Stephens, J. D. (1979). *The Transition from Capitalism to Socialism.* London: Macmillan.

Stephens, J. D., Huber, E., and Ray L. (1999). "The Welfare State in Hard Times." In Kitschelt, H., Lange, P., Marks, G., and Stephens, J. D. (eds.), *Continuity and Change in Contemporary Capitalism.* Cambridge: Cambridge University Press.

United Nations. (2000). *Public Sector Indicators: Report Prepared by the Secretariat.* New York: United Nations Secretariat.

Willmore, L. (1998). Social Security and the Provision of Retirement Income. Pensions Institute Working Paper. London: Birkbeck College.

8

Globalization and Social Adjustment: The Case of the Small Developed Countries. A Comparative View of New Zealand, Sweden, and Switzerland

François-Xavier Merrien

The majority of economists are convinced that globalization necessarily entails the decline of welfare states. To neoclassical economists, and to certain Marxist and radical authors as well, globalization eventually signifies the end of welfare states and the convergence towards a liberal-residual social model. Nevertheless, the argument about globalization and the impossibility of sovereignty by the modern state over social matters merits closer examination. The 1980s and 1990s saw an unmistakable convergence in social policy reforms, but the reforms were not general and did not erase the differences between the various forms of the welfare state. Although it is indeed undeniable that external pressures create a need for action and stimulate attempts to find appropriate responses, they do not stipulate the policies that should be adopted. Many analysts have stressed the influence of existing institutions and the brake on reform which they represent (Weaver and Rockman, 1993; Pierson, 1994).

In this debate on the relative importance of economic and political issues in welfare state reform, an analysis of the reform policies of small countries is particularly interesting, since they are more sensitive to international pressure than larger countries.[1]

There are, of course, great differences among these small countries, particularly in the level and structure of social expenditure. Switzerland and New Zealand seem quite backward in comparison with the Nordic countries or the Netherlands. Nevertheless, all these countries have a high per capita income and relatively small income inequalities. What they have in common is that they have developed a form of society distinctly different from the model of the pluralist, segmented, and inegalitarian market. Until the early 1970s, the small countries adopted effective strategies to adapt to international pressures. Their per capita Gross Domestic Product (GDP) was high, unemployment was low, and social protection was relatively well guaranteed. However, during the 1980s and the 1990s, the small countries went into a severe crisis, one after the other. It became increasingly difficult for them to simultaneously maintain full employment, a stable public budget, and a constant level of social protection. The timing of the appearance of these problems varies, of course, from country to country. The crises in New Zealand, Denmark, and the Netherlands reached a peak starting at the beginning of the 1980s. In contrast, until the beginning of the 1990s, Sweden and Switzerland seemed capable of surmounting the crisis. But sooner or later, the crisis arrived, economic competitiveness decreased, and unemployment and public deficits increased.

According to Herman Schwartz (1994a), the transformation of the international economic situation constitutes the main reason for the reorientation of public policy: administrative reorganization according to the principles of New Public Management and policies to reframe social protection programs in a more "neoliberal" direction. These reforms, taken as a whole, show a desire for restructuring[2] that goes well beyond a pragmatic adaptation to the problems encountered. Everything is happening as if, with a few exceptions, late twentieth-century governments, whatever their political colors, have completely abandoned any belief in the possibility of preserving a Keynesian welfare state and decided to move towards a "liberal Schumpeterian" model of society (Jessop, 1994). The great weakness of this analysis is that it is mainly based on a functionalist view of policy convergence. Many authors have pointed out that, despite fifteen years of continuous reform, very great differences between welfare states continue to exist.

Any explanation of the neoliberal policy reorientation (Jobert, 1994) must therefore both measure developments and establish the reasons for the change and for the persistence of differences. The analysis which we offer here is based on consideration of four factors.

The first variable is the new international economic situation. The transformation in external conditions (internal conditions, too, if de-industrialization is considered an internal factor) destroys the foundations of previous policies and makes it difficult or impossible for policy-makers to maintain their existing policies. External shocks come more or less quickly, depending on the country's position in the international division of labor. Their effects are more or less brutal. In any case, they are among the major factors affecting changes in political direction.

The second variable concerns the effects of "globalization" on the interests of the actors (Keohane and Milner, 1996). Over the last twenty years, history shows that the international situation is tending to work against the agreements between employers and trade unions which have prevailed up to now. From this point of view, it could be argued that internationally minded employers have an "objective" interest in opposing the development of the welfare state, and even campaigning for its destruction.

Nevertheless, external pressures alone are not enough to explain the radical policy reorientations that have taken place.[3] The influence of the new liberal theory on government policy must be taken into account as well. Although it was the new international situation that sparked off the reforms, it is the new interpretation of the world by neo-liberal epistemic communities that have determined the new directions that have been taken. However, if we are to gauge the influence of these new ideas, we must also take into account the conditions that have allowed their progressive hegemony to prevail.

The fourth and last variable is that of existing policies. Every government has to administer an institutional, political, and social heritage which, from the point of view of reform, may be an advantage or a hindrance. A Bismarckian welfare state, which enshrines social benefits as an acquired right, is more difficult to reform than a residual welfare state based principally on means-tested assistance. The groups that benefit from the welfare state (retired people or the staff and beneficiaries of the public services) may successfully oppose the implementation of radical policies, but their capacity for action also depends on the institutional rules that allocate the power of veto. A majority government is stronger than a coalition government when it comes to promoting radical reforms.

In order to evaluate the accuracy of these hypotheses, I have chosen to examine three small countries, New Zealand, Sweden, and Switzerland,[4] each of which represents a specific form of the welfare state[5]: a strong universalistic welfare state in Sweden, a weak universalistic welfare state in New Zealand,[6] and a liberal corporatist welfare state in Switzerland.[7] My analysis covers three points: identifying the neo-liberal program for the transformation of the welfare state; analyzing the reforms in the three countries and their consistency with the new credo; and identifying the factors responsible for the specific developments in each country and thus the dialectic between change and historical continuity.

New Zealand, Sweden, and Switzerland: Similarities and Differences[8]

We should say straight away that, except for their small size, the three countries differ radically. According to the Esping-Andersen classification, Sweden is a highly developed welfare state. Fiscal and social pressure is high (53.3 percent of GDP). Social security expenditure is also high (34.7 percent of GDP). New Zealand belongs to the liberal family of welfare states (Castles, 1996), and Switzerland is related to that family in many ways. With a fiscal and social pressure rate of 34.6 percent of GDP, Switzerland has one of the lowest rates among Organisation for Economic Cooperation and Development (OECD) countries. New Zealand follows closely, at 36.4 percent.[9] As regards social security expenditure, New Zealand at 19.2 percent and Switzerland at 25.9 percent of GDP are also "weak" welfare states.

Nevertheless—and this undoubtedly constitutes a fundamental similarity between them—the three countries have all been integrated into the international economy for many years. Even in the 1960s, the percentage of exports and imports accounted for more than 50 percent of GDP in Sweden, Switzerland, and New Zealand. In 1995, the percentage rose to 52.8 percent in Switzerland, 62.5 percent in Sweden, and 46.5 percent in New Zealand.[10]

In addition, Sweden, Switzerland, and even New Zealand have long been famous for their capacity to adapt in a positive way to the international economy and for their skill in creating a social consensus that allows a relatively equitable distribution of national revenue. In what have become classic analyses, Cameron (1978) and Katzenstein (1984, 1985) have argued that it is precisely this great exposure to international constraints that has pushed employers, unions, and governments to reach compromises on the policies they should adopt and to put in place social and salary compensation policies. The two authors also agree on the hypothesis that a high degree of economic openness leads to high public expenditure. However, the cases in question are not good tests of this hypothesis: it is not applicable to Switzerland at all, let alone to the small Antipodean countries. All the same, the hypothesis may not be false, provided that the full range of possible ways of protecting an open society against "the destructive forces of the market" are taken into account. From this viewpoint, the policies adopted by the small European countries are merely one example of the "great transformation" described by Karl Polanyi (1944). The point specific to the small countries is that they were not in a position to avoid international competition. As a result, they all have a large export sector and their level of imports has always been high, even before the breakdown of Bretton Woods and the liberalization of trade under the aegis of the General Agreement on Tariffs and Trade (GATT) and now the World Trade Organization. On the other hand, throughout this period, they sought to protect their domestic economies and their populations from erratic market effects. This strategy included tariff protection for their "non-internationalist" sectors and also specific labor policies, and has been applied in Sweden, New Zealand, and Switzerland.

The contrast between these two economic sectors is borne out by the three examples discussed here. In the case of Sweden, there is a situation full of contrasts. On the one hand, there is a highly competitive export sector composed essentially of large international-level firms subject to international competition[11] and on the other, a relatively large public sector that covers protected national economic sectors (agriculture, fisheries, transportation, services, and certain industrial branches), which, moreover, benefited from well-known social and salary advantages until the 1990s. In Switzerland, we find the same contrast between the export-oriented and the protected sectors. The former covers the financial and insurance sector and a few specialized industries: the chemical and pharmaceutical sector, engineering, and electronic equipment, to which we may add precision instruments and the watchmaking industry.[12] The protected sector basically comprises the agricultural sector, building, and craft industries. New Zealand presents exactly the opposite picture. At the beginning of the 1980s, just four products—wool, meat, dairy products and timber—accounted for 75 percent of all exports. The other side of the economy consisted of the industrial sector and services protected from international competition by successive governments, which developed an ineffective strategy of substituting domestic products for imported ones. It must be said that these policies for the protection of important economic sectors (ranging from customs protection—weak in Switzerland—to regulations and subsidies) are in themselves "social policies" because, by protecting whole sectors of the economy from international competition, these policies guarantee employment, high wages which are not related to labor productivity, and generous company social policies, contributing to what Esping-Andersen (1990) has called the "decommodification" of the labor force.

Moreover, in all three countries, including New Zealand and Switzerland, this policy has been supplemented by a second policy aimed at the direct protection of labor.

In the Swedish case, there are two elements to this second policy: wage policy and social policy. The Swedish model can thus be characterized as featuring two indissoluble factors: on the one hand, a policy of wage solidarity based on the establishment of a centralized system of wage bargaining and an active employment policy[13]; and, on the other hand, a universal and generous social policy with redistributive aims.

New Zealand's social policies are very different from the Nordic model although, as Francis Castles (1993) has emphasized, similar results have been achieved by a range of social measures including the system of arbitration and collective conciliation of interests, which has the explicit aim of ensuring that employees receive sufficient remuneration to support their families.[14] Social policies in the strict sense of the term consist of family benefits, a fixed, universal retirement pension, a generous range of public services including free state education and health care, housing subsidies, and finally, a series of social benefits basically restricted to needy unwaged persons.[15]

The situation in Switzerland may seem more in line with the "liberal" norm, although this evaluation needs to be qualified. It should certainly be emphasized that, unlike many other countries, collective bargaining is extremely decentralized, generally at the sector level, and the negotiators are not bound by any salary norms. We should also note that only 60 percent of the labor force in the industrial sector and 45 percent in the service sector are covered by collective agreements. However, this freedom is tempered by the tradition of "peace at work,"[16] which means that the partners do everything to ensure that they reach an agreement. In general, this results in relatively high wages that, nevertheless, take account of economic conditions. Another important characteristic of Swiss labor policy is its strong dependence on a workforce made up of immigrants and commuters from neighboring countries. The foreign workforce accounts for over 25 percent of the entire labor force. There is a real duality in the labor market in respect of jobs and, to a lesser extent, in respect of salaries and rights. This immigration policy also reinforces the protection of Swiss workers, who generally receive higher salaries and are less vulnerable to unemployment. Furthermore, Swiss social policies paint a picture full of contrasts: old-age pensions and unemployment insurance are relatively generous; in contrast, the health system is mostly liberal and family policies are underdeveloped.

Until the crises of the 1970s, the strategies followed by the three countries were basically effective. All three are among the richest countries in the world (judged by GDP per capita), although this is true to a lesser degree for New Zealand, and their levels of unemployment and poverty are low. However, during the 1980s and 1990s, it became increasingly difficult for them simultaneously to maintain full employment, a stable public budget, domestic currency exchange rates, and the existing level of social protection. As a result, a period of political and ideological controversy began about ways of resolving the crisis, and social policy reforms, whether radical or incremental, were introduced which could be seen as direct effects of the new international situation.

Globalization and Social Adjustments: The Theoretical Question

The relationship between economic globalization and the need to "downsize social protection" is principally based on economic arguments. The first argument is related to the international economy. Its main variable is the new economic framework (globalization). The question is whether, during a period of increased globalization of trade, countries can maintain high levels of social expenditure and taxation without provoking a backlash that will damage the national economy. The second analysis highlights the negative "microeconomic and social" effects of generous social benefits. According to this theory, globalization merely exacerbates effects that are already observable in a semi-closed economy.

The first argument calls for an analysis of the transformation of preferences in an open economy (Frieden and Rogowski, 1996). According to the theory, three factors contribute to the fact that states can no longer safely pursue autonomous expansionist social policies. The first factor is loss of competitiveness. The second is direct sanctions by the financial markets. The third is the increasingly dominant influence of capital-holders on a country's policies.

According to Frieden and Rogowski (1996), the internationalization of trade is a self-perpetuating process, since it reduces the costs of trade while increasing the associated benefits. Reductions in transportation (and communication) costs make international trade more attractive. International trade also produces economies of scale. From an analytical point of view, the globalization of trade may be compared with a trend towards an international reduction in the price of goods. International competition produces a world price and, in the absence of national protection (customs protection, quotas, etc.), encourages the international division of labor, following the Ricardo model, as modified by Heckscher, Ohlin, and Samuelson. Countries can put up only token resistance to this trend without suffering damaging effects (e.g., increased costs to the consumer, deficits in trade balance, loss of market share, bankruptcies). Increased international competition encouraged by rapid reductions in transportation and communication costs, has allowed countries with low salary levels to enter into economic competition. These countries can produce labor-intensive manufactured goods at a lower cost.

Secondly, the end of the Bretton Woods system of fixed exchange rates and the general lowering of customs and regulatory protection spurred on by the GATT make states very vulnerable to short-term capital movements. It is no longer possible to introduce expansionist Keynesian economic policies, which are synonymous with higher budget deficits and the risk of inflation, without soon being punished by the international markets. The great mobility of short-term capital hampers the state's ability to implement policies that investors do not like, such as a lax budgetary policy, an increase in fiscal pressure or social charges or generous social policies.[17] The opening-up of the international economy has led to great vulnerability to international movements of capital, as shown by the European monetary crises of September 1992 and August 1993.

Thirdly, this new international context also marks the end of the postwar social consensus. In a period of accelerated international competition and rapid economic change, it is in companies' interests to challenge existing social agreements. Now that capital is more mobile than ever and the labor market itself has become international, there is little advantage for employers in accepting centralized agreements. Companies seek to rationalize their productive activities and limit the fiscal and social costs that hamper their competitiveness. Agreements on social issues with trade unions become less important. Their actions are dictated by the need to seek the lowest possible production costs and new market share. In these conditions, campaigning by internationally minded employers against the development of the welfare state or even for its destruction makes a great deal of sense. Conversely, the unions find themselves forced to resume the social struggle in a power context far less favorable than before (Keohane and Milner, 1996).

In the global context, the national dimension disappears. The threat of "exit"[18] by holders of volatile capital is now more influential than the "voice" of the citizens or trade unions. Social and union coalitions have less weight than the companies on which employment and revenue depend. Businesses can move their centers of activity, threaten to leave in order to blackmail the coalitions or impose a global reduction in production costs, while the unions are reduced to a purely defensive position. States are called upon to provide an attractive economic framework: low social charges, low fiscal pressure and labor laws that are flexible and non-restrictive. From this point of view, the new situation is full of risks. Although today a non-negligible proportion of employers still remain attached to the welfare state, we should not forget that globalization is increasing the relative importance of the exposed sector, compared with the protected sector. Following the trade liberalization agreements, the protected sector has found itself in a more or less rapid decline, whereas the exposed sector has benefited fully from the new opportunities. The new and dominant actors in favor of economic deregulation are tending to take over the leadership.

However, external pressures alone are not enough to explain this radical policy reorientation. The cognitive factors involved should not be underestimated.[19] The stagflationist crisis of the 1970s severely undermined people's faith in the virtues of Keynesian macro-economic policies. The recognition of persistent anomalies such as the failure of economic aims, the deterioration of productive investment, deepening deficits, persistent inflation and growing unemployment is leading to a crisis of confidence in the regulatory mechanisms introduced after the Second World War as well as offering a window of opportunity to neo-liberal "outsiders." This crisis of the Keynesian paradigm is bringing the classical liberal theory back to prominence. The "neo-liberals" point out the perverse effects of state action when thwarted by the ploys of private actors (growth of an underground economy, disincentives for work, crowding-out effect, etc.). They emphasize the perverse effects of social policies on the behavior of the social actors. All social policies are liable to produce unwanted effects: in particular, they are liable to reduce the incentive to work (e.g., benefit, disability, sickness insurance and unemployment schemes) or to save (e.g., retirement pensions). They must be reformed in order to remove these negative effects (in particular by reducing the "moral hazard") (Gilbert, 2001).

Because these recipes from policies inherited from the past no longer work, governments are obliged to seek new solutions in order to resolve the deadlock. The first factor thatenabled the new arguments to develop and become dominant is undoubtedly related to the crisis of the Keynesian economic model that occurred in the late 1970s. In most countries, the neo-liberal "box of ideas" is the source for innovations in economic, financial or social policy (Jobert, 1994). Nevertheless, the new theories never have a direct effect. Borrowings from the "new" doctrines are generally partial, adapted to suit their new context and take account of social power relationships and institutionalized interests. They are, moreover, integrated into a more or less conscious process of searching for appropriate solutions.

We will now try to determine the relative influence of the above factors by describing the reforms undertaken over the last two decades in Sweden, New Zealand, and Switzerland.

The Reorientation of Social Policies in New Zealand, Sweden, and Switzerland[20]

New Zealand

The transformation of social policy in New Zealand clearly illustrates the most radical neo-liberal path. Admittedly, even before the 1980s, the social policy of New Zealand was more of a residual nature. However, the application of universal and fixed-rate social laws and the relatively slow, but distinct, extension of social policy between 1940 and 1970 seemed to indicate that New Zealand was tending toward a slow convergence with European countries.

Nevertheless, throughout this period, the New Zealand economy became less and less competitive. Unemployment and inflation increased. The Conservative government (1975-83), confronted with the deterioration in the economic situation, resorted to typical devices of the period (monetary control and wage and price freezes), but was unable to resolve the problems. During the 1983 elections, the flight of capital caused a huge financial crisis. The New Zealand currency had to be devalued by 20 percent.

The 1980s marked an abrupt break with the past. Political leaders made no secret of their desire to destroy the foundations of the welfare state. Social protection, presented as contrary to individual freedom and responsibility, was denounced as the main reason behind the economic stagnation. Against this background, the Labour Party, which was returned to power in 1984, broke with the traditional statist protectionist policy followed by Labour and the Conservatives alike since the 1930s and began to implement a policy inspired by neo-liberalism. All these policies were continued with increased vigor when the Conservatives returned to power in 1990. The policy of international openness and deregulation gained ground.[21] However, the most fundamental turnaround was the Employment Contracts Act of 1991, which abolished compulsory union membership.[22] Unions only represented workers who had explicitly joined the union. Negotiations at the company level took the place of industry-level bargaining. Employers were able to negotiate with individual workers. Accident insurance benefits were drastically reduced. Many public institutions (hospitals, institutions for elderly people and the mentally ill, and childcare centers) were closed. The level of social benefits was reduced even further than under the previous government. Traditional assistance to the poor underwent radical change. The conditions for eligibility were tightened up and recipients were required to act in a certain way,[23] especially in order to gain unemployment benefit.[24] Whereas, at the beginning of the 1980s, approximately 50 percent of benefits were targeted, the percentage rose to 70 percent at the end of the 1990s (Boston, 1999: 519-520)., and, in this field, eligibility requirements have become much stricter. The household, rather than the individual, has become the unit of reference. In many cases, spouses (mainly wives) no longer have the right to unemployment, sickness or other benefits. The poverty threshold is set very low and as a result, the right to claim assistance is reduced. All benefits are counted as income and subject to taxation. The conditions for claiming benefits have become more and more numerous and complex, thus reducing the number of beneficiaries.

The only area where the neo-liberal revolution met with utter failure was that of pensions. The plan to privatize the pension system completely[25] was rejected by 92 percent of voters in the 1997 referendum.

The Case of Sweden

Until the 1980s, the Swedish model could be characterized, on the one hand, by the institutionalization of collective salary bargaining that preserved economic competitiveness and, on the other, by an egalitarian social policy, based on fiscal redistribution, which freed the individual from social insecurity.

The economic crisis of the 1980s changed everything. The centralized and egalitarian salary policy was the first to give way. From 1983, the employers' federation broke with the system of salary compromise. By the end of the 1980s, the centralized bargaining system was dead (Pontusson and Swenson, 1996). There was increasing tension between the sectors subject to strong economic competition and those that were less exposed, as well as between public-sector white-collar unions and blue-collar unions. Collective bargaining became fragmented and social conflict increased. But the welfare state suffered from the crisis as well. The monetary and social crises (increasing unemployment, rising to 8.5 percent by 1993) helped to undermine people's belief in the virtues of the welfare state and forced the Social-Democratic government to adopt an austerity policy from 1990. However, the decision was taken at a very bad time, during the large-scale international recession. Sweden's GNP fell by 5 percent between 1991 and 1994 and went into deficit. In 1994, the budget deficit amounted to 14 percent of GNP.[26] Unemployment rose from 1.6 percent in 1990 to 9.5 percent in 1993, then to 10.3 percent in 1997. A bourgeois coalition was elected in 1991 on a liberal platform of opposition to fiscal pressure, bureaucracy, and immigration by foreign workers. When the Social-Democratic party returned to power in 1994, it set out to reform the welfare state according to liberal principles and, as in all the European countries, began to implement a policy of cutting back on social expenditure, decreasing the earnings replacement rate for unemployment and retirement benefits, changing the eligibility criteria for benefits, increasing social contributions and reducing health benefits.[27] In order to reduce unemployment, Sweden resorted to an early retirement policy for the first time. Private services began to appear in areas that had previously been the monopoly of the state: health and services for children and the elderly. Reforms clearly inspired by New Public Management methods were also introduced into public service management (Schwartz, 1994b; Olson and Sahlin, 1998). A 1992 law allowed and encouraged municipalities, which enjoy a large measure of autonomy, to experiment with new forms of management. Experiments using "management by results," service mandates, the introduction of vouchers[28] and other innovations inspired by liberal ideas on public management were especially frequent, and show many similarities with the innovations implemented in Great Britain or the Netherlands.

The most significant reforms apply to retirement pensions and unemployment insurance (Ploug, 1999; OECD, 1998; Anxo and Erhel, 1998). The first step, in 1993, was to make unemployment insurance compulsory. A contribution of 1.5 percent of salary was laid down. The same year, the level of unemployment benefits was reduced to 80 percent of the previous income and benefit was not payable for the first five days. However, in 1994, when the Social-Democratic government returned to power, it abolished compulsory insurance and social contributions, but tightened up other conditions. Consequently, taking part in employment programs no longer restored a person's right to social benefits.

The old-age insurance law is even more radical. The Swedish reform seeks a formula guaranteeing equal pension rights and allows greater resistance to demographic and economic fluctuations. The amount of the pension is now based on the average income over the person's lifetime and not, as before, the best years. The contributions and benefits of the pay-as-you-go scheme were dependent on economic growth. At retirement age, the amount of the pension was calculated as a function of average life expectancy at that age (i.e., it was not predefined). People who had not paid in enough contributions receive a basic pension. In fact, the great Swedish reform signaled the passage from a defined-benefits scheme to a defined-contribution scheme.[29] It will take effect over the next twenty years.[30] In addition, widows' pensions are now means-tested (1997 legislation).

The Case of Switzerland

It is tempting to try to explain Swiss social policy transformation by citing the new international pressures that emerged in the early 1990s (Mach, 1999). But this would be to forget that a number of major social policy reforms had already been introduced and that, from the 1980s onwards, Switzerland was one of the model pupils of the OECD. Thus, in respect of pensions, reforms of the first pillar (a pay-as-you-go system[31] had been introduced over several decades to take account of emerging concerns (demographic, financial, gender equality). On the other hand, the compulsory second pillar, a capital formation system (1985) introduced in response to concerns about financing pensions, took the form of a market solution in line with ideas already proclaimed by OECD experts. The health insurance reform of 1994 remained faithful to liberal theories on health policy, as can be seen by the maintenance of competition between insurance companies and per capita contributions, even though certain factors, such as the compulsory nature of insurance, regulations preventing companies from separating various degrees of risk, and subsidies for households of modest means, also served a social purpose (but not necessarily different from that proclaimed by the World Bank).

On the other hand, unemployment reforms responded more directly to economic pressures. Between 1991 and 1996, the Swiss economy shed 95,000 jobs. The unemployment rate, which had remained below 1 percent since the end of the Second World War, gradually increased to 5.2 percent by 1997. At the same time, the budget surpluses, which were a constant feature until 1990, were transformed into deficits amounting to 3 percent of GNP in 1993-94. This decline in economic performance provoked heated debates, a resurgence of neo-liberal ideas and the desire to reduce the burden of the welfare state,[32] and the introduction of—or at least an attempt to introduce—new measures. Thus, the new unemployment law (1996) introduced significant changes: penalties if the unemployed person does not cooperate, a more restrictive definition of "suitable" work, and an obligation to take part in employment programs after the first 150 days, and finally, participation in such programs no longer prolonged the unemployed person's entitlement to benefits. The cantons were obliged to organize employment programs and a system of unemployment counseling and placement. The government also attempted to introduce new legislation regulating working conditions, but that was rejected in a referendum. It is thus at the level of collective labor contracts that new trends towards greater decentralization and individualization of the contracts have become apparent (ILO, 1999).

The Countries' Paths Compared

Several more general conclusions can be drawn from an examination of policy reorientations in these three small countries.

Firstly, radical reforms sometimes follow directly on from periods of crises, but this is not always the case. Ambitious reforms in line with newly dominant ideas may be undertaken in periods of stability and economic growth. Thus, whether we look at New Zealand or Sweden, there is no doubt that economic transformation played a major role in the destabilization of the economic and social system. In both cases, the breakdown of the Bretton Woods system of fixed exchange rates and the first and second oil crises were among the most important destabilizing factors. To those should be added long-term factors such as the internationalization of trade and financial flows, which, by provoking reactions from international financial actors, placed these governments in a deadlock and forced them, as a matter of urgency, to take measures that conformed to the expectations of "the international economic community." Similarly, the rise in unemployment and social exclusion forced these governments to implement reforms in accordance with the "new" economic theory, in Sweden, New Zealand, and Switzerland. However, other reforms were introduced without external pressure, for example, the extension of the second pillar by capital formation in 1985 and the new health insurance legislation of 1994 in Switzerland, the introduction of the new pension law in Sweden, and the administrative reforms in accordance with the principles of New Public Management (Hood, 1991, 1995; Pollitt, 1990; Merrien, 1999). These laws undoubtedly constitute "orthodox" responses to emerging concerns about demographics, finance, efficiency, and social security. Yet they were not introduced during an emergency, nor was the choice of solution imposed by changes in the external situation.

Secondly, when external factors do seem to act as a catalyst for change, this is often because of the earlier implementation of "unsuitable" domestic policies. Thus, in the case of New Zealand, the loss of the UK market,[33] a more general reduction in competitiveness, and the rise in interest rates led to economic deadlock, thus making it impossible to pursue either economic policies of supporting exports of a limited range of agricultural products and subsidizing the protected sector, or social policies guaranteeing wage levels and improving social protection. In the case of Sweden, the Rehn-Meidner model would have enabled the state to deal effectively with the new international constraints. It was the impossibility of maintaining neo-corporatist discipline in the long term, then the desperate but sustained attempt to maintain employment by extending the public sector that led to failure. In the case of Switzerland, the deciding factor was the change in immigration policy that no longer allowed it to act as a buffer at times of crisis.[34]

Thirdly, although the economic and social deadlocks partially explain the need for a change of policy, it is the influence of ideas that defines the content of the new direction taken. In all three countries, the neo-liberal "box of ideas" is the source of most innovations. In New Zealand, the employers' organization *New Zealand Business Roundtable* acts as the main "reservoir of ideas," but its ideas are also defended by employers' associations in the protected sector and by a number of economists in the Treasury. A number of elected Labour Party members are also convinced that traditional "statist" policies are doomed and that deregulation of the economy is inevitable,[35] even though many of them come from a working-class background and made their careers in the trade unions. There is undeniably a similar influence in the case of Sweden. Admittedly, at first it was anti-socialist groups that led the debates against the welfare state. But, from the middle of the 1980s, many economists in the ranks of the Social Democrats and the L.O. union supported the new orthodox economy (Stephens, 1996: 44). In Switzerland, too, neo-liberal ideas are very influential among employers, high-level civil servants, and experts.

Fourthly, the exact nature of the reforms depends partly on the political weight of the unions and parties of the left, partly on the influence of welfare state "clients," and partly on the type of political system. Clearly, the New Zealand labor reforms were much more rapid and radical than those of the Swedish socialists or the Swiss government. The first reason for this lies in the political system itself. The majority-rule system in New Zealand makes alternations of power inevitable and accentuates the competition between the parties to gain power. Since the Conservative government had failed to resolve the crisis using traditional methods and was not capable of proposing an alternative, the new Labour leaders were inclined to advocate a real political break. Labour won the elections in 1984 by exploiting the crisis in public finances and the deterioration of the economic situation, calling for a new type of policy. Yet it was clearly their Labour roots that limited their policy of deregulating the labor market. The Conservatives, more recently converted, had no such scruples and were able to complete the program initiated by their predecessors. The other reason is the absence of an organic link between the unions and the Labour Party (Bray and Neilson, 1996). According to New Zealand tradition, the unions were concerned with salary matters, not politics, especially when Labour was in power. The emergency situation that culminated in the 1984 monetary crisis offered a window of opportunity to those who wanted to act quickly. The unions, having lost a great deal of influence over the preceding ten years, did not have the means to oppose them.

The case of Sweden is entirely different. The Social Democrats had to cope with the consequences of their own mistakes. The impossibility of maintaining the global salary compromise led to economic instability and made it unprofitable to maintain the neo-corporatist accords. The economic sectors with the highest levels of exports no longer perceived any advantage in maintaining salary agreements and put the government under pressure. The Conservatives were able to return to power and institute an advanced liberal program. But the Swedish Social Democrats have been back in power since 1994. Their program has three main points: firstly, aggressive economic policies in tune with the world economy; secondly, a policy of modernization and decentralization of public services in accord with the aspirations of the new middle class; and finally, moderate social policies careful to avoid any split with their social base. Sweden was forced to abandon its centralized salary bargaining, but it remains—but for how long?—anchored in its social universalist-egalitarian heritage, even though it has had to cut its social programs.

The case of Switzerland can be analyzed classically as the result of a policy of seeking consensus in a new international context. In other words, all parties have been influenced by the new social policy paradigm: the necessity of reducing work disincentives, the importance of competition in the health sector, and the necessity of developing a second pillar using capital formation alongside the first, pay-as-you-go pillar. They do differ, however, because their social base is different and because, in the end, direct democracy precludes their pushing too far on reforms that might frighten off their electoral base or the citizenry.

Conclusions

A certain number of lessons can be learned from a comparison of developments in the three countries within the new international context. The first is that the internationalization of trade has profoundly changed the potential for conducting expansionist and independent policies. Financial constraints and the power of business are very real. Secondly, the variable of ideology cannot be overlooked. Similar ideas have strongly influenced policy in dissimilar countries and under different governments.

What is at stake today, going beyond mere technical adjustments, is the preservation or destruction of a social philosophy that creates a social relationship of rights between the individual and the state. The philosophy of the classic welfare state may be defined as a philosophy of the rights of citizens. Access to social rights depends neither on individual merit nor on specific behavior. The "new philosophy of social protection" implies a complete reversal of outlook or, in other words, a new paradigm. This implies a reduction in objective rights, an increase in individual risk and the subordination of the social dimension to economic orthodoxy.

Nevertheless, the influence of ideology is never total. The neo-liberal aspects of policy are neither generalized nor identical. Political leaders and social elites continue to select the problems and to adopt strategies in line with their institutionalized culture, taking into account the preferences of their electoral base. Political systems have authorized breaks with the past that are more or less radical and more or less rapid. They have favored some options over others. Yet the results have sometimes been quite different from what had been expected. The "top-down" clean-break policy of New Zealand governments has failed, whereas the more moderate Swedish policies seem to be on the path to success.

Table 8.1
Basic Information on Sweden, New Zealand, and Switzerland, and
Comparison with France, the United Kingdom, and the United States

	Sweden	New-Zealand	Switzerland	France	UK	USA
Population, 1995 (thousands)	8,827	3,580	7,081	58,141	56,613	263,057
Total civilian employment, 1995	3,926	1,560	3,772	21,744	25,579	123,060
% in the agriculture sector	3.4	10.4	4	5.1	2.1	2.9
% in the industry sector	25	24.9	28.8	27.8	27.7	24
% in the services sector	71.6	64.6	67.3	67.3	70.2	73.1
General government expenditures (% of GDP), 1995	25.8	14.3	14	19.3	21.4	16.2
Exports as % of GDP, 1995	34.5	23.1	26.6	18.7	22	8.4
Imports as % of GDP, 1995	28	23.4	26.2	17.4	24.1	10.7
GNP per capita ($ PPP), 1997	19,010	15,780	26,580	22,210	20,710	29,080
Labor Force Participation (LFP: age: 15-64), 1995	83.4	74.3	77.2	67.7	75.5	75.6
LFP (over 64 years old), 1995	4.6	6.1	5.3	1.7	4.8	10.5
Total social security expenditure (% of GDP), 1996	34.7	19.2	25.9	30.1	22.8	16.5
Taxes and social security as % of GDP, 1997	53.3	36.4	34.6	46.1	35.3	28.5

Sources: OECD (1997, 2000); ILO (2000).

When all is said and done, globalization does not mean certain death for the welfare state. There is still room for maneuver in social policy, but certainly less than there has been in the past.

Notes

1. Generally, the smaller the country, the more it is inclined towards international division of labor, since it has fewer of the natural resources and production conditions within its own borders that would allow it to produce the entire range of goods of a modern economy. The import and export of goods and services are thus particularly crucial. Small countries are particularly sensitive to capital flows.
2. And not just in social policy. University education policy is another very good example of these developments (Braun and Merrien, 1999).
3. We should remember that stagflation, interest-rate rises, and the internationalization of trade preceded the wave of deregulation by at least a decade.
4. Herman Schwartz (1994b) is studying developments in Australia, Denmark, New Zealand, and Sweden.
5. We prefer these terms to those used by Titmuss (1974) or Esping-Andersen (1990). For the distinction between strong and weak universalism, the reader is referred to Merrien (2000a: 99-100); the second term is taken from Katzenstein (1984).
6. New Zealand is classified as an example of the liberal model of welfare state by Gøsta Esping-Andersen (1990). This classification is debatable if we remember the details of the "Antipodean welfare state" emphasized by Francis Castles (1996), particularly the strict social regulation of the labor market and the many universal or means-tested benefits.
7. Switzerland has been classified in many different ways. Esping-Andersen (1990) included Switzerland in the "corporatist-conservative" category, but with reservations. In his 1999 book, he classified Switzerland as liberal.
8. Other figures for comparison are shown in table 8.1, annexed to this chapter. In order to enhance the comparison, we have included comparable data for France, the United Kingdom, and the United States.
9. For the sake of comparison, the figure for the United States is 28.5 percent and that for France is 46.1 percent.
10. For the sake of comparison, the figure for the United States was 19.1 percent in 1995 (OECD, 1997).
11. The engineering and metallurgical industries account for the majority of exports, comprising cars, lorries, machinery, electrical equipment, and telecommunications from a number of large companies, such as Volvo, Electrolux, Saab-Scania, Asea, Sandvik, SKF, and Ericsson.
12. These areas account for more than four-fifths of Swiss exports.
13. Wage policy is designed to establish a norm for wage increases which is lower than the norm for increases in productivity in the most dynamic sectors of the economy, but still greater than increases in less competitive sectors and the service sector. The solidary wage policy lays down the principle of equal pay for equivalent work, regardless of the sector, industry or region.
14. The arbitration and conciliation procedure is compulsory. The Court of Arbitration defines the "social wage" as a level of wage sufficient to provide for a family with two children with only the wage of the head of household. When an arbitration judgment is reached, it is applied to the whole of the industry in question.
15. Retirement pensions (retirement benefits) were introduced as early as 1895.

16. The principle of "peace at work" was introduced in 1938 in an agreement between unions and employers. Today, a clause laying down an absolute obligation to respect peace at work is included in most collective labor agreements. It prohibits any action detrimental to the other partner, whatever the purpose of the restriction. In particular, a signatory to the agreement may not cause any harm to the partner in order to oblige that partner to act in a particular way in respect of matters not covered by the agreement. Nor can the signatory cause harm to the partner in order to oblige a third party to act in a particular way (e.g., strikes, lock-outs). As a result, strikes are very rare. For example, looking at the years 1990, 1995, and 1996, we see that, in Switzerland in 1990, there were only two strikes, as compared with 232 for a country such as Denmark. In 1995, there were two strikes in Switzerland and 424 in Denmark, and in 1996 three strikes in Switzerland and 930 in Denmark (ILO, 1999: 78).

17. The fall of the Euro in December 1999 can probably be attributed to the intervention of the German Chancellor, Gerhard Schröder, calling upon the banks to intervene to save Philipp Holzmann AG, the leading construction and public works company in Germany, from bankruptcy. The *International Herald Tribune* commented on the incident in the following terms: "Departing from the usual circumspect language of central bankers, Wim Duisenberg, the ECB's president, complained of the 'fallout to the image of Europe' in the wake of Mr Schröder's government-led bailout for Philipp Holzmann AG, a 150-year-old company and Germany's second-largest builder.... As Mr Duisenberg spoke, the Euro was falling to a record low.... The European Union competition commissioner, Mario Monti, directly linked Mr Schröder with the Euro's slump." (Schmid, 1999: 4).

18. The economist Hirschman (1970) distinguishes three possible strategies when individuals or groups are dissatisfied: "exit" (e.g., changing to another supplier), "voice" (protest), and "loyalty" (i.e., staying with the same choice for normative or emotional reasons).

19. We are referring here to the flow of ideas that emerge or spread at times of great crisis and to the way the authorities choose from a set of "ready-made solutions." In periods of crisis, the previously prevailing definition of reality is swept away by the emergence of sets of anomalies that are difficult to integrate into the intellectual scheme which organizes the social design of reality. These anomalies, which may be very diverse, generally take the form of theoretical or practical antinomies. At such a time, heterodox theories are the ones with the best chance of producing a reaction and—possibly—becoming the new orthodoxy of theory (and policy) (Merrien, 1999). In this way, Keynesianism became the orthodoxy in the late 1930s, and neoclassical liberalism returned in the early 1980s (Hall, 1989).

20. For these country analyses, we have relied upon the following works: (1) *New Zealand:* Boston et al. (1996, 1999); Castles (1993, 1996); Castles et al. (1996); Kelsey (1995); Miller (1997); Roper and Rudd (1993). (2) *Sweden:* Anxo and Erhel (1998); Baldwin (1990); Dröpping et al. (1999); Esping-Andersen (1990, 1996); Kautto et al. (1996); Olsson (1993). (3) *Switzerland:* Bonoli (1997); Gilliand (1986); Mach (1999); ILO (1999); Merrien and Bonoli (2000); Merrien (2001). We naturally assume full responsibility for any errors which may have crept into our text.

21. The textile and automobile assembly sectors, previously protected, have completely disappeared.

22. The proportion of members fell from 45 percent in 1989 to 20 percent in 1996.

23. In the middle of an economic recession, the number of benefit recipients fell from 1.25 million in 1990 to 825,000 in 1995.

24. The "Community Wage" (1998) represents a major transformation of the unemployment benefit system. This solidary income replaces the existing unemployment benefit. In exchange for this income, the unemployed person agrees to make a contribution in exchange. In particular, the unemployed person is required to undertake community work, if requested. He/she must actively seek paid work. If he/she does not abide by the contract, penalties are applied, up to and including the withdrawal of benefit.
25. In other words, to move from a system of fixed old-age benefits, financed from taxation, to a system of individual capital formation.
26. We should recall that the Maastricht Treaty allows for a maximum deficit of 3 percent.
27. For the first three days of sick leave, the earnings replacement rate was reduced from 90 to 65 percent, then to 80 percent until the 90th day (1991); the following year, employers were obliged to assume the costs of the first fourteen days of sick leave.
28. Parents can now choose between public and private schools. They receive a voucher equivalent to 75 percent of education costs.
29. This should really be called a "notional defined-contribution" system. Under the new system, the insured person pays individual contributions to the social assistance system. These are converted to a notional savings fund when the contributor reaches pensionable age. Thereafter, the defined-contribution procedure is followed. In this kind of system, the state does not guarantee the level of benefits, which depend on the contributions paid and the resources of the system. Italy copied the Swedish reforms in its own reform in 1995.
30. A critical discussion of the Swedish reforms may be found in Cichon (1999).
31. The first pillar (old-age and survivors' insurance) is a fully contributory system. Launched in 1948, it offers old-age benefits that are not fixed, but which fall between a minimum (floor) and a maximum (ceiling) (the ceiling set at twice the level of the floor).
32. Nevertheless, we should emphasize that throughout this period, despite an appreciation of the Swiss franc (1991-94) of approximately 20 percent against other European currencies, the Swiss balance of payments remained positive. From 1998, growth resumed (3.5 percent in 2000) and unemployment fell rapidly (1.8 percent in June 2000). Overall, and compared with the two other countries, the Swiss crisis seems much less serious.
33. Mainly due to the UK's entry into the European Community.
34. By granting increasing numbers of regular work permits during the 1980s, Switzerland deprived itself of the possibility of expelling large numbers of foreign workers, as it had done during the crisis of the 1970s.
35. The neoliberal movement was called "Rogernomics" after the finance minister, Roger Douglas, who masterminded the reforms.

References

Anxo, D., and Erhel, C. (1998). "La politique de l'emploi en Suède: nature et évolution (Employment policy in Sweden: nature and evolution)." In Barbier, J.-C., and Gautié, J. (eds.), *Les politiques de l'emploi en Europe et aux États-Unis (Employment policies in Europe and the United States).* Paris: P.U.F.
Baldwin, P. (1990). *The Politics of Social Solidarity.* Cambridge: Cambridge University Press.

Bonoli, G. (1997). "Social Insurance in Switzerland." In Clasen, J. (ed.), *Social Insurance in Europe*. Bristol: The Policy Press, 107-129.

Boston, J. (1999). "Targeting Social Expenditure in New Zealand." *Social Policy and Administration*, 5 (December), 516-533.

Boston, J., Martin, J., Pallot, J., and Walsh, P. (1996). *Public Management: The New-Zealand Model*. Oxford: Oxford University Press.

Boston, J., Dalziel, P., and St John, S. (eds.) (1999). *Redesigning the Welfare State in New Zealand*. Oxford: Oxford University Press.

Braun, D., and Merrien, F.-X. (1999). *Towards a New Governance for Universities? A Comparative Perspective*. London: Jessica Kingsley.

Bray, M., and Neilson, D. (1996). "Industrial Relations Reform and the Relative Autonomy of the State." In Castles, F. G., Gerritsen, R., and Vowles J. (eds.), *The Great Experiment: Labour Parties and Public Policy Transformation in Australia and New Zealand*. St Leonard: Allen and Unwin.

Cameron, D. (1978). "The Expansion of the Public Economy: A Comparative Analysis." *American Political Science Review*, 72, 1243-1261.

Castles, F. (ed.). (1993). *Families of Nations: Pattern of Public Policy in Western Democracies*. Dartmouth: Aldershot.

___. (1996). "Needs-based Strategies of Social Protection in Australia and New Zealand." In Esping-Andersen, G. (ed.), *Welfare States in Transition: National Adaptations in Global Economies*. London: Sage, 88-115.

Castles, F., Gerritsen, R., and Vowles J. (eds.). (1996). *The Great Experiment: Labour Parties and Public Policy Transformation in Australia and New Zealand*. St Leonard: Allen and Unwin.

Cichon, M. (1999). "Notional Defined-contribution Systems: Old Wine In New Bottles?" *International Social Security Review*, 52 (4), 87-105.

Dröpping, J., Hvinden, B., and Vik, K. (1999). "Activation Policies in the Nordic Countries." In Kautto, M., Heikkilä, M., Hvinden, B., Marklund, S., and Ploug N. (eds.), *Nordic Social Policy*. London: Routledge, 133-158.

Esping-Andersen, G. (1990). *The Three Worlds of Welfare Capitalism*. Cambridge, Mass.: Polity Press.

___.(ed.). (1996). *Welfare States in Transition: National Adaptations in Global Economies*. London: Sage.

___. (1999). *Social Foundations of Post-industrial Economies*. Oxford: Oxford University Press.

Frieden, J., and Rogowski, R. (1996). "The Impact of the International Economy on National Policies: An Analytical Overview." In Keohane, R., and Milner, H. (eds.), *Internationalization and Domestic Politics*. Cambridge: Cambridge University Press.

Gilbert, N. (ed.). (2001). *Targeting Social Benefits: International Perspectives and Trends*. New Brunswick, N.J.: Transaction Publishers.

Gilliand, P. (1986). *Les politiques sociales en Suisse (Social policy in Switzerland)*. Lausanne: Réalités sociales.

Hall, P. (ed.). (1989). *The Political Power of Economic Ideas: Keynesianism Across Nations*. Princeton, N.J.: Princeton University Press.

Hirschman, A. (1970). *Exit, Voice, Loyalty: Responses to Decline in Firms, Organizations and States*. Cambridge, Mass.: Harvard University Press.

Hood, C. (1991). "A Public Management for All Seasons." *Public Administration*, 69, 3-19.

___. (1995). "The New Public Management in the 1980s: Variations on a Theme." *Accounting Organizations and Society*, 20, 93-109.

ILO. (1999). Switzerland: Studies on the Social Dimension of Globalization. Geneva: ILO.
___. (2000). World Labour Report. Geneva: ILO.
Jessop, B. (1994). "The Transition to Post-Fordism and the Schumpeterian Workfare State." In Burrows, R., and Loader, B. (eds.), *Towards a Post-Fordist Welfare State?* London: Routledge.
Jobert, B. (ed.). (1994). *Le tournant néo-libéral en Europe (Neoliberal policy reorientation in Europe)*. Paris: L'Harmattan.
Katzenstein, P. (1984). *Corporatism and Change: Austria, Switzerland, and the Politics of Industry*. Ithaca, N.Y.: Cornell University Press.
___. (1985). *Small States in World Markets: Industrial Policy in Europe*. Ithaca, N.Y.: Cornell University Press.
Kautto, M., Heikkilä, M., Hvinden, B., Marklund, S., and Ploug N. (eds.). (1999). *Nordic Social Policy*. London: Routledge.
Kelsey, J. (1995). *The New Zealand Experiment: A World Model for Structural Adjustment?* Auckland: Auckland University Press.
Keohane, R., and Milner, H. (eds.). (1996). *Internationalization and Domestic Politics*. New York: Cambridge University Press.
Kitschelt, H., Lange, P., Marks, G., and Stephens J. (eds.). (1999). *Continuity and Change in Contemporary Capitalism*. Cambridge: Cambridge University Press.
Lange, P. (1984). "Unions, Workers, and Wage Regulations: the Rational Bases of Consent." In Goldthorpe, J. (ed.), *Order and Conflict in Contemporary Capitalism*. Oxford: Clarendon Press.
Mach, A. (ed.). (1999). *Globalisation, néo-libéralisme et politiques publiques dans la Suisse des années 1990 (Globalization, Neo-liberalism and Public Policy in Switzerland in the 1990s)*. Zurich: Seismo.
Merrien, F.-X. (1998a). "Governance and Modern Welfare-state." *International Social Science Review*, March, 57-67.
___. (1998b). "Les figures de l'Etat-providence. L'Etat-providence entre marché et service public" (Figures of the Welfare State. The Welfare State between Market and Public Service). In Decreton, S. (ed.), *Service public et lien social [Public Service, Social Bond]*. Paris: L'Harmattan.
___. (1999). "La Nouvelle Gestion Publique: une mythologie" (New Public Management: A Mythology). *Revue RIACC/Lien Social*, 41 (July), 95-103.
___. (2000a). *L'Etat-providence* (The Welfare State). Que-Sais-Je (2nd ed.). Paris: Presses Universitaires de France.
___. (2000b). "La restructuration des États-providence: 'sentier de dépendance,' ou tournant néo-libéral? Une interprétation néo-institutionaliste" (Restructuring the Welfare State: "Path Dependence" or Neo-liberal Policy Reorientation? A Neoinstitutionalist Interpretation). *Recherche sociologique*, XXI (2), 29-44.
___. (2001). "The Emergence of Active Policy in Switzerland." In Gilbert, N., and van Voorhis, R. (eds.), *Activating the Unemployed: A Comparative Appraisal of Work-oriented Policies*. New Brunswick, N.J.: Transaction Publishers.
Merrien, F.-X., and Bonoli, G. (2000). « Implementing Major Reforms of the Welfare State: France and Switzerland Compared." In Kuhnle, S. (ed.), *Survival of the European Welfare State*, London: Routledge.
Miller, R. (ed.). (1997). *New Zealand Politics in Transition*. Oxford: Oxford University Press.
OECD. (1994). *The OECD Jobs Study: Facts, Analysis, Strategies*. Paris: OECD.
___. (1996). *Economic Survey: New Zealand*. Paris: OECD.
___. (1997). *Economic Survey: Switzerland*. Paris: OECD.
___. (1998). *Economic Survey: Sweden*. Paris: OECD.

___. (2000). *Revenue Statistics*. Paris: OECD.

Olson, O., and Sahlin, K. (1998). "Accounting Transformation in an Advanced Welfare State: The Case of Sweden." In Olson, O., Guthrie, J., and Humphrey, C. (eds.), *Global Warning*. Oslo: Cappelen Akademisk Forlag.

Olsson, S. (1993). *Social Policy and the Welfare State in Sweden*. Lund: Arkiv Förlag.

Pierson, P. (1994). *Dismantling the Welfare State? Reagan, Thatcher and The Politics of Retrenchment*. Cambridge, Cambridge University Press.

Ploug, N. (1999). "Cuts and Reform of the Nordic Cash Benefit Systems." In Kautto, M., Heikkilä, M., Hvinden, B., Marklund, S., and Ploug N. (eds.), *Nordic Social Policy*. London: Routledge.

Polanyi, K. (1944). *The Great Transformation*. New York: Farrar and Rinehart.

Pollitt, C. (1990). *Manageralism and the Public Service*. Oxford: Blackwell.

Pontusson, J., and Swenson, P. (1996). "Governing Labor Markets: Employers, Wage Bargaining, and the Politics of Institutional Change in Sweden." *Comparative Political Studies*, 29 (April): 223-250.

Roper, B., and Rudd, C. (eds.). (1993). *State and Economy in New Zealand*. Auckland: Oxford University Press.

Schmid, J. (1999). "Euro: Schroeder is Blamed for a Loss of Confidence in Currency." *International Herald Tribune*, 3 December: 1, 4.

Schwartz, H. (1994a). "Public Choice Theory and Public Choices: Bureaucrats and State Reorganization in Australia, Denmark, New Zealand, and Sweden." *Administration and Society*, 26(1), 48-77.

___. (1994b). "Small States in Big Trouble: State Reorganization in Australia, Denmark, New Zealand, and Sweden in the 1980s." *World Politics*, 46, 527-555.

Stephens, J. (1996). "The Scandinavian Welfare States: Achievements, Crisis and Prospects." In Esping-Andersen, G. (ed.), *Welfare States in Transition: National Adaptations in Global Economies*. London: Sage.

Titmuss, R. (1974). *Social Policy*. London: Allen and Unwin.

Weaver, K., and Rockman, B. (eds.). (1993). *Do Institutions Matter? Government Capacities in the US and Abroad*. Washington, D.C.: The Brookings Institution.

9

Income Distribution and Social Security in an OECD Perspective*

Koen Caminada and Kees P. Goudswaard

Introduction

In recent years considerable progress has been made in empirical research on income inequality in industrialized countries (see e.g., Gottschalk et al., 1997). An important development has been the launching of the Luxembourg Income Study (LIS) in which micro data sets from various countries have been harmonized. Thus, there are good possibilities for studying how income inequality varies cross-countries (see Atkinson et al., 1995). However, the advancement in methods of measurement and in empirical knowledge is contrasted with the lack of insight into causes for differences in equality over time (Gustafsson and Johansson, 1999). This should perhaps not come as a surprise as the distribution of income in a country is the outcome of numerous decisions made by households, firms, organizations, and the public sector. One could think of an almost infinite number of micro-level causes for differences and changes in income inequality (Gottschalk and Smeeding, 1997; Atkinson et al., 1995).

In this chapter, we investigate whether social policy measures have contributed to changes in inequality among Organisation for Economic Cooperation and Development (OECD) countries. Our hypothesis is that reforms of the social system, such as benefit cuts or more strict eligibility criteria, have made the income distribution more unequal. Of course, this is only the case when (pre-reform-) social transfers are mainly directed at lower income groups (or when the transfers to lower income groups are cut more than the transfers to higher income groups). When, on the other hand, the benefits of the welfare system are rather evenly spread between income groups, reforms will not have a strong impact on income (re)distribution.

Using comparative international time-series data we will analyze whether there is some correlation between changes in social expenditures and welfare generosity, and changes in the income distribution. A more detailed study will be performed for the Netherlands, which is an interesting case, because the Dutch welfare system has been reformed rather fundamentally in recent years. Also income inequality has increased relatively more than in most other OECD countries (Gottschalk and Smeeding, 1998). We use the traditional budget incidence approach to study the combined effects of all taxes and transfers on the income (re)distribution. The distribution of primary or wage and salary income is compared with the distribution of income after tax and after social transfers.

The chapter is organized as follows. In the following section we summarize literature on the (changes in the) income distribution in OECD countries. Then we investigate the proposition that social policy is one of the causes of increasing inequality. The fourth section presents a more detailed budget incidence approach for the Netherlands, before the fifth section concludes the chapter. Details on the comparative databases used are listed in Table 9.6 in the Annex.

Empirical Evidence

Data on Income Inequality

Data availability, data consistency, and many factors in different studies make it hard to compare levels or even trends of income inequality across countries (differences in income concepts, the income units, (summary) measures, equivalence adjustments and other factors).[1] The most promising tool to analyze changes in the income distribution are high quality time-series panel data. However, cross-national studies based on several years of panel data are just beginning to appear (see e.g., Headey et al., 1997).[2] Second-best seems the cross-nationally comparable collection of the Luxembourg Income Study (LIS). LIS was created specifically to improve consistency across countries. The LIS data are a collection of micro data sets obtained from the range of income surveys in various countries. The advantage of these data is that extensive effort has been made by country specialists to make information on income and household characteristics as comparable as possible across a large number of countries. The LIS data sets can be used to compare the distribution of disposable income in twenty-fivr nations over a twenty-year period, though not all periods are available for all nations.[3]

Differences in Inequality across OECD Countries

This section reviews the evidence on cross national comparisons of annual disposable income inequality over twenty wealthy nations. The analysis is mainly descriptive and relies on the empirical evidence from Gottschalk and Smeeding (1997 and 1998), and others using data from the Luxembourg Income Study (LIS).[4] We summarize empirical results by both analyzing absolute *levels* and *trends* of income inequality across countries. We start by comparing levels (around the mid-1990s) and short-run trends in inequality (1980s) and then shift to trends from 1979 onwards.

Levels of Income Inequality around the Mid-1990s

Levels of inequality can be shown in several ways, e.g., by Lorenz curves, specific points on the percentile distribution (P10 or P90), decile ratios (P90/P10), and Gini coefficients or many other summary statistics of inequality. All (summary) statistics of inequality can be used to rank income inequality in OECD countries, but they do not always tell the same story.

Table 9.1 shows two summary measures of the income distribution—the P90/P10-ratio and the Gini coefficient. Countries are listed in order of their P90/P10-ratio from smallest to largest.

The highest inequality is found in the United States, while Nordic countries are the most equal nations. Although other inequality indices would alter the country-ranking to some extent, roughly the same pattern of overall inequality is observed in other analyses of inequality (Atkinson et al., 1995)

We see that according to the Gini coefficient, the Netherlands is grouped with four other countries (Luxembourg, Germany, France, and Taiwan) with quite low coefficients compared to Switzerland, Canada, Spain, Israel, and Japan with somewhat larger coefficient, and five other countries with the largest coefficients, indicating the highest degree of inequality.

Table 9.1 indicates that a wide range of inequality exists across rich nations, with the nation with the highest inequality coefficient (United States) almost twice as high as the nation with the lowest coefficient (Sweden).

Trends in Income Inequality during the 1980s

Table 9.2 summarizes the results of cross-national comparisons of earnings and income inequality. Note that disposable income is equal to market income plus transfers minus taxes. So, Table 9.2 gives some information on social policy as well. Countries have been listed in order of changes in disposable income inequality as measured by the change in the Gini coefficient from largest to smallest change. It should, however, be noted that this country-ranking depends rather strongly on the inequality index used (Gini) and the specific time-intervals applied. Any (small) difference in specification could alter both the magnitude of inequality and the country-ranking to a wide extent. However, the direction of the changes in inequality as shown in Table 9.2 is more or less in line with results of other analyses (Ruiz-Huerta et

Table 9.1
Summary Measures of the Income Distribution

Country	P90/P10 ratio	Gini coefficient
Sweden 1995	2.59	0.222
Finland 1995	2.68	0.226
Belgium 1992	2.76	0.230
Norway 1995	2.84	0.240
Denmark 1992	2.84	0.240
Luxembourg 1994	2.92	0.235
Netherlands 1994	3.08	0.282
Germany 1994	3.18	0.300
France 1994	3.32	0.290
Taiwan 1995	3.36	0.277
Switzerland 1982	3.39	0.323
Canada 1994	3.90	0.286
Spain 1990	3.96	0.306
Israel 1992	4.12	0.305
Japan 1992	4.17	0.315
Ireland 1987	4.20	0.330
Australia 1994	4.22	0.317
United Kingdom 1995	4.52	0.346
Italy 1995	4.68	0.346
United States 1997	5.64	0.375

Note: Data refer to adjusted disposable income based on data from LIS; Gini coefficients are based on incomes which are bottom-coded at 1 percent of median disposable income and top coded at 10 times the median disposable income.
Source: Gottschalk and Smeeding (2000: 211)

al., 1999). As far as disposable income is concerned, it is certainly wrong to think in terms of a worldwide trend towards increased income inequality in the 1980s (Atkinson, 1996: 43).

The extensive survey by Gottschalk and Smeeding (1997) covers many aspects of income inequality. The following stylized facts can be traced from their study:

1. Almost all countries experienced some increase in wage inequality during the 1980s. Changes in household income inequality in most countries were smaller than changes in earnings inequality. In all OECD-countries post-tax and transfer disposable income is more equally distributed than market income.
2. Changes in taxes paid and transfers received—due to changes in tax and transfer structures in many countries—largely offset the changes in the distribution of markets income (pre-tax and pre-transfer).

Table 9.2
Changes in Market and Disposable Income Inequality during the 1980s

Country	Years	Market Income Inequality	Disposable Income Inequality
United Kingdom	1981 - 91	+++	++++
United States	1980 - 93	+++	+++
Sweden	1980 - 93	+++	+++
Australia	1980 - 90	+	+
Denmark	1981 - 90	+	+
New Zealand	1981 - 89	+	+
Japan	1981 - 90	+	+
The Netherlands	1981 - 89	+	+
Norway	1982 - 89	+	+
Belgium	1985 - 89	+	+
Canada	1980 - 92	+	0
Israel	1979 - 92	+	0
Finland	1981 - 92	+++	0
France	1979 - 89	0	0
Portugal	1980 - 90	0	0
Spain	1980 - 90	n.a.	0
Ireland	1980 - 87	+	0
West Germany	1983 - 90	+	0
Italy	1977 - 91	-	-

Note: Change is based on the disposable income Gini coefficient (income concept, method of equivalence scale and computation may differ by country). Designation range of change in Gini coefficient: - = 5 percent or more, 0 = -4 to +4 percent, + = 5 to 10 percent, ++ = 10 to 15 percent, +++ = 16 to 29 percent, ++++ = 30 percent ore more. Methodology: the above result emerges from extensive reading and interpretation of comparative studies of the level and trend in inequality by Gottschalk and Smeeding (1997: 666).

3. However, the changes in the distribution of income are the result of a complicated set of forces. The links between changes in tax and transfer policy and the distribution of disposable income in different countries are not well understood at this stage.

Trends in Income Inequality, 1979-1995

When we turn to long-run trends in inequality, the picture as set in Table 9.2, alters substantially for several countries. We rely on data from another paper by Gottschalk and Smeeding (1998) who list countries in order of *yearly* percentages changes in disposable income inequality (as measured by the change in the Gini coefficient) from largest to smallest change. Disposable income inequality increased dramatically in a number of countries, but

Figure 9.1

Trends in Disposable Income Inequality 1979-1995: Average Percentage Change of Gini Coefficient per Year

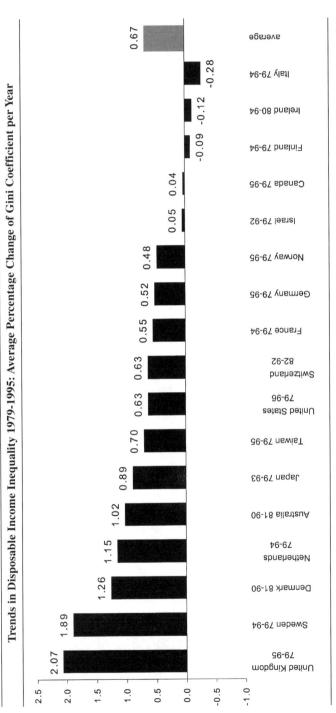

Note: Average percentage change per year equals the percentage change in the Gini coefficient over the time frame indicated divided by the number of years in the interval.

Source: Gottschalk & Smeeding (1998: 56, 64); own calculations.

this trend was not universal. Income inequality did *not* rise in five of the seventeen nations examined from 1979 to 1995 (see Figure 9.1).

Inequality increased by more than 1 percent a year in five countries over this period. The United Kingdom, Sweden, Denmark, the Netherlands, and Australia are on top of the list in descending order. Compared to Table 9.2, the United States fall back dramatically, while e.g., the Netherlands show a remarkably sharp increase. Moreover, household income inequality increased in several countries in the period 1979-95, but the timing of changes was markedly different.

While even the LIS-data are by no means perfect, they produce some consistent patterns. The range of income inequality in OECD countries seems very wide at any point in time. The Gini coefficient in the most unequal country (United States) is almost twice as large as that found in the most equal country (Sweden). Income inequality has increased dramatically in a number of countries, particularly in the United Kingdom, but also in the Netherlands, Denmark, Sweden, Australia, and seven other nations. While income inequality rose in twelve of the seventeen nations examined from 1979 to 1995, this trend was not universal. In almost all countries inequality declined through the 1970s and started to increase in the 1980s and 1990s. Country specific trends in income inequality are more similar, though not universally so. The large majority of nations have experienced rising income inequality over the last decade or longer.

The Role of Social Policies

Causes of Change: Is It Social Policy?

The increasing income inequality observed for most—but not all—Western economies over the last decades has coincided with many structural changes in the economic system. The world economy has been hit by oil crises twice, there has been a tendency towards more free market oriented policies, and more women have been participating in the labor market. For many countries the main forces behind growing disposable income inequality are the growth of inequality of earned market income, demographic changes, changes in household size and composition, and other endogenous factors. Atkinson (2000: 17) concludes that we should not expect the same development in all countries, because the distribution of income is subject to a wide variety of forces. The evolution of income inequality is not simply the product of common economic forces: it also represents the impact of institutions and national policies. We focus on social policy to that end, and look for a relationship, if any, between social policy and income inequality.

One could argue that one of the explanations of the dissimilarity in country-ordering in Table 9.2 compared to Figure 9.1 could be the welfare state reform. In some countries the welfare state (tax and transfer systems) has been reformed rather drastically in recent years. Cutting back public spending and increasing income inequality could be correlated.

On basis of the LIS-data presented by Ervik (1998) we find mixed evidence. Ervik presents for eight countries the trend in the Gini coefficients corresponding with several income concepts; moving from earned market income, via gross income (also including social transfers) to net disposable income (gross income minus social contributions and taxes). For any year (and country) the magnitude of welfare states' total redistributive effort is represented by the reduction of the Gini coefficient between market income and net disposable income (Ervik 1998: 30). This budget incidence approach indicates that the tax and transfer system does redistribute income in such a way that a substantial reduction in overall income inequality is accomplished in all of the eight countries under consideration. How did this distributing effort by social policy vary over time in different countries? In some countries the redistributive effect of transfers and taxes decreased in the last ten to fifteen years (Sweden, the United Kingdom, Finland, and the United States), whereas in other countries the redistributive effect of transfers and taxes increased (Denmark, Australia, Germany, and Norway). However, this study does not deal with the possible relationship between welfare state *policies* and changes in the income distribution.

Empirical Evidence from a Straightforward Approach

How do we measure changes in social policy or changes in "generosity" of social security systems? A range of indicators are used in comparative studies (Whiteford, 1995). We look at only two of these indicators in our straightforward approach (see also below): *(a)* social security expenditures as percentage of Gross Domestic Product (GDP), and *(b)* replacement rates of unemployment benefits.

Social Security Transfers as Percentage of GDP

It is well known that social security systems are very difficult to compare. Countries often use different definitions of social security and of specific social risks, such as unemployment or disability. Moreover, benefits may be provided by either public institutions or market institutions. In the latter case, market provision may be regulated by government in such a way as to make it equivalent to public provision. These different forms of social protection may not be included consistently in national statistics. A specific statistical problem is related to the tax treatment of social benefits. In some countries benefits are taxable as a rule, in others not. Also, benefits can take the form of tax relief. These tax features can make a big difference in the statistics.

Also, changes in expenditure ratios often do not reflect policy changes. Higher outlays can simply be the result of aging, rising unemployment, et ceteras. Expenditure ratio's can thus only be considered as rough indicators of welfare state policies.

Gottschalk and Smeeding (1997) use this indicator to analyze the impact of social policy in the 1980s. They conclude that there is a noticeable correlation between public cash transfer expenditures and disposable income inequality. While the level of social spending is negatively correlated with changes in income inequality, they found little relationship between retrenchment and increases in inequality in most countries (Gottschalk and Smeeding 1997: 673). Reductions in social welfare spending for the non-aged and regressive changes in the structure of income taxes for some countries during the 1980s account for only a small part of the trend in post-tax and transfer inequality in most nations.

Following Gottschalk and Smeeding, we look at expenditure ratios for a somewhat longer period. Table 9.3 shows that in almost all modern welfare states social security transfers as percentage of GDP rose in the period 1979-94. Using the Comparative Welfare State Data Set (LIS/OECD), we found only two countries with a non-positive change in social security transfers over this time interval: Germany and the Netherlands.

The expansion of social security systems and/or safety nets in most countries mitigated the observed trend of increasing (market) income inequality to some extent during the period under consideration. Although for most countries both income inequality and social security transfers rose (this seems to contradict with our hypothesis), the growth rates of social security transfers show variation across countries. Rising inequality in some countries *could* be associated with a *below average* change in social security transfers as percentage of GDP. This is analyzed in Figure 9.2.

We have plotted the average percentage change of social security transfers as percentage of GDP and the average percentage change in the Gini coefficient for countries, where both data-items are available. Both averages are calculated over the period indicated (total change divided by the number of years in the interval) and are represented by the cross of both axes: 0.67 for Gini and social security transfers rose on average approximately 0.3 percentage-points per year among these fifteen countries. Several countries show growth rates in social security transfers above this average: Canada, France, and the four Nordic countries. Other countries show below average growth rates: Australia, Germany, Ireland, Italy, Japan, the Netherlands, Switzerland, the United Kingdom, and the United States.

Table 9.3
Social Security Transfers as a Percentage of GDP

	Around 1979	Around 1994	Total change	Average annual change
Australia 81-94	19.5	21.8	+2.3	+0.18
Canada 79-94	9.6	15.2	+5.6	+0.37
Denmark 81-94	17.8	22.0	+4.2	+0.32
Finland 79-94	9.4	25.1	+15.7	+1.05
France 80-93	18.6	23.3	+4.7	+0.31
Germany 79-94	16.5	16.1	-0.4	-0.03
Ireland 80-93	12.6	15.4	+2.8	+0.22
Italy 79-94	15.7	19.5	+3.8	+0.25
Japan 79-93	9.8	12.1	+2.3	+0.16
Netherlands 79-94	25.5	25.5	0.0	0.00
Norway 79-94	15.5	20.5	+5.0	+0.42
Sweden 79-94	17.6	24.9	+7.3	+0.49
Switzerland 82-92	13.2	15.9	+2.7	+0.27
United Kingdom 79-94	11.1	15.4	+4.3	+0.29
United States 79-93	10.0	13.2	+3.2	+0.23
average (unweighted)	*14.8*	*19.1*	*+4.3*	*+0.30*

Note: total change equals the change in social security transfers as percentage of GDP over the time frame indicated; average annual change is total change divided by the number of years in the interval.
Source: LIS/OECD Comparative Welfare State Data Set (http://lissy.ceps.lu/compwsp.htm); and own calculations.

The plotted results for the United Kingdom, the Netherlands, Japan, and Australia seem in line with our hypothesis. These countries combine an above average rise in income inequality with a below average growth rate of social security transfers over the time interval indicated. Furthermore, Norway, Canada, France, and Finland combined an above average growth rate in social security transfers with a below average rise in income inequality. However, for the other countries we do not find a noticeable negative correlation between the change in the level of social security transfers and disposable income inequality. Especially Sweden and Denmark combine both an above average growth rate in social security transfers with a relatively large rise in income inequality. Note that a weak positive relationship between social security transfers and inequality can also be the result of the fact that social security transfers are not well-targeted towards the poor.

Figure 9.2
Cross Country Changes in Social Security Transfers and Gini Index, 1979-1994

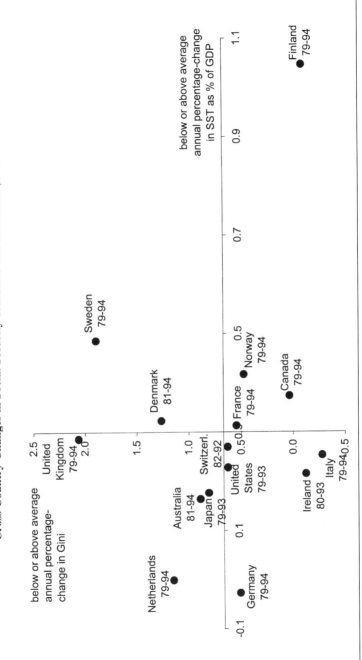

Source: Gini coefficient: see Figure 9.1; Social Security Transfers: LIS/OECD Comparative Welfare State Data Set; own calculations.

Replacement Rates

Comparative studies of social security systems have increasingly turned to the use of replacement rates as measures of the level of benefits in different countries and therefore of the degree of social protection offered by different welfare systems. However, also replacement rates can only be seen as limited indicators of the generosity of benefit systems (Whiteford, 1995). Some of the limitations are: (1) replacement rates are based on entitlement rules and often represent only the maximum payment available in the circumstances specified; (2) benefits are often not fully indexed, implying that benefits represent a decreasing percentage of wages; (3) not all relevant benefits may be reckoned with (such as housing subsidies or health care); (4) taxation can blur the picture; and (5) to monitor social policy developments in the OECD area, one should calculate a variety of replacement rates (differentiated to e.g., social security schemes, earnings levels, family situations, duration of spells). Bearing these limitations in mind, we can look at Figure 9.3, which presents only the gross replacement rates for unemployment benefits for twenty-one OECD countries in 1985 and 1997. All replacement rate calculations are based on the level of previous earnings defined with reference to the Average Production Worker (APW), taking as the two most significant cases the APW level of earnings and two-thirds of the APW level of earnings.

Seven countries show a decline in the replacement rates in the period 1985-97: the Netherlands, Belgium, Spain, the United States, the United Kingdom, Germany, and Sweden. All these countries are faced with an increasing income inequality as measured by the Gini coefficient (Figure 9.1). This gives some support for our hypothesis.

In line with Figure 9.2 we have plotted the annual average percentage change of the gross replacement rates and the annual average percentage change in the Gini coefficient for countries, where both data-items are available for the time interval indicated. Again, both axes cross at these averages: 0.67 for Gini and the replacement rose on average approximately two percentage points per year among these countries. Figure 9.4 shows some indications that support our hypothesis. A negative relationship between the change in replacement rates and the change income inequality can be found for the United Kingdom and the Netherlands. Other countries with a relatively sharp increase in income inequality (Sweden and Denmark) show relatively modest positive changes in the replacement rates. However, it is certainly wrong to think in terms of a worldwide explanation for the upward trend towards increased income inequality since the 1980s.

Relationship

The comparative data used in the analysis above are by no means perfect. They do not accurately indicate (the direction of) changes in social policy.

Figure 9.3
Gross Replacement Rates Unemployment Benefits in the OECD, 1985 and 1997

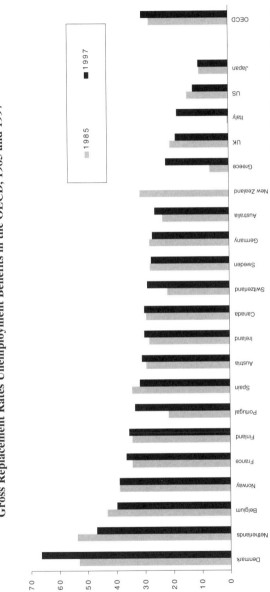

Note: Replacement rates (i.e. benefits before tax as a percentage of previous earnings before tax) as defined by legislated entitlements averaged across various circumstances in which an unemployed person may be. Countries are ranked in descending order of this average in 1997. Benefit entitlements have been estimated for two earnings levels (average earnings and two-thirds of average earnings), three family situations (single, with dependent spouse, with spouse in work) and three durations of unemployment spells (one year, 2 to 3 years, 4 to 5 years out of work). For every datayear between 1961 and 1997 the unweighted averages of these replacement rates are computed. The computations assume standard circumstances such as 40 years of age, involuntary loss of the former job, long previous work record, etc.

Source: OECD (data provided by Glenn Cooper).

Figure 9.4
Changes in Gross Replacement Rates and Gini Index, around 1979 and 1994

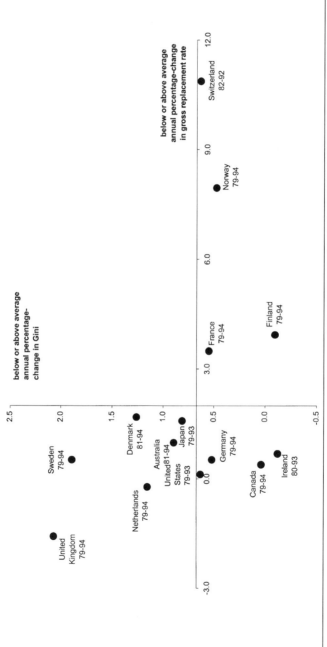

Note: Italy is excluded due to a strongly downward biased figure for the replacement rate in 1979.

Source : Gini coefficient: see Figure 9.1; gross replacement rates: see Figure 9.3; own calculations

The material presented is only descriptive, does not explain changes in the household income distribution, and therefore can not establish a *causal* relationship between changes in social policy and changes in the income distribution. Obviously, this straightforward analysis is much too simple to draw far-reaching conclusions.

Nevertheless, for some countries the data produce patterns for the period 1979-94, which are consistent with our hypothesis; for others not though. Especially the UK and the Netherlands are interesting cases: these countries combine a relatively large increase in inequality with lower replacement rates and for the Netherlands also a non-positive change in the expenditure ratio. These are indications that support our hypothesis on a negative relationship between changes in income inequality and changes in social policies. A much more elaborate country-approach is needed, however, to be more conclusive, which we attempt for the case of the Netherlands.

A Budget Incidence Analysis for the Netherlands

Social Security Reform

The Dutch social protection system used to be characterized by generous open-ended benefits and lax administrative control. However, the expansion of the system caused severe and growing problems, starting in the 1970s. The number of benefit recipients and the financial burden of inactivity rose dramatically, as can be seen in Table 9.4. Combined with a number of adverse macro-economic shocks, a vicious cycle of increasing (non-wage) labor costs, erosion of employment and growing benefit dependency was set in motion. Reform of the social system was called for and was indeed initiated in the early 1980s. Actually, the change in policy stance occurred at a relatively

Table 9.4
Key Figures on Social Security in the Netherlands

	1970	1980	1990	1999
Public expenditure on social security as % of GDP [a]	17.2	26.4	25.8	20.7
Number of benefit recipients in millions	2.0	3.1	4.0	4.1
Same under age 65	0.7	1.4	2.0	1.9
Benefit recipients as % of employment	45	66	82	69
Real disposable income of welfare and old age benefit recipients (index: 1973 = 100)		124	114	112

[a] Excluding supplementary labor pensions and housing subsidies, including public expenditure on health care.
Source: Ministry of Social Affairs (1995: 5) and (1999).

early stage, compared to other European countries, because of the severity of the problems (Bovenberg, 2000).

In the 1980s reform strategy was almost exclusively directed at cutting benefit levels. The (legally required) indexation of social benefits to wage development was suspended during almost the entire 1980s and partly in the first half of the 1990s. Actually, in many years no adjustment for inflation took place, that is, benefits were frozen in nominal terms. Also, unemployment and disability benefits were cut from 80 percent to 70 percent of previous wages. As a consequence of these and other measures, real disposable income of many beneficiaries strongly fell since 1980, as shown in Table 9.4.[5] The strategy was successful in containing expenditure growth. Public expenditure on social protection roughly stabilized in the 1980s, despite continuing growth of benefit volumes.

In the 1990s the reform strategy has been primarily directed at reducing the number of beneficiaries, through encouraging labor force participation, and discouraging and preventing benefit dependency. Important policy measures in this context have been the tightening of eligibility requirements in the unemployment and disability schemes, reform of the benefit administration, and the introduction of stronger financial incentives for employees and—especially—employers. The sickness benefit scheme has been privatized in the period 1994-96, which means that employers are now fully responsible for paying sickness benefits of 70 percent of wages during the first year of sick leave. This risk can be privately insured, which has actually occurred on a large scale. The disability scheme has also been changed fundamentally, through the introduction of experience rating. Also, the option was introduced for employers to private coverage of the disability risk during the first five years of disability. Radical changes have been made in the survivors scheme. Most people are now expected to privately insure against the risk of death of relatives.

The reduction in statutory benefits has been offset mostly, because trade unions have negotiated supplementary benefits, especially sickness benefits and disability benefits. However, employees (and others) not taking part in these collective contracts do not profit from this.

The figures in Table 9.4 show that these policies had some success in terms of halting the rise in claimants under 65 years, but so far the rising trend has not been clearly reversed. A more positive development is that the ratio of benefit recipients to the number of employed is falling in recent years, as a consequence of rapid employment growth. Also, total expenditure on social security is declining in recent years. It goes without saying, however, that the reforms discussed will have a substantial impact on the income distribution (see following).

Methodology

Social security schemes in the Netherlands, as in many countries, make low-income earners better off after social policy than before. In general, income is transferred from high-income earners to poor ones through taxes and transfers. We analyze the effect of social policy on the distribution of income in line with the work of Musgrave et al. (1974). The distribution of primary or wage and salary income is compared with the distribution of income after tax and after social transfers. Summary statistics of income inequality before and after social policy are used to indicate the amount of distribution by social policy (Ervik, 1998, and Duclos, 2000). Our measure of the redistributive impact of social security on inequality is straightforwardly based on a formula developed by Kakwani (1986) and Ringen (1991).

$$\text{Redistribution by government} = \frac{(\text{primary income} - \text{disposable income})}{(\text{primary income})}$$

This formula is used to estimate the reduction in inequality produced by social security, where primary income inequality is given by a summary statistic of pre-tax, pre-transfer incomes, and disposable income inequality is given by the same summary statistic of disposable equivalent incomes. The measures of both pre- and post-social security income are far from ideal. At a conceptual level, no conceivable measure of pre-social security income could indicate what the income distribution would look like if social security did not exist.

The unit of analysis is an important issue in income distribution studies. Equivalence scales are widely used.[6] In our analysis for the Netherlands we use the results obtained by other researchers, where equivalence scale elasticity is around 0.5 (most OECD-studies). Moreover, we analyze data for a long time period in which data-consistency for the adjustments for household size and composition for market income is troublesome. For this reason we separately analyze the whole trajectory from original or market income to net disposable income with non-adjusted incomes to approach the impact of the tax and benefit system as part of the overall trend in income distribution.

We use the Mean Log Deviation (Theil index) as a summary measure of income inequality. It is generally agreed upon that this statistic is best suited to identify components of the change in inequality, that is, for assessing the impact of taxes and benefits on inequality. The lower this statistic the more equal is the distribution. Mean Log Deviation can be meaningfully added and subtracted from another in a way that most other indices of inequality cannot. Of course, many other summary measures can be found in the literature and all imply some a priori value judgments about the distribution itself.

The important issue of tax/transfer shifting is totally ignored in analyses on budget incidence in such a classical framework. However, models that include all behavioral links are beyond the scope of existing empirical work (Gottschalk and Smeeding, 1998: 3). Therefore, researchers have restricted themselves largely to accounting exercises that decompose changes in overall inequality into a set of components. Despite the problem of tax shifting, analyses on statutory and budget incidence can be found for decades in literature on public finance.[7]

Results

We perform a budget incidence analysis for the period 1981-1997, because we measure the lowest level of inequality in the early 1980s (as most studies for the Netherlands do). Inequality especially rose during the 1980s. We analyze the trajectory from primary income to adjusted disposable income. Table 9.5 illustrates the main characteristics of the trend in inequality in the Netherlands.

As expected, adjusted disposable incomes are distributed much more equally than primary incomes. In the years shown, inequality was reduced by some 80 percent. By far the largest part of the overall reduction in inequality (about sixty percentage points) is due to social transfers. Note, however, that the redistributive effect of transfers has become smaller in the period under consideration. Taxes and social security contributions reduce inequality by some seven to ten percentage points. Finally, the use of equivalence scales reduces inequality by another ten percentage points.

Which are the main factors behind the changes in the income distribution? These are shown in the right part of Table 9.5. In the period considered, the Mean Log Deviation for disposable income increased by thirty-six points, which is equivalent to a rise in overall inequality by 25 percent (29 percent when adjusted income is taken).

A major force behind the rise in overall inequality of disposable household income is a more unequal distribution of primary income (13 percentage points or 36 percent of the total change). This is partly caused by the strong rise in the labor force participation of secondary earners (women). Another factor behind the increase in inequality is lower progressivity of the tax system (9 percentage points or 25 percent).[8] But social transfers explain the largest part of the total increase in inequality (39 percent).[9]

We conclude that the change in social policies since the early 1980s has indeed made the income distribution less equal. Social transfers are a main force behind the rise in overall income inequality. It should be noted, however, that our results are only rough estimates (which depend rather strongly on the data used) given the limitations of the budget incidence method. Including the effect of behavioral responses would probably provide a different result. Transfers cuts have reduced replacement ratios which has stimu-

Table 9.5
Decomposition of Inequality in Household Income: Mean Log Deviation

		Level			Change	Share in change
	1981	1991	1997		1981-1997	1981-1997
Primary income	0.532	0.540	0.545		+0.013	36%
effect transfers	-0.334	-0.324	-0.320		+0.014	39%
Gross income	0.198	0.216	0.225			
effect taxes	-0.054	-0.040	-0.045		+0.009	25%
Disposable income	0.144	0.176	0.180		+0.036	100%
adjustment for household size						
and composition	-0.048	-0.057	-0.056		-0.008	
Disposable income						
equivalence scale	0.096	0.119	0.124		+0.028	

Source: Data on the partial effects of transfers and taxes for 1981 are from Odink (1985); for 1991 from Jeurissen (1995) and for 1997 are own calculations. The partial effects of household size and composition are taken from Trimp (1993) and De Kleijn (1998). The data mentioned did not (always) correspond. For all data years we have postulated the same income concepts and used the same income units as Jeurissen (i.e. definitions from before a major tax reform in 1990) to arrive at identical decomposition of income inequality for all data-years. Thereafter we re-weighted the partial effects (of taxes, transfers and household size and composition). Because of these transformations values in the table will differ from values as presented by Statistics Netherlands (and other studies).

lated labor force participation of benefit recipients.[10] This may have reduced income inequality. Moreover, one would analyze some effects in more detail (by scheme), for example, the effect of shifting responsibility for social schemes from state to market institutions. Our analyses indicate that the reforms of the Dutch social system have made the Dutch income distribution more unequal *overall*. However, the partial effects of reforms of specific social schemes on inequality may have been dissimilar, depending on the altered conditions on benefits and eligibility (retrenchment or not) and the targeting of the pre- and post-reform social scheme (transfers mainly directed to lower or higher income groups).

Conclusions

In this chapter, we investigated whether changes in the overall distribution of incomes in OECD countries can be attributed to social policy measures. Income inequality rose in two out of seventeen OECD countries since the early 1980s. In some countries this rise was rather dramatic, especially in the United Kingdom and in Sweden and—to a lesser extent—in Denmark and the Netherlands. For some countries we find a relationship between changing welfare state policies (as measured by expenditure ratios and replacement rates) and changes in income inequality, but for others not. Especially the United Kingdom and the Netherlands combined and above average rise in inequality with a reduction in the generosity of the welfare system.

We performed a more elaborated country approach for the case of the Netherlands, which is interesting because this country combined a relative sharp increase in income inequality with a quite fundamental reform of the welfare state. We used the traditional budget incidence approach—despite some methodological problems—to study the combined effects of all taxes and transfers on the income (re)distribution. The distribution of primary or wage and salary income is compared with the distribution of income after tax and after social transfers. Summary statistics of income before and after social policy are used to indicate the redistributive effect of social policy. We find that inequality of disposable household income increased in the period 1981-97 by roughly 25 percent as measured by the Mean Log Deviation. Almost 40 percent of the increase in inequality can be attributed to changes in transfers. Our budget incidence analyses indicate that social security reforms have had an important impact on increasing income inequality in the Netherlands.

Annex

Table 9.6
Comparative Database: Availability of Data around 1979 and 1994

Countries	(1) Income inequality around 1995 (LIS)	(2) Trend in income inequality around 1979-1995 (LIS)	(3) Gross replacement rates (OECD)	(4) Comparative welfare state data set (LIS/OECD)	(5) Gross social transfers as % of GNP (OECD Economic Outlook)	Qualified
1 Austria	n.a.	n.a.	x	x	X	No
2 Australia	X	X	x	x	X	Yes
3 Belgium	X	n.a.	x	x	X	No
4 Canada	X	X	x	x	X	Yes
5 Denmark	X	X	x	x	X	Yes
6 Finland	X	X	x	x	X	Yes
7 France	X	X	x	x	X	Yes
8 Germany	X	X	x	x	X	Yes
9 Greece	n.a.	n.a.	x	n.a.	X	No
10 Israel	X	X	n.a.	n.a.	n.a.	No
11 Ireland	X	X	x	x	X	Yes
12 Italy	X	X	x	x	X	Yes
13 Japan	X	X	x	x	X	Yes
14 Luxembourg	X	n.a.	n.a.	x	n.a.	No
15 Netherlands	X	X	x	x	X	Yes
16 New Zealand	X	n.a.	x	x	n.a.	No
17 Norway	X	X	x	x	X	Yes
18 Portugal	n.a.	n.a.	x	n.a.	X	No
19 Spain	X	n.a.	x	n.a.	X	No
20 Sweden	X	X	x	x	X	Yes
21 Switzerland	X	X	X	x	X	Yes
22 Taiwan	X	X	n.a.	n.a.	n.a.	No
23 United Kingdom	X	X	X	x	X	Yes
24 United States	X	X	X	x	X	Yes
Coverage	21	17	21	19	21	15

Sources: (1): Gottschalk and Smeeding (2000: 211), (2): Gottschalk and Smeeding (1998: 56, 64), (3) OECD (data provided by Glenn Cooper, May 2000), (4): LIS/OECD Comparative Welfare State Data Set (http://lissy.ceps.lu/compwsp.htm), (5): Data Set OECD Economic Outlook (December 1998).

Table 9.7

Trends in Disposable Income Inequality, around 1979 and 1994

	Year 1	Year 2	Number of years	Index (1979=1)	Annual % change
Australia	1981	1990	9	1.0730	0.81
Canada	1979	1995	16	1.0056	0.04
Denmark	1981	1990	9	1.1136	1.26
Finland	1979	1994	15	0.9858	-0.09
France	1979	1994	15	1.0820	0.55
Germany	1979	1995	16	1.0827	0.52
Ireland	1980	1994	14	0.9830	-0.12
Italy	1979	1995	16	0.9556	-0.28
Japan	1979	1993	14	1.1250	0.89
Netherlands	1979	1994	15	1.1731	1.15
Norway	1979	1995	16	1.0760	0.48
Sweden	1979	1994	15	1.2837	1.89
Switzerland	1982	1992	10	1.0632	0.63
United Kingdom	1979	1995	16	1.3306	2.07
United States	1979	1996	17	1.1071	0.63
Average qualifiers	*1979.5*	*1993.7*	*14.2*	*1.0960*	*0.67*

Source: See Table 9.9.

Table 9.8

Social Security Transfers as Percentage of GDP, around 1979 and 1994

	Year 1	Year 2	Social security transfers (% GDP) Year 1	Year 2	Index (1979=1)	Change per year
Australia	1981	1994	19.5	21.8	1.1179	0.18
Canada	1979	1994	9.6	15.2	1.5833	0.37
Denmark	1981	1994	17.8	22.0	1.2360	0.32
Finland	1979	1994	9.4	25.1	2.6702	1.05
France	1979	1994	18.6	23.3	1.2527	0.31
Germany	1979	1994	16.5	16.1	0.9758	-0.03
Ireland	1980	1993	12.6	15.4	1.2222	0.22
Italy	1979	1994	15.7	19.5	1.2420	0.25
Japan	1979	1993	9.8	12.1	1.2347	0.16
Netherlands	1979	1994	25.5	25.5	1.0000	0.00
Norway	1979	1991	15.5	20.5	1.3226	0.42
Sweden	1979	1994	17.6	24.9	1.4148	0.49
Switzerland	1982	1992	13.2	15.9	1.2045	0.27
United Kingdom	1979	1994	11.1	15.4	1.3874	0.29
United States	1979	1993	10.0	13.2	1.3200	0.23
Average qualifiers	*1979.5*	*1993.5*	*14.83*	*19.06*	*1.2855*	*0.30*

Source: See Table 9.9.

Table 9.9
Gross Replacement Rates, around 1979 and 1994

	Year 1	Year 2	Gross replacement rates		Index (1979=1)	Change per Year
			Year 1	Year 2		
Australia	1981	1995	22.1	27.0	1.2217	1.58
Canada	1979	1995	25.6	27.2	1.0625	0.39
Denmark	1981	1995	54.2	67.0	1.2362	1.69
Finland	1979	1995	26.5	43.2	1.6302	3.94
France	1979	1995	24.0	37.4	1.5583	3.49
Germany	1979	1995	25.1	27.2	1.0837	0.52
Ireland	1979	1993	28.1	30.8	1.0961	0.69
Italy	1979	1995	1.0	19.3	19.3000	114.38
Japan	1979	1993	8.7	9.9	1.1379	0.99
Netherlands	1979	1995	47.5	45.8	0.9642	-0.22
Norway	1979	1991	19.9	38.9	1.9548	7.96
Sweden	1979	1995	25.1	27.2	1.0837	0.52
Switzerland	1981	1993	12.8	29.5	2.3047	10.87
United Kingdom	1979	1995	23.8	17.8	0.7479	-1.58
United States	1979	1993	11.7	11.9	1.0171	0.12
Average qualifiers	*1979.4*	*1994.2*	*23.74*	*30.67*	*1.2921*	*1.97*

Source: Gottschalk and Smeeding (1998: 56, 64); LIS/OECD Comparative Welfare State Data Set (http://lissy.ceps.lu/compwsp.htm); OECD (data provided by Glenn Cooper, May 2000); and own calculations.

Notes

*   In an earlier stage of our research project on this topic we have benefited from discussions with, and helpful comments from Erik Fjaerli, René Goudriaan, Thor Olaf Thoressen, Henk Vording, and participants of The Year 2000 International Research Conference on Social Security, 26 September 2000, Helsinki. The views expressed as well as any remaining shortcomings are, of course, our own responsibility. This research is part of Leiden Social Security Incidence Project, which is supported by a grant of Reaal Verzekering NV.

1.   Several studies try, however, to overcome the cross-country data-differences. See e.g.,, Dollar and Kraay (2000). The advanced econometric procedure used in their paper does not generate very precise estimates for the adjustments needed (see the authors' note 8). Atkinson and Brandolini (1999) therefore criticized these types of adjustments and this type of large "secondary" datasets.

2.   Presently, there are a few countries for which panel data have been collected for ten years or more. Fully comparable data are available only for the United States, Germany, and the Netherlands and only for a few data years (1985-89). Nevertheless, the approach by Headey et al. (1997) seems an attractive route in this kind of empirical research.

3.   It is very useful for measuring differences in inequality at a point in time, but is less well suited for measuring changes in inequality over time across countries (Smeeding, 2000). Ideally, data collection on income inequality is both consistent over time and

across countries. However, such a project is daunting at this time (Atkinson et al., 2000: 1). In assessing trends across countries one should be aware of noisy data due to definitional differences in income, definitional differences in population coverage (immigrants), differences in survey collections practices, and differences in periodicity related to the business cycle (Smeeding, 2000: 214-219).

4.   We do not review conceptual and measurement issues that should be addressed in any cross national comparison of survey-based household income data (e.g., the definition of income, the unit of analysis, income sharing rules, the period of analysis, and income data quality and measurement errors), although some of this issues are addressed in the fourth section.

5.   On the other hand, the increases of real disposable income of social security beneficiaries had been large in the 1970s.

6.   An equivalence scale is a function that calculates adjusted income from income and a vector of household characteristics (Figini, 1998). The general form of these equivalence scales is given by the following expression: $W = D / S^E$, where W is adjusted income, D is income (disposable income), S is size (number of persons in households) and E is equivalence elasticity. E varies between 0 and 1. The larger E, the smaller are the economies of scale assumed by the equivalence scales. Equivalence scales range from E=0 (no adjustment or full economics of scale) to E=1 (zero economies of scale). Between these extremes, the range of values used in different studies is very large, strongly affecting measured inequality. It has been shown that, within a wide range, choice of equivalence scales affects international comparisons of income inequality to a wide extend. Alternatively, adjustment methods would definitely affect the ranking of countries, although the broad pattern remains the same (Atkinson et al., 1995: 52).

7.   See, for example, Dalton (1936), Musgrave and Thin (1948), Gillespie (1965), Kakwani (1977a, 1977b), Reynolds and Smolenskey (1977), Kiefer (1984) and Silber (1994), and more recent analyses based on the Luxembourg Income Study database (some of them are also listed in our references). See Smolensky et al. (1987) for a critical survey of efforts to measure budget incidence.

8.   This is consistent with other research we did, see Caminada and Goudswaard (1996).

9.   The growth in the number of one-person households since 1981 has made the non-adjusted distribution of disposable household income more unequal (Trimp, 1999 and Social en Culturel Planbureau, 1998: 109).

10. See, for example, Gelauff and Graafland (1994, chapter 10 on "Cutting Back the Welfare State").

References

Atkinson, A. B., Rainwater, L., and Smeeding, T. M. (1995). "Income Distribution in OECD Countries: Evidence from the Luxembourg Income Study." *OECD Social Policy Studies* 18, Paris: OECD.

Atkinson, A. B. (1996). "Explaining the Distribution of Income." In Hill, J. (ed.), *New Inequalities*. Cambridge: Cambridge University Press.

___. (2000). "The Changing Distribution of Income: Evidence and Explanation." *German Economic Review,* 1 (1), 3-18.

Atkinson, A. B., and Brandolini, A. (1999). *Promise and Pitfalls in the Use of "Secondary" Data-Sets: Income Inequality in OECD Countries*. Oxford: Nuffield College, and Rome: Banca d'Italia.

Atkinson, A. B., Brandolini, A., van der Laan, P., and Smeeding, T. M. (2000). Producing Time Series Data for Income Distribution: Sources, Methods, and Techniques. Paper prepared for the 26th General Conference of The International Association for Research in Income and Wealth. Cracow, Poland, 27 August-2 September.

Bovenberg, A. L. (2000). "Reforming Social Insurance in the Netherlands." *International Tax and Public Finance,* 7 (3), 345-371.

Caminada, K., and Goudswaard, K. P. (1996). "Progression and Revenue Effects of Income Tax Reform." *International Tax and Public Finance,* 3 (1), 57-66.

Dalton, H. (1936). *Principles of Public Finance*, third edition, London: George Routledge and Sons.

De Kleijn, J. P. (1998). "Inkomensverdeling, 1996" (Income Distribution 1996). *Sociaal-economische maandstatistiek,* 15 (3), 18-22 and 75-85.

Dollar, D., and Kraay, A. (2000). *Growth is Good for the Poor.* World Bank, Development Research Group, Washington, D. C.: World Bank.

Duclos, J.-Y. (2000). "Gini Indices and Redistribution of Income." *International Tax and Public Finance,* 7 (2), 141-162.

Ervik, R. (1998). *The Redistributive Aim of Social Policy: A Comparative Analysis of Taxes, Tax Expenditure Transfers and Direct Transfers in Eight Countries.* LIS Working Paper Series No. 184, Luxembourg: Luxembourg Income Study.

Figini, P. (1998). *Inequality Measures, Equivalence Scales and Adjustment for Household Size and Composition.* LIS Working Paper Series No. 185, Luxembourg: Luxembourg Income Study.

Gelauff, G. M. M., and Graafland, J. J. (1994). *Modelling Welfare State Reform.* Amsterdam: Elsevier Science.

Gillespie, W. I. (1965). "Effects of Public Expenditures on the Distribution of Income." In R. Musgrave (ed.), *Essays in Fiscal Federalism.* Washington, D.C.: The Brookings Institution.

Gottschalk, P., Gustafsson, B., and Palmer, E. (eds.) (1997). *Changing Patterns in the Distribution of Economic Welfare.* Cambridge: Cambridge University Press.

Gottschalk, P., and Smeeding, T. M. (1997). "Cross-National Comparisons of Earnings and Income Inequality." *Journal of Economic Literature,* 35 (June), 633-687.

___. (1998). *Empirical Evidence on Income Inequality in Industrialized Countries.* LIS Working Paper Series 54 (revised), Luxembourg: Luxembourg Income Study.

___. (2000). "Empirical Evidence on Income Inequality in Industrialized Countries." In Atkinson, A. B., and Bourguignon, F. (eds.), *Handbook of Income Distribution*, New York: Elsevier-North Holland Publishers, Vol. 1, 262-307.

Gustafsson, B. A., and Johansson, M. (1999). "In Search of Smoking Guns: What Makes Income Inequality Vary over Time in Different Countries?" *American Sociological Review*, 64 (4), 585-606.

Headey, B., Goodin, R. E., Muffels, R., and Dirven, H.-J. (1997). "Welfare Over Time: Three Worlds of Welfare Capitalism in Panel Perspective." *Journal of Public Policy,* 17 (3), 329-359.

Jeurissen, P. C. J. (1995). "Robin Hood in Nederland" (Robin Hood in the Netherlands). *Sociaal-economische maandstatistiek,* 12 (4), 17-21.

Kakwani, N. C. (1977a). "Measurement of Tax Progressivity: An International Comparison." *Economic Journal,* 87, 71-80.

___. (1977b). "Applications of Lorenz Curves in Economic Analysis." *Econo-metrica,* 45 (3), 719-727.

___. (1986). *Analyzing Redistribution Policies.* Cambridge: Cambridge University Press.

Kiefer, D. W. (1984). "Distributional Tax Progressivity Indexes." *National Tax Journal,* 37, 497-513.

Ministry of Social Affairs. (1995). *Sociale Nota 1996.* The Hague: Sdu Publishers.

___. (1999). *Sociale Nota 2000.* The Hague: Sdu Publishers.

Musgrave, R. A., and Thin, T. (1948). "Income Tax Progression, 1929-1948." *Journal of Political Economy,* 56, 498-514.

Musgrave, R. A., Case, K. E., and Leonard, H. B. (1974). "The Distribution of Fiscal Burdens and Benefits." *Public Finance Quarterly,* (2), July, 259-311.

Odink, J. G. (1985). *Inkomensherverdeling-enkele aspecten van de inkomensherverdeling door de overheid in Nederland.* Groningen: Wolters-Noordhoff.

Reynolds, M., and Smolensky, E. (1977). "Post Fisc Distributions of Income 1950, 1961, and 1970." *Public Finance Quarterly,* 5, 419-438.

Ringen, S. (1991). "Households, Standard of Living and Inequality." *Review of Income and Wealth,* 37, 1-13.

Ruiz-Huerta, J., Martínez, R., and Ayala, L. (1999). *Inequality, Growth and Welfare: An International Comparison.* LIS Working Paper Series 215, Luxembourg: Luxembourg Income Study.

Schiepers, J. M. P. (1998). "Equivalentiefactoren: methode en belangrijkste uitkomsten'" (Equivalence Scales for the Netherlands: Methodology and Main Results). In CBS *Jaarboek Welvaartsverdeling 1998.* Deventer: Kluwer/CBS, 117-121.

Silber, J. (1994). "Income Distribution, Tax Structure, and the Measurement of Tax Progressivity." *Public Finance Quarterly,* 22 (1), 86-102.

Smeeding, T. M. (2000). "Changing Income Inequality in OECD Countries: Updated Results from the Luxembourg Income Study (LIS)." In Hauser, R., and Becker, I. (eds.), *The Personal Distribution of Income in an International Perspective.* Berlin: Springer-Verlag, 205-224.

Smolensky, E., Hoyt, W., and Danziger, S. (1987). "A Critical Survey of Efforts to Measure Budget Incidence." In van de Kar, H. M., and Wolfe, B. L. (eds.), *The Relevance of Public Finance for Policy-Making*, Proceedings of the IIFP Congress 1985, Detroit, 165-179.

Sociaal en Cultureel Planbureau. (1998). *Sociaal en Cultureel Rapport 1998. 25 jaar sociale verandering* (Social Cultural Report 1998). Rijswijk: SCP.

Statistics Netherlands. (1999). "Inkomensverdeling 1977-1997. Tabellen" (Income Distribution 1977-1999. Tables). *Sociaal-economische maandstatistiek,* 16 (5), 107-119.

Trimp, L. (1993). "Inkomens van huishoudens, 1977-1990" (Income of Households, 1977-1990). *Sociaal-economische maandstatistiek,* 10 (7), 16-18.

___. (1999). "Inkomensverdeling 1977-1997" (Income Distribution 1977-1997). *Sociaal-economische maandstatistiek,* 16 (5), 21-27.

Whiteford, P. (1995). "The Use of Replacement Rates in International Comparisons of Benefit Systems." *International Social Security Review,* 48 (2), 3-30.

Part 3

Migration

10

Non-Discrimination, Free Movement, and Social Citizenship in Europe: Contrasting Provisions for EU Nationals and Asylum-Seekers

Deborah Mabbett and Helen Bolderson

In the extensive literature on the effects of "globalization" on the welfare state, the analysis of the movement of people has developed quite differently to the analysis of the impact of free trade in goods and services and free movement of capital. The study of migration is dominated by political rather than economic language: the concept of citizenship, the continuing significance of nationalism (Bommes and Geddes, 2000). There are several obvious reasons why the economic pressures that count so highly in the study of globalization play a lesser role in understanding labor movement. There has been no general liberalization of labor movement analogous to the freer movement of capital. States do not conceive of there being unmitigated benefits from labor inflow, whereas they compete to attract capital. Labor movement is regulated within a more manifestly political framework than capital movement. While capital movement is as much a political as an economic phenomenon, the negotiation between states, which underpins the globalization of capital markets, is much less overt and transparent than that relating to labor.

Nonetheless, migration can be expected to have significant economic effects. One important argument is that unrestricted migration is liable to have negative effects on welfare provision because, if people can move freely, states offering high levels of provision will be "welfare magnets." The belief that these effects are significant, and that free movement can therefore compromise states' ability to implement their preferred welfare policies, appears to have motivated the inclusion of a provision permitting states to discriminate against recent arrivals in the 1996 U.S. welfare reform (Schram and Beer, 1999). (This provision has since been struck down as unconstitutional by the Supreme Court.)

Applied to Europe, the same arguments would suggest that freedom of movement for people will further reduce the sovereignty of European welfare states, already gravely compromised by the development of a single market in goods and services and the free movement of capital. However, the lessons to be drawn from the U.S. case are rather complicated. It is notable that discrimination against recent arrivals in U.S. states was part of a package of measures to restrict access to welfare provision more generally. Discrimination was, therefore, part of an intensification of "entitlement policing" (Klausen, 1995). This leads us to examine the relationship between rules that discriminate against migrants and other entitlement rules, such as contribution requirements, category membership rules, and needs and means tests. We suggest that, contrary to the U.S. case, these entitlement rules can incorporate fundamental legitimating principles of social policy that are consistent with non-discrimination and do not have to be supported by the exclusion of migrants. We argue against drawing inevitable connections between the exclusion of migrants, the maintenance of social solidarity, and the legitimization of welfare provision. We suggest that the symbolic politics of citizenship and belonging are a long way from the realities of administrative control over the allocation of resources through social security. The politics of social solidarity have only a tenuous connection with the administrative and judicial principles and practices affecting migrants' access to social security.

This chapter is organized as follows. First, the current coordination arrangements governing migrants' access to social security are described briefly. We show that the insurance nature of many benefits has provided a relatively uncontentious basis for the coordination of social security provision for migrants. The main aspect that has caused contention concerns access to non-contributory benefits. However, the issues that arise relate primarily to the exportability of these benefits, rather than from claiming by resident non-nationals.

We then turn to examine the situation of non-nationals who stay in, and endeavor to claim benefits from, the host state, rather than returning to their home state. There are long-standing provisions on the rights of migrant workers, but less clarity about the rights of those who have ceased working or have never worked in the host state. Access to benefits may be conditional on obtaining a particular legal residence status, and this may be refused, delayed or terminated in certain circumstances. The European Court of Justice (ECJ) appears to be inclined to establish a "Community concept" of residence for benefit purposes which is based on the facts of a person's living arrangements rather than the legal rules prevailing in each member state. Combined with the extension of the principle of non-discrimination from workers to all EU nationals, this would remove the main channels by which states currently prevent non-nationals from claiming social benefits.

In the last section, we contrast the situation of asylum-seekers in Europe with that of EU nationals. European states have put forward "welfare magnet" arguments to justify the exclusion of asylum-seekers from mainstream social provision in their country of stay. These limitations on access to welfare have been accompanied by (rather than being an alternative to) measures to constrain asylum-seekers' freedom of movement. Furthermore, there are some signs of a competitive "race to the bottom" in states' provisions for asylum-seekers, which suggests that some harmonization might be in member states' interests.

Our discussion is based on the legal position in Europe in mid-2000. Some elements are evolving rapidly, particularly policy towards asylum-seekers, both in the member states and at the European level. The "Community concept" of residence is still far from being established, and the application of the principle of non-discrimination to non-workers rests on just a few cases. There may be new moves in the future to limit EU migrants' access to benefits in their country of stay and to extend home state responsibility, but we think that the trends outlined in the discussion are those most likely to be followed.

Migration and Benefits in the European Economic Community (EEC)

The two main regulations relating to access to social benefits in Europe, Regulations 1612/68 and 1408/71, were formulated to meet concerns related to the movement of workers. They reinforced the central aim of promoting economic integration by enabling nationals of EEC states to take up work anywhere in the community. Their primary concerns were to prevent exploitation of migrant workers by ensuring that their pay and conditions were the same as those of national workers, and to ensure that migrant workers did not lose access to benefits through moving around. There were particular issues about the relationship between residence and eligibility for benefits, as migrant workers were seen as vulnerable to losing benefits through losing, or giving up, residence. One solution was to make some benefits exportable. The other solution was to protect workers' right to remain in the host state. Regulation 1251/70 "on the right of workers to remain in the territory of a Member State after having been employed in that state" offered a degree of protection.

In practice, exportability assumed primary importance as a way of protecting workers' rights, relative to regulation of the right to residence. One explanation is that migrant workers often wanted to export their benefits and return to their home state. Another is that the right to residence for non-nationals who were not currently employed was not very secure, and remains somewhat contested (Veil, 1997: 22). Since nationals have an undisputed right of residence, while non-nationals have to establish their claim, it follows that residence requirements in the benefit system can operate as implicit nationality requirements. Alert to indirect discrimination against non-nationals, the European Court of Justice has tended to view residence requirements with suspicion, and has promoted the exportability of benefits.

Exportability also fitted well with the contributory basis of the social security systems of the main host states for migrant workers. The contributory principle embodies the idea that the worker earns the right to benefit through economic participation. It was natural, given the emphasis on free movement of labor, to focus on rights acquired through employment. The emphasis on contribution enabled those rights to be detached from other bases of social obligation and claimed outside the social context of the national social security system. Furthermore, despite the technical problems involved in aggregating rights and preventing overlapping, the contribution basis made benefits divisible, so that claims could be made and allocated among several states.

A further attraction of the contributory principle was that it was well suited to resolving the allocation of social security responsibilities when the pattern of migration was highly asymmetrical. Given unequal levels of development in the member states and a strong unidirectional pattern of migration for employment purposes, it would be hard for the states to agree to pay benefits to each other's nationals as if they were their own ("common citizenship"). A wealthy host state would fear an influx of migrants claiming benefits (instead of working), while the reciprocal possibility of its nationals claiming in poorer, less developed states would be of little value. The export of contributory benefits does involve an asymmetrical flow of payments towards the poorer states that supply migrant workers, but this is acceptable to richer states as it is based on the work activity of the poorer states' nationals.

The same logic meant that, in bilateral agreements, wealthier states tend to resist the export of "unearned" (non-contributory) benefits. Issues also arose about benefits linked to the cost of living in the host state, given that living costs were generally lower in the poorer home states which provided most migrant workers. Both these considerations led host states to divide benefits between insurance and assistance, or, more precisely, to calculate an amount owing on the basis of contributions paid ("insurance") which is exportable, but deny the migrant benefits related to the cost of living in the host country ("assistance").

One reading of Regulation 1408/71 is that it accepted the utility of the insurance-assistance distinction, and merely set out to codify and standardize a practice that was already current in a number of bilateral agreements. It required workers to contribute to the social security schemes of their state of employment (with the exception of "posted" workers, engaged temporarily in another state) and it assigned to the state or states of employment the responsibility for paying social security to the worker when he or she became eligible. It only applied to social security; social assistance was excluded. We can see this as a minimal and undemanding approach to the coordination of social security. It is firmly attached to its economic base (mobility of workers) and the use of the contributory principle surmounts issues about the extent of social solidarity between the worker and the host state.

However, the coordinating provisions have developed considerably beyond this minimal basis. In a succession of decisions, the ECJ expanded the rights acquired by workers beyond a narrow economic focus on the rights that workers might be said to have earned through employment. The ECJ was faced with questions about the treatment of social security rights that accrued, not to workers specifically, but to people generally. For example, a right to a minimum pension may accrue to a worker through the "entry point" of membership of a social insurance scheme, while the same right may accrue to a non-worker through a different entry point, such as a residence requirement. The question that then arose was whether residence requirements for such provisions could be struck down, enabling migrant workers to export the minimum pension of the state of employment.

The gist of the case law is that the ECJ has answered "yes" to this question. In the leading case of *Frilli* and the cases that followed it, the Court looked in effect to make exportable all benefits that would accrue to a resident worker with the same work history and contributions record as the migrant worker. These could include benefits with a "double function," covering those (residents) who had not worked as well as those who had. In particular, supplements to insurance benefits, which are intended to ensure that workers with inadequate contributions have a sufficient pension to live on in their retirement, were deemed exportable (Steiner 1985).

In interpreting the range of exportable benefits expansively and the social assistance exemption restrictively, the ECJ established a wide social, as opposed to narrowly economic, basis for the rights of migrants. The Court defined a social security benefit, in contrast to "social assistance" (excluded by Art 4(4) of Reg. 1408/71) as "a benefit payable by virtue of a situation that has been legally defined, without any individual and discretionary assessment of personal needs." The fact that a benefit was tax-financed did not exclude it from social security; nor did means-testing, provided that the test was applied in a sufficiently non-discretionary, rule-based way to be characterized as a social right.

One way of explaining the Court's approach is that its primary concern was with countering economic inequality between states. Exportability served to achieve a flow of transfers from richer to poorer states. Arguably this flow compensated the poorer states for the costs of supporting the young and old, reducing the exploitation inherent in the use of working-age labor by the richer states. However, the justice of this inter-state redistribution was not always accompanied by resilient legitimacy for the patterns of redistribution that resulted for individuals. Benefits intended for the most needy in the host community could be exported by some of the more wealthy in the home community. Furthermore, the coordination rules were not always helpful to the development of social policy in the home states. For example, in the case of *Stinco and Panfilo* (Case C-132/96, ECJ 24 September 1998), the applicants argued that the applicable amount for calculating the Italian share of their pension should be the minimum pension in Italy rather than a lower amount based on their contributions. They won, despite the fact that, once pro-rata pensions from Britain and France were added in, their total pensions were in excess of the Italian minimum pension. The Court applied a principle of contribution to a benefit based on needs, and the applicants won benefit payments that bore no connection to the needs standard. The result was that Italian taxpayers had to pay two Italian pensioners more than they "need" (and more than the Italian legislature intended).

New provisions introduced in 1992 (Reg. 1247/92) enabled states to put limits on the export of non-contributory benefits. This regulation amended Articles 4 and 10 of Reg. 1408/71 by creating a separate category of non-contributory social security benefits that would not be exportable. Instead, such benefits would be granted by and at the expense of the institution of the place of residence. The amendment made a succession of provisions designed to ensure that the benefits could be accessed by residents who may recently have migrated from another state, for example by requiring that periods of employment or residence completed in other member states shall be treated as if they were in the current state of residence. In effect, the *quid pro quo* of allowing a state to refuse to export a benefit is that it must award the benefit to its residents who have lived and worked in other states.

The discussion so far has indicated the utility of relying on contribution and exportability in coordination in the early stages of European integration. However, times have changed in at least two important ways. First, the main host states in the "guest worker" era had substantial contributory systems, and migrant workers participated in these. Nowadays, increasing numbers of people (both migrants and non-migrants) do not belong to contributory systems, whether because of unemployment, low-waged work in unregulated areas, or use of the "posted worker" exemption. Second, the pattern of migration was both clear and asymmetric, being dominated by guest workers. Now, patterns are more complex. Economic inequality between the states has fallen, making the rough and ready justice of maximizing exportability less acceptable. Furthermore, guest workers did not always seek to return to their home state as keenly as the model assumed, and other migration patterns have emerged, including migration by non-workers (e.g., retirement by northern Europeans to southern Europe). More generally, a social security coordination system based, fundamentally, on economic citizenship sits increasingly uneasily alongside wider efforts to expand the social dimension of European citizenship.

All these factors suggest that less reliance on exportability and more host state responsibility in the social security coordination arrangements could be desirable. However, such a move arouses some major fears and concerns. First, the coordination arrangements for insurance-based systems have enjoyed relatively high legitimacy and acceptability, as they rest on economic participation rather than social solidarity. The legitimacy of host state responsibility for non-nationals may be more vulnerable to challenge. Second, host states may try to avoid responsibility, particularly by denying resident status to claimants who are not their own nationals, since only nationals have an undisputed right of residence.

These two issues are clearly connected by the theme of nationalism. If social solidarity is a bond between nationals, then extension of welfare entitlements to non-nationals may undermine solidarity. States may endeavor to secure the bonds of solidarity by excluding non-nationals, which they can do indirectly by denying them resident status. From this perspective, the extension of host state responsibility might bring to the surface underlying nationalistic tensions in European welfare states.

However, there is a great gulf between rhetoric and reality in welfare state policy as it relates to issues of migration and national identity. The rhetoric of the welfare state invokes the solidarity of the national community, yet explicit nationality requirements are not widespread in social security (Roberts and Bolderson, 1999; Guiraudon, 2000). As Guiraudon argues, this is partly the result of judicial intervention; we also see administrative aims and constraints playing a part. In the next section, we show that host state responsibility is a resilient approach to coordination from a social policy perspective, and we suggest some reasons why this approach may prevail against political concerns.

Extending Host State Responsibility

From a social policy perspective, the principle that a state should be responsible for the provision of social benefits to the people who live in it has much to recommend it. Most obviously, as already mentioned, needs are affected by the claimant's place of residence, as the cost of living varies between states. Needs may also be affected by differences in the structure of the welfare state, for example reflecting the combination of cash benefits and services in kind adopted by the state. Furthermore, the ability of the paying state to maintain administrative controls is enhanced by locational proximity, enabling the administration to check on qualifying conditions such as job search, disability, the means of other household members and the application of rules about employment and other income. Administration by the agencies of another state is rarely satisfactory to the paying state, as the agent lacks incentives to invest resources in administrative control.

These points are illustrated by the developments that led to the 1992 amendment to the coordination rules. One of the key preceding events was a decision by the ECJ on several joined cases in which Italian nationals won the right to export the French minimum pension (*Giletti, Giardini, Tampan and Severini* ([1987] ECR 955)). One could say that the outcome was unacceptable to France because it meant that French taxpayers were subsidizing Italian pensioners, but we would argue that the problems generated by the Court's approach are better understood as problems of conflicting allocative principles, not as problems of nationality. After all, the applicants had been in receipt of the minimum pension when they resided in France, without any objection from the French authorities that, as Italians, they should not call on French communal solidarity. By contrast, France resisted the export of the benefits because it cut across the administrative requirements of needs- and means-testing, and because the amount of the French minimum pension bore no necessary relationship to the minimum necessary for an adequate living standard in Italy.

While the social policy rationale for the 1992 amendment would seem to be sound, it relies on migrants being able to establish full rights of residence in the place where they live. For host state responsibility to be consistent with free movement in Europe, some of the current restrictions limiting migrants' legal residence status have to be resolved. The main rights of residence of nationals of EU member states are set out in Directive 68/360/EEC "on the abolition of restrictions on movement and residence within the Community for workers of Member States and their families." This directive establishes a procedure whereby a worker holding a confirmation of engagement or a certificate of employment must be given a residence permit. Once a person is employed and resident, he or she can claim access to all the "social advantages" that a national worker could access (Reg. 1612/68). This provision is restricted to workers.

Despite some expansive interpretations by the ECJ of the concept of a "worker," the ability of people without a contract of employment to obtain access to social provisions is limited. Even within the economic sphere, there are problems with the situation of job-seekers. On one hand, Community law establishes the right of EU citizens to travel in search of work; on the other, it makes limited provision for their means of support. This issue was considered in detail by the Veil Panel on the free movement of persons (Veil, 1997). The approach adopted by the Veil Panel was to propose extension of the current system for free movement of tourists and other travelers. While a worker becomes part of the social system of the employing state, tourists and other travelers exercising the right of free movement remain attached to their state of permanent residence. Coordination arrangements for providing health care and other urgent aid, chargeable to the home state, apply to stays of up to three months. The Veil Panel proposed that the unrestrained right of community nationals to stay in another member state should be extended from three months to a year, but, instead of creating new benefit obligations for the host state, Veil favored implementation of a Commission proposal to amend Reg. 1408/71 to allow the export of unemployment benefit for up to one year (Veil, 1997: 23). The common theme of the Veil proposals is that freedom of movement is exercised without creating the opportunity to claim benefits from the host state.

The previous discussion suggests several reasons why the Veil approach has not been implemented. The export of unemployment benefits for long periods presents major problems of administrative control for the paying state, which has to rely on the host state's agencies to check that the claimant is actively seeking and available for work. The Veil approach does not resolve the tension between free movement and benefit entitlement for those job-seekers who do not have exportable benefit rights (who would rely on social assistance in their home state). Furthermore, mobile workers may face problems establishing which state should be deemed to be their home state, and this may mean that they have to have recourse to their state of nationality, thereby heightening the importance of nationality in the coordination arrangements.

The ECJ has rejected some attempts to condition rights of residence on exclusion from claiming benefits. For example, in *Antonissen* (Case C-292/89 ([1991] ECR I-745), a Belgian national resisted deportation from the UK, claiming that he had the right to reside in the UK as a job-seeker under Community law. The UK government and the Commission argued that the right of residence of those seeking work was subject to time limits. While no time limit was established in European regulations, the Commission drew attention to the provision in Reg. 1408/71 that unemployment benefits could be exported for three months as both confirming that a work-seeker has the right to seek work in another state and indicating the possible duration of this search. In other words, the exportability of unemployment benefits could be seen as underpinning the right of temporary residence, given that an unemployed person is likely to be reliant on social security benefits. However, the Court rejected this attempt to link the duration of the right of residence to the duration for which unemployment benefits could be exported, and accepted the Advocate General's view that there was no "necessary legal connection" between the availability of an exportable unemployment benefit and the right of residence.

The position of non-workers who are not seeking work is different again. Directive 90/365/EEC expanded the rights of this group, but it, nonetheless, provides that non-workers can be required by the host state to establish that they have adequate means of support before a residence permit is granted.

This creates a conditional freedom of residence which is open to, for example, pensioners with adequate exportable benefits. One reason for the ECJ to promote and defend exportability is, therefore, that it enhances citizens' effective freedom of choice of residence. However, in *Snares'* case, the ECJ itself recognized the limitations of this approach.

Snares (Case C-20/96, ECJ 4 Nov 1997) was a British man who became disabled due to an accident and sought to move to Spain to live with his mother, who could care for him. Snares' disability entitled him to an insurance-based benefit (Incapacity benefit, IB) and a non-contributory benefit (Disability Living Allowance, DLA). Snares found that he could export IB but not DLA, which was classed as a non-exportable benefit under Regulation 1247/92. If IB had been less than the minimum income Snares needed in Spain, the Spanish authorities would be able to deny him residence. Snares' lawyers argued that Regulation 1247/92 contravened the principle of free movement, as Snares was more likely to have a sufficient income in Spain if he could export DLA as well as IB. However, the ECJ noted that, in the absence of harmonized benefit rates across the EU, IB might be adequate by itself, or indeed IB plus DLA might be inadequate. Exportability was neither a necessary nor a sufficient condition to protect Snares' right of residence in another member state. In effect, the ECJ recognized that exportability is a poor basis on which to establish freedom of residence, compared with more direct routes such as extended rights of family unification.

In practice, the idea that a state can prevent non-national non-workers becoming dependent on its welfare system will not be workable in many cases. Suppose, for example, that Snares did join his mother, and his exportable benefits provided an adequate income. At some later stage, Snares' condition could worsen or his mother's circumstances could change. The family's residence status would then come into question: was their residence permanent or temporary, conditional or not? Could Spain press them to return to the UK?

Some insight into the ECJ's likely answer to this question comes from the decision in *Martinez Sala* (Case C-85/96, ECJ 12 May 1998). In this case, the Court struck down an attempt by the German authorities to deny a benefit to a Spanish national because she did not have the requisite residence permit. The substantive fact that Martinez Sala was resident was not disputed. She had lived in Germany since 1968, and held residence permits until 1984. From 1984 to 1994, the authorities provided only documents certifying that she had applied for extension of her residence permit, so that technically she was without a permit, although legally resident. The Court held that it was discriminatory to require resident non-nationals to have a document that was not required of resident nationals. A significant feature of the case was that the Court found that Martinez Sala could benefit from the non-discrimination provisions of the EC Treaty because she was a citizen of the Union, although not a worker.

Commentators on the case have agreed that one of its problematic features is that the fact of Martinez Sala's residence was not disputed, so the Court did not get the opportunity to set out its views on how residence should be established and to develop the idea of a "Community concept" of residence that could be detached from the legal procedures of each state. However, in *Swaddling* (Case C-90/97, ECJ 25 Feb 1999), the ECJ ruled that member states were not free to make up their own definitions of residence for benefit purposes. The Court held that, since the amendment of Reg. 1408/71 in 1992, residence has become a crucial factor in the coordination system for social security, and it followed that it cannot be acceptable to have "marked differences in the meaning ascribed by the various national systems to the concept of residence. [...] [T]he concept of residence is a Community notion and as such its meaning cannot be adapted to suit the unilateral and uncoordinated preferences of the various national systems" (Opinion of Advocate General Saggio, 29 September 1998, paras. 15-16).

The decision in Swaddling challenged the operation of the "habitual residence test," introduced by the Conservative government in the UK with the intention of preventing recent arrivals in the country from claiming Income Support. The test proved to be very difficult to administer, as it involved a complex weighing-up of factors to determine whether a person was resident or not, and therefore proved very difficult to apply consistently (Adler, 1995). Furthermore, the test became a political embarrassment. To comply with the principle of non-discrimination, the test applied to returning British nationals (such as Swaddling) as well as non-nationals, and many British nationals failed the test.

Notwithstanding the decision in Swaddling, the EU is still some way from establishing a Community concept of residence. However, the outlines of a factual test of whether a person lives in a state are beginning to emerge, and the ECJ's unwillingness to allow member states to operate forms of second-class citizenship for nationals of other member states on their territories is evident. We have argued that there is a strong basis in social policy for the principle that each state should have responsibility for those living on its territory, but this principle is only operable if the question of where a person is living is answered by looking at their actual conditions, not at their legal status as residents under each state's distinctive and different laws.

The Implications of Free Movement and Non-Discrimination

The central idea of welfare magnet theory is that states offering generous benefits attract poor migrants. The previous discussion indicated that there have been two major barriers to welfare magnet processes in Europe. First, the most generous benefits are insurance-based, requiring migrants to establish a contribution record through employment. Second, non-working migrants cannot freely establish residence in a state other than that of which they are a national. Both these features of the European coordination arrangements are subject to change. More rights to non-contributory benefits have been established for non-workers living outside their state of nationality.

Some commentators have criticized these developments as overreaching the economic foundations of the EU and exposing the welfare provisions of member states to unwarranted pressure. Tomuschat (2000), commenting on the Martinez Sala decision, has argued that access to financial benefits should depend on inclusion in the economic life of the state, and it is therefore fair that non-discriminatory access is confined to workers. This would mean that people seeking financial assistance, who could not claim as workers or family members of workers, would have to reside in their state of nationality. While states might provide for such non-nationals on their own volition and pursuant to international conventions, non-working non-nationals would not have the right to non-discriminatory treatment under Community law.

Tomuschat's analysis accepts the basic idea of welfare magnet theory, that people will be strongly influenced in their decisions on where to live by their benefit entitlement. To the extent that he envisages that people might stay on in a state despite being denied benefits, he argues that it is for each state to find its own preferred solution to this problem. In practice, the European states are committed to providing social assistance to non-nationals under the European Convention on Social and Medical Assistance, adopted by the Council of Europe in 1953, and Martinez Sala received assistance under this measure (the case arose because she was denied child benefits).

O'Leary (1999), commenting on the same case, adopted the opposite value position, that the wide application of EU non-discrimination provisions is desirable. Her concern was that the principle of non-discrimination was being extended without sufficient support in Union law for freedom of residence. She feared that, if all residents have the rights accorded to Martinez Sala, member states may become more active in "chas[ing]...from their territories other states' nationals who are not workers and are not covered by the other residence directives" (1999: 78). In other words, if states are unable to deny migrants equal access to benefits, they might seek to close the doors of migration as an alternative "safeguard" against welfare magnetism. Tomuschat also concluded that member states are liable to respond to the Martinez Sala decision by administering residence controls more rigorously.

In our view, these predictions are implausible. It is unlikely that member states will revert en masse to a Poor Law regime, whereby paupers are returned to their parish (state) of birth (nationality). States' accession to the European Convention on Social and Medical Assistance signals their acceptance that repatriation, with all that it involves in policing, the use of force and the criminalization of the poor, is an inappropriate instrument against EU nationals (as we show below, quite the opposite situation prevails in the treatment of asylum-seekers). While member states will no doubt defend their powers to prevent recent arrivals gaining resident status, the reality is that states already have to accept people who may exercise claims against their non-contributory social security systems, including job-seekers, workers whose earnings are inadequate to live on, workers who have stayed on after stopping work, and family members of workers. (In another recent German-Spanish case, *Gómez Rivero* (Case C-211/97, ECJ 3 June 1999), the ECJ confirmed the right of a worker's family members to claim benefits, regardless of the social security affiliation of the worker himself.) The importance of the Swaddling and Martinez Sala decisions is that states will be prevented from operating forms of "second class" residency for non-workers, just as Regulation 1612/68 prevents them from treating guest workers as second-class citizens. States do discriminate against non-nationals by differentiating between different classes of residence, but these practices will gradually be challenged so that non-discrimination becomes established in this area as in others.

The developments we envisage are incremental and almost covert, and the institutions promoting them are administrative and judicial, not political. Could there be a political backlash against these developments, and what form might it take? In the USA, the threat that welfare provisions may attract poor immigrants may have fuelled the process of welfare state retrenchment. However, it is notable that measures discriminating against recent arrivals from other states have been introduced within wider packages of retrenchment policies (Schram and Beer, 1999). Far from protecting the welfare state, the exclusion of migrants has been an integral part of a wider attack on it.

Several features of the U.S. case distinguish it from the European situation. The U.S. states provide highly-discretionary social assistance benefits; the main insurance benefits are provided under a uniform Federal scheme. Thus the U.S. experience tells us nothing about the effect of migration on the operation of insurance as a legitimating principle. We have seen that contributory benefits have proved adaptable to the participation of guest workers and the export of benefits. The posted worker issue shows that, far from excluding migrants, host states are concerned to ensure that migrants participate in insurance schemes.

The 1996 welfare reform in the U.S. increased the ability of states to adopt intensified modes of "entitlement policing," particularly through work requirements. Prior to the reform, states had adopted such measures subject to Federal scrutiny, which aimed to ensure that reasonable standards of fairness, consistency and impartiality in administration were maintained. Non-discrimination towards recent arrivals was one of these standards. We have seen that the European coordination rules on social security are concerned with benefits that can be seen as "social rights." Most European states provide a much richer set of social rights than the U.S. states, and the use of the language of rights signifies that, within the European states, principles of fair administration are established. Social security administrations do undertake entitlement policing; however, this policing need not necessarily be arbitrary and discriminatory. On the contrary, some level of policing is necessary to maintain the legitimacy of the social security system, by ensuring that benefits go to those whose circumstances are envisaged and described in the law. Non-discriminatory access for migrants should not threaten the domestic administration of benefits where social rights are firmly established and sufficiently legitimated.

We can summarize our main conclusions as follows. Concern about welfare magnet effects is intensified when migration cannot be controlled administratively, and is, therefore, free to respond to incentives. European states retain formal control over long-term migration (residence) by EU nationals, and forms of second-class residence status are used to discriminate against non-nationals in the provision of benefits. These measures contravene the principle of non-discrimination and will gradually have to be reformed. As this happens, the formal obstacles to welfare magnet effects will be removed. However, states will not chase people from their territories to prevent them achieving residence under a "Community concept," as deportation and repatriation is far too cumbersome and costly. The threat of welfare magnet effects may be used as a political instrument for challenging the legitimacy of the whole welfare state, but this threat will be marginal so long as states can maintain the basic legitimating principles of welfare provision.

Asylum-seekers

In the discussion above, we have seen how the aim of economic integration of the European states has been given social content, primarily through the prohibition on discrimination. This prohibition means that migrants generally enjoy similar social conditions in their state of residence to non-migrants. However, third-country nationals do not have the same rights and protections. The result is an anomalous situation where European law promotes the social integration of one set of strangers (nationals of other EU states) while allowing the persistence of exclusion for another. In this section, we illustrate the different issues affecting non-EU nationals by examining the European dimension of the evolution of policy towards asylum-seekers. The comparison highlights two main differences: the willingness of European states to expend substantial resources in controlling the movement and living arrangements of this group, and their creation of separate and discriminatory welfare provisions, which are then susceptible to competition between states to make these provisions as unattractive as possible.

While all the member states of the EU are subject to the same international obligations, stemming from the 1951 Geneva Convention, they vary both in their interpretations of the Convention (e.g., on the definition of a refugee) and in their reception conditions for asylum-seekers. The provisions made for the care of asylum-seekers in the reception phase may be "inclusionary" or "exclusionary." Inclusionary measures allow asylum-seekers to work, move around and utilize existing welfare systems which are also accessed by the rest of the population. Exclusionary measures ensure the social separation of asylum-seekers through restrictions on employment and accommodation, and by making separate welfare provision. All the member states have exclusionary aspects to their rules and structures for the reception of asylum-seekers. Access to the job market is not generally granted, with the result that most asylum-seekers are dependent on social benefits. Access to these benefits may be linked to stays in reception centers or designated accommodation, so that the conditions of access are not compatible with freedom of movement within the territory of the host state.

The implementation of exclusionary measures became more draconian in the 1990s, notably in two of the main receiving states, Germany (Bank, 2000) and the UK. The UK has recently made the transition from a (more or less) inclusionary system to an exclusionary system. Until 1996 asylum-seekers in the UK were entitled to claim Income Support, the mainstream social assistance benefit for British residents, although at a slightly reduced rate. In 1996 this entitlement became restricted to asylum-seekers who declared their status on arrival ("at port"). Asylum-seekers who declared themselves after arrival were left without protection. More recent legislation (Immigration and Asylum Act 1999) has deprived all asylum-seekers of access to UK social security and replaced it with an entirely separate system of vouchers and accommodation in designated areas.

The UK's moves were justified by its government as means of "deterring" asylum applications and preventing would-be asylum-seekers from seeing it as "soft touch" (Home Office, 1998, para. 1.10; Home Office, 1999, para. 4.20). Generally, it appears that there has been "a tendency towards restriction...arising from deterrence and financial motives" (Bank, 2000; see also European Council of Refugees and Exiles, 1999, para. 3.4 for restrictions that serve as deterrents). The European Commission has drawn attention to potentially competitive aspects of member states' deterrence of asylum-seekers. It notes that the variation "in the extent and standard of reception arrangements in the Member States...encourages some of those applying for the status of refugees either to choose the Member States which appear to offer the best reception conditions or move from one Member State to another" (European Commission, 2000a: 2).

It is arguable that competition between states to deter asylum-seekers may result in an outcome which is worse for everyone than the policy which would be adopted in the absence of competition (e.g., if there was only one state giving asylum). Competition may mean that each state adopts a suboptimal level of provision because of its "fear" of the competitive advantage that other states might achieve by undercutting it. Two sub-optimal aspects of exclusion, from the host state's point of view, are that it is administratively expensive and may contribute to social tension. Exclusion is more likely than inclusion to lead to tension and alienation between asylum-seekers and local communities, as it is in the very nature of exclusionary policies that asylum-seekers will not be able to integrate into the community.

However, states also have internal, non-competitive motives for the adoption of exclusionary policies. One such motive is that exclusion and prevention of social integration might facilitate the eventual expulsion of asylum-seekers, by making it easier to locate them when their applications are turned down. Another motive for the creation of separate systems of social provision may be that separation makes it possible for provision to be adapted and cut without affecting the main system, minimizing the political response to any cuts.

If member states are subject to strong competitive pressures in their policies towards asylum-seekers, it would follow that they might see benefits from cooperation and harmonization of policies. The Commission's view is that such competition exists and that therefore there is a justification for Community action. The Amsterdam Treaty created an opportunity for the harmonization of treatment of asylum-seekers by moving asylum and immigration matters from the intergovernmental (third) pillar to the sphere of community action (the first pillar) (Stetter, 2000; Kuijper, 2000). At a special meeting of the European Council on justice and home affairs in Tampere in October 1999, heads of state reaffirmed their respect for people's absolute right to seek asylum and agreed to move "towards establishing a common European asylum system based on the full and inclusive application of the Geneva Convention" (European Commission, 2000b). The Tampere meeting's short-term aim was to establish common standards for the fair and efficient adjudication of asylum claims, common minimum conditions of reception, and the approximation of rules on the recognition and content of refugee status (para. 14). The longer-term aim was that "Community rules should lead to a common asylum procedure and a uniform status for those who are granted asylum valid throughout the Union" (para. 15). Furthermore, the Commission was "invited to explore the possibilities [.. for..] some form of financial reserve available in situations of mass influx of refugees for temporary protection" (para. 16).

The main initiative of the Commission came in February 2000 with a proposal for a European Refugee Fund. The Fund would be activated in situations where temporary protection for large groups of refugees is called for. The proposal "seeks to redress the balance between the efforts of the Member States in matters of asylum, by creating a system for dividing resources in proportion to the burden of expenditure on each Member State, while at the same time encouraging those member States with the least developed infrastructure and services for asylum and refugees to make good the disparities in this area" (European Commission, 2000a). As noted above, the Commission suggested that there was a competitive element in the variation in reception standards in member states. The creation of a Refugee Fund would ameliorate competitive externalities, as those states receiving large numbers of people would be financially assisted. The Commission has proposed that minimum standards would be set, implying that competition has gone too far if some conditions now fall below these standards. The creation of a fund signals the possibility of raising standards where they are poorest.

We can see that the existence of significant externalities in the reception of asylum-seekers may mean that member states are willing to accept harmonization (and contribute to the proposed fund), whereas the externalities arising from the movement of EU nationals, discussed in previous sections, are not sufficiently strong to create incentives for harmonization. Furthermore, the existence of separate, exclusionary provisions for asylum-seekers within each state increases the prospects for a harmonized asylum policy in Europe. If member states allowed asylum-seekers access to work and social benefits on the same basis as residents, there would be substantial differences between states in the opportunities and benefits available. The separation of asylum provision means that asylum policies can be more easily harmonized while mainstream provisions remain diverse. Such harmonization would also mean that the segmentation of domestic welfare would be institutionalized, with one area under European competence and another (mainstream social policy) under national competence.

However, there are some major obstacles to the harmonization of asylum policies. While the Tampere meeting indicated that there was the political will to increase cooperation in immigration policy, there appears to be more will in some areas than others. In Kuijper's analysis, minimum standards of reception for asylum-seekers are low on the list (2000: 360). Much more activity has been seen in police-related areas, such as the development of a fingerprinting system ("Eurodac"). Asylum is linked to the "high politics" of common immigration and security policies, rather than the "low politics" of welfare, ensuring that provision for asylum-seekers is framed as a question of how they may be policed, rather than how they are provided for.

Conclusion

This chapter has endeavored to analyze the policy effects of the movement of people in Europe by identifying the pressures on social security systems that movement may generate and examining the possible responses. One possible response is discrimination, whereby states erect barriers to the participation of migrants in their economic and social systems. Another response is to reduce the attractiveness of social provisions (a "race to the bottom") to deter migration by potential claimants. A third response is to find the appropriate combination of eligibility conditions (contribution, needs, means, and category membership), and the means of implementing these conditions, to ensure that the legitimacy of social provisions is preserved in the face of migration.

Our comparison of the situations of asylum-seekers and EU nationals has shown that discrimination and the "race to the bottom" can be connected. Where discrimination is possible, social provisions for migrants may more readily be cut. If discrimination is prohibited, any cuts in provision will affect home nationals as much as migrants, and therefore the domestic political forces that maintain social provisions will be mobilized in their defense. The British experience of the habitual residence test shows that it is now difficult for member states to discriminate against the nationals of other EU states, and this greatly reduces the political benefits of making an issue of migrants' claims on the welfare system. Clearly, the opposite situation prevails in the case of asylum-seekers.

It is not clear to what extent competitive factors have driven provisions for asylum-seekers below the level that would be chosen by a state acting in isolation. There are signs that cuts are damaging to the states' own interests, in so far as the exclusion of asylum-seekers from work and social security is accompanied by increased social tension and conflict. However, that there are mixed pressures in operation is indicated by the EU's difficulties in combating competition through harmonization. States have internal political motives for engendering the social exclusion of asylum-seekers, and their ability to find a cooperative solution is limited by the political salience of the issue.

We have shown that the coordination arrangements for social security initially focused on promoting the exportability of benefits. However, this approach is much better suited to insurance-based benefits than non-contributory benefits. For the latter, it has proved necessary to develop principles of entitlement for non-nationals in the host state. Contribution is a powerful legitimating principle, and it functioned not only as a rationale for exportability but also to justify access to social provisions for non-national resident workers, who could be seen as contributing to the national economy through their employment. The next stage being faced by the European welfare states is the application of the right of non-discrimination to non-national residents who are not employed and not contributing. The legitimacy of this right rests on the same social policy principles that legitimize welfare provisions generally.

Failure to extend non-discrimination to non-working non-nationals has unacceptable consequences, in heightening the importance of nationality and implying that the state of nationality has the residual "duty of care." A feature of the current coordination arrangements for social security in Europe is that they refrain from using nationality as an organizing principle. Raising the salience of nationality would bring emotive issues about the granting of citizenship to the fore. It could have adverse consequences for people with ties to more than one state, and the current moves towards acceptance of dual citizenship (Hall, 1999: 600) could not be sustained. Most importantly, however, the principle requires levels of policing and administrative control that are incompatible with the social structures of a market economy. This incompatibility is all too evident in the treatment of asylum-seekers.

It is received wisdom that welfare states must defend their boundaries by deploying principles of exclusion. However, it is equally the case that exclusionary policies must be reconciled with the basic principles of social policy and the freedoms of the market economy within which the welfare state functions. The establishment of freedom of movement for economic purposes within Europe has spillover effects on the maintenance of national barriers for social provisions. Exclusionary policies within Europe are inconsistent with wider principles, particularly the principle of non-discrimination. As a result, the relevant exclusionary boundary for the European states has become Europe as a whole, not the national borders within Europe.

References

Adler, M. (1995). "The Habitual Residence Test: A Critical Analysis." *Journal of Social Security Law*, 2, 179-195.

Bank, R. (2000). "Europeanising the Reception of Asylum-Seekers: The Opposite of Welfare State Politics." In Bommes, M., and Geddes, A. (eds.), *Immigration and Welfare: Challenging the Borders of the Welfare State*. London: Routledge.

Bommes, M., and Geddes, A. (eds.) (2000). *Immigration and Welfare: Challenging the Borders of the Welfare State*. London: Routledge.

DG V. (1999). *Employment Policies in the EU and in Member States*. Brussels: European Commission (http://europa.eu.int/comm/dg05/empl&esf/emp99/jer98_en.pdf).

European Commission (2000a). *Proposal for a Council Decision Creating a European Fund*, Community preparatory acts, Doc 599PC0686. Brussels: European Commission.

___. (2000b). *A Common European Asylum System*, Bulletin EU 10-199, Conclusions of the Presidency [4/16]: II. Brussels: European Commission.

European Council of Refugees and Exiles. (1999). *Country Reports for 1999*. London and Brussels: ECRE.

Guiraudon, V. (2000). The Marshallian Triptych Reordered: The Role of Courts and Bureaucracies in Furthering Migrants' Social Rights. In Bommes, M., and Geddes, A. (eds.), *Immigration and Welfare: Challenging the Borders of the Welfare State*. London: Routledge.

Hall, S. (1999). "The European Convention on Nationality and the Right to Have Rights." *European Law Review*, 24, 586-602.

Home Office (UK). (1998). *Fairer, Faster and Firmer—A Modern Approach to Immigration and Asylum*. CM 4018, London: The Stationery Office.

___. (1999). *Report of the Asylum Seekers Support Project Team*. Croydon: Immigration and Nationality Directorate.

Klausen, J. (1995). "Social Rights Advocacy and State Building. T. H. Marshall in the Hands of Social Reformers." *World Politics*, 47, 244-267.

Kuijper, P. J. (2000). "Some Legal Problems Associated with the Communitarization of Policy on Visas, Asylum and Immigration under the Amsterdam Treaty and Incorporation of the Schengen Acquis." *Common Market Law Review*, 37, 345-366.

O'Leary, S. (1999). "Putting Flesh on the Bones of European Union Citizenship." *European Law Review*, 24, 68-79.

Roberts, S., and Bolderson, H. (1999). "Inside Out: Migrants' Disentitlement to Social Security Benefits in the EU." In Clasen, J. (ed.) *Comparative Social Policy: Concepts, Theories and Methods*. Oxford: Blackwell.

Schram, S., and Beer, S. (eds.). (1999). *Welfare Reform: A Race to the Bottom?* Washington, D.C.: Woodrow Wilson Centre Press.

Steiner, J. (1985). "The Right to Welfare: Equality and Equity under Community Law." *European Law Review*, 10, 21-41.

Stetter, S. (2000). "Regulating Migration: Authority Delegation in Justice and Home Affairs." *Journal of European Public Policy*, 7(1), 80-103.

Tomuschat, C. (2000). "Casenote on Case C-85/96 *Maria Martinez Sala v. Freistaat Bayern.*" *Common Market Law Review*, 37, 449-457.

Veil, S. (1997). *Report of the High Level Panel on the Free Movement of Persons*, 18 March 1997. Brussels: European Commission.

11

Migration and Social Security: Parochialism in the Global Village

Simon Roberts

The increasingly global characteristic of migration has considerable implications for social security. This chapter examines entitlement to social security in the European Union (EU) for migrants who are not nationals of an EU member country (sometimes referred to as third-country nationals).

The chapter looks at both the direct effect of immigration status on benefit eligibility, and the effect of benefit entitlement conditions themselves on third-country nationals in the fifteen member countries at different stages of settlement. It then examines the extent to which international social security agreements mitigate exclusion from benefit entitlement.

The chapter draws attention to the lack of agreements between EU member countries and some sending countries with large stocks and flows; and argues that if the gaps in coverage are to be closed it is necessary to rethink the obligations of the receiving country.

Sources of Migrants' Rights

The chapter examines five sources of social security rights for migrants within the EU. These are:

- The domestic arrangements of the member states;
- The plethora of bilateral agreements entered into separately by the member states;
- EU Regulations;
- The various association and cooperation agreements entered into by the EU and the member states in partnership; and
- Council of Europe instruments.

The Domestic Arrangements of the Member States

The domestic arrangements of the member countries include both immigration rules and benefit entitlement conditions.

Direct Effects of Immigration Policies

Each of the EU member countries accords different immigration statuses to newcomers, with asylum-seekers and those granted exceptional leave to remain the least secure at the bottom rung of the "ladder" and those who have been naturalized the most established at the top. The ease with which immigrants may move up the ladder to acquire settlement and/or nationality varies from country to country (Roberts, 1998a).

The member countries differ in the social security arrangements they make for third-country nationals at the different stages of settlement (North et al., 1987; Brubaker 1989; Roberts and Bolderson, 1993, 1999; Roberts, 1995, 1998a, 2001a, 2001b; von Maydell and Schulte, 1995; Bolderson and Roberts, 1997; Jorens, 1997). Some of the countries discriminate directly against third-country nationals in that immigration status disallows a claim to benefit or a claim jeopardizes the right to remain in the country. For example, entitlement to social assistance in Denmark for more than a temporary period is reserved for people who have lived in Denmark for the previous three years. Social assistance for people who have lived in Denmark for a shorter period of time is decided by local authorities acting under guidance laid down by the Ministry of Social Affairs. If a claim for social assistance is made by a person who has lived in Denmark for less than three years, she/he may be deported.

Immigration policies also restrict access to benefits for spouses. A claim by the relative to social assistance before a long-term permit is granted may jeopardize his or her right to remain in each of the countries. For example, in Belgium, the Netherlands, and the UK a claim for social assistance within the first year of arrival may result in the person being refused continuing leave to stay.

Effect of Benefit Entitlement Conditions

Nationality. In other cases the benefit entitlement conditions themselves discriminate directly against third-country nationals in that they reserve entitlement for the nationals of the receiving country only. Although none of the fifteen EU member countries reserve contributory benefits for nationals only, almost half require that somebody be a national of their country in order to claim at least some of their non-contributory benefits. Austria, Belgium, Denmark, France, Greece, Italy, and Portugal all have nationality conditions attached to some of these benefits (Bolderson and Roberts, 1997; Roberts, 1998a; Roberts and Bolderson, 1999).

Although there is no discrimination by nationality with respect to contributory benefits claimed domestically, there is, however, discrimination by nationality with regard to contributory benefits when it comes to exporting them (Bolderson and Gains, 1993). Some countries do not allow non-nationals to claim some of their benefits from abroad. This is the case with France, for example, where pensions cannot be claimed from abroad by non-nationals.

Residence. In many cases the benefit entitlement conditions discriminate indirectly against third-country nationals in that they require the satisfaction of a lengthy past period of residence or the satisfaction of criteria that may be more difficult for a migrant to satisfy than it is for a national of the receiving country.

Although there are no residence conditions attached to contributory benefits, many of the countries attach residence conditions to tax-financed benefits.

In the UK, receipt of Income Support, Income-Based Job Seekers Allowance, Council Tax Benefit and Housing Benefit are restricted to those who are "habitually resident." This term is not defined in the legislation but determined with reference to subjective criteria to do with the person's intentions, reasons for coming to the UK, employment record, length and continuity of residence in another country and "centre of interest" (Bolderson and Roberts, 1994; Roberts, 1995, 1997, 2001c).

A number of countries require a prior period of residence as a condition for the receipt of some non-contributory benefits. For example, in Finland, in order to be eligible for invalidity benefit it is necessary to have lived in the country for a total of five years. Here Finland discriminates directly between Finnish nationals and third-country nationals in that a Finnish national only has to have been resident in Finland for three years after the age of sixteen.

Asylum-Seekers

Asylum-seekers fall, in part, outside the main social security arrangements. The social security entitlements of asylum-seekers not only vary considerably from country to country but also within the same country. Some countries house a proportion of asylum-seekers in reception centers while the remainder must enter the housing market. In other countries there are no coordinated reception policies.

The provision made for those staying in reception centers where they exist may include free food, clothing, and accommodation. In some countries, additional one-off payments may be made on arrival to take account of immediate special needs of asylum-seekers. Those staying outside reception centers may either receive a cash allowance paid at a rate equivalent to national benefits or more often an amount paid at a rate lower than the rate paid to nationals. In some countries the assistance is payable for a limited period only. In a few countries there is no obligation on the state to provide either social assistance or accommodation. As a consequence, asylum-seekers await-ing the result of their application must rely on charity or sleep rough on the streets.

International Social Security Agreements

Bilateral Agreements

The traditional way of overcoming some of the disadvantages experi-enced by migrants is through international agreements. Each of the member countries has signed a plethora of bi-lateral social security agreements (Holloway, 1981; ILO, 1992; Tamango, 1994; Nagel and Thalamy, 1994; Pizarro, 1995).

International social security agreements use five methods to ameliorate the disadvantages faced by migrants. These are equality of treatment, or the prohibition of discrimination on grounds of nationality in respect of rights and obligations under the legislation of each of the contracting parties; pro-visions to ensure that migrant workers are not insured in either country's scheme and thus without any social security protection and to prevent them being insured in both; aggregation of periods of insurance spent in each of the countries when calculating entitlement to benefits; proratarization—that each of the countries pays a proportion of the pension determined by the period of insurance spent in each. Proratarization differs from aggregation in that the latter is concerned with adding together periods of insurance, resi-dence, and presence in order to satisfy the qualifications for benefit paid by one or the other of the countries. Aggregation in general is applied to short-term benefits where the costs falling on one or the other countries are not likely to be considerable. The principle of proratarization is applied to long-term benefits to distribute the costs in accordance with the perceived respon-sibility for meeting them; and export of benefits.

The History of International Social Security Agreements

The history of international social security treaties goes back to the begin-ning of the twentieth century, although international treaties affecting the rights of aliens have a much longer history (Holloway, 1981; Dummett, 1986; ILO, 1992; Nagel and Thalamy, 1994). The first treaties were concerned with accidents at work. The 1882 agreement and 1897 convention between France and Belgium introduced the fundamental principle of all ensuing interna-tional social security agreements—that of equal treatment.

In 1904 France and Italy signed an international social security treaty that allowed people who had suffered an industrial accident to export their compensation to their home country. The exportability of employment injury compensation broke through the territorial restrictions of the national social security systems of the two countries (Watson, 1980; Nagel and Thalamy, 1995). In 1919 another Franco-Italian treaty introduced the principle of aggregation of periods of insurance so that periods of insurance in one country were counted towards the satisfaction of conditions of entitlement to benefit in the other (Holloway, 1981).

Between the wars agreements relating to equality of treatment for work accident benefits became quite common. However, it was usual for other aspects of social security to be included in general labor conventions (Watson, 1980). Gradually, the scope of social security agreements, in terms of both the people and the benefits covered, widened towards comprehensive agreements covering all benefits (Watson, 1980). In addition to equality of treatment, aggregation of periods of insurance, and export of benefits, the principle of proratorization for long-term benefits was introduced. After the Second World War there was an expansion in international agreements affecting migrants in general and social security in particular (Dummett, 1986).

Most of the expansion of bilateral social security agreements that has taken place since the Second World War has happened between European countries in response to the large-scale intra-European labor migration that took place during the 1950s, 1960s, and early 1970s (Berger and Mohr, 1989; Thomas, 1982; Clout et al., 1985; King, 1990; Castles and Miller, 1993).

In the twenty years between 1946 and 1966, 401 bilateral agreements concerning social security were signed worldwide; in 94 percent of these treaties both parties were European (Holloway, 1981). Although these postwar treaties were more sophisticated than their prewar counterparts, they were still founded on the principles of removing direct discrimination through the principle of equal treatment and indirect discrimination through aggregation of insurance and the export of benefits, and the apportionment of responsibility through the determination of which country should pay what proportion of the benefit.

The Countries Covered by an International Social Security Agreement

Large numbers of people in the world are actually or potentially not protected by an international social security agreement should they choose to migrate to an EU member country. Indeed the lack of a bilateral social security agreement might be a factor in deciding not to migrate. Countries that do not have a bilateral agreement with any EU member country are mainly, but not exclusively, developing countries. Intuitively, one might expect that the countries without an agreement would be those between which migration flows have been historically nonexistent or small. If this were the case there would either be no need for an agreement, or the administrative costs of negotiating and maintaining a bilateral agreement might outweigh the gain of a relatively small number of its own migrants.

However, a number of countries with large stocks of migrants in an EU country do not have a bilateral agreement. Apart from an agreement between France and Senegal, there are no agreements with sub-Saharan Africa. Yet Belgium, France, and the UK all had long-standing African empires, and each has a long history of migration flows from their former African colonies. There are nearly 16,000 Zaireians in Belgium, and 82,000 West Africans and 48,000 East Africans in the UK. These figures include people from Nigeria, Ghana, the Sudan, Uganda, and Kenya. In addition to migrants from these ex-colonial countries there are over 26,000 Senegalese, 19,000 Somalians, 14,000 Ethiopians, and 14,000 Ghanaians in Italy; and 9,000 Ethiopians in Sweden.

There is only one agreement with the Indian subcontinent, that between Denmark and Pakistan, despite there being 151,000 Indians, 98,000 Pakistanis, and 73,000 Bangladeshis in the UK, over 14,000 Indians in Spain, and almost 6,000 Sri Lankans in Denmark (SOPEMI, 1999).

Apart from the agreements between the Philippines and Italy and the Philippines and Spain, there are no agreements with any other Asian countries. This is despite significant populations of Vietnamese in Denmark, Finland, France, and Sweden, Thais in Denmark, Chinese in Finland, Italy, and Spain, Cambodians and Laotians in France, and Filipinos in Denmark.

Of the countries of Eastern Europe, only Poland has an agreement with any of the EU member countries. Poland has agreements with France, Germany, and Sweden, but not with Denmark, Finland, or Italy. Despite significant populations of Romanians in Germany, Italy, and Sweden; Bulgarians in Germany, Hungarians in Germany, Finland, and Sweden; and Albanians in Italy, there are no agreements between any of these countries.

Of the Middle Eastern countries, only Egypt has an agreement with a member country, Italy. Iraq, Iran, and the Lebanon, despite significant populations in Denmark, Germany, and Sweden, do not have an agreement with any of these countries.

It might be argued that some of these populations are refugees who do not anticipate returning to the country from which they fled and so would not benefit from a bilateral agreement. However, regimes change, and significant numbers of refugees then wish to return home. Following the restoration of democracy in Chile in 1992, for example, many refugees were apparently deterred from returning home from the UK because of the lack of inflation proofing of UK pensions and non-entitlement for those with less than eleven years of UK contributions.

The Benefits Covered and the Mechanisms of Coordination

Where bilateral agreements do exist, the protection provided is variable. Bilateral agreements are extremely heterogeneous despite model agreements having been produced by international bodies such as the International Labour Office (ILO) and the Council of Europe or by the individual countries themselves (Bolderson and Gains, 1993; ILO, 1996; Council of Europe, 1995).

All bilateral agreements provide for equal treatment in respect of rights and obligations under the legislation of each contracting party. However, in some cases the equal treatment is not complete. For example, Denmark's agreements include conditions requiring the satisfaction of past periods of residence or availability for work that do not apply to Danish nationals.

Whom the equal treatment applies to varies from agreement to agreement. Some countries favor agreements that are restricted to the nationals of the two countries. Others have agreements that are open to all people who have been insured in one of the two countries. In a few countries, for example, Finland, the same bilateral agreement may be open to all insured for some benefits, but restricted to nationals for others.

The definition of who is a "national" is a matter for the country concerned. As a result of historical connections some agreements include nationals of third countries. For example, the agreement between Belgium and the UK covers a "person having Belgian nationality or a native of the Belgian Congo or Ruanda-Urundi," while that between France and the UK refers to "a person having French nationality and any French protected person belonging to French Togoland or the French Cameroons." Who is actually covered by these agreements is a matter for the Belgian and French authorities.

While most bilateral agreements cover all nationals or all insured persons who move between the two countries, others are narrower, applying only, for example, to seconded or "detached" workers or to frontier workers. In other cases, specific provision is made within an agreement for detached workers who are sent by an employer in one of the bilateral partner countries to work in the other. Detached workers will remain insured in the "home" country only as long as the secondment is not expected to last for longer than an agreed period, which may vary between one year and up to five years.

New agreements concluded by the UK provide even more limited cover, being confined to arrangements for coordinating contributions. Scope for new agreements between the UK and other countries is limited because of the UK's "frozen" pension policy under which pensions are not uprated. To pay annual cost-of-living increases to pensioners and widows living in another country under new agreements, which would normally be expected, would lead to pressure to "unfreeze" pensions for UK nationals who are retired and living in Canada, Australia, and New Zealand. The UK Government regards this as too costly. As a result, Australia has this year suspended its agreement with the UK.

All bilateral agreements between countries that have insurance-based schemes contain provisions to ensure that migrant workers are not insured in either country's scheme and to prevent them being insured in both.

Most of the bilateral agreements provide for the aggregation of periods of insurance. Where each country's social security system is based on contributions, aggregation of periods of insurance involves adding together paid contributions. However, not all social security schemes are contributory. Where one country's scheme is based on paid contributions and the other is based on periods of residence or employment, aggregation rules provide for the aggregation of different types of periods. For example, the agreement between Portugal and Australia aggregates Portuguese periods of insurance with Australian periods of residence.

Even agreements that are open to all people moving between two countries do not always provide for all contingencies. The benefits included are, in the main, insurance-based benefits. At the heart of most of the agreements are arrangements for long-term benefits that provide for invalidity, retirement, and widowhood. Periods of insurance for these benefits are aggregated, the principle of "proratorization" is employed to distribute costs between the countries according to insurance, and the benefits are exportable. Fewer of the agreements cover short-term benefits for sickness and maternity. These benefits are not paid on a pro rata basis and are generally not exportable. Of the insurance-based benefits, those for unemployment are the least likely to be included in a bilateral agreement.

The majority of bilateral social security agreements are between countries that are now members of the EU. For EU nationals, bilateral agreements between member countries are largely redundant, having been superseded by Regulation (EEC) 1408/71.

Multilateral Agreements

Regulation (EEC) 1408/71. This regulation coordinates social security for EU nationals who move between member countries. It ensures that migrants are subject to only one country's legislation and provides for equal treatment, aggregation of contributions, proratorization, and export of benefits within the Community. However, it provides only very limited cover for third-country nationals as the Regulation is restricted to member country nationals, stateless persons or refugees who are residing within the territory of one of the member countries, as well as to the members of their families and their survivors.

The Association and Cooperation Agreements. The EU has concluded Association and Cooperation Agreements with most third countries, mainly establishing economic cooperation. However, the Community has concluded cooperation agreements with Algeria, Morocco, and Tunisia and association agreements with Turkey, Poland, Hungary, and the Czech and Slovak Federal Republics, all of which include provisions in respect of social security (Guild, 1992; Jorens and Schulte, 1998).

The EU-Turkey Agreement, and the Maghreb Agreements provide for non-discrimination between workers and members of their families living with them who are nationals of the contracting countries; periods of employment, insurance, and residence spent in different member countries of the EU to be aggregated for retirement, invalidity, and death benefits and medical care; retirement, death and industrial injuries benefits to be exported to the country of origin at the rate payable in the exporting country; and for family benefits to be paid to members of the worker's family who are resident in the Community.

While on the face of it these agreements appear to give substantial social security rights to Turkish nationals and nationals of the Maghreb countries, in practice the only right to social security so far created by any of these agreements is to equal treatment with the nationals of the receiving country for Algerian, Moroccan, and Tunisian nationals. This is because the EU member countries have argued that the agreements are not capable of creating rights and obligations for individuals under their national laws (Gacon-Estrada, 1998; Roberts, 1998b; Sieveking, 1998).

Migrants' rights under the newer "Europe Agreements" with Poland, Hungary, and the Czech and Slovak Federal Republics are reduced in comparison with the older Maghreb and Turkey agreements. As a result of the Court's finding that the principle of equal treatment has direct effect in the Morocco agreement, the principle has been omitted from the "Europe Agreements." In addition, in these newer agreements, family benefits are only payable if the family is living with the worker and are not exportable if they are living in another EU member country, as is the case with the earlier agreements. This represents a reduction of the (theoretical) rights of these migrants in comparison to those granted by the earlier agreements (Guild, 1998).

The EU has also concluded the Lomé IV Convention with sixty-nine states in Africa, the Caribbean, and Pacific that includes provisions about workers. Annex VI of the Final Act provides that:

> workers who are nationals of an ACP (Africa, Caribbean and Pacific) state legally employed in the territory of a Member State and members of their families living with them shall, as regards social security benefits linked to employment in that Member State, enjoy treatment free from any discrimination based on nationality in relation to nationals of that Member State.

At present the Lomé Convention does not give any rights to social security in any of the member countries. The scope and effect of the treaty have yet to be tested before the European Court of Justice (ECJ) (GISTI, 1995).

The only agreement of this type to be made fully effective is that with the EFTA countries, which are now Iceland, Liechtenstein, and Norway, setting up the EEA. People from these countries are fully covered by social security arrangements that are parallel, and identical to Regulation 1408/71 (Sakslin, 1998).

Council of Europe Instruments

The two Interim Agreements on Social Security Schemes and the European Convention on Social and Medical Assistance (ECSEMA) have been in force since 1954. One interim agreement deals with old age, invalidity, and survivors' benefits, the other with sickness, maternity, unemployment, industrial injury, death grants, and family benefits. ECSEMA requires ratifying states to provide assistance in cash and kind to nationals of other ratifying states who are lawfully present in their territory and without sufficient resources on the same conditions as their own nationals. The only country outside the EEA that is a signatory to these three agreements is Turkey, and so their usefulness is limited to Turkish nationals.

Conclusion: Beyond Reciprocity

The conditions of entitlement attached to social security benefits in the member countries of the European Union deny access to social security for many migrants.

International social security agreements have gone some way to meeting the challenges posed by labor migration. However, international social security agreements leave large numbers of people in the world either actually or potentially not protected should they choose to migrate to an EU member country.

The explanation for the lack of a bilateral agreement with so many developing countries with large migrant populations in the EU concerns the principle of reciprocity. The important theoretical characteristic of the principle is that each party shares the costs and benefits on a reasonably equal basis (Tamango, 1994). Thus, reciprocity requires that the nationals (or insured) of one country must receive treatment in the other country that is roughly equal to that received by that country's nationals (or insured persons) in the first. That would suggest that for an agreement to be concluded each of the social security schemes must be reasonably compatible. This is the case, to a greater or lesser extent, with the social security systems of developed countries. Even where different principles apply, as in the case of the contributory Bismarckian schemes of most of Western Europe and the tax-financed residence-based schemes of the Scandinavian countries, it has proved possible to apply the basic principles of bilateral agreements effectively, with a little modification.

However, there may be structural problems when it comes to coordinating the schemes of developed countries with those of the developing countries. Some developing countries have provident funds, paying out a lump sum in the event of the contingency, for example, sickness or injury, occurring. Such a scheme may be incompatible with one that pays out a continuing benefit, as reciprocity would not exist between the two schemes. Even those countries with social security schemes that pay weekly or monthly benefits may yet be incompatible with reciprocity if the amount paid does not provide a reasonable benefit taking into account the standard of living and does not cover a significant proportion of the population or workforce (Tamango, 1994).

The ILO reported recently that

> more than half of the world's population (workers and their dependants) are excluded from any type of statutory social security protection. They are covered neither by contribution-based social insurance schemes nor by tax-financed social assistance. In sub-Saharan Africa and South Asia, statutory social security coverage is estimated at 5 to 10 percent of the working population and decreasing. In India for example, not more than 10 percent of workers were in the formal sector in the mid-1990s, compared to more than 13 percent in the mid-1980s. In Latin America, coverage lies roughly between 10 and 80 percent, and is mainly static or more often stagnating (van Ginneken, 1999).

Under these circumstances it is unlikely that social security agreements based on reciprocity will be able to fill the gaps in coverage for migrants. To fill the gaps it will be necessary to move beyond the principle of reciprocity and rethink the obligations of the receiving country.

There are technical difficulties in providing some arrangements for migrants in the absence of an international agreement. It is not possible to aggregate periods of insurance paid, or time spent, in the sending and receiving countries, and there may be obstacles to exporting benefits that require administrative checks such as unemployment, sickness, and perhaps incapacity benefits in some circumstances. However, there are no technical obstacles to extending equal treatment to migrants unilaterally or to exporting retirement pensions.

Arguments against granting equal treatment and exporting pensions unilaterally tend to be based on a particular view of welfare which can be characterized as "communitarian" (Roberts, 2001a). In this view welfare is founded in the "solidarities implicit in a common tax and public service system...and...this solidarity is necessarily bounded" (Coughlan, 1992: 112). From this perspective people do not feel a sense of solidarity with the whole world, but rather only with other members of the community. According to communitarians, the community is the national community and "the solidarities that exist within the nation state do not, or rarely, exist cross-nationally or between states. It is this fact above all that ties the re-distributive welfare state irrevocably to the national level" (Coughlan, 1992: 112).

Such a parochial perspective is inadequate to meet the challenges of globalization. Citizenship as a bundle of reciprocal rights and obligations has grown up in the context of the development of the nation state (Marshall and Bottomore, 1992). However, the growing economic interdependence of the world is making the boundaries of the nation state less relevant. If economic mechanisms are transnational, so, too, should be economic justice (Heater, 1990).

Migrants pay taxes, including indirect taxes from the moment of arrival, and contribute to the financing of the social security system of their country of residence. It is hard to make a fair case for allowing migrants to contribute economically, but then refuse to share the economic benefits and risks.

References

Berger, J., and Mohr, J. (1989). *A Seventh Man*. Cambridge: Granta.

Bolderson, H., and Gains, F. (1993). *Crossing National Frontiers: An Examination of the Arrangements for Exporting Social Security Benefits in Twelve OECD Countries*. London: HMSO.

Bolderson, H., and Roberts, S. (1994). "New Restrictions on Benefits for Migrants: Xenophobia or Trivial Pursuit?" *Benefits* (December), 123-131.

____. (1997). "Social Security Across National Frontiers' in Social Security and Population Movement." *Journal of International and Comparative Welfare: Special edition "New Global Development,"* XIII, 412-430.

Brubaker, W. (1989). "Membership without Citizenship: The Economic and Social Rights of Noncitizens." In Brubaker, W. (ed.), *Immigration and the Politics of Citizenship in Europe and North America*. Lanham: University Press of America.

Castles, S., and Miller, M. (1993). *The Age of Migration*. London: Macmillan.

Clout, H., Blacksell, M., King, R., and Pinder, D. (eds.). (1985). *Western Europe: Geographical Perspectives*. Harlow: Longman.

Coughlan, A. (1992). *The Limits of Solidarity: Social Policy, National and International*. Paper given to "50 Years after Beveridge" Conference at University of York, 27-30 September, Vol. 2. York: SPRU.

Council of Europe. (1995). *Model Provisions for a Bilateral Social Security Agreement and Explanatory Report*, Strasbourg: Council of Europe.

Dummett, A. (ed.). (1986). *Towards a Just Immigration Policy*. London: Cobden Trust.

Gacon-Estrada, H. (1998). "The Cooperation Agreements Concluded between the European Community and the Maghreb Countries." In Jorens, Y., and Schulte, B. (eds.), *European Social Security Law and Third Country Nationals*. Brussels: Die Keure la Charte.

GISTI. (1995). *La Circulation des etrangers dans l'espace europeen*. Paris: Groupe d'information et de soutien des immigrés.

Guild, E. (1992). *Protecting Migrants' Rights: Application of EC Agreements with Third Countries*. Brussels: Churches Committee for Migrants in Europe.

____. (1998). "The Europe Agreements: Natural Persons and Social Security." In Jorens, Y., and Schulte, B. (eds.) *European Social Security Law and Third Country Nationals*. Brugge: Die Keure.

Heater, D. (1990). *Citizenship*. London: Longman.

Holloway, J. (1981). *Social Policy Harmonisation in the European Community*. Farnborough: Gower.

ILO. (1992). *Repertoire des instruments internationaux de securite sociale.* Geneva: International Labour Office.

___. (1996). *International Labour Conventions and Recommendations.* Three Volumes. Geneva: International Labour Office.

Jorens, Y. (1997). *De rechtspositie van niet-EU-onderdanen in het Europese socialezekerheidsrecht.* Brugge: Die Keure la Charte.

Jorens, Y., and Schulte, B. (eds.). (1998). *European Social Security Law and Third Country Nationals.* Brugge: Die Keure la Charte.

King, R. (1990). "The Social and Economic Geography of Labour Migration: from Guestworkers to immigrants." In Pinder, D. (ed.), *Western Europe: Challenge and Change.* London: Belhaven.

Marshall, T H., and Bottomore, T. (1992). *Citizenship and Social Class.* London: Pluto Press.

Nagel, S., and Thalamy, C. (1994). *Le droit international de la securite sociale.* Paris: Presses Universitaires de France.

North, D., Whitol de Wenden, C., and Taylor, C. (1987). Non-Citizens' Access to Social Services in Six Nations. Unpublished paper for the German Marshall Fund. Washington, D.C.: German Marshall Fund of the United States.

Pizarro, S. (1995). "The Agreements on Social Security between the Community and Third Countries: Legal Basis and Analysis." In Commission for the European Communities (ed.), *Social Security in Europe: Equality between Nationals and Non-Nationals.* Lisbon: Departamento de Relações Internacionais e Convenções de Segurança Social.

Roberts, S. (1995). "Nationality and Equal Treatment: Access to Social Security Benefits and the National Health Service for Non-EEA Nationals under British Law." In von Maydell, B., and Schulte, B. (eds.), *Treatment of Third-Country Nationals in the EU and EEA Member States in Terms of Social Security Law.* Leuven: Peeters.

___. (1997). "Anspruchsvoraussetzungen fur Leistungen der Sozialen Sicherheit, des Sozialen Schutzes und der Gesundheitsversorgung fur Drittstaatsangehorige in Grossbritannien." In Barwig, K., Sieveking, K., Brinkmann, G., Lörcher, K., and Röseler, S. (eds.). *Sozialer Schutz von Ausländern in Deutschland.* Baden-Baden: Nomos.

___. (1998a). "Not One of Us: Social Security for Third Country Nationals in the European Union." Ph.D. thesis, Brunel University, Uxbridge.

___. (1998b). "The Rulings of the European Court of Justice on the Association and Co-operation Agreements in Matters Concerning Social Security". In Jorens, Y., and Schulte, B. (eds.), *European Social Security Law and Third Country Nationals* Brussels: Die Keure la Charte.

___. (2001a). "Crossing Frontiers: Migration and Social Security." In Schokkaert, E. (ed.), *Ethics, Poverty, Inequality and Reform in Social Security.* Aldershot: Ashgate Publishing.

___. (2001b). "Migración y Seguridad Social: redibujando las fronteras de la previsión del bienestar." In F. Ortíz (ed.), *Contratación Laboral de Extranjeros. Régimen Jurídico.* Murcia: Laborum.

___. (2001c). "A Strong and Legitimate Link." The Habitual Residence Test in the UK. Paper originally presented at the conference in Helsinki "From Citizenship to Residence. Access to Social Protection in the Nordic and EU Countries" 10-11 March 2000, Helsinki.

Roberts, S., and Bolderson, H. (1993). How Closed are Welfare States? Migration, Social Security and National Frontiers: Social Security Provisions for Non-EU

Nationals in Six EU Countries. Paper given to the Annual Conference of the International Sociological Association, 23 September, Oxford.

——— (1999). "Inside Out: A Cross-National Study of Migrants' Disentitlements to Social Security Benefits." In Clasen, J. (ed.), *Comparative Social Policy*. Oxford: Blackwell.

Sakslin, M. (1998). "The Agreements on the European Economic Area." In Y. Jorens and B. Schulte (eds.), *European Social Security Law and Third Country Nationals* Brussels: Die Keure la Charte.

Sieveking, K. (1998). "The Rulings of the European Court of Justice on the Legal Position of Non-European Union Nationals under Labour Law and Social Security Law." In Jorens, Y., and Schulte, B. (eds.), *European Social Security Law and Third Country Nationals* Brussels: Die Keure la Charte.

SOPEMI. (1999). *Trends in International Migration*. Paris: OECD.

Tamango, E. (1994). "Coordination of Social Security Programmes of Developed and Developing Countries." *International Social Security Review,* 47 (1), 3-13.

Thomas, E. J. (ed.) (1982). *Immigrant Workers in Europe: Their Legal Status*. Paris: UNESCO.

van Ginneken, W. (1999). *Social Security for the Excluded Majority. Case Studies of Developing Countries.* Geneva: International Labour Office.

von Maydell, B., and Schulte, B. (1995). *Treatment of Third-Country Nationals in the EU and EEA Member States in terms of Social Security Law*. Leuven: Peeters.

Watson, P. (1980) *Social Security Law of the European Communities*. London: Mansell.

Part 4

Labor Markets and Social Security

12

Changing Rights and Obligations in Unemployment Insurance*

Jon Kvist

Changing rights and obligations are at the heart of much European policy-making. Since the early 1990s many governments have expressed intentions to change their unemployment policies. For example, in 1994, the Norwegian government in its Welfare White Paper *Welfare Towards 2030* declared that the "Work Approach":

> constitutes a vital element in the Government's strategy to establish a firm basis for our welfare schemes. We must create the basis for the welfare we desire…. The Government wants to emphasise that work is to be regarded as valuable for the individual person himself. The Work Approach entails that as many as possible shall be able to support themselves by their own work, and that persons with social problems and health problems shall be helped in order to manage their daily activities themselves as far as possible. Work must consequently be the obvious preference for persons of occupationally active age. (Norwegian Government, 1994: 2)

More recently, the British Prime Minister, Tony Blair, presented the views and values of New Labour:

> For too long, the demand for rights from the state was separated from the duties of citizenship and the imperative for mutual responsibility on part of individuals and institutions. Unemployment benefits were often paid without strong reciprocal obligations…. The rights we enjoy reflect the duties we owe: rights and opportunity without responsibility are engines of selfishness and greed (Blair, 1999: 4).

In Denmark, the slogan "from passive to active" adapted by the Social Democratic coalition government in the 1990s signaled a concern to change not least the unemployment policies from a "passive doling out of money" to a proactive system helping and expecting able-bodied to work. Most Western

European governments have made use of similar rhetoric and initiatives in the 1990s. With the help of hindsight it is often possible even in countries without a master plan, like the Netherlands, to find a "crooked path towards an active labor market policy" (Visser and Hemerijk, 1997: 155ff).

The nexus between social rights and obligations has always been crucial in unemployment insurance. Rules governing the personal scope of application and eligibility criteria delimit the group having the right to unemployment insurance. Rules concerning claimants' capability of and availability for work as well as willingness to work is everywhere obligations for claimants. The debate in recent years, however, indicates that established thinking and policy-making are challenged, that the proper forms and levels of rights and obligations and their balancing is up for discussion (Standing, 1990; Gilbert, 1992; Carroll, 1999). In particular it seems governments place a greater emphasis on obligations, independent of whether they have a Liberal policy tradition like the US, a mixed tradition of Liberal and Labour policies as in Britain, a Social Democratic inheritance as the Nordic countries, or a Conservative one as many continental European countries (Esping-Andersen, 1990; Mishra, 1990; Janoski, 1998; King, 1999).[1]

Whether recent political rhetoric translates into actual change of unemployment insurance is the topic of this chapter. The following section briefly sets out the method and material used. This is followed by a cross-national analysis of the development of social rights and obligations in unemployment insurance in seven European countries during the 1990s. First, we analyze changing rights and obligations in unemployment insurance. The last part of the analysis focuses on the configuration of rights and obligations and in this way identifies emerging models of unemployment insurance. In total, this enables us to shed light on whether countries are converging or not in the area of unemployment insurance, as may be signaled by the political slogans cited earlier.

Method and Material

Social rights are often portrayed as epitomizing the realization of full citizenship, the triumph of modern societies (Marshall, 1964 [1950]). Today it is largely uncontested that social rights constitute the cornerstone of the welfare state (Esping-Andersen, 1990; Barbalet, 1988). Citizenship is "a status bestowed on those who are full members of a community. All who possess the status are equal with respect to the rights and duties with which the status is endowed" (Marshall, 1964 [1950]: 84), and social rights refer to "the whole range from the right to a modicum of economic welfare and security to the right to share to the full in the social heritage and to live the life of a civilized being according to the standards prevailing in the society" (Marshall, 1964 [1950]: 72). Marshall is less clear about the obligations, duties, and responsibilities associated with social rights besides that citizens should pay taxes, do military service, and live the lives of gentlemen. But obligations are not only vague expressions of duties, but are backed by laws and state's enforcement of such laws, just like social rights (Janoski, 1998: 66ff).

In investigating how social rights and obligations are changing, we make use of a new method in social sciences, fuzzy sets, that is particularly useful in assessing diversity among a small number of cases (for an introduction to the use of fuzzy sets in social science, see Ragin, 2000). Diversity in this chapter concerns similarities and differences in unemployment insurance schemes, and our cases are seven Northern European countries in the 1990s. In contrast to crisp sets where things are either out of or in a set (equal to a score of, respectively 0 or 1), fuzzy sets allows for partial membership (equal to scores between 0 and 1, where 0.5 is the cross-over point from being more in than out of a set). Accordingly, a given object like an unemployment insurance scheme can be assessed according to its membership of various sets reflecting concepts like benefit generosity. Fuzzy set theory demands a high degree of correspondence between concepts and fuzzy membership scores in sets established to reflect such concepts. Therefore it is essential that great attention is paid to the analytical construction of the concepts, the criteria for establishing qualitative breaking points, and the empirical evidence. These crucial decisions should be made on the basis of theories, substantive knowledge, and the availability and nature of data. In any case, the decisions made should be explicit to allow for scientific dialogue and replication of the analysis.

In our analysis we use three sets for concepts related to the accessibility of unemployment insurance benefits, the generosity of unemployment insurance benefits, and, finally, the obligations of unemployment insurance claimants. This leads to the identification of empirical indicators, criteria for qualitative breaking points, and procedures for translation of raw data into fuzzy membership values along the following lines:

- *Accessibility* of unemployment benefits is measured by an index based on scores for the personal scope of application and various eligibility criteria (e.g., work demands, definition of work, and membership requirements, if any). Two observations should be kept in mind when using such an index of accessibility to unemployment insurance benefits. First, unemployment insurance is only but one scheme that may provide cash transfers to people out of work. Other schemes like social assistance, early exit benefits, and sickness and disability benefits all provide benefits to people who are not employed. Ideally, one would want to study the whole system of possible schemes and their accessibility features simultaneously, but this is not possible in one chapter. Second, per definition unemployment insurance cannot be universal, as it would then be a citizen wage. Thus, no country has "fully" universal unemployment insurance schemes. Instead one may talk of the degree to which such benefits are accessible (see also Clasen et al., 2000). The starting point for our index is that people between eighteen and official retirement age should be able to qualify for benefits within twelve months by six months of work, taking into account what activities counts towards eligibility besides ordinary work (e.g., training, child caring, and so forth). If qualification is possible under these conditions, the scheme is seen as being more easy than difficult to access (i.e., membership score greater than 0.5). When this is not the possible, the scheme is difficult to access (i.e., membership scores lower than 0.5). The translation of raw data, index scores, into fuzzy membership scores and verbal labels can be seen in Table 12.1.

- *Generosity* of unemployment benefits is measured by net replacement rates that express the ratio of benefits compared to former wages after taxation. This measure of generosity has become commonly accepted in the literature (see, for example, Esping-Andersen, 1990; Martin, 1996; Carroll, 1999; Salomäki and Munzi, 1999). Again we look only at unemployment insurance. This makes the measure less representative of the empirical reality when unemployment compensation consists of other elements than the tax system and unemployment insurance. In particular, British claimants of unemployment insurance (Job Seeker's Allowance) may simultaneously receive other cash transfers like housing allowance and supplementary social assistance. However, in the other countries this is less of a problem. We use the net replacement rate for a single person with previous earnings at the level of the Average Production Worker (APW). This measure has two main caveats. First, net replacement rates calculated at other points in the income interval may give other expressions of generosity. Second, the net replacement rates may differ between persons in single individual households and non-single households due to the existence of tax allowances and/or supplements for children. In short, the problem in both cases is how to find an appropriate measure for a country's social protection system when, in fact, this system works very differently for different socioeconomic groups (Kvist, 1998). Aggregate measures like an average net replacement rate for different income and family situations (see, for example, Scarpetta, 1996) does not give an indication of how the national system works for any one population group, but simply conflates otherwise useful information. As most national unemployment insurance schemes are strongly individualized and as unemployment is concentrated among groups with shorter education, if any (OECD, 2000a), we stick with the net replacement rate for a single APW as our empirical indicator for benefit generosity. The next issue is how to establish qualitative breaking points for when a benefit is fully generous, fully not-generous and more generous than not. According to national consumption surveys persons cannot maintain any attained standards of living if they got their income reduced to a fifth; they would soon have to rearrange their financial affairs dramatically (Hansen, 1998). Hence, if the net replacement rate is below 20 percent we deem it to be fully not-generous. Having a job or participating in an active labor market policy (ALMP) placement involves costs for mobility and various other types of expenses.

In most countries, Denmark, for example, workers have tax allowances to cover partially for such costs and ALMP participants may earn something extra before their benefit is reduced. Both the earnings disregard and the tax allowances amount to approximately 10 percent of the APW earnings in the Danish example. For this reason we deem net replacement rates of 90 percent and more to be fully generous. It is more difficult to establish; when benefits are more generous than not, we have put the point at 55.5 percent. For the specific translation of net replacement rates into fuzzy scores and verbal labels, see Table 12.1.

- *Obligations* of unemployment claimants can be measured in numerous ways, but it is immensely difficult to derive a good index of strictness of sanctions (Kvist, 1998; Ministry of Finance, 1998; OECD, 2000b). We have decided to opt for a measure on negative sanctions, as they are stipulated in legal texts. That is, an index that measure the negative sanctions that may be imposed if a person becomes unemployed voluntarily or because of fault, and, when claiming benefits, refuses to accept a job or ALMP offer first, second, and subsequent times. Recognizing that implementation may not always follow the letter of the law, legal stipulations do give an important signal to both administrative authorities and claimants, and can be seen as a reflection of politicians' stance on the issue of obligations. Hence, our fuzzy set concerns the severity of negative sanctions measured by an empirical indicator on the number of weeks claimants may have their benefits suspended. The logic behind the index is that the earlier strict sanctions are imposed, the higher the score. For example, a temporary sanction period for the first refusal weighs twice as much as for a similar period imposed for a second refusal, which, in turn, weighs twice as much as sanction periods for subsequent refusals. Also the longer, and thus more severe, the sanctions, the higher index score. For this reason scores for permanent exclusion have been set equal to a 26-weeks period of sanction, and, again, the weight is twice as big for exclusion at the first refusal as for exclusion at the second refusal, etc. Where countries apply different rules for refusal of job and ALMP offers, respectively, the average of these two scores have been used as the index score. Similarly, an average is found when countries make use of different rules for refusals depending on timing in benefit spell (e.g., Denmark) or discretion to decide between temporary or permanent benefit cut-offs (e.g., Finland and Sweden). In the latter case, the average takes into account the actual use of the permanent withdrawal informed by national statistics and experts. Finally, consideration has been made to the normal timing of offers in the benefit period; the earlier offers, and hence potential sanctions are imposed, the higher index scores.

Table 12.1 reports empirical indicators for three fuzzy sets on concepts or aspects, and procedures for translating raw data into fuzzy membership scores. Also Table 12.1 shows how fuzzy membership scores are translated into nine verbal labels, ranging from, for example, "fully accessible" to "fully not

Table 12.1

**Specification of Empirical Indicators and the Translation of Data into
Fuzzy Membership Scores and Verbal Labels**

Empirical indicators:			Translation of data into:	
Accessibility to unemployment benefits measured, by an index taking into account personal scope of application, age groups & eligibility criteria	*Generosity* of unemployment benefits measured by net replacement rate for single person with earnings at level of APW (%)	*Obligations* of claimants measured by an index of the negative sanctions imposed if claimants refuse to accept job and ALMP offers	Fuzzy membership scores	Verbal labels
>90.0	>90.0	>85.0	1	Fully in the set
82.0-90.0	79.3-89.9	69.5-85.0	0.84-0.99	Almost fully in the set
72.0-81.9	67.7-79.2	54.9-69.4	0.68-0.83	Fairly in the set
60.0-71.9	55.6-67.6	41.3-54.8	0.51-0.67	More or less in the set
59.0-59.9	54.5-55.5	40.2-41.2	0.50	Cross-over point
47.0-58.9	42.4-54.4	27.6-40.1	0.34-0.49	More or less out of the set
37.0-46.9	30.8-42.3	16.0-27.5	0.18-0.33	Fairly out of the set
28.9-36.9	20.1-30.7	5.4-15.9	0.01-0.17	Almost fully out of the set
<28.9	<20.0	<5.4	0	Fully out of the set

accessible," which are used throughout the chapter. For example, if a benefit scores 70.2 in the set on generosity this is translated into and presented as a "fairly generous" benefit.

After having established empirical indicators and procedures of translating raw data into fuzzy scores and verbal labels, we may now proceed to the specification of cases' membership in fuzzy sets. That is, we can now analyze the development in social rights and obligations based on our empirical evidence.

Changing Rights and Obligations in Unemployment Insurance

Table 12.2 shows fuzzy membership scores in the accessibility of unemployment insurance, one of the two aspects of social rights we have chosen to investigate. As can be seen, all the Nordic countries and the United Kingdom had accessible unemployment insurance schemes throughout the 1990s just as it was more difficult in Germany and the Netherlands. No country experienced a qualitative shift from difficult to easier accessible unemployment insurance or the other way. But this masks important quantitative national changes and cross-national differences.

Table 12.2
Fuzzy Membership Scores in Accessibility (A) of Unemployment Insurance, 1990-1998

Country	1990	1991	1992	1993	1994	1995	1996	1997	1998
Denmark	.98	.98	.98	.98	.74	.74	.65	.53	.53
Finland	.66	.66	.51	.51	.51	.71	.71	.58	.58
Norway	.78	.78	.78	.78	.78	.78	.71	.64	.64
Sweden	.92	.92	.92	.92	.77	.77	.77	.77	.77
Germany	.45	.45	.45	.45	.45	.45	.45	.45	.45
Netherlands	.41	.41	.41	.41	.41	.28	.28	.28	.28
United Kingdom	.52	.52	.52	.52	.52	.52	.52	.52	.52

All the Nordic countries made access to unemployment insurance more difficult in the 1990s. In 1990, Denmark and Sweden were almost fully accessible, Norway was fairly accessible, and Finland more or less accessible. By 1998, Denmark was only more or less accessible because of the new "activation line" in Danish unemployment policy initiated in the late 1980s and given new impetus by the labor market reforms of 1994 and subsequently. Since 1994, participation in training and job offers no longer qualifies people for re-entitlement to unemployment insurance. Previously there was a virtual recycling mechanism as the unemployed at risk of losing their benefits were made an offer that in turn re-qualified them for a new benefit period. From having perhaps the most relaxed work requirement among Western welfare states, things changed in 1997 when 52 weeks of work instead of 26 weeks within a three-year period became a requirement. Sweden moved from an almost fully accessible unemployment insurance system to a fairly accessible one. In 1994, the work requirement was raised from four to five months of work within a year. The Swedish work concept, however, is still broad and includes de facto participation in labor market programs and leave schemes. Unemployment insurance in Finland was fairly accessible in 1990, mainly because the Finnish self-employed were excluded from coverage. In 1992, it became less accessible as participation in active labor market programs was no longer a qualification for a renewed benefit period. The self-employed became covered in 1995. And in 1997, the minimum contribution period for unemployment insurance was increased from six to ten months, and the work requirement from 26 weeks to 43 weeks of work within a two-year period. As a result Finland's unemployment insurance is now more or less accessible. The Norwegian scheme moved from being fairly accessible to become more or less accessible in 1996 when there was an increase in the amount of previous earnings required before becoming eligible. In sum, access to Nordic unemployment insurance today is not as relaxed as it was a decade earlier.

The Netherlands also made access more strict. Eligibility for the Dutch unemployment insurance benefit became increasingly difficult as it moved from a more or less not-accessible to a mostly not-accessible system. In 1995, the relatively tough working requirement became 39 weeks of work rather than 26 weeks within 52 weeks, coupled with four years of some employment (or child minding) within the last five years. In contrast, access conditions remained stable in Germany and the United Kingdom. Germany retained a more or less not-accessible unemployment insurance mainly because, on the one hand the self-employed are excluded from coverage and there are relatively strict working requirements, and, on the other, compulsory coverage. Because of comparatively lax working requirements in the form of paid or credited National Insurance contributions within two years, the UK unemployment insurance scheme was more or less accessible throughout the 1990s.

Benefit generosity has decreased in all countries, except Norway, in some countries more than others, but nowhere leading to a qualitative shift in this aspect of unemployment insurance, see Table 12.3. Among the Nordic countries, Sweden has reduced its generosity the most, falling from almost fully generous in 1990 to fairly generous in 1998 as it reduced its earnings-replacement rate gradually from 90 to 75 percent (and now 80 percent). Finnish cuts were less visible through the lack of indexation and by reducing the earnings base for calculating the benefit. Nevertheless, Finland was more or less generous the whole period. In fact, there has been no changes made to the Danish unemployment benefit itself, but changes made in the tax system made benefit generosity fall gradually nevertheless. Denmark was fairly generous from 1990 to 1993 and more or less generous afterwards.

Table 12.3
Fuzzy Membership Scores in Generosity (G) of Unemployment Insurance,
1990-1998

Country	1990	1991	1992	1993	1994	1995	1996	1997	1998
Denmark	.71	.71	.69	.69	.65	.63	.62	.61	.60
Finland	.62	.62	.62	.62	.62	.62	.60	.58	.57
Norway	.65	.65	.65	.65	.65	.65	.65	.65	.65
Sweden	.96	.96	.95	.85	.85	.81	.74	.72	.71
Germany	.58	.58	.58	.58	.55	.55	.55	.55	.54
Netherlands	.75	.75	.75	.75	.76	.75	.75	.74	.72
United Kingdom	.04	.04	.04	.04	.04	.03	.02	.01	.00

Both the Netherlands and Germany remained stable in their generosity of unemployment benefits. Germany retained more or less generous benefits and the Netherlands fairly generous benefits. With net replacement rates around 21-22 percent the British unemployment insurance scheme was almost fully not-generous, and in 1998 it became fully not-generous when its replacement rate dropped to 20 percent. However, this replacement rate does not take into account the possibility of supplementary benefits in the United Kingdom.

Social rights come with obligations. Unemployment claimants' obligations span a wide specter. In all countries, unemployed have to be willing, capable, and searching for work, the so-called ILO criteria. There are cross-national differences as to how these obligations are translated into laws and administrative practice. For example, the willingness to work is often stipulated in terms of occupational, geographical, and wage mobility requirements that may vary between countries, regions, branches of industry, and over time. Authorities often test willingness to work by stipulating that unemployment claimants must accept work offers and ALMP placements. Work capability may be checked by doctors. Search obligations are sometimes tested by requiring unemployment claimants to document job search activity, for example by showing that they have made actual job applications at interviews with case officers. If unemployment claimants do not meet their obligations, they are typically subjected to some sort of negative sanctioning. This may be in the form of having their unemployment benefits withdrawn temporarily or permanently. Vice versa, if unemployment claimants fulfill their obligations, they may be met with positive sanctioning, for example, benefit increase or extension of benefit period. In short, social rights are intrinsically linked with obligations that are stipulated in legal texts and enforced through positive and, more often, negative sanctions.

Table 12.4
Fuzzy Membership Scores on Obligations (o) in Unemployment Insurance, 1990-1998

Country	1990	1991	1992	1993	1994	1995	1996	1997	1998
Denmark	.22	.22	.22	.22	.73	.73	.84	.89	.94
Finland	.38	.38	.38	.38	.38	.38	.38	.38	.48
Norway	.75	.75	.75	.75	.75	.75	.75	.75	.75
Sweden	.22	.22	.22	.22	.22	.22	.81	.81	.81
Germany	.66	.66	.66	.66	.66	.66	.66	.66	.66
Netherlands	.40	.40	.40	.40	.40	.40	.92	.92	.92
United Kingdom	.48	.48	.48	.48	.48	.48	.51	.51	.51

Danish claimants' obligations have undergone dramatic changes in the 1990s from fairly weak in 1990 to almost fully strong in 1998, see Table 12.4. Until 1994, claimants refusing to accept job and ALMP placements were subjected to a one- or three-week sanction period for first and second refusal, respectively, and possible exclusion for subsequent refusals. With the labor market reform of 1994 and its subsequent modifications, ALMP placements have been offered increasingly to test claimants' willingness to work. At the same time, refusing an ALMP offer in the so-called activation period means an exclusion from benefits. Initially, the activation period started after four years of unemployment, but has gradually been put forwarded to start after two years in 1998 (and after one year in 2000). Since 1994 claimants have also been excluded from benefits if they refuse their second job or ALMP offer, independent of the timing in their unemployment spell. The reasoning behind the stricter rules governing obligations and their implementation is that ALMP helps unemployed get into work and will deter people not wanting to work from drawing benefits.

Finland had more or less weak obligations during the 1990s, see Table 12.4. Claimants refusing job and ALMP placements were subject to a six-week sanction period, independent of the number of refusals. In the light of the improved economy in the second half of the 1990s, obligations became stricter in 1998. A two-month sanction period was imposed for claimants refusing job offers, and authorities got the possibility to withdraw benefit permanently. Refusing ALMP placements was penalized by a sanction period varying from zero to two months. At the second refusal and subsequent refusals of both job and ALMP offers a fixed two-month period is applied, with the possibility of permanent exclusion or until the person in question has been in a job or occupational education for eight weeks. Whereas temporary sanctions are used frequently, the use of permanent benefit withdrawal is very rare. This may in part be explained by ALMP participation in 1990 and 1991 counting towards qualification for a new benefit period, as in Denmark before 1994; today this is only the case for a minor part of Finnish ALMP measures.

Sweden, however, has retained the practice of letting ALMP participation count as ordinary work towards new unemployment benefit periods throughout the 1990s. As used to be the case in Denmark, Swedish ALMP authorities have designed their activities so as to avoid large number of unemployment insurance claimants falling out of the system. The existence of fairly weak obligations from 1990 to 1996 to accept job and ALMP offers should be judged on this background. Claimants lost their benefit between one and four weeks (five to twenty compensation days) depending on the length of the job and ALMP offers made with the possibility of exclusion for repeated refusal until the person had taken work for four weeks. Rules were made stricter in 1996 when sanction periods were tripled or more. Since sanction periods last four weeks for offers lasting at maximum one week, eight weeks for offers that last up to two weeks, and twelve weeks for offers lasting longer than two weeks, still with the possibility of exclusion until a person has had work for four weeks. As a result of the tougher sanctioning rules, Sweden today has fairly strong obligations for claimants.

Norway has not made any changes to the lengths of sanction periods during the 1990s. The first refusal of a job or ALMP offer results in a sanction period of eight weeks, second refusal in twelve weeks, and subsequent refusals in twenty-six weeks. Norway has fairly strong obligations as measured here.

Germany also made no changes to the rules governing its sanction periods during the 1990s. Claimants declining the first job or ALMP offer experience a twelve-week sanction period that may be reduced in some circumstances. Claimants are excluded from benefits when they have had their benefits withdrawn for twenty-four weeks. As a result Germany has more or less strong obligations.

The Netherlands has markedly changed claimants' obligations. Obligations were more or less weak until 1996 when they became almost fully strong as a result of the 1996 Law on Sanctions and Penalties. Before claimants refusing the first offer suffered a month benefit withdrawal with authorities having the possibility of permanent exclusion until the person accepted the offer. The exclusion possibility was rarely applied. This all changed in 1996 when authorities got obliged to impose sanctions for claimants' refusals and exclusion became the rule for first refusal of job and ALMP offers. Today Denmark and the Netherlands have the strongest obligations for unemployment claimants.

When claimants refuse a job offer in the United Kingdom they risk losing their benefit between one and twenty-six weeks, based on the case officers' discretion. Claimants lose their unemployment benefit for two weeks when refusing ALMP, but this period was doubled to four weeks after 1996. In short, the United Kingdom seems to place less importance on withdrawal of benefit periods due to refusal of ALMP than any other country included. Instead the United Kingdom imposes obligations by demanding high degrees of wage mobility and documentation of job search to be demonstrated on a frequent basis. The latter type of enforcing obligations results in relatively high shares of benefit sanctions. However, these dimension of obligations are not caught with our measure here that focus on the link between rights and obligations with regard to accepting job and ALMP offers, and not with regard to mobility requirements nor job search demands.

Emerging Models of Unemployment Insurance

How are we to make sense of the development of rights and obligations? To make sense of such changes it is useful not only to distinguish between different types and levels of rights and obligations, but also between different *combinations* of rights and obligations. If rights and obligations act together in meaningful ways, it does not suffice to only assess the development on either of these two dimensions of unemployment insurance alone; they should be assessed together and simultaneously. Inspired by the growing literature in comparative welfare state research we may distinguish between different types of unemployment insurance models (Esping-Andersen, 1999; Gallie and Paugam, 2000). Each model is characterized in Weberian ideal typical terms by distinct conceptions and balances of social rights and obligations (Weber, 1949 [1904]). By ideal typical is meant that no one country will be a perfect match to the ideal type, but may conform more or less to one rather than another type of ideal type.

In the Social Democratic welfare state model, social rights follow the egalitarian principle that people ought to be equal in some respect. The state actively attempts to undo market-induced differentials or hereditary privilege. The goal of the state is to damper inequalities in living conditions between families and persons with and without jobs, between men and women, between skilled and less-skilled, and to secure employment for all. To achieve these lofty goals, the state takes on an active role by not only providing easy accessible, generous unemployment benefits, but also intervenes more broadly in the economy. On this background, the Social Democratic unemployment insurance model is ideal typically characterized by the combination of easy accessible, generous unemployment benefits combined with weak obligations for claimants.[2]

The merit principle dominates the conception of rights and obligations in the Conservative welfare state model. Rights are derived from employment and occupational status. The state has a limited active role in trying to maintain status differentials so redistribution occurs within occupational groups where social provisions reflect previous status in the labor market and does not aim to damper existing inequalities. Citizens have strong obligations to take part in community and to take care of themselves. However, as social rights are earned through employment, they are more like property rights and inviolable than in the other models. Therefore, claimants of social provision have few obligations to take on work and ALMP offers, to the extent they are offered by the state at all, at least initially in their benefit period. On this background, the Conservative unemployment insurance model can ideal typically be characterized by the combination of hard to access benefits, that are generous, with weak obligations for claimants.

In the Liberal welfare state model rights and obligations are guided by the principle of equity or need. The state does not have an active role in trying to damper inequalities or maintain status differentials, but should merely try to compensate for market failures and alleviate poverty. The state should not interfere with the market and individuals who, according to the dominant liberal ideas, can better decide and provide welfare. Therefore, the state has, in the area of social policy, to exclude itself to temporary relief of poverty for deserving groups of the population. This model is supposed to characterize countries like the United States (King, 1995, 1999).

In the European context, however, the work of, not least, Beveridge, has resulted in a Liberal model with a social reminiscence in that all citizens should be guaranteed some insurance against the vagaries of the market through a minimum income for a limited period (see Room, 1979; King, 1995, 1999). In the lack of better terms we will call this a Labour model. Since the state has no active role in helping people into work through job offers, ALMP claimants of, for example, unemployment insurance, have weak obligations to accept such offers, but strong obligations to search for work. As a result, the Labour unemployment insurance model can be ideal typically characterized by the combination of easy accessible, not-generous unemployment benefits coupled with weak obligations on behalf of claimants to accept work or ALMP offers. In contrast, the access to benefits is hard in the Liberal model.

In sum, we have four different unemployment insurance models labeled according to their dominant political ideologies. However, as indicated in the introduction to this chapter, governments have recently stressed the importance of stronger obligations, independent of their ideological tradition. For this reason, we will make a simple distinction between what we will call "new" and "old" models, where the new models are characterized by strong obligations, and the old models by weak obligations. Through this distinction we may judge whether the political rhetoric is matched by actual policy changes resulting in qualitative shifting of the national unemployment insurance model from an old to a new version.

As a consequence, we have, for the sake of simplicity, identified the same three concepts or aspects of unemployment insurance to constitute a total of eight distinct models of unemployment insurance, see Table 12.5.

Table 12.5
Models of Unemployment Insurance

Accessibility to benefits (A)	Generosity of benefits (G)	Obligations to accept job or ALMP offers (O)	Model
A (easy)	G (high)	O (strong)	A*G*O (New Social Democratic)
A (easy)	G (high)	~O (weak)	A*G*~O (Old Social Democratic)
A (easy)	~G (low)	O (strong)	A*~G*O (New Labour)
A (easy)	~G (low)	~O (weak)	A*~G*~O (Old Labour)
~A (difficult)	G (high)	O (strong)	~A*G*O (New Conservative)
~A (difficult)	G (high)	~O (weak)	~A*G*~O (Old Conservative)
~A (difficult)	~G (low)	O (strong)	~A*~G*O (New Liberal)
~A (difficult)	~G (low)	~O (weak)	~A*~G*~O (Old Liberal)

The New Social Democratic unemployment insurance model in this presentation of the analytical property space is equal to the first model in Table 12.5. If we transform the aspects in the analytical property space into fuzzy sets, as described earlier, we get that this model, expressed in fuzzy set terms, equals the ideal typical location: A*G*O, or the combination of easy accessible unemployment insurance benefit *and* generous unemployment benefits *and* strong obligations to accept job or ALMP offers. The Old Social Democratic model equals the ideal typical location: A*G*~O, and so forth. If, and to what extent, individual countries actually belong to this or that model can be studied empirically with fuzzy set theory.

On the basis of the unemployment insurance models identified in the analytical property space and the preceding analysis of countries' fuzzy membership scores in the accessibility (A) and generosity (G) of unemployment benefits and claimant's obligations (O), we may now analyze countries' conformity to unemployment insurance models. Table 12.6 sets out countries' fuzzy membership scores in the eight models. Scores in bold indicate countries' membership of a model (i.e., fuzzy membership score greater than .5), scores in bold and italics indicate more or less membership (i.e., membership score between .34 and .49), and scores in italics indicate fully and almost fully out of the model (i.e., scores between .00 and .17). Using these qualitative distinctions we can analyze not only which model a country belongs to and its degree of membership, but also which models the country is closest to and furthest away from. This enables us to make judgments on the (shifting) character of the national unemployment insurance models.

From Table 12.6 we can see countries' membership of the four unemployment insurance models in their old and new versions, respectively, with weak and strong obligations. It can be seen that Denmark and Sweden have put action behind the words in the sense that both countries move from belonging to an Old Social Democratic model to belong to a New Social Democratic model. Moreover, these were not incremental shifts in the area of great ambiguity. Both Sweden and Denmark moved from being fairly out of the New Social Democratic model to become fairly in and more or less in, respectively. Indeed the greater emphasis on obligations in the two Nordic countries can be interpreted as resulting in a qualitative change of their unemployment insurance models. Also, as indicated by the Danish and Swedish scores in italics, these two countries are almost fully out of many of the other model during large parts of the 1990s. In other words, their unemployment insurance policies are pretty distinct most of the time.

In contrast, Finland presents a more ambiguous case. Throughout the 1990s, Finland belonged to the Old Social Democratic model, although to a varying degree. However, as can be seen from the Finnish scores in bold and italics in Table 12.6, the country is only more or less out of a number of other models. This can be interpreted as Finland not having as distinct an unem-

Table 12.6
Fuzzy Membership Scores in Unemployment Insurance Models, 1990-1998

Country	Model	1990	1991	1992	1993	1994	1995	1996	1997	1998
Denmark	New Social Democratic (A*G*O)	.22	.22	.22	.22	.65	.63	.62	.53	.53
	Old Social Democratic (A*G*~O)	.71	.71	.69	.69	.27	.27	.26	.11	.06
	New Labour (A*~G*O)	.22	.22	.22	.22	.35	.37	.38	.39	.40
	Old Labour (A*~G*~O)	.29	.29	.31	.31	.27	.27	.16	.11	.06
	New Conservative (~A*G*O)	.02	.02	.02	.02	.26	.26	.35	.47	.47
	Old Conservative (~A*G*~O)	.02	.02	.02	.02	.26	.26	.16	.11	.06
	New Liberal (~A*~G*O)	.02	.02	.02	.02	.26	.26	.35	.39	.40
	Old Liberal (~A*~G*~O)	.02	.02	.02	.02	.26	.26	.16	.11	.06
Finland	New Social Democratic (A*G*O)	.38	.38	.38	.38	.38	.38	.38	.38	.48
	Old Social Democratic (A*G*~O)	.62	.62	.51	.51	.51	.62	.60	.58	.52
	New Labour (A*~G*O)	.38	.38	.38	.38	.38	.38	.38	.38	.43
	Old Labour (A*~G*~O)	.38	.38	.38	.38	.38	.38	.40	.42	.43
	New Conservative (~A*G*O)	.34	.34	.38	.38	.38	.29	.29	.38	.48
	Old Conservative (~A*G*~O)	.34	.34	.49	.49	.49	.29	.29	.42	.42
	New Liberal (~A*~G*O)	.34	.34	.38	.38	.38	.29	.29	.38	.42
	Old Liberal (~A*~G*~O)	.34	.34	.38	.38	.38	.29	.29	.42	.42
Norway	New Social Democratic (A*G*O)	.65	.65	.65	.65	.65	.65	.65	.64	.64
	Old Social Democratic (A*G*~O)	.25	.25	.25	.25	.25	.25	.25	.25	.25
	New Labour (A*~G*O)	.35	.35	.35	.35	.35	.35	.35	.35	.35
	Old Labour (A*~G*~O)	.25	.25	.25	.25	.25	.25	.25	.25	.25
	New Conservative (~A*G*O)	.22	.22	.22	.22	.22	.22	.29	.36	.36
	Old Conservative (~A*G*~O)	.22	.22	.22	.22	.22	.22	.25	.25	.25
	New Liberal (~A*~G*O)	.22	.22	.22	.22	.22	.22	.29	.35	.35
	Old Liberal (~A*~G*~O)	.22	.22	.22	.22	.22	.22	.25	.25	.25
Sweden	New Social Democratic (A*G*O)	.22	.22	.22	.22	.22	.22	.74	.72	.71
	Old Social Democratic (A*G*~O)	.78	.78	.78	.78	.77	.77	.19	.19	.19
	New Labour (A*~G*O)	.04	.04	.05	.15	.15	.19	.26	.28	.29
	Old Labour (A*~G*~O)	.04	.04	.05	.15	.15	.19	.19	.19	.19
	New Conservative (~A*G*O)	.08	.08	.08	.08	.22	.22	.23	.23	.23
	Old Conservative (~A*G*~O)	.08	.08	.08	.08	.23	.23	.19	.19	.19
	New Liberal (~A*~G*O)	.04	.04	.05	.08	.15	.19	.23	.23	.23
	Old Liberal (~A*~G*~O)	.04	.04	.05	.08	.15	.19	.19	.19	.19
Germany	New Social Democratic (A*G*O)	.45	.45	.45	.45	.45	.45	.45	.45	.45
	Old Social Democratic (A*G*~O)	.34	.34	.34	.34	.34	.34	.34	.34	.34
	New Labour (A*~G*O)	.42	.42	.42	.42	.45	.45	.45	.45	.45
	Old Labour (A*~G*~O)	.34	.34	.34	.34	.34	.34	.34	.34	.34
	New Conservative (~A*G*O)	.55	.55	.55	.55	.55	.55	.55	.55	.54
	Old Conservative (~A*G*~O)	.34	.34	.34	.34	.34	.34	.34	.34	.34
	New Liberal (~A*~G*O)	.42	.42	.42	.42	.45	.45	.45	.45	.46
	Old Liberal (~A*~G*~O)	.34	.34	.34	.34	.34	.34	.34	.34	.34
Netherlands	New Social Democratic (A*G*O)	.40	.40	.40	.40	.40	.28	.28	.28	.28
	Old Social Democratic (A*G*~O)	.41	.41	.41	.41	.41	.28	.08	.08	.08
	New Labour (A*~G*O)	.25	.25	.25	.25	.24	.25	.25	.26	.28
	Old Labour (A*~G*~O)	.25	.25	.25	.25	.24	.25	.08	.08	.08
	New Conservative (~A*G*O)	.40	.40	.40	.40	.40	.40	.72	.72	.72
	Old Conservative (~A*G*~O)	.59	.59	.59	.59	.59	.60	.08	.08	.08
	New Liberal (~A*~G*O)	.25	.25	.25	.25	.24	.25	.25	.26	.28
	Old Liberal (~A*~G*~O)	.25	.25	.25	.25	.24	.25	.08	.08	.08
	New Social Democratic (A*G*O)	.04	.04	.04	.04	.04	.03	.02	.01	.00
	Old Social Democratic (A*G*~O)	.04	.04	.04	.04	.04	.03	.02	.01	.00
United Kingdom	New Labour (A*~G*O)	.48	.48	.48	.48	.48	.48	.51	.51	.51
	Old Labour (A*~G*~O)	.52	.52	.52	.52	.52	.52	.49	.49	.49
	New Conservative (~A*G*O)	.04	.04	.04	.04	.04	.03	.02	.01	.00
	Old Conservative (~A*G*~O)	.04	.04	.04	.04	.04	.03	.02	.01	.00
	New Liberal (~A*~G*O)	.48	.48	.48	.48	.48	.48	.48	.48	.48
	Old Liberal (~A*~G*~O)	.48	.48	.48	.48	.48	.48	.48	.48	.48

ployment insurance model as the other Nordic countries. The last Nordic country, Norway, had a fairly strong New Social Democratic unemployment insurance model during the 1990s. And Norway was not close or very distant from many other models. In short, the Nordic countries live up to the expectation that they should have Social Democratic unemployment insurance models, and with the exception of Finland they today belong to the version we have earlier called the New Social Democratic model stressing strong obligations.

Germany also performs more or less as would be expected. It demonstrates a stable membership of the New Conservative model. However, as can be seen from Table 12.6, Germany only has more or less membership in this model, and is only more or less out of all the other models. Seen in this perspective it is hard to say that the German unemployment insurance model is very distinct.

Like Denmark and Sweden, the Netherlands also witnessed a fundamental change in the 1990s. The Dutch shifted from an Old to a New Conservative unemployment insurance. On the one hand, this qualitative change is perhaps less marked than in Denmark and Sweden as the Netherlands was only more or less out of the new model before the change. On the other hand, the country got a fairly strong membership in the new model, and it moved to become almost fully out of the Old Conservative model.

If action follows rhetoric, we may expect the greatest changes to have occurred in the United Kingdom, that is, a shift from an Old to a New Labour unemployment insurance model, although this may not be thoroughly investigated yet as our data ends in 1998 and Labour only took office in 1997. The United Kingdom does make a shift from an Old to a New Labour model, which dates to 1996—a year before the current Labour party got into government. However, the shift is marginal in nature. From being only marginally in the Old Labour model the United Kingdom moves to become marginally a member of the New Labour model. This can hardly be said to constitute a real change. A more interesting story unfolds if we look at how the United Kingdom belongs to other unemployment insurance models. Then we find that the United Kingdom does not share much with its European counterparts. The country is fully or almost fully out of both the Social Democratic and Conservative unemployment insurance models, as is indicated by the scores in italics for the United Kingdom in Table 12.6. What is more, it is only marginally out of the Liberal unemployment insurance models. The empirical evidence presented here in this way supports the idea that the United Kingdom has important commonalities with policies across the Atlantic rather than with policies in the European Union (Walker, 1999). There is in other words a strong liberal reminiscence in British unemployment insurance policy that is not shared to the same extent by the other European countries in this study.

Concluding Remarks

The study on the development in European unemployment insurance policies in the 1990s provided a number of insights. First, access to unemployment insurance has become increasingly difficult in the 1990s in nearly all countries. Although sometimes markedly stricter, no country can be said to have transformed their access criteria fundamentally. Second, most countries have also made benefits less generous. This was particularly the case in the Nordic countries, except Norway, less so in Germany, whereas benefit generosity in the Netherlands and the United Kingdom was pretty stable. Third, claimants' obligations were increased dramatically in three countries leading to qualitatively changing their national unemployment insurance model. Denmark and Sweden thus changed from an Old to a New Social Democratic model, and the Netherlands from an Old to a New Conservative model. Finland and, less so the United Kingdom also made obligations stronger, but these changes were more marginal in nature. Norway and Germany retained their level of obligations, but these were already comparatively strong at the beginning of the 1990s. Fourth, despite general tendencies to stricter access, reduced generosity, and stronger obligations, country developments remained within model-specific trajectories. The Danes and Swedes joined the Norwegians in having a New Social Democratic unemployment insurance model. Similarly, the Dutch joined the Germans in having a New Conservative unemployment insurance model. And the British got their own New Labour model, but this is very close to the Old Labour and Liberal models. The overall development in unemployment insurance may on this background be characterized by some cross-national commonalities in policy changes across countries belonging to different models, and some convergence between countries having the same underlying ideology in social policy. All national governments are, to varying degrees, actively adapting their unemployment insurance policies in what seems a concern to link social protection more firmly with work, changing the nature of citizenship, but at the same time governments pay due attention to their ideological and institutional legacies.

The Nordic countries and the Netherlands have introduced most changes, whereas the German and British policies have been largely the same. Generally, however, it has become more difficult in all countries to become, be, and remain a claimant of unemployment insurance. The big question today, therefore, is whether the tougher situation for jobless people is complemented by similarly active government efforts to help unemployed (back) into work. Unemployment insurance will always be an important part of modern welfare states, but unemployment amelioration is a more ambitious agenda that points towards a more inclusive form of citizenship, of balancing both passive and active rights with obligations.

Notes

* The author thanks Karen M. Anderson, Christina Behrendt, Bjørn Hvinden, Jürgen Kohl, and Charles Ragin for valuable comments.
1. Liberal tradition denotes the European usage of the term that in the U.S. is called a Conservative tradition.
2. Long duration of unemployment benefit periods could have been added as one of Social Democratic models' special features just as there are perhaps other, and more important, constitutive features of the Conservative and Labour models. Formal rules on benefit duration are, however, partly invalidated in the presence of strict obligations that result in fictitious maximum benefit periods.

References

Barbalet, J. M. (1988). *Citizenship*. Minneapolis: University of Minnesota Press.

Blair, T. (1999). "The Third Way: New Politics for the New Century." *Fabian Pamphlet*, No. 588.

Carroll, E. (1999). *Emergence and Structuring of Social Insurance Institutions*. Stockholm: Swedish Institute for Social Research.

Clasen, J., Kvist, J., and van Oorshot, W. (2001). "On Condition of Work." In Kautto, M., Fritzell, J., Hvinden, B., Kvist, J., and Uusitalo, H. (eds.), *Nordic Welfare States in the European Context*. London: Routledge.

Esping-Andersen, G. (1990). *The Three Worlds of Welfare Capitalism*. Cambridge: Cambridge University Press.

____. (1999). *Social Foundations of Postindustrial Economies*. Oxford: Oxford University Press.

Gallie, D., and Paugam, S. (eds.). (2000). *Employment Precarity, Unemployment, and Social Exclusion*. Oxford: Oxford University Press.

Gilbert, N. (1992). "From Entitlements to Incentives: The Changing Philosophy of Social Protection." *International Social Security Review*, 45 (3), 5-18.

Hansen, F. K. (1998). "Forbrugerstyrelsens Familiebudget." *Råd and Resultater*, No. 8, 13-20.

Janoski, T. (1998). *Citizenship and Civil Society: A Framework of Rights and Obligations in Liberal, Traditional, and Social Democratic Regimes*. Cambridge: Cambridge University Press.

King, D. (1995). *Actively Seeking Work?* Chicago: Chicago University Press.

____. (1999). *In the Name of Liberalism: Illiberal Social Policy in the USA and Britain*. Oxford: Oxford University Press.

Kvist, J. (1998). "Complexities in Assessing Unemployment Benefits and Policies." *International Social Security Review*, 51 (4), 33-55.

Marshall, T. H. (1964 [1950]). *Class, Citizenship, and Social Development*. New York: Doubleday.

Martin, J. P. (1996). "Measures of Replacement Rates for the Purpose of International Comparisons: A Note." *OECD Economic Studies*, No. 26, 99-114.

Ministry of Finance. (1998). *Availability Criteria in Selected OECD-Countries*, Working Paper No. 6. Copenhagen: The Ministry of Finance.

Mishra, Ramesh. (1993). *The Welfare State in Capitalist Society: Policies of Retrenchment and Maintenance in Europe, North America and Australia*. London: Harvester Wheatsheaf.

Norwegian Government. (1994). *Welfare Towards 2030*, White Paper No. 35, Oslo.

OECD. (2000a). *Education at a Glance*. Paris: OECD.

___. (2000b). *Employment Outlook*. Paris: OECD.

Ragin, C. (2000). *Fuzzy-Set Social Science*. Chicago: Chicago University Press.

Room, G. (1979). *The Sociology of Welfare*. Oxford: Basil Blackwell.

Salomäki, A., and Munzi, T. (1999). *Net Replacement Rates of the Unemployed. Comparisons of Various Approaches*, Economic Papers, No. 133, European Commission: Directorate-General for Economic and Financial Affairs.

Scarpetta, S. (1996). "Assessing the Role of Labour Market Policies and Institutional Settings on Unemployment: A Cross-Country Study." *OECD Economic Studies*, 26, 43-98.

Standing, G. (1990). "The Road to Workfare: Alternative to Welfare or Threat to Occupation?" *International Labour Review*, 129 (6), 677-691.

Visser, J., and Hemerijk, A. (1997). *"A Dutch Miracle"—Job Growth, Welfare Reform and Corporatism in the Netherlands*. Amsterdam: Amsterdam University Press.

Walker, R. (1999): "The Americanization of British Welfare: A Case Study of Policy Transfer." *International Journal of Health Services*, 19 (4): 679-97.

Weber, Max. (1949 [1904]): "Objectivity" in Social Science and Social Policy." In Max Weber, *The Methodology of the Social Sciences*. Glencoe, Ill.: The Free Press.

13

Combating Unemployment:
What Can Be Learned from Whom?

Karl Hinrichs

Apparently, the number of "employment miracles" has grown during the second half of the 1990s. Countries still struggling with comparatively high unemployment rates and employment levels considered as too low, like France, Germany, Italy, Belgium, and Spain, enviously look at others performing much better. Policy-makers, academics and, not the least, the media in these countries where the labor market situation has deteriorated until the mid-1990s or even beyond have been very receptive to foreign success stories and what could or should be *learned* from them. The now spluttering "Great American Job Machine" was the first success story receiving much attention, although European observers and local scholars recurrently pointed to the darker sides accompanying the impressive job growth in the U.S. (e.g., Schäfer, 2000; Mishel et al., 2001: chap. 7). The Netherlands provided the next "miracle" as it began to recuperate from the "Dutch disease" by the mid-1980s and attained full employment at the end of the last decade. In the late 1990s the sudden turnaround of the Danish economy became widely admired, almost at the same time as the "Celtic tiger" superseded the Asian "tiger states" when they suddenly lost very much of their appeal in 1997. Indeed, during its catch-up process, Ireland's record in bringing down unemployment stands out in the second half of the 1990s. Finally, the recent return of Switzerland to an almost "accustomed" full employment situation after a steep increase in unemployment around the mid-1990s gave rise to speak of another "miracle." These countries in particular have obviously disproved assumptions about an inevitable "jobless growth," albeit approaching full employment has not come at the terms of the *Golden Age* when jobs corresponding to the "standard employment relationship" clearly prevailed (Hinrichs, 1991).

A number of further small states with an open economy have not enjoyed attention to that extent as the Netherlands or Denmark although their employment performance has been even more impressive: after "full employment" vanished in the wake of the oil price shocks of 1973 and 1979, only Norway and Austria have *constantly* experienced unemployment rates well below the Organization for Economic Cooperation and Development (OECD) average. Sweden, remaining one of the few "full employment" countries until the late 1980s, fell into a deep labor market crisis at the beginning of the next decade, and even deeper fell Finland after being hit by the most severe economic recession of all OECD countries. However, the two latter countries achieved a turnaround and almost halved their peak level unemployment rates. While Norway, because being blessed with "manna from the sea" and thus still able to switch to expansionary fiscal policies if necessary, can hardly act as a "model" for other European countries, Austria's employment performance was not paid much attention since no spectacular policy shifts happened beyond incremental adjustments (Hemerijck et al., 2000; Pichelmann and Hofer, 1999). In contrast, the "miracles" in the Netherlands, in Denmark and, to some extent, in Ireland were attributed to comprehensive changes in welfare state, labor market, and macro-economic policies. Although the "streamlining" of the Swedish welfare state that preceded and accompanied the improvement of the labor market situation during the 1990s was looked upon with much interest from outside, the once coherent *Swedish Model* had lost much of its appeal after its gradual erosion started well before the upsurge in unemployment in 1991.

"Policy transfer," "transnational learning," "policy borrowing," "policy diffusion," or "lesson drawing" are related, although not identical concepts in comparative politics, referring to a process in which knowledge about policies, administrative arrangements, institutions, and ideas in one political system is gained and used to develop corresponding policies, administrative arrangements, etc. in another political system (Dolowitz and Marsh, 2000: 5). Such a process when it occurs becomes an element of social learning, eventually resulting in policy changes (Hall, 1993). Whether processes of ("crosscutting") transnational learning, always picking the "best practice," lead to policy *convergence* is not of particular interest here.

Rather, in this chapter, it is asked what can be learned from which "employment miracle" in order to attain a better labor market performance in countries doing worse so far. An optimistic notion rests upon the "suggestive analogy" (Offe, 1996: 213) of what has worked elsewhere will be a superior solution in general. Such a conception ignores, however, that somehow "copied" and transplanted policy instruments, programs, institutions, etc. are likely to yield very different and often counter-intentional results when removed from their structural context and, hence, lack the moral and cultural infrastructure on which the "original" can rely (Offe, 1996: 217). [1] *Within* a "family of nations" showing many similarities, those risks are smaller, but in order to avoid the pitfalls of an uninformed, incomplete or inappropriate policy transfer, a "prospective evaluation" (Rose, 1993: 32-34, 114-117; Dolowitz and Marsh, 2000: 17-20) is indispensable. It starts with inquiring how a program operates in another country and then develops a model of what is necessary to produce the same desired effects in another setting. Among others, a prospective evaluation includes an assessment of whether the policy change or "innovation" in question is part of a sequence of changes in related policy areas or whether political actors involved in the importing country and bound to a certain national culture would deal with the prospective change in similar manner. These prerequisites are easier to fulfill in case of a *tabula rasa* than when the policy has to be fitted in an already established and tightly coupled institutional structure which has to be adapted accordingly. In any case, it assumes a high degree of rationality of actors involved in the process of policy transfer or, more concretely, expecting policy-making to be a rational process which it usually is not.

If it is true that, with regard to combating unemployment, the lessons that can be drawn are not of a generalized "one-size-fits-all" type then one has to relate them to a concrete country. The non-universal application of the standard recipes of the OECD "Jobs Strategy" emanating from market liberal doctrines shows that they are hardly appropriate in every situational context and/or not feasible due to the specific national politics. Therefore, the focus of this chapter is on a single country, namely Germany, as one of the "poor performers" of Continental Europe. Taking Germany as a reference country requires us to analyze the institutional, historical, and other idiosyncrasies in some detail. Over and above such an inspection of the causes and the degree of the comparatively unfavorable labor market development, only a focus on a concrete country can show why sweeping policy changes that occurred in the "miracle" countries have not taken place in Germany (or any other country with similarly poor employment performance) and, hence, why policy transfers have played a limited role so far. A next step, however completely neglected in this chapter, could be to investigate what the "poor performers" possibly have in common when it comes to reform inertia and obstacles to ideational change, re-framing issues, reordering interests and, finally, remodeling institutional arrangements.

Despite considerable skepticism about which lessons can be learned from obviously more successful others, those reservations do not imply that corresponding attempts are pointless. Overcoming introversion the lessons may be encouraging as to a search for innovative (and possibly quite different) changes which fit the given institutional context because the countries regarded as "models" themselves could not rely on superior models to borrow from and, what is more, they had no homemade blueprint to follow, but rather "puzzled" single reforms in a sequence which only in retrospective combine to an apparently coherent strategy (Visser and Hemerijck, 1997; Green-Pedersen et al., 2001). Hence, the will to reform as such may be strengthened and the respective learning capacities improved when there are others having tackled a comparable problem already. [2]

I will proceed as follows: in the subsequent section, different criteria of "successful" labor market development will be discussed. As labor supply is not solely determined by demographic changes anymore and, ever less regularly, having a "job" means full-time employment yielding a "family wage," the evaluation of "success" in comparative perspective requires to apply more than one yardstick and also has to take into consideration possible trade-offs and concomitants. In the third section I will look into the "employment miracles," thereby focusing largely on the Netherlands, Denmark, and the United States, and the policies and policy changes which are commonly ascertained as having been conducive for their respective success story. The next section firstly deals with the peculiarities of the German labor market development especially after unification in 1990, and, moreover, arguments will be brought forward why Germany failed politically to embark in a timely manner upon a vigorous reform enterprise, similar to some of the more successful countries. In the second part of this section, I will come back to the question of what Germany and possibly other countries of the European continent as well can actually learn from foreign experiences. Finally, it is asked whether the strong emphasis on increasing commodified work should at least be accompanied by deliberate strategies to promote non-commodified forms of work and production.

What is Successful Employment Performance?

The level and change of the unemployment rate are regularly used as central indicators defining the need to take political action or to measure the success of state policies. Among those countries listed in Table 15.1 a clear division can be ascertained: during the last economic downturn hitting the OECD countries (1990 to 1994) in Belgium, France, Germany, Italy unemployment surged considerably and, up to now, not *very* much improvement can be noted compared to the peak levels which all happened to be in the 1990s (in Belgium the 10.0 percent figure in 1994 was only slightly lower than the 1984 record high). The increase was even steeper in Spain (starting from an already high level), Finland and Sweden, but afterwards the unemployment rate went down significantly. In contrast, in Austria, Denmark, Ireland, the Netherlands, Norway, and the U.S. the unemployment rate rose much less during the last economic downturn; the increase was much smaller than during the two preceding worldwide recessions before (Table 15.1, columns 1 and 2). Moreover, in these countries the unemployment rate has fallen substantially below the respective peak levels. However, if one was looking into

Table 13.1
**Increase in Unemployment Rates ("Commonly Used Definitions")
in Selected OECD Countries (Difference in Percentage Points), Peak
Level and Figure for 2000**

	(1) 1974/1978	(2) 1980/83	(3) 1990/94	(4) Peak	(year)	(5) 2000	(6) May 2001
Germany	1.5	4.7	2.0	9.5	(97)	7.8	7.8
Belgium	4.7	5.3	3.3	11.1	(84)	7.0	6.9
France	2.4	2.0	3.3	12.4	(97)	9.7	8.5
Italy	1.8	1.8	2.1	11.9	(98)	10.7	-
Spain	3.8	5.9	8.0	23.7	(94)	14.1	12.9
Denmark	4.8	4.5	0.5	10.2	(93)	4.8	4.6
Netherlands	2.6	5.8	1.6	11.0	(83)	2.4	2.3
Ireland	2.9	6.7	1.9	17.0	(86)	4.3	3.8
United States	0.5	2.5	0.5	9.7	(82)	4.0	4.3
Austria	1.0	2.2	1.1	5.7	(98)	4.6	3.7
Norway	0.3	1.8	0.2	6.0	(93)	3.4	-
Finland	5.5	0.8	13.4	16.7	(94)	9.8	8.9
Sweden	0.2	1.5	6.7	8.2	(93)	4.7	5.0

Sources: Columns (1) and (2): OECD (1997b: 32-33); columns (3) to (5): OECD (2001: 251); (6): SU (2001).

differentiated statistics—long-term or youth unemployment, both implying a special social problem, or regional distribution—the picture described above is somewhat less clear-cut.

Apart from the methodological problem of how the number of unemployed is ascertained (and how the procedures changed over time), those figures do not inform us about the number of persons presently included in labor market programs (e.g., retraining or public work), involuntarily working part-time, and thus being "part-time unemployed" (OECD, 1999: 32-34) or who gave up searching for a job ("discouraged workers") or are no longer counted as workless due to political manipulations of the unemployment statistics. The most important reason for questioning the unemployment rate as an appropriate indicator of (un)successful labor market performance is that the size of the labor force not only fluctuates according to demographic changes, [3] rather, and only partly related to labor demand, is also dependent on *behavioral* changes (particularly, women's increased inclination to continuous labor market participation which, to some extent, again indicates an "added-worker effect") and influenced by *political* measures (e.g., opening or closing pathways into early retirement or providing options for a paid parental leave).

As a result of simple arithmetic, at any given *number* of jobless the unemployment *rate* is inversely related to the share of actually employed persons among the population of working age (15 to 64 years). This *employment/population ratio* and how it developed is a more meaningful indicator of success. Therefore, the European Commission and national governments focus on the employment rate as a prime benchmark (70 percent overall, 60 percent for women). At any time since 1974 it has differed very much among the countries listed in Table 15.2.[4] The employment rate has remained largely constant at around 70 percent or has risen (clearly) above this level in Austria, Denmark, Norway, and the U.S. In both the Netherlands and Ireland the employment rate continuously increased since the mid-1980s, but surpassed the 70 percent threshold in the Netherlands only recently. At least until 1995, the long-term trend in France, Germany, Belgium, and Italy was unequivocally downward (although interrupted by an increase between 1984 and 1991 in Germany). In Sweden, until 1990 being top of the OECD league, and Finland the decline was steepest after 1990 (CEC, 2000: 86-100).

Table 13.2
Employment Rates in Selected OECD Countries,
Various Years between 1974 and 2000

	(1) 1974	(2) 1980	(3) 1985	(4) 1990	(5) 1995	(6) 2000
Germany	67.7	66.3	62.2	64.8	64.9	66.3
Belgium	61.2	58.0	54.3	57.1	56.6	60.9
France	66.0	63.8	59.1	60.4	59.4	61.1
Italy	55.7	56.2	53.7	54.9	51.2	53.4
Spain	59.6	50.8	44.1	50.7	47.2	56.1
Denmark	73.9	75.1	75.1	77.1	74.5	76.4
Netherlands	55.6	54.2	52.2	61.7	64.8	72.9
Ireland	59.7	57.8	50.7	53.9	55.3	64.5
United States	64.8	66.9	68.5	74.3	74.7	74.1
Austria	68.0	63.4	63.4	65.5	69.2	67.9
Norway	67.6	74.0	75.5	76.5	75.0	77.8
Finland	71.6	72.9	73.9	74.2	61.4	67.0
Sweden	75.3	79.4	79.7	84.4	73.5	74.2

Source: Columns (1) to (3): OECD (1992: 42); columns (4) and (5): OECD (1997b: 163); column (6): OECD (2001: 209).

Again, a differentiation of the employment rate by age (especially the development in the age brackets 15 to 24 and 55 to 64 years) and sex provides further insights into the effective utilization of the employment potential but blurs a clear-cut picture (CEC, 2000: 45-47). However, almost nowhere in Europe does a lower employment rate of older workers (attained by politically defined pathways into various forms of early retirement) go along with high rates of younger workers (or lower youth unemployment, cf. OECD, 2001: 212-220). If the "head-count" approach of employment rates shows an extraordinary positive performance for some countries it could possibly hide that the development is largely due to an increase in part-time jobs. Indeed, when this performance indicator is recalculated at "full-time equivalents" (FTE) the ranking list for EU countries changes somewhat: Denmark, Finland, Sweden, and Austria (in that order) still had the highest FTE-employment rate in 1999. In the Netherlands this rate was *lower* than in Ireland, Germany or France, but exceeding the figures for Spain and Italy by far (CEC, 2000: 86-100). On this account, the Dutch employment "miracle" was tantamount to a leap in the labor force participation rate of women working part-time (see below).

Related to this, information on the development of the aggregate volume of working hours and the average annual working hours per person of employable age would supplement the performance indicators in a meaningful way. Unfortunately, somewhat reliable and comparable data on annual hours worked are not available for all countries in question (OECD, 1998: 207, 154-157, 185). If nevertheless a simple recalculation of the figures on average annual working hours per employed, as given by the OECD (2001: 209, 225), is carried out the differences are quite impressive: per person of *employable age*, annual hours worked in the year 2000 amount to 952 in the Netherlands, 981 in Germany, 1,205 in Sweden, and 1,391 in the U.S., which is almost 1.5 times more paid employment performed per capita than in the Netherlands.

Good or poor employment performance, however, has to be evaluated against other (un-)employment-related features that precondition a positive development, occur as a trade-off or simply show as unintended concomitants—although, very often, a causal relationship should be hard to establish empirically. If it is true that higher profits are a prerequisite for enterprises' increased investment abilities and, hence, employment growth, a change in the functional distribution of national income at the disadvantage of labor could be expected to happen in countries that are moving out of an "employment crisis."

Such a change being the result of a "moderate" wage policy is more important when it comes to the development of *real* wages: are (temporarily) stagnating or decreasing real wages for all dependent employees (as in the Netherlands) the "price" for increasing their numbers or, *vice versa*, are increased real earnings of the "insiders" coming about at larger numbers of "outsiders"? If not *all* employed workers experienced constant or reduced real wages, have those in the lower deciles of earnings distribution suffered most while high-wage workers actually gained? According to widely held assumptions, an enlarged wage spread is required in order to improve the employment opportunities of unskilled job seekers especially in the service sector when being paid according to their lower productivity. As earnings inequality increased in all OECD countries (most extreme in the U.S. and UK), except for Germany and Belgium (OECD, 1996: 59-76), an improved labor market situation has to be weighed against two criteria: (a) has the number/share of full-time workers earning less than the nationally defined poverty level increased? Since governments in some countries attempt to contain the number of those "working poor" by in-work benefits (e.g., the Earned Income Tax Credit (EITC) in the U.S.; Pearson and Scarpetta, 2000) or subsidizing low-wage employment by other means, a change in the relative poverty rate of households of employable age would be another meaningful indicator to judge success; (b) if the number of low-wage jobs increased (and/ or unemployment of low-skilled workers decreased) are those workers "trapped" or is there considerable upward mobility of earnings? High out-flow figures would indicate that improved job opportunities are paid for with only temporary hardships (OECD, 1996: 76-94, 1997a: 29-43).

Furthermore, it is widely assumed that labor market performance will be improved if the chances to be offered a job are heightened when employment regulation is relaxed or if incentives for unemployed, particularly those with unfavorable earnings prospects, to take up a job offer are strengthened. There-fore, changes in the unemployment benefit system (entitlement criteria, level and maximum duration of benefits, sanctions for refusing job offers, etc.) and how these materialize in the financial situation of households with an unem-ployed member represent further indicators of success. For those impairments will not only make employment more attractive (as it is intended) but also affect the income of those who remain unemployed involuntarily or lose their job for no self-inflicted reason.

Success in pure *quantitative* terms has also to be valued against criteria as to whether the number or proportion of jobs deviating from terms that are commonly considered as "normal" or "desirable" has risen. Among others this could be measured by changes in the proportion of temporary jobs, of workers not covered by collective agreements, excluded from firms' fringe benefits or enjoying less protection against dismissals, or an increase of jobs demanding to work "unsocial hours" (e.g., at weekends or shift work). Some-times those developments may be the intended outcome of deliberate poli-cies to deregulate the national labor market. However, they may not only benefit the unemployed or entrants in a more flexible labor market but possi-bly also affect a larger number of employees in a negative way if a change in working conditions occurs that is not in accordance with their preferences. Thus, the development of job satisfaction in general would be one indicator or, more concretely, changes in the perceived job security another (OECD, 1997a: 129-137). Further indicators, which are somewhat less directly related to a positive/negative development of the employment situation, are changes in crime rates, the number of homeless people, suicide rates, frequency of violent protests and other forms of societal disorganization and disintegration.

Finally, the permanence (or sustainability) of the "employment miracle" is a central criterion. Is it merely a short-lived episode or have those economies presently admired for their performance also been successful in coherently readjusting the institutional design of economic, social, wage and labor market policy(-making) so that the return to a much-lamented *status quo ante* will not be likely? The "Dutch miracle" lasted not much longer than one decade, and the Danish and Irish success stories are even more recent ones so that it remains to be seen what will happen to the "miracles" when hit by a worldwide (or regional) recession. The other way round, what can be expected if the (almost) full employment situation endures? Will a hitherto moderate wage policy be continued and no vigorous demands for welfare state expansion be raised? Or will the social dialogue that emerged (Ireland) or was revitalized (Netherlands) be abandoned when single collective actors put their immediate interests first and retreat to more adversarial practices? In the latter case, among others, resurgent inflation and increased government expenditure may lead to growing imbalances and uncoordinated reactions, putting full employment in jeopardy.

All in all, if one looks into different measures of success it is not unequivocal *from* whom the other countries should learn. However, this still incomplete examination demonstrates that before one ties oneself down to a certain "model" it is indispensable to learn *about* it in great detail.

Different Routes to Become an "Employment Miracle"

It is not possible here to track down the strategies, the stepwise implementation of innovative reforms and the linking of policies/policy areas in detail that have led to a considerable improvement of employment performance in a number of countries. Rather, pointing to certain elements, generally regarded as cornerstones of positive development, is meant to emphasize the starkest contrasts to Germany (and possibly other unemployment-stricken countries) and, subsequently, to ask whether they may instruct a reorientation.

The labor market recovery in the United States, the Netherlands, Denmark, and Ireland succeeded because they strove to create a *virtuous cycle*. Macro policies caused a continuous labor demand, and this dynamics developed in different institutional configurations. Among OECD countries, there was more than one route either to fail or become successful (Alber, 2000; Schettkat, 2001). Likewise, micro-level policies were not uniform. In different ways the successful countries shaped the micro conditions for the (re-)integration of low-skilled, (potentially) long-term unemployed who are in the focus of political efforts everywhere, and the service sector is generally regarded as the main job reservoir.

Although having reached the lowest figure in thirty years, the most impressive feature of the U.S. "miracle" was probably not the decline in the unemployment rate (particularly not if the large number of people in prison and without a regular "job" is taken into consideration), but rather the almost uninterrupted increase in employment and total volume of annual hours worked for more than two decades. According to Solow (1999), besides comparatively less *product*-market regulation and better chances for start-up firms to develop in the U.S., it was pragmatic and skillful monetary policy in combination with fiscal policy committed to attain a balanced budget that maximized potential aggregate output and increased labor demand without bursting inflation. If the demand-induced job creation (and thus the minimization of cyclical—Keynesian—unemployment) due to macro-economic policy has been so relevant it is questionable whether those features of the U.S. labor market, which are hard to accept in most European countries, like increased wage inequality and numbers of *working poor*, meager unemployment benefits and weak restriction on discharging workers, are (always) essential parts of an "employment miracle."

On that account the successful small economies in Europe show different, albeit not homogeneous features: Austria, Denmark, and the Netherlands are still strong welfare states after mainly removing certain "overshooting" and offer a long-lasting, high replacement rate for unemployed; legal job protection is strict (not Denmark); organized labor plays a pivotal role in the (corporatist) wage-setting process; and wage dispersion remained moderate or extremely low (Denmark) (for a compilation of data on these features, see Schettkat, 1999: 161; Auer, 2000).

For both Denmark and the Netherlands the route to the "miracle" status meant a transformation of their hitherto "passive" welfare states which paid generous social transfers to the "redundant" (unemployed or "disabled") parts of the labor force, but lacked an institutional commitment to full employment as an autonomous policy goal. However, the actual employment rate was extremely low in the Netherlands, while in Denmark it remained at a level already attained in the 1970s that was attained by the U.S. only in the 1990s. Maintaining such a high rate of the working age population actually occupying a job may be regarded as a success as such. However, Denmark is admired for having halved its unemployment rate (1993 and 1994: about 12 percent) within the subsequent five years. After having pursued a stability-oriented, tight budget policy, the government was able to give a substantial anti-cyclical fiscal impetus for increasing economic growth and employment. The economic upswing, being utilized to reduce budget deficits, was supported by a moderate wage policy occurring in a context of "centralized decentralization" allowing for more flexible wage structures (due to wage drift on the firm level) within the framework of a low wage spread (for a more detailed account, see Madsen, 1999).

However, employment growth can only partly explain the reduction of unemployment since the employment rate is back where it was in 1990 and only about three percentage points higher than in 1994. The reduction of lifetime working hours was a second element: firstly, labor supply was reduced by giving elderly workers and unemployed the chance to early retirement pensions. The introduction of the now terminated "leave schemes" represent an equivalent instrument to relieve the labor market when workers on parental or educational leave (and receiving social transfers) are temporarily replaced by unemployed. In this case, the specific Danish combination (Kvist, 2001) of labor market flexibility (except for the UK, Denmark has the least regulated labor market in Europe) and easily accessible, generous unemployment benefits (at least for previous low-wage workers) is obviously advantageous. In an environment where "employers who shall hire have to be given the opportunity to fire," the actual turnover on the labor market is high (OECD, 1997a: 49-51), so that in a "job-rotation" process the unemployed have better chances to acquire and improve functional *and* extra-functional skills on the job, even if they are only temporarily employed, and do not fall into an abyss when being out of work (again). The complement, obviously indispensable to maintain generous unemployment benefits, was strengthened during the 1990s: following the traditional Swedish and more recent Norwegian approach, the "active turn" in labor market policy meant that the unemployed became obliged (as well as entitled) to participate in training and counseling measures (individual action plans) and to (regional) mobility. Sanctions for not taking up an appropriate job offer were strengthened, and (renewed) access to benefits was made more difficult. The recommodification strategy was accompanied by more decentralized responsibility of the (local) employment service agencies (for details, see Kvist, 2001). Although it is exactly this "activation" element of the Danish "miracle" that received much attention abroad, in fact and despite economic prosperity, many participants are stranded in "artificial jobs" and do not enter a regular job in the *private* sector.

Moreover, one might question whether the Danish success story rests upon coherent action that was "fine-tuned" among the relevant political and societal actors. It seems, however, that the Dutch story is even more an *ex post* constructed "model" and not a well-ordered and deliberate sequence of politically reconstructing the welfare state and the employment system. At the end of the 1980s the declining generosity of the welfare state was regarded as simple "retrenchment," not different from what was going on elsewhere, and the now famous "Wassenaar accord" of 1982 was *then* not seen as the starting-point for a revived corporatism facilitating "negotiated" social reform and to which the unions willingly agreed to but, because being confronted with a rapidly declining membership and in view of the omnipresence of unemployment, were on the defensive and not left with many alternatives (Visser and Hemerijck, 1997; Cox, 2001).

Compared to the United States and Denmark, the Netherlands does not stand out due to its current employment rate (see below), but rather its level of *un*employment. Even more than in Denmark it was accomplished by a redistribution of employment in various dimensions: Due still to the considerable numbers of disability pensioners and early retirees the average working life in the Netherlands is rather short, showing up in a below EU-average employment rate in the age bracket 55 to 64 years (CEC, 2000: 46). As one of the results of the "Wassenaar accord," the standard working week was reduced by 5 percent in the 1980s, accompanied by the start of working-time flexibilization. Job growth, however, stemmed largely from the increase in part-time work which made it possible to reduce unemployment and to attain a steep rise of female labor force participation *at the same time*. Although many female part-timers work very short hours, within about fifteen years the Netherlands accomplished a transition towards a "post-male breadwinner model." In no other OECD country is there such a high share of female and male workers that are part-timers, and the pattern, "one spouse is working full-time, the other part-time," now clearly dominates among the various distributions of employment within families (OECD, 1999: 240).

This expansion of (predominantly part-time) jobs, only recently resulting in a higher total volume of working hours, was facilitated by action taken by the government and the social partners; as well it was a prerequisite for gaining broad social acceptance of these actions: the extremely moderate wage policy, almost continuously pursued since the early 1980s, meant a decline in real wages but also a recovery of profits and international competitiveness (not the least due to a *real* depreciation of the currency against the German Mark). Subsequently, rising investments and more jobs in the private sector when economic activity picked up made decreasing real wages less felt within the family income context as did a reduced inflation rate. Freezing the level of social benefits (and restricting access) and even cutting public sector pay by 3 percent (in 1984) helped the government to reduce budget deficits, and after a positive development of economic output and employment was set in motion it was able to reduce taxes and social security contributions—thus supporting a continued moderate wage policy of the social partners—and to expand benefits targeted on individuals and families at the lower end of the income scale without public deficit again growing. In varying the (real) level of social transfers the government benefited from the existence of a legal minimum wage to which several benefits (e.g., the basic pension and social assistance) are linked. For it provides one central lever for budget-relevant changes in one blow while not changing the relative position of various claimant groups. Beside making social insurance financing more "employment-friendly" (integrating contributions into the income tax schedule in 1990), the government forced employers to internalize the costs of sick pay and disability pensions (a prime cause for speaking of the "Dutch disease"), which they were formerly able to improperly externalize to all social insurance contributors and taxpayers, and, moreover, it curtailed the power of the social partners in the administration of social security. The so far final step of government's institutional reform aims at greater effectiveness of labor market policy—somewhat resembling the Danish "active turn," including new tasks and more responsibility of the public (now competing with private) employment service.[5]

The recovery of the "Dutch patient" is considered to be the outcome of a negotiated change brought about by coordination between the government and the social partners and a not always easily attainable consensus among the social partners to give job growth priority over wage growth. The admiration by foreign observers is not only for the *results* but likewise for the *mode* of how the change in political priorities and the institutional reforms actually occurred. Within the framework of preexisting bipartite (*Stichting van de Arbeid*) and tripartite (*Sociaal-Economische Raad*) institutions and based on scientific expertise, conflicts were resolved and the strategies that should be brought into force were concerted and consented. As part of a revived corporatism, the central coordination of the terms of wage policy and its decentralized implementation, adjusted to the specificities of the branch and firm level, was particularly relevant. By and large, it is the consensual manner how these decisions were brought about that is regarded as impressive because, for a long stretch of time, no real gains were distributed. Within a traditional Dutch "consensus culture" the broad acceptance of (temporary) sacrifices was facilitated by almost equally sharing them, what can be read off from a not substantially increased income inequality.

Germany: In Need of Lessons Taught?

The Peculiar Development of the Labor Market in the 1990s

After sixteen years, in the Federal Republic "full employment," defined as an unemployment rate of less than 3 percent, ended in 1975. More interesting than the subsequent decade is the period 1984 to 1991, which includes the two-year "unification boom": the downward trend in the employment rate that already had begun in the late 1960s was temporarily reversed when the number of employed persons in *West* Germany grew by 2.6 million (which was 10 percent). Due to the growth of labor supply (married women and substantial immigration) unemployment reduction was less, albeit the (unstandardized) rate came down from 7.9 percent to 5.5 percent. Thus, in 1991 the rate was (considerably) lower than in the United States, Denmark ,and Ireland and about the same level as Austria, the Netherlands, and Norway. Moreover, on the eve of unification the general government's financial deficit was reduced to almost zero, and a "smooth consolidation" (Offe, 1991) of the German welfare state had led to social expenditures (as percentage of GNP) well below the peak levels of the mid-1970s and early 1980s. *Potentialities* for a coordinated attack on the remaining unemployment problem existed.

It is undeniable that the turnaround in employment performance during the 1990s has very much to do with unification (Czada, 1998), an event and process to which nothing compares in any other (traditional) OECD country. Therefore, a counterfactual question might be asked: what would the German labor market situation have looked like at the turn of the century without unification, given an as strong determination of the government and other political actors to combat unemployment by whatever means appropriate as it was shown to master the challenge of unification? Most likely, all performance indicators would look (much) more favorably than they actually do in *West* Germany.

Viewed in retrospective, the foundation of the aggravating employment problems in the whole of Germany was laid in July 1990 when, as the first step of the unification process, the *German Mark* was introduced in the former GDR. At that time, misconceptions about the true state of the GDR economy as well as unrealistic expectations to repeat the "economic miracle" of West Germany in the 1950s and 1960s prevailed, and political considerations dominated as against economic rationality when extremely overvalued exchange rates were adopted. This appreciation shock led to the immediate bankruptcy of many East German enterprises since productivity was generally low (30 percent of the West German level) and, moreover, demand for products of the COMECON-integrated GDR economy dropped away. De-industrialization was furthered by the subsequent wage policy aimed at catching up with the West German wage level but being unresponsive to employment and productivity development in East Germany (Lindlar and Scheremet, 1998: 3-9). Like the *Deutschmark* introduction before it meant a steep increase in purchasing power, it thus contributed to a slowdown of mass migration from East to West Germany, and relieved West German enterprises from facing competitors in an otherwise emerging low-wage region. As a result, the number of employed persons in *East* Germany decreased from 9.8 million in 1989 to 6.4 million in 2000 (minus 35 percent), and registered unemployment rose from zero to 1.35 million. Additionally, about 500,000 East Germans were engaged in various measures of active labor market policy.

Manow and Seils (2000) argue that the economic slump following the short-lived "unification boom" triggered a routine response pattern from the political system, again boosting the vicious "welfare without work" cycle. In order to cushion the collapse of employment and to maintain the legitimacy of the new economic and social order in East Germany, enormous public transfers (among others to finance large-scale early retirement and public works programs) were made available, including large funds from the social insurance schemes. About half of the increase in the total contribution rate to these schemes—from 35.2 percent in 1991 to more than 42 percent in the late 1990s—was due to those West-East transfers and the other half largely caused by declining covered employment in West Germany. According to Manow and Seils (2000) higher non-wage labor costs in East and West Germany contributed to increased unemployment in overall Germany and the slow growth of low-productivity service jobs. Since federal government's transfers for social purposes and for improving the physical infrastructure in East Germany were financed through tax increases (and shifts in spending priorities) to only a small extent and generous tax incentives for private investors in East Germany deteriorated the revenue side, public debt grew to levels that made it difficult to meet the Maastricht criteria. The 50 percent increase in public debt during the 1990s reduces the scope of action, especially to fight the non-structural part of unemployment by means of fiscal policy. [6]

It is contested whether Germany actually has a "service gap" and that this is caused by high payroll taxes. With regard to the level and growth of employment in service industries, (West) Germany obviously lags behind other countries, particularly, if compared to the "good performers" (OECD, 2000: chap. 3). However, in Germany due to less outsourcing the number of workers performing service activities is underestimated (Wagner, 1999): when classifying services not by "sector" but rather by "job activity," compared to the U.S., no significant difference in the share of service employment remains but reappears when a "service employment rate" is calculated. Wagner (1999) argues that the growth potential of particularly consumer-oriented and personal service jobs beyond the present level is limited since in Germany a "service culture" is underdeveloped. It can be overcome only in an "overworked economy" with long working hours and/or when women are integrated into the labor market to a higher degree than in Germany so that "household production" (in the broadest sense) is increasingly replaced by paid services.

According to Lindlar and Scheremet's (1998: 26-27) estimations an almost one percent decline of the employment level is due to the increase of the combined rate of contributions to the social insurance schemes in the 1990s while another study (Bauer and Riphahn, 1998) finds only minimal employment effects of social insurance contributions. Others regard the mode of financing social security and the recent rate leaps as particularly harmful to the level and growth of low-productivity, consumer-oriented service employment, and the reemployment chances of unskilled people out of work which constitute the bulk of long-term unemployed. On a disaggregated level, the comparative analyses by Scharpf (2000) and Jochem and Siegel (2000) find the tax wedge, caused by social insurance contributions, to be the central variable for explaining the change of employment in these *sectors* of the economy, whereas in high-skilled, business-oriented service jobs (like with highly productive manufacturing jobs) tax-wedge considerations do not play a prominent role.[7] In Germany, the high total wage costs necessary to provide employees with a disposable net income exceeding the "reservation wage" determined by the social assistance level (and collectively agreed wage levels for unskilled full-time workers regularly being beyond it) make it unprofitable for employers to offer jobs yielding low productivity. Where social security payroll taxes as such are low (U.S.), social transfers are almost exclusively financed out of general taxation (Denmark) or social insurance contributions are to a larger extent paid by employees but, because integrated into the income-tax schedule, exempt low earnings (Netherlands), employers' total wage costs can more easily match the low productivity of certain jobs without being unattractive for unskilled workers to take them.

Demands for somehow subsidizing a low-wage sector (that is facilitating a larger wage spread without negatively affecting workers net income) resulting from these findings are contested due to their small labor market effects and high fiscal costs (Klammer, 2000; Buslei and Steiner, 2000). In particular, it is argued (Karr, 1999) that in Germany the bulk of unskilled jobless with a high risk to become long-term unemployed would not benefit very much from this policy instrument: in general, they are older and very often suffer from health problems which reduces their chances for re-employment anyway. Different from the profile of low-skilled unemployed in most countries performing better, in Germany they are largely the victims of structural change in the *manufacturing* sector when disproportionally affected by the dramatic job losses during the 1990s.

This leads to the question of whether wage policy has been adequately responsive to the level and change of unemployment and to the needs of a postindustrial economy where job growth, if at all, occurs predominantly (or solely) in the service sector. A "high-wage, high-productivity strategy" with long job tenure and a relatively small wage spread has traditionally been a central element of the "German Model" of capitalism specializing in "diversified quality production" (Streeck, 1997). The "productivity whip" exerted on the core of an export-oriented manufacturing industry by the social partners' wage policy has indeed led to a comparatively high overall wage level that is, however, matched by an likewise high skill level of the work force. On whether wage-bargaining institutions have been sufficiently responsive to the (un)employment level during the last two decades, commonly used indicators give no clear-cut evidence: with the exception of the Netherlands and Ireland, no other European country, including the U.S., has—measured as an increase of unit labor costs—experienced less wage inflation than Germany (OECD, 1997a: 5-6). Moreover, wage increases should not have strangled enterprises' possibilities for investments—on the contrary: profitability has almost constantly increased since the early 1980s (while taxes on profits have decreased since then; Lindlar and Scheremet, 1998: 9-14).

Wage inequality in Germany is comparatively low and has even declined (OECD 1996: chap. 3). Since employees in all sectors are (still) broadly covered by the results of collective bargaining, full-time workers at the lower end of the wage scale also regularly attain a "family wage" and thus the problem of "working poor" hardly exists (despite the absence of a legal minimum wage). However, the OECD (1996: 76) found "little solid evidence to suggest that countries where low-paid work is less prevalent have achieved this at the cost of higher unemployment rates and lower employment rates for the more vulnerable groups in the labor market" (see also OECD, 1996: 94). In the same vein, the European Commission (CEC, 1998: pt. 1, chap. 4) could not detect a clear relationship between the wage spread and employment rates in the service sector. Nevertheless, Scharpf's (2000) arguments concerning the poor prospects of the German employment system to generate more jobs in the service sector are convincing: the "American way" of increased *private* service employment is precluded due to much lower income inequality and higher taxation (particularly indirect taxes and social security contributions). Likewise, the "Scandinavian way" is not feasible since already high taxes and contributions in order to finance a transfer-biased welfare state can hardly be increased for the sake of more publicly provided social services.

Finally, labor market *rigidities* are regarded as most relevant for persisting disequilibria (Siebert, 1997): comprehensive employment protection (for "insiders") implies high costs for employers to dismiss workers, and a generous replacement level of unemployment benefits and/or a long duration of entitlement increases the reservation wage and prolongs unemployment spells. While the German labor market is indeed highly regulated, in comparison, unemployment benefits in Germany are not overly generous (OECD, 1996: 28-43; Martin, 2000) and an increasing share of long-term unemployed may be regarded as endogenous to high unemployment independent of its cause. Moreover, unemployment in Germany (and other European countries) surging in the early 1980s and 1990s was not precedented by changes toward *more in*flexibility (or more generous unemployment benefits)—on the contrary, employers' external adjustment flexibility was enhanced (Solow, 1999: 5; OECD, 1999: 54-66).

Why has Germany abstained from initiating comprehensive reforms when until 1997 the unemployment rate climbed to ever new record highs? Apart from the "agenda overload" argument (see note 6), which can claim some truth for the first years after unification, Scharpf's (1987) findings on how successfully the UK, Sweden, Austria, and Germany coped with the "crisis" of the 1970s still hold for the 1990s given a substantially different environmental context (globalization). While Austria then "won" the contest due to its favorable institutional configuration facilitating a proper macro-economic policy (Sweden scored second), Germany's problems to pursue a consistent and coordinated fiscal, monetary, and wage policy again became virulent in the 1990s. The contradictory and procyclical macro-economic policies—beginning with the overheating of the economy (when the rest of Europe was already in recession), followed by monetary restraint, budget consolidation (in view of meeting the Maastricht criteria), and, finally, isolated wage restraint—were identified as central causes for not utilizing the potentialities for economic and employment growth and thus a considerable portion of existing unemployment (Lindlar and Scheremet, 1998: 36-46; Solow, 1999).

Related to the preceding argument, the political inability to resolutely take reform action has to be considered as a reason for Germany's poorer employment record. "Reform blockade" became a prominent catchword during the last years of the Kohl government, describing a discrepancy between reform pressures and actual reform activities. Bicameralism, the independence of the *Bundesbank*, constitutionally guaranteed autonomy of collective bargaining, vested interests integrated in the governance of the German *social insurance state*, etc. offer numerous "veto points," "joint decision traps" or opportunities to benefit from "budget particularisms" and which make Germany comparatively more susceptible to institutional rigidity and that can hardly be overcome by naive appeals to "reason" and "good will" or reference to working corporatist pacts elsewhere (Theisen, 1998), particularly, after increased party competition (opposing majorities in the *Bundestag* and *Bundesrat* arose again in 1991) made negotiated reforms rare events and stalemates more frequent (Lehmbruch, 2000). Germany is not a "consensus society" like the Scandinavian countries or the Netherlands, but needs much consensus to get things going.

What Can/Should Be Transferred?

One may safely assume that only in rare cases can policies be transnationally transferred on a one-to-one basis and even if it happens do not lose in effectiveness in another institutional setting. The prospects of successfully "learning from others" should be better the more a direct link can be constructed between a unanimously defined problem and a concrete policy. With regard to the employment problem, the most instructive example is that labor market policy can be made more effective when it comes to labor market *de*segmentation. Despite ascertained deficits, the Danish and

Dutch examples show that timely activation of unemployed, particularly the targeting of weak groups (young and long-term unemployed), and the reorganization of employment service (that is foremost: decentralization to better adapt to local circumstances and more emphasis on counseling job seekers) can help to improve the functioning of the labor market and, hence, support a smooth, non-inflationary job growth when labor demand actually picks up.

Although Germany had institutionalized an active labor market policy already in 1969 and devotes an above average share of GNP to the various measures (Martin, 2000), it has only been recently that its effectiveness has been studied more intensively, also by looking into evaluation studies produced in some of the "miracle" countries (Schmid et al., 2001; MittAB, 2000; Rabe, 2000). The results show that contrary to widespread beliefs they are not equally effective and sometimes do more harm than good. Apparently, the most effective measure to dissolve a structuration of unemployment is subsidized work with a private employer combined with in-work training. The imminent reform of labor market policy in Germany is going to take into account a number of promising policy innovations already practiced abroad.

Moreover, the review of the success stories revealed that there is not a single best way, starting from a well-defined blueprint and time schedule, to bring envisaged reforms into force. Rather, a significant reduction of unemployment and a high(er) employment rate are feasible within differently configured institutional settings, and it is hardly possible to exactly determine which reconfigured element has delivered what. Other than possibly being helpful in overcoming political immobilism, the "miracles" may provide some further conclusions, of which some are clearly trivial. The problem which particularly the Netherlands and Denmark as originally high-unemployment countries solved was to start with changed political priorities facilitating an escape from a vicious cycle. They managed to attain a turnaround in employment figures that made possible a reduced tax grip (on workers and employers) and lower public deficits and, in turn, less wage pressure. A further expansion of jobs then improved the employment intensity of economic growth (Schettkat, 1999) since higher private demand primarily favored private service jobs less accessible for productivity growth. Where labor market regulation was still high (as in the Netherlands) rising employment itself made more flexibility socially acceptable and, thereby, possibly effected more jobs in the service industry.

What were the ingredients for bringing about the turnaround? A stability-oriented macro-economic policy and attempting to reduce public deficits was pursued not only in Denmark and the Netherlands, but also in the United States, Ireland, and Austria as well as in Sweden, on its way to recovery during the 1990s. Fiscal consolidation and low inflation enlarge the scope of action and help to build up stable, consistent expectations among market actors. Therefore, a reliable and somewhat predictable wage policy is a further ingredient. On this account, the European countries and the U.S. differ. In the almost non-unionized U.S., with extreme decentralized wage setting, monetary policy needs not to reckon with labor unions exploiting expansionist moves. In the European countries in question, strong(er) unions have to be somehow integrated in the macro-economic management to be coherent and effective. Austria with its long-standing tradition of central coordination of wage policy among the social partners and concerted with the government represents one route (also entered in Ireland when after 1987 several tripartite agreements materialized). The "shadow of hierarchy" (Visser and Hemerijck, 1997), effective in Denmark and particularly in the Netherlands, is another, namely, that governments have the legal ability to intervene in the social partners' negotiations or conflicts although a negotiated compromise is prioritized. In Germany the situation is more complicated due to the complete autonomy of the social partners in collective bargaining (*Tarifautonomie*, see above) and which relieves the government from becoming involved in distributional struggles. The price, however, is a loss in governance capacity. Although the social partners—or more specific: organized labor—can hardly be accused of having acted "irresponsibly" or unresponsively (in *West* Germany), the unions were able (and sometimes threatened) to "do differently" and were less committed to show wage restraint over a longer period.

If the willingness of the Dutch unions to agree to continuous wage restraint was less a deliberate decision, but rather stemmed from their weakness as against the employers, it might well be—and contradicting common wisdom—that German unions are (still) too strong to become reliably integrated into a long-term corporatist "investment project" attaining higher employment when overcoming "local maxima" and shifting to "global maxima." Another Dutch "lesson"—and again indicating why Germany can hardly "follow"—is that cooperation and negotiated reforms need a government determined and *able* to bring change into force. The more fragmented political powers limit this ability, particularly since internally more divided social partners against the background of a worsened "climate" between them hinder the renewal of a welfare state *reform* consensus and favor the utilization of veto power.

In the Netherlands such an adversarial stalemate situation was resolved through the "unemployment explosion" (Cox, 2001; Hemerijck et al., 2000). A credible "crisis rhetorics" helped to reframe issues and get things moved also in Ireland, Denmark, and Sweden when unemployment soared and concomitant economic figures (public deficit) changed dramatically. In these small and largely homogeneous countries a common understanding of the problems as well as a consensus on the necessity and direction of change was easier to accomplish, including to generate relevant actors' acceptance of an impairment of hitherto vested positions and properties. In Germany, unification meant a "shock" but not immediately a "crisis," and collective actors were anxious to avoid or limit repercussions on the established institutional structures. Hence, before November 1989, the preconditions for a coordinated attack on the unemployment problem were better than thereafter when it became a much larger problem in an enlarged and even less homogeneous country. Thus, Germany is not only lagging behind the "miracle" countries by ten years or so when it comes to budget consolidation, reforms of the tax system or labor market policy, etc. Having missed the "right" moment and thus not experiencing a comparably strong employment growth can hardly be made good when the worldwide boom phase is obviously over.

That leads to a final, rather practical problem: unemployment levels in one country regularly differ by region, and in Germany, like in Italy, Spain, or Belgium, they vary quite considerably (OECD, 2000: 34-50). The most recent unemployment figures (July 2001) show a rate of 7.3 percent in *West* and 17.4 percent in *East* Germany (not to speak of even larger differences between the states of, for example, Bavaria on the one hand and Sachsen-Anhalt on the other). In view of such a "split economy," which, most likely, will last for several decades, the question is whether it is possible to design and pursue particularly macro-economic policies that are adequately targeted according to region and whose outcomes will not violate expectations of the public (e.g., regarding equal pay for equal work) or other policy objectives (e.g., equalizing living conditions).

Conclusion

The success stories dealt with in this chapter have obviously been proven wrong, those "jobless growth" scenarios and presumptions on the "end of employment" that gained ground during the late 1970s and early 1980s. These scenarios and presumptions were not altogether pessimistic. The total work volume being stagnant or declining—due to productivity growth usually exceeding output expansion—was assumed to lead to an aggravating *quantitative* "crisis" if not redistributed more fairly among the work force. Shorter working hours thus became a central demand of labor unions in France, Germany, Belgium and other countries. At the same time, a *qualitative* "crisis" was expected since changed work values meant increased demands on the content of paid work and on opportunities to better integrating it into extended and revalued life spheres outside employment and into life course events. Shorter and more flexible working hours would provide options for an enlarged involvement in unpaid (decommodified) work for the benefit of oneself, one's family and the community—ranging from housework, care work, do-it-yourself, productive activities performed in networks to civic engagement and beyond (see e.g., Matthes, 1983). This optimistic, partly utopian notion of the "future of work" in which waged labor would have lost its pivotal role in social integration and structuring individual life courses largely disappeared from the debate. Instead, the focus shifted back to a fixation to paid employment and political strategies that would maximize its volume and, furthermore, make able-bodied transfer recipients "employable" and prepared to perform most dull and unpleasant service jobs—at least temporarily. Corresponding efforts are mainly targeted at the low-skilled labor force and work where the interchangeability of "make or buy"—being performed as either unpaid or commodified labor—is quite high.

If one considers the U.S. route to employment maximization as either impracticable or not desirable, it might again be the Dutch development that teaches an interesting lesson (despite recent critical reviews—e.g., van Oorschot, 2001). Although "jobs, jobs, jobs" was the strategy successfully pursued, factually a departure from the objective of "full-time full employment" took place. The rapid growth of predominantly preferred and thus voluntary part-time and other non-standard types of employment has been a most effective way of redistributing work (and income) and definitely improved the flexible integration of paid work and unpaid activities into the individual life course and increased the plurality of time-use patterns among families. These variable combinations would be once again enhanced if plans for (partly remunerated) parental, educational or unspecified leaves become materialized as they are already in place in Denmark, Sweden, and Germany. Those developments can be expected to further deplete the monopoly of paid employment on meaning (*Sinnmonopol*) and on securing a living (*materielles Existenzmonopol*). Possibly, those still experimental and not yet firmly institutionalized approaches to promote socially and/or individually "useful" activities outside employment—and how they might be used to politically influence the volume of labor supply—provide various opportunities for transnational policy transfers.

Notes

1. Joseph Schumpeter (1962: 325), who had analyzed the first steps of Swedish "socialism" in the 1930s, pointed to "the stuff the Swedish nation is made of and to its exceptionally well-balanced social structure." He added, "That is why it is so absurd for other nations to try to copy Swedish examples; the only effective way of doing so would be to import the Swedes and to put them in charge."

2. Obviously, this was the effect of the "Bismarck model" after it had been studied in Scandinavia and the UK (see Hennock, 1987; Petersen, 1990; Kuhnle, 1996): quite different approaches, fitting the specific national contexts, were pursued in order to attain similar ends.

3. Therefore, Beveridge's (1944: 125-9) definition of "full employment," a 3 percent unemployment rate among the *male* labor force denoting the borderline, is no longer meaningful. See Auer (2000: 99-101) for a discussion of the need for a "new notion of full employment."

4. The development and actual level of the employment rate is also open to statistical manipulation (or methodological problems). For example, Alber (2000: 562) re-

ports an unexplained break (plus 5.6 percentage points) in the series for the Netherlands, and after a more complete counting of marginal part-time jobs in Germany the recent revision of national accounting showed the largest positive difference in employment for this country (CEC, 2000: 17, 44). Including a further revision by the Federal Statistical Office in 2000 it means a plus of 4 million employed (about 11 percent) for the year 1999 compared to the formerly published figures (Autorengemeinschaft, 2001: 15-6). It would add about 3.5 percentage points to Germany's most recent employment rate figure presented in Table 15.2.

5. For details on the social policy, labor market policy, and wage policy, see Visser and Hemerijck (1997); Green-Pedersen et al. (2001); Schmid and Helmer (1998); and Hartog (1999).

6. Although it might be true that serious political mistakes were made in managing the transformation process, it is generally admitted that not many alternatives existed in view of tremendous time pressure, the lack of blueprints on how to merge two countries, and an "agenda overload" that prevented a (partly overdue) reform of West German institutions before becoming transplanted completely to East Germany. In order to minimize the repercussions of unification on West German institutions and (collective) actors' interests, it was also ruled out to engage in a process of evaluating which elements of the GDR's institutional structure were worth retaining and then to transfer these to West Germany.

7. Recent regression analyses done by the OECD (2000: 97-105) show less clear-cut results with regard to the tax wedge and service employment (overall and disaggregated by subsectors).

References

Alber, J. (2000). "Sozialstaat und Arbeitsmarkt. Produzieren kontinentaleuropäische Wohlfahrtsstaaten typische Beschäftigungsmuster?" *Leviathan*, 28, 535-569.

Auer, P. (2000). *Employment Revival in Europe*. Geneva: International Labour Office.

Autorengemeinschaft. (2001). "Der Arbeitsmarkt in der Bundesrepublik Deutschland in den Jahren 2000 und 2001." *Mitteilungen aus der Arbeitsmarkt- und Berufsforschung*, 34, 5-27.

Bauer, T., and Riphahn, R. T. (1998). Employment Effects of Payroll Taxe—An Empirical Test for Germany. Forschungsinstitut zur Zukunft der Arbeit, IZA Discussion Paper, No 11. Bonn: IZA.

Beveridge, W. H. (1944). *Full Employment in a Free Society*. London: George Allen and Unwin.

Buslei, H., and Steiner, V. (2000). "Beschäftigungseffekte und fiskalische Kosten von Lohnsubventionen im Niedriglohnbereich." *Mitteilungen aus der Arbeitsmarkt- und Berufsforschung*, 33, 54-67.

CEC (Commission of the European Community). (1998). *Employment in Europe 1998: Jobs for People—People for Jobs: Turning Policy Guidelines into Action*. Luxembourg: Office for Official Publications of the European Communities.

___. (2000). *Employment in Europe 2000*. Luxembourg: Office for Official Publications of the European Communities.

Cox, R. H. (2001). "The Social Construction of an Imperative: Why Welfare Reform Happened in Denmark and the Netherlands but Not in Germany." *World Politics*, 53, 463-498.

Czada, R. (1998). "Vereinigungskrise und Standortdebatte." *Leviathan*, 26, 24-59.

Dolowitz, D. P., and Marsh, D. (2000). "Learning from Abroad: The Role of Policy Transfer in Contemporary Policy-Making." *Governance*, 13, 5-24.

Green-Pedersen, C., Kersbergen, K. van, and Hemerijck, A. (2001). "Neo-liberalism, the "Third Way" or What? Recent Social Democratic Welfare Policies in Denmark and the Netherlands." *Journal of European Public Policy*, 8, 307-325.

Hall, P. A. (1993). "Policy Paradigms, Social Learning, and the State: The Case of Economic Policymaking in Britain." *Comparative Politics*, 25, 275-296.

Hartog, J. (1999). *The Netherlands: So What's So Special about the Dutch Model?* Employment and Training Papers, No. 54. Geneva: ILO.

Hemerijck, A., Unger, B., and Visser, J. (2000). "How Small Countries Negotiate Change: Twenty-Five Years of Policy Adjustment in Austria, the Netherlands, and Belgium." In Scharpf, F. W., and Schmidt, V. A. (eds.), *Welfare and Work in the Open Economy. Vol. II*. Oxford: Oxford University Press.

Hennock, E. P. (1987). *British Social Reform and German Precedents*. Oxford: Clarendon Press.

Hinrichs, K. (1991). "Irregular Employment Patterns and the Loose Net of Social Security." In Adler, M., Bell, C., Clasen, J., and Sinfield, A. (eds.), *The Sociology of Social Security*. Edinburgh: Edinburgh University Press.

Jochem, S., and Siegel, N. A. (2000). "Wohlfahrtskapitalismen und Beschäftigungsperformanz—Das "Modell Deutschland" im Vergleich." *Zeitschrift für Sozialreform*, 46, 38-64.

Karr, W. (1999). *Kann der harte Kern der Arbeitslosigkeit durch einen Niedriglohnsektor aufgelöst werden?* IAB-Kurzbericht, No. 3. Nuremberg: Institut für Arbeitsmarkt- und Berufsforschung.

Klammer, U. (2000). "Low Pay—Challenge for the Welfare State." *Transfer. European Review of Labour and Research*, 6, 570-591.

Kuhnle, S. (1996). "International Modelling, States, and Statistics: Scandinavian Social Security Solutions in the 1890s." In Rueschemeyer, D., and Skocpol, T. (eds.), *States, Social Knowledge, and the Origins of Modern Social Policies*. Princeton, N.J.: Princeton University Press.

Kvist, J. (2001). "Activating Welfare States: How Social Policies Can Promote Employment." In Clasen, J. (ed.), *What Future for Social Security?* The Hague: Kluwer Law International.

Lehmbruch, G. (2000). "Institutionelle Schranken einer ausgehandelten Reform des Wohlfahrtsstaates." In Czada, R., and Wollmann, H. (eds.), *Von der Bonner zur Berliner Republik. 10 Jahre Deutsche Einheit*. Wiesbaden: Westdeutscher Verlag.

Lindlar, L., and Scheremet, W. (1998). Germany's Slump: Explaining the Unemployment Crisis of the 1990s. Deutsches Institut für Wirtschaftsforschung, Discussion Paper No. 169. Berlin.

Madsen, P. K. (1999). *Denmark: Flexibility, Security and Labour Market Success*. Employment and Training Papers, No. 53. Geneva: International Labour Office.

Manow, P., and Seils, E. (2000). "Adjusting Badly: The German Welfare State, Structural Change, and the Open Economy." In Scharpf, F. W., and Schmidt, V. A. (eds.), *Welfare and Work in the Open Economy. Vol. II*. Oxford: Oxford University Press."

Martin, J. P. (2000). What Works Among Active Labour Market Policies." *OECD Economic Studies*, No. 30, 79-113.

Matthes, J. (ed.). (1983). *Krise der Arbeitsgesellschaft?* Frankfurt/New York: Campus.

Mishel, L., Bernstein, J., and Schmitt, J. (2001). *The State of Working America, 2000-2001*. Ithaca, N.Y.: Cornell University Press.

MittAB. (2000). *Mitteilungen aus der Arbeitsmarkt- und Berufsforschung*, 33 (3) (special issue on "Evaluation of Active Labor Market Policy").

OECD. (1992). *Historical Statistics 1960-1990*. Paris: OECD.

___.(1996). *Employment Outlook. July 1996*. Paris: OECD.

___.(1997a). *Employment Outlook. July 1997*. Paris: OECD.

___. (1997b). *Labour Force Statistics 1976-1996*. Paris: OECD.

___. (1998). *Employment Outlook. June 1998*. Paris: OECD.

___. (1999). *Employment Outlook. June 1999*. Paris: OECD.

___. (2000). *Employment Outlook. June 2000*. Paris: OECD.

___. (2001). *Employment Outlook. June 2001*. Paris: OECD.

Offe, C. (1991). "Smooth Consolidation in the West German Welfare State." In Piven, F. F. (ed.), *Labor Parties in Postindustrial Societies*. Cambridge, Mass.: Polity Press.

___. (1996). "Designing Institutions in East European Transitions." In Goodin, R. E. (ed.), *The Theory of Institutional Design*. Cambridge: Cambridge University Press.

van Oorschot, W. (2001). Miracle or Nightmare? A Critical Review of Dutch Activation Policies and Their Outcomes. Paper prepared for the Conference "Old and New Social Inequalities: What Challenges for Welfare States?," ISA, RC 19, Oviedo (Spain), 6-9 September.

Pearson, M., and Scarpetta, S. (2000). "An Overview: What Do We Know About Policies to Make Work Pay?" *OECD Economic Studies*, No. 31, 11-24.

Petersen, J. H. (1990). "The Danish 1891 Act on Old Age Relief: A Response to Agrarian Demand and Pressure." *Journal of Social Policy*, 19, 69-91.

Pichelmann, K., and Hofer, H. (1999). *Austria: Long-term Success Through Social Partnership*. Employment and Training Papers, no. 52. Geneva: International Labour Office

Rabe, B. (2000). *Wirkungen aktiver Arbeitsmarktpolitik. Evaluierungsergebnisse für Deutschland, Schweden, Dänemark und die Niederlande*. Discussion Paper FS I 00-208. Berlin: Wissenschaftszentrum Berlin für Sozialforschung.

Rose, R. (1993). *Lesson-drawing in Public Policy: A Guide to Learning across Time and Space*. Chatham, N.J.: Chatham House Publishers.

Schäfer, C. (2000). "Lower Pay—a Better World?" *Transfer. European Review of Labour and Research*, 6, 687-716.

Scharpf, F. W. (1987). *Sozialdemokratische Krisenpolitik in Europa*. Frankfurt/New York: Campus.

___. (2000). "The Viability of Advanced Welfare States in the International Economy: Vulnerabilities and Options." *Journal of European Public Policy*, 7, 190-228.

Schettkat, R. (1999). "Small Economy Macroeconomics: The Success of Ireland, Denmark, Austria and the Netherlands Compared." *Intereconomics*, 34, 159-170.

___. (2001). "Beschäftigungsentwicklung im internationalen Vergleich: Eine Renaissance der europäischen Wohlfahrtsstaaten?" *Zeitschrift für Sozialreform*, 47, 310-339.

Schmid, G., and Helmer, M. (1998). "The Dutch Employment Miracle? A Comparison of Employment Systems in the Netherlands and Germany." In Delsen, L., and de Jong, E. (eds.), *The German and Dutch Economies: Who Follows Whom?* Heidelberg: Physica Verlag, 52-85.

Schmid, G., Speckesser, S., and Hilbert, C. (2001). "Does Active Labour Market Policy Matter? An Aggregate Impact Analysis for Germany." In de Koning, J., and Mosley, H. (eds.), *Labour Market Policy and Unemployment*. Cheltenham: Edward Elgar.

Schumpeter, J. A. (1962). *Capitalism, Socialism and Democracy*. Third ed. New York: Harper and Row.

Siebert, H. (1997). "Labor Market Rigidities: At the Root of Unemployment in Europe." *Journal of Economic Perspectives* 11 (3), 37-54.

Solow, R. M. (2000). *Unemployment in the United States and in Europe: A Contrast and the Reasons*. CESifo Working Paper Series, No. 231. Munich: Center for Economic Studies/ifo Institute.

Streeck, W. (1997). "German Capitalism: Does It Exist? Can It Survive?" In Crouch, C., and Streeck, W. (eds.), *Political Economy of Modern Capitalism*. London: Sage.

SU. (2001). *Sozialpolitische Umschau*, No. 224 (13 August).

Theisen, H. (1998). "Korporatismus und Konfliktkultur als Ursachen der 'Deutschen Krankheit.'" *Aus Politik und Zeitgeschichte*, 48 (29-30), 9-15.

Visser, J., and Hemerijck, A. (1997). *A Dutch Miracle: Job Growth, Welfare Reform and Corporatism in the Netherlands*. Amsterdam: Amsterdam University Press.

Wagner, G. (1999). "Einige Bemerkungen zur Diskussion einer 'Dienstleistungslücke'" in (West)Deutschland." *Arbeitsmarkt. Beihefte der Konjunkturpolitik*, 48, 77-92.

14

Is There a Trade-off between Employment and Social Protection in Europe's Economic and Monetary Union?

Nadine Richez-Battesti and Audrey Koulinsky

The trend of economic globalization is accompanied by a simultaneous growth in regionalization. Against this background the European Union (EU) has launched a process of monetary integration and it has also introduced guidelines for employment. Whilst the national states remain dominant in matters of social protection, the integrationist dynamic, which is a feature of the European Union, reflects an underlying normative model of social protection. On the one hand this is because it is impossible for the various countries individually to reconcile objectives of low public spending deficit, high employment, and a significant redistribution of resources (the Iversen and Wren "trilemma," or triangle of incompatibility). Given the pressing need for budget restraint (stability pact), one suspects that this may result in a trade-off between employment and social protection. The other reason for the EU's desire for harmonization stems from general a priori approval of disengagement by the state, largely prompted by recent developments in economic theory. The purpose of this chapter is to show that the triangle of incompatibility in the Economic and Monetary Union (EMU) ultimately means a trade-off between employment and social protection.

In the first part of the chapter we shall show how this three-way trade-off leads to difficulties, by testing the hypotheses of Iversen and Wren (1998) in the context of European integration. Then, by tracing the progress of the Community agenda, we shall show how employment objectives put pressure on the redistribution of resources. In part two, using an econometric study of the 14 Member states of the European Union, we shall try to ascertain whether or not the "trilemma" referred to earlier actually exists.

Triangle of Incompatibility or Trade-off between Employment and Social Protection in Europe?

Steady progress on the building of Europe, together with globalization, places significant constraints on governments in their choice and conduct of macro-economic policies. The development of competition tends to encourage the search for economic efficiency, sometimes to the detriment of objectives of equality, fuelling the debate on the role of the State (Leibfried and Pierson, 1998). Some authors have shown that quite apart from a crisis over funding, the crisis facing the welfare state is also defined in terms of efficacy and legitimacy (Rosanvallon, 1981). Others have pointed to contradictions between efficiency and social protection (Okun, 1975). In effect, changes in the international environment further exacerbate the challenges created by demographic changes, changing family models, the labor market, and employment systems, in short the new forms of social insecurity. The report by Supiot (1999) concludes that changing patterns of work create a new need for security, specifically social security, which can no longer depend solely on the fact of being in (continuous) employment (Supiot, 1999: 298), and which cannot either offer a response of solidarity to the needs of the individual (Supiot, 1999: 305). We see here a loss of stability in the two pillars of the twentieth-century welfare state, the first being employment–"thanks to social security, employment allows the employee to benefit from financial solidarity in meeting these risks" (Supiot, 1999: 230)—and the second being public service and citizens' rights. None of the various models of social protection or, as Esping-Andersen puts it (1990), "welfare state regimes," meaning the specification of relatively stable institutional arrangements between the private sphere, the market, and the state, is now immune to a measure of fragility. Challenges to the welfare state concern its function as a redistributor of resources, largely driven by commercial concerns driven by globalization, and its function as an insurer. We need, therefore, to look at the choices of action in economic and social matters that are open to governments within a context of the Economic and Monetary Union (EMU), and then to show how the impulses provided by the Community institutions influence choices and trade-offs in social protection and employment.

A Triangle of Incompatibility?

Examining the decline in the industrial sector in the Organization for Economic Cooperation and Development (OECD) member countries in the 1970s and 1980s, partly offset by the growth of the service sector, Iversen and Wren (1998) set out to show that there is a triangle of incompatibility between equality of incomes between the sectors, growth in employment, and fiscal discipline. They emphasize that the determining feature of the triangle of incompatibility is the passage from an economy dominated by industrial activity to one that is service-based (Iversen and Wren, 1998: 508). On the question of institutions they contend that, given the gap between the productivity of labor in manufacturing (where it is high) and in the services (where it is lower and rises less quickly), if earnings in the services continue to be based on those in industry this will lead to a slowing down of job creation in the private service sector. They argue that this trade-off can be countered in part by a government policy of developing public services, which means an easing of budget restraint. Thus, more private-sector jobs in the services means greater income inequalities, whilst attempts to establish greater income equality means that public-sector jobs have to be created, which are paid at levels higher than the marginal productivity of labor and so affect budget equilibrium.

Iversen and Wren (1998) show that the governments of the industrialized nations cannot concurrently pursue all three objectives of fiscal discipline, growth in employment, and the reduction of income inequalities, but only two out of the three. So one objective has to be sacrificed. Depending on which objectives have priority, they identify three ideal models of the welfare state, using the definitions of Esping-Andersen (1990):

- The first model gives priority to fiscal discipline and increasing employment. This is the "neo-liberal" model.
- The second model emphasizes fiscal discipline and income equality. This is the "christian democratic" model.
- The third favors income equality and increased employment. This is a "social democratic" model.

Figure 14.1
The Trilemma of the Welfare State

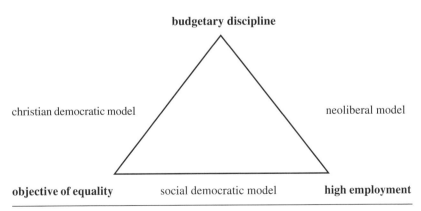

Source: Iversen & Wren (1998).

This analysis enables us to identify the types of collective choices made by the different European governments and their economic policy priorities. But it underestimates the constraints imposed by macro-economic strategies at European level and those imposed by globalization which significantly limit the choices open to countries. From this point of view we believe that whilst the three combinations were feasible in the early 1990s, they no longer are, except in very marginal cases.

One explanation of the smaller number of combinations possible between the three points of the triangle lies in an understanding of the effects of increasing globalization. This affects the distribution of incomes both within countries and between countries (Atkinson, 1999; Leamer, 1999; Haskel and Slaughter, 1999; Tanzi, 2000). Thus, the objective of reducing inequalities supposedly becomes increasingly expensive at the domestic level, requiring the state to play an increasingly active role, whilst the phenomenon of globalization, which changes the way in which taxation can be used due to fiercer fiscal competition, makes it harder for the state to do this. Governments are, in fact, in danger of ultimately losing one of the instruments whereby they can promote income equality, namely a high level of social protection. The only alternative would be to promote regional strategies of cooperation which would get around the problem of international fiscal competition.

The progress of integration is a second factor that reduces the range of available choices. Our analysis assumes the background of EMU, understood here as an area of integration that has a single currency and a restricted capacity to adjust to economic upsets. We focus on changes brought about by the process of integration and not, as Iversen and Wren do (1998), on sectoral changes in manufacturing and employment.

Under EMU monetary policy is conducted centrally by the European Central Bank, whose objective is price stability. Responsibility for budgetary policy rests with the nation states but is coordinated at European level within the terms of the stability pact which sets a ceiling for budget deficits (less than 3 percent of Gross Domestic Product (GDP) and closer to balance). The macro-economic margin of the various member states is thus limited given that the classic instruments of economic policy are not available to them. Not only do the EMU member states no longer have any autonomy in monetary policy (control over through interest and exchange rates), they are also losing much of their ability to determine budgetary policy. Given this situation, and given the low mobility of labor (Eichengreen, 1990; Decressin and Fatas, 1994; Masson and Taylor, 1992) and the curtailment of freedom in budgetary spending, any adjustment in the event of a macro-economic crisis will be made through two channels:

- prices and more specifically direct and/or indirect wage conditions, in other words wage levels and/or indirect incomes: for an economy that faces a competitive disadvantage this will mean that flexible exchange rates are replaced as an instrument of adjustment by a mechanism of wage flexibility.[1] Taken to its extreme, this argument suggests that monetary devaluation will be replaced by social devaluation, which will provide a fertile breeding ground for social dumping.

* quantitative variations in the factors of production: if we accept that mobility of physical and financial capital is not very effective in coping with economic crises and disparities (Farvaque et al., 1995: 73) it is reasonable to suppose, given the low level of labor mobility between the members of EMU, that adjustment will be via variations in unemployment (Masson and Taylor, 1992).

At the present stage of building Europe, the clear priority is budgetary discipline. Membership of EMU thus requires countries to give priority to the first "corner" of the triangle. So there is a trade-off between wage flexibility (and thus a lesser degree of social protection) on the one hand, and unemployment on the other hand (Richez-Battesti, 1997). But at Community level the emphasis has been firmly placed on increasing employment, implicitly reflecting the desire to prioritize employment at the expense of efforts to reduce income inequalities. So it would seem that the triangle of incompatibility is reduced to over-determination by a neo-liberal-type model, with the countries concerned having only minimal freedom to act in trying to reduce income inequalities.

To sum up, all other things being equal, if the single currency is to endure, it presupposes a dismantling of previous social compromises and radical changes in the behavior of economic players which would appear to be irreconcilable with a high level of social protection and distribution of resources.

We shall now endeavor to show, by tracing the Community's agenda and procedures over the last ten years, how the trade-off between employment and social protection seems to be resolved by an over-determination of welfare state models by employment.

The Position of the Community Institutions: A Trade-off Partly Resolved by the Priority Given to Employment

The scale of unemployment in Europe during the 1990s compared with the other parts of the "Triad" (Table 14.1) partly explains the priority given at Community level to employment and the construction of an employment strategy.

Against this background, account was taken throughout the 1990s of the social dimension (employment, social protection, social relations), but the most significant progress was achieved on employment. Up to the end of the 1980s employment had been the preserve of the United Nations, but the 1990s saw the European Union laying down principles for action in this area.

Table 14.1

Change in Employment and Unemployment in the Areas of the "Triad"

Total Employment	1986-1990	1991-1995	1996-2001*	1997	1998	1999*	2000*
Eur-15	1.4	-0.4	1.0	0.8	1.3	1.2	1.2
USA	2.1	1.3	1.6	2.3	1.5	1.7	1.2
Japan	1.0	0.7	0.2	1.1	-0.7	4.1	1.1
Unemployment	1986-1990	1991-1995	1996-2001*	1997	1998	1999*	2000*
Eur-15	8.9	10.0	9.5	10.6	9.9	9.2	8.6
USA	5.9	6.6	4.7	4.9	4.5	4.2	4.4
Japan	2.5	2.6	4.2	3.4	4.1	4.9	5.0

* Forecasts; Total employment: employment in the whole of the economy (all sectors), annual percent change; Unemployment: number of persons unemployed as a percentage of the civilian population of working age.

Source: Autumn 1999 Forecasts, European Commission.

It all began with Jacques Delors' white paper on "growth, competitiveness, employment" (CEC, 1993), adopted at the Brussels summit of December 1993. The European Council held in Essen in December 1994 converted this initiative into a common strategy based on recommendations and the identification of priority actions, with progress on the policies implemented by member states being reviewed every year at one of the European Council meetings. The stability pact of June 1996 declared that all players were committed to and would work to promote measures to combat unemployment and in 1997 the Amsterdam Treaty recognized employment as "a matter of common concern," giving formal status to the coordinated strategy through guidelines for employment which would be adopted annually by the Council, acting by qualified majority. Every year, each member state reports on its strategies and results in the light of the guidelines previously set.

At the same time, as regards social protection, a strategy for the convergence of social protection policies was proposed in 1992, centering on common objectives and endorsed by a Council recommendation. This text was complemented the same year by another Council recommendation on measures to combat social exclusion. Since then there has been no significant action on this, apart from references in the Amsterdam Treaty that provide for incentive-based action programs at the Community level. Three other documents were added to the 1992 recommendation on social protection. In 1995 the Commission opened a debate on the future of social protection which gave rise to a strategy for consultation. Then in 1997 a communication on "Modernizing and improving social protection in the European Union" affirmed the central place of social protection in the European model. In 1999 a new Commission communication, entitled "A concerted strategy for modernizing social protection," sought to strengthen the process of cooperation to that end. In this latter document the Commission proposes that social protection should, like employment, become a matter of common concern (though questions of social security require unanimity in the Council) and be coordinated more closely by a group of high-level national officials.

As a result, in the early 1990s, fresh impetus was given to the coordination of employment and social protection matters in connection with projects to deepen the process of integration (Quintin and Favarel-Dapas, 1999). We see, in fact, that coordination is a shared principle applied in aligning national systems of employment and social protection (cf. Box 14.1). But the differing paces at which this coordination is applied and formalized reflect the greater priority given to employment. For social protection, this coordination uses a mechanism without penalties, based on the member states regularly reporting on their policies and results. This process is supposed to produce a "scoreboard" of performance and so spread good practice by pooling information and experience and by consultation. Thus, reporting and peer pressure are considered as adequate motivating factors, possibly reinforced by Council recommendations.

Box 14.1
Three Models for Building Social Europe

The Community considered three models for building social Europe. They reflect three different views of the integration process.

The first aimed to unify the European social dimension "from the top down," applying an integration principle that national systems should be harmonized on the model of the "best system." The second was built on the principle that a new European system should be devised which would help to spread a more homogeneous social model, limiting the transaction costs needed to set it up. The aim here was to combine existing systems into a new supranational model. The third was built on the idea that the integrity of national social systems and thus of national social "frontiers" should be preserved. The structure underlying this model is one of coordination, and the supranational dimension would be simply to provide supranational regulation of the national systems.

At the end of the 1970s, and emphatically since then, it is the third model that has been adopted. It allows national differences to be respected and gives governments the necessary margin in regard to the subsidiarity principle.

Given the interrelationships between employment systems and social security systems, strategies for employment also affect the direction followed by reforms of social protection systems. At Community level the choice of assessing national strategies for employment on the basis of a priority indicator of growth in employment means that preference is given to a quantitative indicator which tells us nothing about the quality of employment or income inequalities. Consequently, social protection has to adjust accordingly, by limiting factors which prevent people from entering the labor market (e.g., payment of excessively generous benefits) and promoting active policies (training and employment incentives) which influence the number of people in work, rather than passive policies that merely provide people with an income.

The 1993 white paper already pointed to the importance of reforming social protection systems to make them more efficient and less costly, by means of greater individual responsibility and selectiveness (CEC, 1993: 16) and by reducing the burden of social contributions on low-qualified work (CEC, 1993: 19). In subsequent years the Community institutions have reaffirmed the need for reform of social protection systems, to make them more appropriate to a new Europe which is more integrated and competitive, but also more burdened by unemployment. The changes advocated are thus aimed essentially at increasing rates of labor market participation. At the same time the Community institutions have recognized the importance of social protection based on the European social model, the need to maintain a high level of social protection (average spending equal to 28 percent of GDP), and the absence of any negative correlation between macro-economic performance and social protection. These undertakings of principle are not neutral in their anticipated effects. They are designed, on the one hand, to reassure people and strengthen popular approval of a dynamic of far-reaching economic and monetary integration and, on the other hand, to "sweeten the pill" of a social model that is broadly centered on the question of employability. But they offer no tangible guarantees that there will not be social competition between countries, leading to a decline in the influence of the welfare state.

There are two dimensions missing from the Community texts on social protection. The first concerns the level of public spending. This omission is due to the fact that member states have committed themselves elsewhere to cutting budget deficits on a sustainable basis. Thus, the constraint of budgetary consolidation and pressure to cut public spending are taken as read (Buti et al., 1997). The second dimension concerns inequalities: the only necessity stressed is the need for safety nets and a guaranteed minimum income, by reference to a principle of equity based on the idea that the most disadvantaged must not be sacrificed. But the widening of inequalities since the 1980s (Atkinson et al., 1995; Picketty, 1997) calls for strategies that are more ambitious, but more expensive, too. Current reforms of social protection aim to make it easier for people to work, whilst ensuring that there is a safety net for the most disadvantaged, without increasing the level of budgetary expenditure. The means whereby this is to be achieved are not stipulated, being a matter for national policy, but the choice is partly dictated by the priority given to rates of labor force participation. Member states thus have considerably less room for maneuver than might appear from a reading of the Community texts on social protection.

Furthermore, current debate and strategy on the part of the different member states continues to contrast the tenets of flexibility and deregulation as ways of restoring growth with those that see revitalized social protection as a guarantee of growth and prosperity. Paradoxically, whilst the compatibility of economic performance and social protection is accepted, it is the theoretical arguments supporting the principle of a contradiction that continue to be adduced. Thus, exhortations to improve the efficacy of social protection systems are built on a desire to limit distortions of the labor and savings markets (Enjolras, 1999). Regarding the labor market we have the arguments and conclusions of authors like Lindbeck (1988) and Atkinson and Mogensen (1993). They point both to employment disincentives and the existence of unemployment or poverty traps (Atkinson and Mogensen, 1993). These factors led to the introduction of a series of reforms designed to make work more advantageous, notably by ensuring that the value of benefits does not seem too attractive compared with the wages paid for work and so discourage people from trying to find a job. Other authors (Feldstein, 1974; Ando and Modigliani, 1963) emphasize the fact that transfers (notably pensions) affect levels of savings by changing people's behavior and making them less likely to save. The introduction and development of a third pillar of retirement is born of this trend, and in the same way it is designed to ensure the continuance of pension schemes which are threatened by the fact of an aging population.

Some reforms are also based on an analysis of the ineffectiveness of government monopolistic regulation and of bureaucratic models. Recent developments in the theory of quasi-markets argue in favor of an association between government funding and commercial regulation through the introduction of competition between service providers. The result is an original combination of a free choice of provider (for the beneficiary) and public funding (Le Grand and Bartlett, 1993), which means that a twofold scrutiny is exercised, by government and users (or clients). From this point of view the mechanism of regulation assumes a threat that people may "exit" (Hirschman, 1970) or "vote with their feet" (Tiebout, 1956)—which is likely to guarantee a better quality of service—and that competing organizations will have to respect the objectives set by government. Defined in this way, quasi-markets would seem to be the answer to the failure of bureaucratic regulation (source of inefficiency) and to market shortcomings (socially less than optimum level of production). This type of regulation has been introduced into the health care systems of a number of European countries, notably the Netherlands and the United Kingdom.

The temptation to introduce into Europe a system inspired by the U.S. model, centered on the cutting of government social protection expenditure by lowering levels of benefit, shortening periods of coverage, and limiting institutional barriers to employment, has not altogether disappeared. But whereas the gap between social protection expenditure in Europe and the United States is considerable when we look at the public portion of it alone, it is almost nonexistent when we add private spending into the equation. So it seems that in the United States the reduction in public spending is offset by an increase in private spending. This polarization is not neutral in its effects, however, since it has repercussions on the distribution of prosperity and levels of poverty, and it reinforces inequalities (CEC, 1997). One bottom-line response to the negative external features of the American model is to take the view that safety nets for the most disadvantaged provide a guarantee that these inequalities will be contained. That is the line taken by the Community.

Implicitly within the Community, or explicitly in the theoretical debates prompted or fed by these initiatives, two avenues of reform are envisaged and may be combined:

- A clear separation between the functions of assistance and insurance. The functions of social assistance will then be designed essentially to redistribute income towards the most disadvantaged, with the introduction of employment incentives. As for insurance, a change in the system of regulation is advocated, to introduce more commercially based incentives and forms of competition subject to government scrutiny and control.
- Greater individual responsibility, through the development of voluntary and private insurance schemes and through employment incentives (progression from a *welfare* to a *workfare* state).

It would thus appear that the Community attaches greater priority to employment than to a redistribution of incomes. This suggests that the various welfare states are conducting their reforms by reference to a model of the predominantly neo-liberal type, a model which, nevertheless, comprises forms of assistance aimed at limiting the undesirable effects of exclusion and poverty. Given this reality, the three welfare state models represented by the EU member states are affected differently by Community policy. Manifestly, the liberal system of the United Kingdom is destabilized very little, though it needs to develop welfare policies to cope with the rise in poverty. The social democratic system typical of the countries of northern Europe is also partially protected by virtue of the high rate of labor market participation in those countries, and despite tensions over the funding of social expenditure.

It is the (christian-democratic) model of continental Europe, with lower rates of employment and public spending deficits, that seems to be the most affected by current reforms.

Existence of the Triangle of Incompatibility

Our approach is consistent with the thinking of Iversen and Wren (1998) who, on the basis of a sectoral study,[2] point to a "trilemma" or triangle of incompatibility between growth in employment, fiscal discipline, and income equality between different sectors of the economy. They, however, are describing a "trilemma" specific only to jobs in the service industry that are not interchangeable,[3] spending by the government as an employer, and income inequalities between major sectors of activity. And this analysis seems to us less and less pertinent, since the service sector, which is to some extent still protected, is rapidly opening up to foreign competition, particularly intra-European competition from other providers of transport, energy, and communications services. Moreover, restricting budgetary policy to fluctuations in spending on public-sector jobs means to neglect a large part of government resources.[4] A proportion of these government resources is used precisely to fund policies for reducing income inequalities that are applied through social transfers to households. We shall now address the question of whether a triangle of incompatibility, in fact, exists between the objectives of increased growth, income equality and budgetary restraint, using a broader canvas than that studied by Iversen and Wren (1998).

Our Approach

We consider total employment, that is to say employment for all sectors together, as a dependent variable, and we hypothesize that its growth is negatively affected by a policy of equalizing gross incomes. We measure that policy roughly as the growth in expenditure on social protection and social transfers (other than those made in kind), as a percentage of GDP. Our second hypothesis is that any restriction of government funding capacity[5] harms the growth of employment throughout the economy as a whole. Thus, our intention is to ascertain, through an empirical study, whether or not there has in the last thirty years and the countries of the EU been a trade-off in the allocation of government funding in favor of employment or the redistribution of income.

The relationship that interests us first is the one between growth in employment and growth in social spending in the EU countries, since in our view the one necessarily precludes the other. But we shall also analyze the relationship between growth in employment and budgetary capacity so that we can relate these to the triangle of incompatibility demonstrated by Iversen and Wren (1998).

Data and Methods

Given that we are seeking to identify and measure the relationship between changes over time, all our variables are presented as rates of annual growth.[6] We thus consider the annual growth in total employment as the dependent variable in our study, which covers the period from 1970 to 2000 and fourteen countries in Europe.[7] The variables used to explain relative annual variations in employment are social transfers other than those made in kind, as a percentage of GDP at market prices, and government funding capacity or net funding requirement as a percentage of GDP at market prices.

The first explanatory variable is an indicator of changes in policies for redistributing incomes at national level: if the percentage of GDP accounted for by social transfers has fallen, this means that monetary transfers to households are rising less quickly or falling more quickly than GDP, suggesting that the policy of redistribution is failing. Unlike a Gini index, which gives a picture of national income inequalities at a given moment in time, our variable provides a picture of the political will of governments to redistribute national income rather than the actual result.[8] We use a different indicator of the political will to equalize incomes: social protection expenditure as a percentage of GDP which encompasses not only social transfers to households but also operating costs and other recurrent expenditure. Since data for this variable are only available for the period 1980-1996, it is useful for statistical analysis of the relationships we are interested in, but cannot be used in the econometric study that follows.

The second explanatory variable represents changes in budgetary equilibrium as a percentage of GDP in the EU member states. The fact of dividing budgetary funding capacity by GDP is designed to remove the effect of economic growth: if budgetary capacity is rising at the same pace as GDP, as fiscal revenue increases due to an improvement in economic activity, then the ratio will remain stable; if, on the other hand, it is falling this reflects a restriction of budgetary capacity in relation to economic growth in the country.

Three other variables will also be taken into account, as instruments, in the econometric estimates that follow. These are real unit wage cost, social security contributions received by government as a percentage of GDP, and the cost of government employees' salary costs as a percentage of GDP.

Descriptive Statistics

In this preliminary analysis we look for correlations between total employment and the explanatory variables, using their time series grouped as panel data. This enables us to multiply the observation points (n = 434) and so identify a dominant trend in space and time. The regression lines in Figures 14.2 and 14.3 thus give a summary picture of the relationship between the variables in question for the fourteen EU countries as a whole (Luxembourg is not included) and for the period as a whole. They do not, however, tell us anything about the reasons underlying these relationships.

The first of our hypotheses suggests that spending on social protection or social transfers as a percentage of GDP correlates negatively with total employment.

At first sight, Figures 14.2 and 14.3, whose regression lines have a negative slope, appear to bear out this hypothesis: annual growth in employment

Figure 14.2
Correlation between Total Employment and Social Protection Expenditure

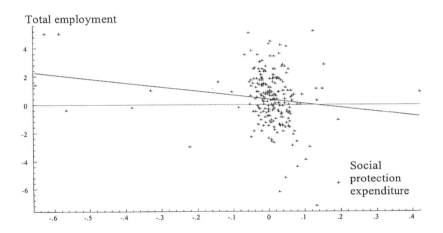

Figure 14.3
Correlation between Total Employment and Social Transfers

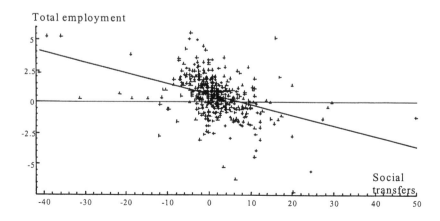

correlates inversely with annual growth in social protection expenditure or social transfers as a percentage of GDP. In Figure 14.2, though, the regression line seems poorly representative of the cluster of points, leaving a presumption of independence between the variables of total employment and of social protection expenditure. This comment is also true of Figure 14.3; here the regression line appears more significant, but the correlation coefficient is small ($r^2 = 0.175$).

Our second hypothesis suggests that any restriction of government budgetary capacity should be accompanied by a slowing of growth in total employment in the economy. In other words, growth in total employment and government funding capacity as a percentage of GDP ought to move in the same direction.

Figure 14.4 shows a regression line that is fairly representative of the cluster of points and with a positive slope. But the correlation coefficient indicates that this relationship is very weak ($r^2 = 0.055$).

In order to be consistent with the analysis of Iversen and Wren (1998), in terms of three-way trade-offs, we estimated the intensity and direction of the relationship between budgetary capacity and public spending on monetary social transfers.

As expected, the correlation appears to be negative, but as in the previous cases, there is in fact a weak correlation ($r^2 = 0.224$).

At this level of our empirical analysis we can conclude that whilst the relationships observed have signs consistent with our expectations, they are so weak that we remain doubtful as to whether a significant trade-off in fact exists.

Figure 14.4
**Correlation between Total Employment and Government Funding
Capacity or Net Funding Requirement**

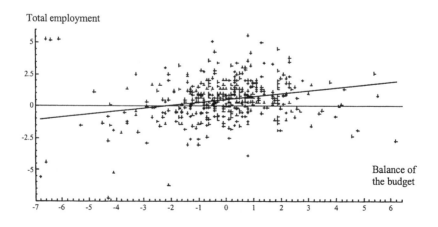

Figure 14.5
Correlation between Government Funding Capacity or Net Funding Requirement and Social Transfers

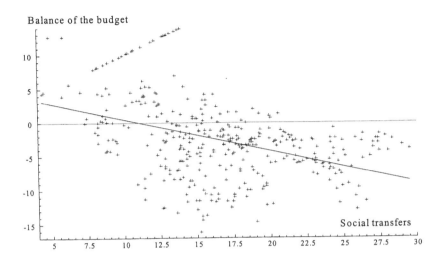

Specification of Estimates and Results

In order to obtain good properties of stationarity, we convert all the variables into rates of annual growth. To estimate the relationships between these variables we use the method of three-stage least squares. This enables us, in part, to avoid the problems of endogeneity in the variables of the model, notably between employment and social transfers on the one hand and employment and budgetary capacity on the other hand. Given that part of social transfers varies automatically with fluctuations in unemployment, it is likely that they increase when employment and GDP decrease. This is a problem commonly reported in the literature on redistribution spending, namely that it is difficult to separate the stabilizing components from the redistribution components. Also, the total fiscal cost of unemployment is three to four times greater than the simple direct cost of payments to the unemployed, bearing in mind the cost represented by future lost tax revenue and social security contributions and the indirect costs of lower productivity. We also include specific national and time effects in the model in the form of dummy variables for each country and year. So we apply the hypothesis of heterogeneous response to the exogenous variables, for each country and each year.

A first estimate, made from panel data and covering all the 14 EU countries, is made in three stages. The first two reduce the interdependence between the variables, regressing the exogenous ones on three instrumental

Table 14.2
Trade-off between Employment, Social Transfers and Budgetary
Capacity in the EU-14[a]

	Coefficient	T-Stat
	Dependent variable: employment (E)	
BC(estimated)$_{t-1}$	0.418**	(2.520)
ST(estimated)	-0.122***	(-3.743)
	Dependent variable: budgetary capacity (BC)	
RUWC$_{t-1}$	0.009	(0.202)
SOCC$_{t-1}$	0.017	(1.259)
GOES$_{t-1}$	-0.114***	(-4.936)
	Dependent variable: social transfers (ST)	
RUWC$_{t-1}$	0.388**	(2.283)
SOCC$_{t-1}$	0.069	(1.282)
GOES$_{t-1}$	0.443***	(5.007)

Notes: E = employment; BC = budgetary capacity; ST = social transfers; RUWC = real unit wage cost; SOCC = social contributions; GOES = government employees' salaries. The asterisks mean: *Significant at 10 percent level ; **Significant at 5 percent level ; ***Significant at 1 percent level.
[a]The country excluded is Luxembourg.
Results obtained from three-stage least squares on panel data, including a group of dummy variables for each country and year. Standardized r^2 is 0.42.

variables. This gives two *estimated* exogenous variables that are introduced into the last equation, as regressors of the explained variable. Of the instruments used, real unit wage cost is an approximate indicator of labor productivity in the economy which, via tax revenue, influences budgetary capacity; social security contributions for their part restrict opportunities for increasing social spending and thus social transfers, and government employees' salaries endanger the balance of the budget and restrict government funding capacity.

The result of the regressions, shown in Table 14.2, indicates that a priori the model is poorly specified (median r^2 = 0.42), that is to say the exogenous variables only partly explain the behavior of the endogenous variable. This is, however, an effect inherent in the method used, so the criticism is somewhat unfair. Then it appears that the instrumental variables of government employees' salaries and wage cost are statistically significant and have high coefficients in the intermediate regressions—except for social transfers—whilst social contributions seem to have no effect either on budgetary capacity or social transfers. The results of the main equation confirm those of our statistical analysis of the signs for relationships and are rather more conclusive as regards the severity of trade-offs, especially between employment and budgetary capacity. The link between social transfers and employment is weak, and the poor results from the intermediate regression for social transfers lead us to assume that a strong bias of endogeneity persists between these two variables. Thus, we cannot conclude from this that a trade-off exists between these two objectives of economic and social policy.

We shall now calculate these same relationships using time series data and the method of "seemingly unrelated regressions" (SUR). This new estimate allows an individualized reading of the results, so that a finer and more differentiated analysis of our question is possible: given the many comparative studies done on the political and institutional similarities and differences between welfare states, it is fair to suppose that there are not necessarily trade-offs in all countries of the EU, or at any rate that their severity varies between countries. With this method we also take account of the hypothesis of a correlation between the residuals of the equations for the various countries. This correlation is explained by the existence of an interaction between national economies which affects the variance of employment in each one but is not explicitly recorded by the main model.

Table 14.3 shows the results. For the most part our hypotheses are confirmed. Specifically, the relationship between employment and social transfers appears to be negative and statistically highly significant in ten of the fourteen countries studied. The coefficients associated with them are, however, low overall (between 5 and 20 percent). For the relationship between

Table 14.3
Trade-off between Employment, Social Transfers, and Budgetary Equilibrium in 14 Countries of the EU

Country	Dependent variable: annual growth in employment (E)				
	Delayed budgetary capacity		Social transfers		r^2
Belgium	0.273***	(5.822)	-0.033**	(-2.650)	0.35
Denmark	0.130*	(1.960)	-0.169***	(-6.382)	0.63
Germany	0.027	(0.306)	-1.140***	(-5.936)	0.46
Greece	0.188**	(2.007)	0.052	(1.389)	0.39
Spain	0.396*	(1.775)	-0.164***	(-3.528)	0.37
France	0.049	(0.871)	-0.056***	(-3.570)	0.38
Ireland	-0.166	(-0.790)	-0.103**	(-1.991)	0.35
Italy	-0.107	(-1.507)	-0.065**	(-2.730)	0.32
Netherlands	0.241**	(2.448)	-0.057***	(-3.761)	0.63
Austria	0.051	(0.832)	-0.020	(-0.927)	0.25
Portugal	-0.004	(-0.055)	-0.003	(-0.212)	0.01
Finland	0.331***	(4.166)	-0.180***	(-9.093)	0.69
Sweden	0.249***	(4.169)	-0.026	(-0.913)	0.35
United Kingdom	0.219*	(1.906)	-0.204***	(-6.769)	0.61

*Significant at 0.10 level; **Significant at 0.05 level; ***Significant at 0.001 level. T-stats in brackets.

employment and budgetary capacity the results are less significant but markedly better in terms of the coefficient values. In just five countries in the sample the variations in employment seem to be clearly explained by variations in social transfers with estimates significant at an error level strictly below 10 percent and positive sign coefficients between 18 and 33 percent. The values for r^2 are low, however, which means that the models tested were poorly specified, except in the case of four countries: Denmark, the Netherlands, Finland, and the United Kingdom, where r^2 was greater than 60 percent.

The trade-off between employment and social transfers seems to be greatest in the United Kingdom (20.4 percent), which is consistent with the liberal thinking behind the British welfare state. Notably the idea that social assistance finds its limitations in the marginal propensity of individuals to opt for welfare rather than work. Starting from this basis in building a system of social protection it was inevitable that the British would give preference to policies which would create jobs most directly and minimize forms of "passive" assistance such as social transfers. Compared with that, the trade-off between growth in employment and restriction of budgetary capacities is statistically not very significant but comparable in severity (21.9 percent) to the trade-off between employment and social transfers.

By comparison, for Finland and the Netherlands the trade-off between the variables of employment and budgetary balance (33.3 and 24.1 percent, respectively) is more severe and low between the variables of employment and social transfers (18 and 5.7 percent, respectively). It thus seems that like the UK model, those in Finland and the Netherlands—which we may term the "social democratic" type (Esping-Andersen, 1990)—combine a high level of employment with a large budgetary capacity, but that in the United Kingdom, budgetary equilibrium is maintained at the expense of increased social spending, whereas in Finland and the Netherlands this is possible thanks to high tax revenues drawn from a broad tax base. Whilst the econometric tests we have conducted are not enough to depict the whole of this trade-off process, they bear out our previous assumptions and are consistent with the idea, mooted in a number of institutionalist comparative studies (Titmuss, 1974; Esping-Andersen, 1990; Boismenu, 1994), that the liberal-style welfare states give priority to growth and economic efficiency, whilst the prime objectives of social-democratic welfare states are to reduce poverty, income inequalities, and unemployment.

Denmark is a case apart, though Esping-Andersen classifies it as one of the social-democratic countries. It appears to react like the United Kingdom: the link between social transfers and employment is more significant and the associated coefficient higher than between employment and restriction of budgetary capacity. These results would seem to show that Denmark is closer to a model of the minimum universalist type like that of the United Kingdom than to a maximum universalist model like that seen in the other Scandinavian countries (Korpi and Palme, 1994; Ferrera, 1994).

In the case of the welfare states of continental Europe (conservative-corporatist, or christian-democratic), the poor results in terms of the specification of their models (R^2 less than 40 percent) suggest that our econometric method is not very good at measuring the trade-offs they experience. This finding forces us to challenge Scharpf's basic criticism: "a lack of clarity over two basic distinctions—between binding constraints and price effects on the one hand, and between effects on policy instruments and policy outcomes on the other hand" (Scharpf, in this volume, p. 86). Economic and social policy objectives resulting from institutional schemes and private policies will not necessarily be reflected in quantitative data, which are, moreover, aggregated at the macro-economic level. This puts one in mind of an observation on methods by Théret that

> [i]t seems that the problem of recognizing and/or constructing the equivalences needed for comparisons is different depending on whether one seeks to establish term-to-term correspondences between simple elements in the various social systems compared, or whether the comparison is done at a higher level of abstraction using simply "functional equivalents," i.e., "structures serving the same purpose" within entities themselves deemed to be conceptually comparable . . . (Théret, 1997: 20)

It would thus appear that our empirical study is too superficial, that is to say based on indicators that represent just the "simple elements" rather than the "comparable structures" in welfare state models, to describe the trade-offs experienced by the countries of continental Europe which have more diffuse objectives and less clear-cut situations.

Conclusion

These results partly bear out the analysis in the first part of our study. It is fair to say that in most European countries the triangle of incompatibility does indeed amount to a dilemma between employment and social protection. But the model of the neo-liberal-type welfare state seems to be less dominant than we implied at the end of our first part. Our econometric analysis covering a thirty-year period unquestionably identifies the trends that are prevalent today.

For the future we need a more detailed analysis of these trade-offs: firstly we must distinguish systematically between indicators of political action and indicators of results; secondly we must use more disaggregated data on employment policies and social protection policies on the one hand and policies on employment and income inequalities on the other hand; thirdly we must use an econometric method that records breaks in trends over time, such as recursive estimates, for example.

We see, however, from the work of Iversen and Wren (1998), but also of Scharpf (2000), or Headey et al. (1999)—who wonder about the existence of trade-offs similar to those examined in this chapter, and on the role of such trade-offs in the reforms being undertaken in the welfare states—that the challenge of social cohesion is likely in the near future to become a challenge of major importance. Whereas Iversen and Wren (1998) do not see economic globalization and tertiarization of the developed economies as factors that challenge the ideal models of social protection, Scharpf (in this volume) describes the many constraints and vulnerabilities of each of these models and says that the models of continental Europe are likely to experience the most severe trade-offs.

Unless proper thought is given to how social cohesion is to be established under the system of Economic and Monetary Union, and unless a proper mechanism for redistribution at Community level is devised (Koulinsky and Richez-Battesti, 2000), European integration may well be accompanied by a process of "social disintegration."

Annex: Definition of Variables and Data Sources Used

Total employment for the whole of the economy (number of persons in employment as a percentage of the civilian population of working age), percent annual change.

Real unit wage costs for the whole of the economy (1991 = 100).

These data are taken from the document published by the European Commission: *Statistical annex, macroeconomic series*, autumn 1999.

Funding capacity (+) or net funding requirement (—) (as percentage of GDP at market prices, percent annual change): this is the net amount of resources that the government makes available to other sectors of the economy, or which other sectors lend to it. It is the difference between total resources and total spending. Total resources include recurrent expenditure (total recurrent taxes, social security contributions, and other current receipts received by general government) and capital transfers received. Total spending is all current expenditure (expenditure for final consumption, transfers other than those made in kind, interest, subsidies and other recurrent expenditure), plus spending on gross capital formation and other capital.

Social security contributions collected by general government as a percentage of GDP at market prices: these are all social contributions paid by employers, employees, the self-employed and unemployed into social security funds; they also include taxes earmarked to finance social security programs recorded in the accounts of general government; they are the counterpart of social benefits (less any employee contributions) which are paid directly by government units (i.e., not linked to contributions paid by government as an employer) to their employees or former employees and other qualifying persons.

General government employees' salaries as a percentage of GDP at market prices: defined as the total remuneration, financial or in kind, payable by the government to its employees in return for their work over a given period. It includes wages and salaries, and paid and notional social contributions.

Social transfers other than those made in kind that are distributed by general government, as a percentage of GDP at market prices: these cover (financial) transfers to households to ease the burden of certain risks or needs, and are based on collective mechanisms. The social risks in question are divided by function: sickness, disability/infirmity, occupational accidents/ illness, old age, survivors, maternity, family, job placement/guidance/mobility, unemployment, housing, miscellaneous.

These data and the definitions of the variables concerned are based on a European Commission document: *General Government Data, General Government Resources, Expenditures, Balances and Gross Debt*, autumn 1999.

Social protection expenditure as a percentage of GDP at market prices: expenditure is divided into benefits, operating costs, and other recurrent expenditure; transfers between administrations, that is, internal flows within the social security system, are excluded. Benefits are transfers to households to cover social risks which, if realized, entail financial cost or loss of income. The risks are divided by function, viz. sickness; disability/infirmity; occupational accident/illness; old age; survival; maternity; family; job placement/ guidance mobility; unemployment; housing, miscellaneous. Operating costs for the administration of social protection comprise three categories of expenditure: wages and salaries, consumption of goods and services, and taxes linked to production.

Other current expenditure includes taxes other than those linked to production, interest paid and transactions with the "rest of the world."

These data are published by Eurostat in *Social Expenditure and Receipts 1980-96*, Luxembourg, 1996.

Notes

1. By wage flexibility we mean adjustment of direct and indirect earnings. For a discussion of the various definitions of flexibility, see Boyer (1998: 222-251).
2. The services sector and industry. Agriculture is excluded from the analysis.
3. The services in question are: wholesale and retail trade, hotels and restaurants, community, social and personal services, plus a broad range of public services. Altogether they account for 80 percent of service jobs.
4. On average, government spending on government employees' salaries is 10-15 percent of GDP at market prices, or less than half the total government budget.
5. We use the variable of government funding capacity or net funding requirement.
6. See Annex for sources and definitions used.
7. Luxembourg is excluded from the study because of incomplete data.
8. Numerous studies using the micro-data of the Luxembourg Income Study (LIS) have shown that social transfer policies do much to reduce income inequalities (Ervik, 1998). But admittedly, most of these studies consider the effects of the tax/

transfer mechanism as a whole on variations in the Gini index (Gottschalk and Smeeding, 1997).

References

Ando, A. and Modigliani, F. (1963). "The Life Cycle Hypothesis of Saving: Aggregate Implication and Tests." *American Economic Review*, 53 (6), 55-84.

Atkinson, A. B. (1999). "Equity Issues in a Globalizing World: The Experience of OECD Countries." In Tanzi, V. et al. (eds.), *Economic Policy and Equity*. Washington, D.C.: IMF.

Atkinson, A. B., and Mogensen, G. (eds.). (1993). *Welfare and Work Incentives*. Oxford: Clarendon Press.

Atkinson, A. B., Rainwater, L., Smeeding, T. (1995). *Income Distribution in OECD Countries*. Paris: OECD.

Boismenu, G. (1994). "Systèmes de représentation des intérêts et configurations politiques: les sociétés occidentale en perspective comparée." *Canadian Journal of Political Science*, XXVII (2), 309-343.

Boyer, R. (1988). "Defensive or Offensive Flexibility." In Boyer, R. (eds.), *The Search for Labor Market Flexibility: The European Economies in Transition*. Oxford: Clarendon Press.

Buti, M., Franco, D., and Pench, L. R. (1997). "Reconciling the Welfare State with Sound Public Finances and High Employment." *European Economy: Reports and Studies*, 4, 7-42.

CEC (Commission of the European Communities). (1993). *Growth, Competitiveness, Employment—the Challenges and Ways Forward into the 21st Century*, White Paper. Luxembourg: CEC.

___. (1997). Social Policy and Economic Performance. Conference organized by the European Commission and Dutch Social Affairs Ministry, 23-25 January, Amsterdam.

___. (2000). *Social Protection in Europe 1999*. European Commission, DG V, Brussels.

Cohen, D. (1997). *Richesse du monde, pauvreté des nations*. Paris: Flammarion.

Decressin, J., and Fatas, A. (1994). Regional Labor Market Dynamic in Europe, *CEPR Discussion Paper*, 1085, December. London: CEPR.

Eichengreen, B. (1990). "One Money for Europe: Lessons from the US Currency Union." *Economic Policy*, April, 117-180.

Enjolras, B. (1999). *Protection sociale et performance économique*, Coll. Sociologie Economique. Paris: Desclée de Brouwer.

Ervik, R. (1998): *The Redistributive Aim of Social Policy: A Comparative Analysis of Taxes, Tax Expenditure Transfers and Direct Transfers in Eight Countries*, Luxembourg Income Study Working Paper Series No. 184, Luxembourg: LIS.

Esping-Andersen, G. (1990). *The Three Worlds of Welfare Capitalism*. Princeton, N.J.: Princeton University Press.

Farvaque, E., Richez-Battesti, N., and Venon, C. (1995). *Intégration monétaire et autonomie des politiques budgétaires*. Paris: CFE-CGC et IRES.

Feldstein, M. S. (1974). "Social Security, Induced Retirement and Aggregate Capital Accumulation." *Journal of Political Economy*, 82 (5), 905-926.

Ferrera, M. (1994). "La comparacion y el estado de bienestar: un caso de exito?" In Sartori, G., and Morlino, L. (eds.), *La comparacion en las ciencias sociales*. Madrid: Alianza Editorial.

Gottschalk, P., and Smeeding, T. M. (1997). "Cross-national Comparisons of Earnings and Income Inequality."*Journal of Economic Literature*, XXXV, 633-687.

Haskel, J. E., and Slaughter, M. J. (1999). "Technological Change as a Driving Force of Rising Income Inequality." In Siebert, H. (ed.), *Globalization and Labor*. Tübingen: Mohr Siebeck.

Headey, B., Goodin, R. E., Muffels, R., and Dirven H.-J. (1999). "Is there a Trade-off Between Economic Efficiency and Generous Welfare State? A Comparison of Best Cases of 'The Three Worlds of Welfare Capitalism.'" *Social Indicators Research*, 50, 115-157.

Hirschmann, A. (1970). *Exit, Voice and Loyalty*. Cambridge,Mass.: Harvard University Press.

Iversen, T., and Wren, A. (1998). "Equality, Employment and Budgetary Restraint: the Trilemma of the Service Economy." *World Politics*, 50 (July), 507-546.

Korpi, W., and Palme, J. (1994). *The Strategy of Equality and the Paradox of Redistribution*. Swedish Institute for Social Research, Stockholm: Stockholm University.

Koulinsky, A., and Richez-Battesti, N. (2000). L'assurance chômage interrégionale dans l'UEM: la question des choix sociaux. *12th Annual meeting on socio-economics*, London School of Economics, London, 7-10 July.

Leamer, E. E. (1999). "Competition in Tradables as a Driving Force of Rising Income Inequality." In Siebert, H., et al. (eds.), *Globalization and Labor*. Tübingen: Mohr Siebeck.

Leibfried, S., and Pierson, P. (1998). "Institutions multiniveaux et production de politiques sociales." In Leibfried, S., and Pierson, P. (eds.), *Politiques sociales européennes: entre intégration et fragmentation*. Coll. Logiques Politiques, Paris: L'Harmattan.

Le Grand, J., and Bartlett, W. (eds.). (1993). *Quasi-markets and Social Policy*. London: Macmillan.

Lindbeck, A. (1988). "Consequences of the Advanced Welfare State." *The World Economy*, March, 19-37.

Masson, P., and Taylor, M. (1992). "Common Currency Areas and Currency Union: An Analysis of the Issue." *CEPR Discussion Paper*, No. 617, London: CEPR.

Maurice, J. (ed.). (1999). *Emploi, négociations collectives, protection sociale: vers quelle Europe sociale*. Rapport pour le Commissariat Général du Plan. Paris: La Documentation Française.

Okun, A. M. (1975). *Equality and Efficiency: The Big Tradeoff*. Washington, D.C: The Brookings Institution.

Picketty, T. (1997). *L'économie des inégalités*. Coll. Repères, La Découverte.

Quintin, O., and Favarel-Dapas, B. (1999). *L'Europe sociale: enjeux et réalités*, Coll. Réflexe Europe. Paris: La Documentation Française.

Richez-Battesti, N. (1997). "Union économique et monétaire et protection sociale: monnaie unique et espaces sociaux fragmentés." *Solidarité-Santé*, 1 (January-March), 95-108.

Rosanvallon, P. (1981). *La crise de l'Etat-Providence*, Paris: Le Seuil.

Supiot, A. (ed.). (1999). *Au delà de l'emploi: transformations du travail et devenir du droit du travail en Europe*. Report for the European Commission. Paris: Flammarion.

Tanzi, V. (2000). *Globalization and the Future of Social Protection*. IMF Working paper, No. 00/12, Washington, D. C.: IMF.

Théret, B. (1997). "Méthodologie des comparaisons internationales, approches de l'effet sociétal et de la régulation: une lecture structuraliste des systèmes nationaux de protection sociale." *L'année de la régulation*, 1 (1), 163-228.

Tiebout, C. M. (1956). "A Pure Theory of Local Expenditures." *Journal of Political Economy*, LXIV, 416-424.

Titmuss, R. (1974). *Social Policy*. London: Allen and Unwin.

15

Family Policy, Work Incentives, and the Employment of Mothers

Katja Forssén and Mia Hakovirta

Over the past thirty years, many countries have seen a major transformation in patterns of family formation and the structure of families, as well as in the employment patterns of mothers. The policies of welfare states in respect to families have also undergone major changes. In the 1990s, many argued that welfare states had become too supportive and provided too much welfare, with the result that individuals and families were no longer taking responsibility for themselves. The system of family policy, combined with taxation and the provision of services, can very easily create a situation in which there is a strong economic disincentive for individuals to work. Mothers and single-parents tend to be confronted by these disincentives more easily than others because of the multiple goals of family policy.

The disincentives created by family benefits are often highlighted in evaluations of family support systems. But the disincentive issue is not simple. Modern family policy systems aim to achieve several goals simultaneously. Their function is not only to provide economic support. Other equally important instruments include the provision of services (day-care services) and measures that make it possible for parents to take time-off work. These elements of family policy vary from one country to another. In some conservative welfare states, mothers with young children are seen more as providers of care than as workers. In the Nordic countries, the role of mothers is seen from a broader perspective and the aim of Nordic family policy is to help parents reconcile work and family life. The manner in which family support systems have developed and the various views of the role of women depend to a great extent on ideological and historical factors.

The debate on the disincentive effects of social security benefits seems to have its roots more in ideological factors than in empirical evidence. Indeed, very few studies have been carried out on the effects of welfare benefits on the employment of mothers. Some studies have indicated that family policy has an important effect on the labor supply of mothers (Gornick et al., 1998; Knudsen, 1999). But the labor supply of mothers is influenced by their preferences and labor market conditions, as well as by family policies. In our earlier study (Forssén and Hakovirta, 1999), it was noted that most single parents in Finland work, despite the fact that they would have the same or a higher disposable income if they stayed at home. In this study, this approach is broadened to cover other OECD countries and both single and two-parent families.

The aim of this chapter is to study the impact of the various family policy models on the incentives of parents (and especially mothers) to participate in the labor market in a number of OECD countries. The main emphasis is on the situation in the 1990s. The Luxembourg Income Study (LIS) is used as the main source of data to chart the connections between the labor market participation of women, their economic situation and the achievement of family policies. The term "family policy" in this context means services, taxation, and income transfers targeted at families with children, including benefits related to unemployment, maternity, sickness, minimum income support and child-related benefits. The economic effects of income transfers are examined from the perspective of poverty. What effects do the labor force participation of women and household structures have on the risk of poverty? The main issue is the effect that the various social security systems have on the incentives of individuals to participate in the labor market.

The study first describes briefly how the various welfare states have structured their family policy systems. In this part of the study, countries are grouped by their main policy targets. An analysis is then made of how the different styles of policy-making encourage women to choose their roles as mothers and workers. The last part of the study focuses on the economic situation of families with children by analyzing the poverty rates of different types of families with differing employment patterns. Finally, the results of the study are placed in a broader context.

Differing Divisions of Responsibility between the State, the Market, and the Family

Most Western governments have played an increasingly important role in providing income support to families with children and subsidized services for education, health care, and the socialization and development of children. Family policies consist of those welfare state support mechanisms that are intended to shield families with children against social risks and to redistribute income between families with children and childless families (Kamerman and Kahn, 1994; Wennemo, 1994; Gauthier, 1996; Forssén, 1998).

The aims of family policies have varied both over time and between different welfare states, ranging from securing population growth to ensuring the welfare of families with children (Wennemo, 1994; Forssén, 1998). However, in some countries, the family has been seen as an institution with which society must not interfere. For this reason, family policy legislation is almost completely lacking in many countries (Ford and Millar, 1998; Forssén, 1998).

Forssén (1998) has categorized welfare states according to their family policies, using Esping-Andersen's (1990) welfare state typology as her starting point. Corporatist family policies are based on gender differences and the ethos of the housewife. Family and employee insurance systems play a central role and social policies are characterized by their direct linkage with labor market performance. Family policies are designed to meet the needs of two-parent families. Liberal family policies highlight the role of markets in producing family welfare. In these countries, the starting point for family policies lies in free markets, which have the task of producing welfare services for citizens. Those who cannot secure their livelihood on the market are offered means-tested benefits. The aim of Nordic family policies is social integration, to be achieved through the provision of extensive public services and benefits of a reasonably high level. All citizens are entitled to social security. The aim of family policies is to redistribute the cost of raising children, harmonize work and family commitments, and enable women to participate in the labor market (Forssén, 1998).

Although almost all countries now have economic support systems for families with children, these systems have developed at different periods and from different starting points. Family policies differ between countries with respect to their extent and level. Support may be provided in the form of income transfers or tax relief (Wennemo, 1994; Forssén, 1998). The aims of family policies also vary and a single support system may be striving to achieve many often conflicting aims.

The manner in which these different views of the family are reflected in family policies in the various countries is now examined through a comparison of the levels of family policy in fourteen countries. The study focuses on the family policies that reflect the commitment of nations or governments to support the employment of mothers. When packaging different family policy arrangements, it is clear that some countries have gone much further than others in making provision for working parents and in helping to reconcile employment and family life. In this section, national policies for reconciling employment and family life are examined by means of a policy index of the different levels of state intervention. The family policy index includes cash transfers for families with children, taxation, and child-care arrangements. To construct the index, the relative values of all the indicators are transferred into plusses and the index scores are then assumed to give a meaningful interpretation of relative national performance in supporting the reconciliation of family life and work for mothers.

Table 15.1 shows that Scandinavian countries, together with Belgium, France, Italy, and Spain, have a fairly wide range of family policy legislation. The Nordic states tend to reject special protection for women as mothers in the labor market on grounds of equality. Generous state provision of child care, paid parental leave for both men and women, and favorable working time arrangements have to be understood as measures thatsupport the access of women to the labor market. Belgium and France also have a long tradition of family policy (Hantrais and Letablier, 1996). Explicit statements have been made about the intention of the state to develop measures to help parents combine employment and family life. In Belgium and France, the focus has been on improving the quality of life for working people, protecting the standard of living of families and achieving greater equality between men and women in the labor market. All these countries have in common the fact

Table 15.1
Family Policy Index in Various Countries in the 1990s

	Paid maternity leave	Extended leave	Financial support during extended leave %	Separate taxation	Leave to care for sick children	Coverage of day care	Family policy index
Finland	+++	+++	+	+	+	++	11
Sweden	+++	+	+	+	+	++	9
Belgium	++	++	+	-	+	++	8
Italy	++	+	+	+	+	++	8
France	+	+++	+	-	-	++	7
Norway	++	++	-	+	+	+	7
Denmark	++	+	-	+	-	++	6
Spain	+	+++	-	-	+	+	6
Germany	+	+	+	-	+	+	5
Netherlands	+	++	-	+	-	-	4
United Kingdom	+	+	-	+	-	-	
Australia	-	++	-	+	-	-	3
United States	+	-	-	+	-	-	2

Source: Millar and Warman (1996): leave to care for sick children, coverage of day care (except for Australia and United States). O'Donoghue and Sutherland (1998): separate taxation (+ = exists). Knudsen (1999): extended leave: 100 or more weeks = +++, 50-99 weeks = ++, 20-49 weeks = +, below 20 weeks = -. Money support for extended leave: yes = +. Work incentive and disincentive indexes are calculated as follows: +++ = 3 points, ++ = 2 points, + = 1 point and - = 0 point.

that family policy is intended to help parents reconcile their family responsibilities with their jobs. The state is generally supportive of economic activity by women and has therefore provided a legislative framework for the employment of mothers with dependent children outside the home.

The countries that are characterized by low levels of intervention to help parents combine employment and family life include some in which governments have deliberately avoided interfering in the private lives of individuals and some where there is a relatively underdeveloped system of social protection. In these countries, the employment of women has largely been seen as a private matter, with public provision of childcare being designed to protect children in need, but not to enable women to engage in paid employment. In Australia, United Kingdom, and United States, paid parental leave is not a universal right, but an area for negotiation between employees and employers.

The Employment of Mothers

The rise in the labor market participation of women in general, and especially of mothers with small children, is a widely illustrated and internationally applicable social phenomenon. Although the participation of women in the labor market has increased everywhere, there are still significant differences between countries. But these differences cannot been explained by any single factor. The labor market behavior of women in each country is a product of a complex mix of factors, including cultural beliefs and social norms. However, there is strong evidence that the family policy model has an effect on the labor market behavior of mothers. Our earlier study (Forssén, 2000) found that the labor force pattern of women in the United States is very similar to that in Nordic countries (see Table 15.2), but that the level of family policy measures is low the United States. In general terms, it would appear that broader family policy measures clearly affect the labor market situation of women.

Mothers have to make various decisions concerning their participation in the labor market. These decisions are affected by economic and social resources, working arrangements, and the availability of private and public day-care services. The values of society in terms of child rearing also influence the employment of mothers. Welfare states differ strongly in terms of how the role of mother is seen. Should mothers be expected to stay at home and care for their children, or are they expected to do paid work outside the home? Are they, as Lewis (1993) has put it, mothers or workers? Although this diversity between welfare states has weakened over the past twenty years, there still exist huge variations in the labor force participation rates of mothers. Table 15.2 shows the employment rates of single mothers and mothers with partners.

Table 15.2
Percentage of Single Mothers and Mothers with Partners Employed
Full time and Part time, circa 1990

	% of single mothers employed			% of mothers with partners employed		
	Full time	Part time	Total	Full time	Part time	Total
Australia	23	20	43	24	32	56
Austria	43	15	58	28	18	46
Belgium	52	16	68	36	22	61
Denmark	59	10	69	64	20	84
Finland	61	4	65	62	8	70
France	67	15	82	49	20	68
Germany	46	21	67	29	28	57
Italy	58	11	69	29	12	41
Luxembourg	61	13	73	32	13	45
Netherlands	16	24	40	13	39	52
Norway	44	17	61	40	37	77
Sweden	41	29	70	42	38	80
United Kingdom	17	24	42	21	41	63
United States	47	13	60	45	19	64

Note: Full time is usually greater or equal to 30 hours a week. Part time is usually less than 30 hours a week.

Source: Bradshaw et al. (1996); Kilkey (2000: 80).

A comparison of the overall employment rates of single and married/cohabiting mothers in Austria, Belgium, France, Germany, Italy, and Luxembourg shows that the overall employment rates of single mothers are higher than those of mothers with partners. In contrast, in Australia, Denmark, Finland, Netherlands, Norway, Sweden, United Kingdom, and United States, mothers with partners have higher employment rates than single mothers.

Countries can be categorized into three groups according to the employment rates of mothers. The first is a group of countries in which both types of mothers have relatively high employment rates, namely the Nordic countries and the United States. In the Nordic countries, the state supports the labor market participation of mothers of small children through universal family benefits. Social policies encourage their labor market participation through the provision of social services and employee rights, extensive maternity leave systems and day-care services. In the United States, it is the lack of family benefits that pushes mothers into the labor market.

The second group of countries includes those in which the employment of single parents is low in comparison with mothers with partners, namely Australia, the Netherlands, and United Kingdom. In these countries, there are hardly any social services to help mothers go out to work, since caring for the family and the home is seen as the women's responsibility.

In addition, there are countries where the labor market participation rates of married mothers are low, but the rates for single parents are high. The lack of family benefits pushes single parents into the labor market and they have a higher labor market participation rate than married mothers. This model is represented by Austria, Germany, Italy, and Luxembourg.

However, the employment rates of mothers provide only a general picture of their working patterns which needs some clarification. Table 15.3 shows in greater detail the *intensity* with which mothers participate in paid work. (Unfortunately, the LIS provides this information for only eleven countries). It shows the weekly working hours of mothers by family structure, number of children, and the age of the youngest child. Women in Finland, Italy, and Sweden work more than in other countries. When comparing Tables 15.2 and 15.3, it could be said that the labor force participation rate of women is low in Italy, but that those women who are in paid employment work more than women in most other countries. Working hours seem to be extremely low in Australia, the Netherlands, and United Kingdom.

Although more and more women are in paid employment, marked differences still exist in both the employment rates of women and the form of their employment. In the first place, Table 15.3 shows that employed single mothers work more than employed mothers in two-parent families. This is the case in most countries, except for Australia, Canada, the Netherlands, and United Kingdom. Secondly, there is a positive correlation between the age of the youngest child and working hours. As the age of the youngest child increases, so do working hours. Countries can be classified into three groups according the manner in which mothers participate in paid work. In general, it would seem that their working pattern in Scandinavia shows no differences for family types. In these countries, single mothers and mothers in two-parent families both work more than mothers in other countries. The second group includes countries where mothers in both family types work less than in other countries. This is the case in Australia, the Netherlands, and United Kingdom. The third group includes countries where single mothers work significantly more than mothers in two-parent families. This is the case in Austria, Belgium, Luxembourg, and United States.

Mothers seem to have adopted different working patterns in different countries. In Scandinavia, the labor force participation rates of women are high and mothers in both family types work equal numbers of hours on average. In the Nordic countries, mothers in both family types find it easier to combine work and family responsibilities than in other countries. The liberal welfare states cannot be grouped as clearly as the Nordic countries. In Australia and the United Kingdom, women in both family types work less than in other countries, but in the United States single mothers work more than mothers in

Table 15.3
Weekly Working Hours of Employed Mothers in Eleven Countries

Country	Mean (total)	Number of children			Age of the youngest child		
		1	2	3 or more	0- 5	6-12	13-18
Finland 91 1A+C	33	33	33	30	29	34	34
Finland 91 2A+C	30	31	30	28	26	34	36
Sweden 95 1A+C	30	31	30	29	29	30	33
Sweden 95 2A+C	29	31	30	27	28	30	31
Austria 87 1A+C	24	27	21	10	20	28	24
Austria 87 2A+C	17	26	14	8	17	16	21
Belgium 94 1A+C	21	24	24	11	13	23	30
Belgium 94 2A+C	18	22	20	11	18	19	18
Netherlands 91 1A+C	8	7	8	8	6	8	10
Netherlands 91 2A+C	9	10	8	9	7	10	11
Luxembourg 94 1A+C	26	36	24	18	26	24	-
Luxembourg 94 2A+C	12	15	9	11	11	13	6
Italy 95 1A+C	37	39	34	-	39	38	36
Italy 95 2A+C	35	36	35	33	34	35	38
United Kingdom 95 1A+C	8	9	11	3	4	11	15
United Kingdom 95 2A+C	13	15	13	11	11	15	18
United States 94 1A+C	25	30	26	19	20	28	30
United States 94 2A+C	13	15	13	11	11	15	18
Australia 94 1A+C	10	9	12	7	6	12	16
Australia 94 2A+C	13	17	13	9	9	18	20
Canada 94 1A+C	16	17	16	13	12	19	22
Canada 94 2A+C	21	23	22	18	18	23	26

1A+C= single-parent family with at least one child under 18 years old.
2A+C= two-parent family with at least one child under 18 years old.

Source: LIS

two-parent families, because single mothers are pushed into the labor market as a result of the lack of family benefits.

Poverty Risk

One way of looking at how the different family policy systems affect work incentives consists of focusing on poverty rates. According to the work incentive approach, paid work should always provide a level of disposable income that is above the poverty line. Although women's employment is a central element in alleviating the risk of poverty, it does not guarantee that poverty is avoided in every case. It has been shown above that countries differ greatly in the way in which they encourage women to participate in the labor force. In this section, the economic incentive effect of family policy systems is analyzed by focusing on poverty rates. Could it be that in some countries there is no significant difference in poverty rates according to the number of earners in the family? Could poverty rates for single parents in some countries be high despite the fact that they work?

Figures 15.1 and 15.2 show poverty rates for different family types by the number of earners in the household. Figure 15.1 focuses on the situation of single-parent families. It has been considered self-evident that a single-parent family without income from employment is at greater risk of poverty than a family with an employed single parent. But this is not the case in all countries. In Norway, the poverty rate is at the same level in both situations. At the beginning of the 1990s, the situation was also similar in Finland and Sweden, but after the recession poverty rates increased for unemployed single parents. In all other countries, there is a wide gap between poverty rates for the employed and the unemployed, and for single-parent families it is obvious that employment alleviates the poverty risk.

One of the main findings is that the poverty rate of single parents is highest in the United States in both situations. This shows that the economic situation of single parents is bleak even if they work. And, as noted above, the labor force participation pattern of single parents in the United States is very close to that of Scandinavia.

Figure 15.1
Poverty Rates of Single-Parent Families by the
Number of Earners, Early 1990s (%)

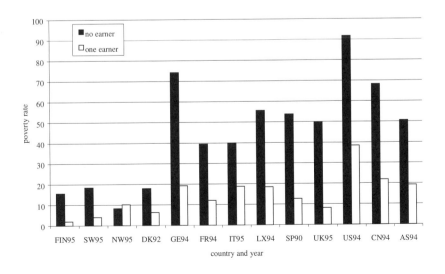

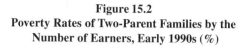

Figure 15.2
Poverty Rates of Two-Parent Families by the
Number of Earners, Early 1990s (%)

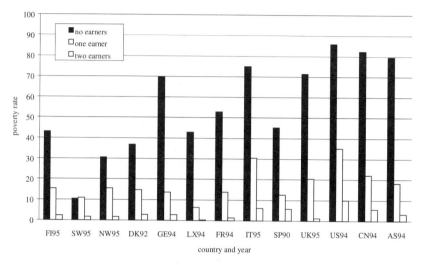

The number of earners in two-parent families is also a significant determinant of the poverty risk. In all countries, the absence of income from work for both parents clearly increases the poverty risk. Moreover, if families have two earners, the poverty rate is very low in all OECD countries. The interesting factor is where families have only one earner in the household. In most continental European countries, the difference between poverty rates for two- and one-earner households is smaller than in Scandinavian countries. This difference reflects the dominant social views concerning breadwinners: in continental Europe, social security and family policy services are structured to support the single earner model, while in the Nordic countries social policy encourages both parents to work.

Employment seems to be an effective shelter against poverty, especially for single-parent families. For two-parent families, employment also plays an important role, although there is diversity among OECD countries as to how many earners are needed to prevent families from falling into poverty. In many continental European countries, two-parent families do well with only one earner in the household. In Scandinavia and liberal welfare states, two earners are needed to keep households above the poverty line.

Discussion

There is growing evidence that social policies have an important impact on the employment of mothers. The labor supply of women is influenced by women's preferences and labor market conditions, as well as by family policies and taxation. The high labor force participation rate of women may be connected to a high level of family policy. In the Nordic countries, families are helped to reconcile family life and employment by a multi-tasked family policy system. However, in some other countries, family policy focuses on supporting mothers to stay at home (Forssén and Hakovirta, 1999).

As shown in this study, most Western governments have played an increasingly important role in providing income support and subsidized services for families with children. Some countries have gone even further by assuring working parents more time for parenting. The effect of these mixed systems can be seen by looking at the labor market outcomes in each country. The employment patterns of women are a product of a complex mix of factors, including cultural beliefs, social norms, taxation, the social security system, and economic factors. Cultural and social factors are connected to the way in which women make decisions concerning paid work and to the manner in which family policy is structured in each society. The family policy system also has an effect on the decisions taken by families, but this effect is not straightforward. One confusing example is that of single-parent families in liberal welfare states. Although these liberal countries all lack a comprehensive family policy system, there are great variations in the participation rates of mothers in the labor force. To understand these variations, it is important to take a broader view of the relevant historical, social, and qualitative factors.

Many studies describe the Nordic welfare state model as "women-friendly." For example, Finland's welfare state has contributed considerably to changes in the social practice of motherhood. The Finnish welfare state is also based on the ideas of the full employment integration of women and of public childhood (Pfau-Effinger, 1999). However, this dual breadwinner policy also includes traps. The question arises as to how women-friendly the state is in practice if a family needs to have two earners to live above the official poverty line. How voluntary is the participation of Finnish mothers in the labor market? Would they prefer part-time jobs if they were available? There is evidence that the participation of women in full-time employment in Finland is based on a voluntary decision. According to Nätti et al. (1994), only 4 percent of women working full time would prefer a part-time job.

As noted above, the linkage between family policy measures and the labor force participation of women is not straightforward. It has been argued, for example, that the availability of universal day-care services in Scandinavia explains the high labor force participation rates of women in these countries. However, an historical overview shows that women began to enter the labor force well before day-care services began to develop (Forssén, 2000). Although the quality and coverage of day care was low in the 1960s and 1970s, it was an economic necessity for many families to have two earners in the household. On the other hand, universal day-care services now make it easier for women to enter the labor market when they choose to do so.

The employment of women and work incentives are very complex issues. Because every country has its own family policy system, the effects of these systems can be evaluated in the first place at the national level. However, if the family policy systems in different countries and their effects on the employment patterns of mothers are to be compared, more detailed studies are needed covering a broader context. But the studies carried out in this area appear to be mainly focused on economic factors, leaving aside equality aspects, such as the preferences of individual families.

References

Bradshaw, J., Ditch, J., Holmes, H., and Whiteford, P. (1993). *Support for Children: A Comparison of Arrangements in Fifteen Countries*. London: HMSO.

Bradshaw, J., Kennedy, S., Kilkey, M., Hutton, S., Corden, A., Eardley, T., Holmes, H., and Neale, J. (1996). *The Employment of Lone Parents: A Comparison of Policy in 20 Countries*. London: Family Policy Studies Centre.

Esping-Andersen, G. (1990). *The Three Worlds of Welfare Capitalism*. Cambridge, Mass.: Polity Press.

Ford, R., and Millar, J. (1998). "Lone Parenthood in the UK: Policy Dilemmas and Solutions." In Ford, R., and Millar, J. (eds.), *Private Lives and Public Responses. Lone Parenthood and Future Policy*. London. Policy Studies Institute.

Forssén, K., and Hakovirta, M. (1999). "Work Incentives in Single Parent Families." In Ringen, S., and de Jong, P. R. (eds.), *Fighting Poverty: Children, Parents, The Elderly and Health*. Series of International Social Security Vol. 6. Aldershot: Ashgate.

Forssén, K. (1998). *Children, Families and the Welfare State. Studies on the Outcomes of the Finnish Family Policy*. Helsinki. STAKES Research Reports 92.

Forssén, K. (2000). *Child Poverty in the Nordic Countries*. Working Paper B: 22/2000. University of Turku, Department of Social Policy.

Gauthier, A. H. (1996). *The State and the Family. A Comparative Analysis of Family Policies in Industrialized Countries*. Oxford. Clarendon Press.

Gornick, J. C., Meyers, M. K., and Ross, K. E. (1998). "Public Policies and the Employment of Mothers: A Cross-national Study." *Social Science Quarterly* 79 (1), 35-54.

Hantrais, L., and Letablier, M.-T. (1996). *Families and Family Policies in Europe*. New York: Longman Publishing.

Kamerman, S. B., and Kahn, A. J. (1994). "Family Policy and the under-3s: Money, Services and Time in a Policy Package." *International Social Security Review* 47 (3-4), 31-43.

Kilkey, M. (2000). *Lone Mothers between Paid Work and Care. The Policy Regime in Twenty Countries*. Aldershot. Ashgate.

Knudsen. K. (1999). *Married Women's Employment Supply and Public Policies in an International Perspective*. NOVA Report 12/1999. Oslo: NOVA.

Lewis, J. (1993). *Women and Social Policies in Europe*. Aldershot: Edward Elgar.

Millar, J., and Warman, A. (1996). *Family Obligations in Europe*. London: Family Policy Studies Center.

Nätti, J., and Julkunen, R. (1994). *Joustavaan työaikaan vai työajan uusjakoon*. Tampere: Vastapaino.

O'Donoghue, C., and Sutherland, H. (1998). *Accounting for the Family: The Treatment of Marriage and Children in European Income Tax Systems.* Occasional papers, Economic and Policy Series EPS 65. Florence: UNICEF.

Pfau-Effinger, B. (1999). "The Modernization of Family and Motherhood." In Crompton, R. (ed.), *Restructuring Gender Relations and Employment.* Oxford:Oxford University Press,.

Wennemo, I. (1994). *Sharing the Costs of Children. Studies on the Development of Family Support in the OECD Countries.* Doctoral Dissertation Series 25. Stockholm. Swedish Institute for Social Research.

Part 5

Social Cohesion

16

The Welfare Pentagon and the Social Management of Risks

Chris de Neubourg

Social welfare is defined as the ability of an economy to satisfy the needs of its members and to manage the risks threatening the well being of the same people. Social (protection) policy has to be defined as all actions taken by public authorities to contribute to the satisfaction of these needs and to address the risks threatening the former. Societies have developed various ways to deal with their basic problems (satisfaction of needs and coping with the risks threatening the satisfaction of needs), and intervention by public authorities is only one, though important, element in this process. Needs and risks have always been taken care of even in the absence of deliberate social (protection) policy (or more narrowly defined "welfare state policy"). The five major institutions (the Welfare Pentagon) that are used to satisfy needs and to take care of risks are: markets, families, social networks, membership institutions, and public authorities. Each of them has different historical and geographical appearances (names), but basically they are found in all societies across time and locations. Economies and societies have blended the five basic elements in different portions and different formats, but the five elements are (almost) always present. The chapter explores the characteristics of the Welfare Pentagon in the next sections by contrasting it to "the simplistic dyad" as inspired by economistic thinking and "baseline triangle" that may be constructed on intuitive grounds. It is then argued that social protection policy has to be (re)defined as the social management of risks. The concepts of needs and risks will be developed consequently in order to round up with the discussion of how strategies and policy instruments in social protection policy are analyzed within risk management framework.

The Simplistic Dyad and the Baseline Triangle

Ever since (nearly) automatically evolving market equilibria were given a central place in economic thinking, all welfare production or welfare distribution outside markets became residual in the analyses. In many cases markets are believed and proved to produce efficient outcomes, guaranteeing the maximum possible attainable level of welfare (and thus the maximum attainable level of satisfaction of needs) and a Pareto-efficient distribution given a set of assumptions and conditions. Whenever the former conditions are not met or whenever the assumptions are violated, there are efficiency arguments for interventions. Besides efficiency arguments, equity arguments (linked to "justice" considerations—including Pareto-optimality—and political preferences) are accepted as another rationale for interventions. It is implied that interventions have to have a public nature and public authorities almost automatically become the sole responsible agent for non-market actions. This reduces the empirical complexity to a simplistic dyad wherein in most cases markets are accepted to deliver efficient levels of social welfare with a set of exceptions wherein the state (as an acronym for public authorities) has to guarantee social welfare and its distribution where markets fail or where equity considerations require some corrective action.

There are two major problems with the simplicity of this analytical framework. Firstly, it fails to recognize that quite a serious quantity of the welfare production and an even bigger part of welfare distribution is realized outside the realm of markets and beyond the scope of public interventions. Secondly, it leaves the state (public authorities) with an assignment that exhausts its power and potential instruments.

The idea that some wealth is produced outside markets and without public intervention is often no more that a token consideration referring to the production goods and services within households or other informal parts of the economy and is treated to have no further implications for economic analyses. It is recognized that its Gross Domestic Product (GDP) may be underestimated by the output of many informal workers, but only feminist economists and development specialists seem to care. However, the output of (and inputs into) unobserved, black, grey, and criminal markets are left out of the analysis. This is not only troublesome when less developed or transition economies are analyzed, but it hampers the analysis seriously in developed

Figure 16.1
The Simplistic Dyad

Markets ——————————————————————— **State**

economies as well especially when we try to understand the dynamics of shifts of economic activities from the household sector to the market sector and vice versa. The shift from commercial laundries to household laundries or from household meal-production to fast-food and prepared food catering, for example, cannot be understood or even estimated in a context with the markets and the state as the only two providers of wealth.

When considering social protection policy, the simplistic dyad is even more harmful to the analysis. The implicit assumption that when markets fail, the sole alternative is the government taking action is not only politically unrealistic but is far from the actual practice in all economies whether developed, less developed or in transition.[1] This is even more relevant when not only the production of wealth but also its distribution is taken into account. It is absolutely incomprehensible how intergenerational transfers within households or how voluntary transfers within social networks and charitable organizations are accounted for when the analysis is limited to markets and the state. In empirical terms it is impossible to explain how people in poverty are able to survive without reference made to other distribution channels than markets or the state (Gassmann and de Neubourg, 2000). This is even more important when social protection policy and social protection actions are analyzed in a multi-period context wherein individuals are risk averse and want to address the risks of not being able to satisfy their needs in the future (see below).

All this is better understood when we try to model individual behavior within what we call the *baseline triangle*.

Let's take a relatively simple problem: every individual needs means to survive. In a monetarized economy this usually implies that an individual needs money to buy the goods and services that are necessary to survive (or, in other words, to satisfy his/her basic needs). Solving this problem means: make sure you get money basically to buy food and protection against the elements (cloths, a shelter). In modern economies the option that most people will opt for, is to look for a job that provides the money that is needed. This is, however, not the only option an individual has. One could also try to produce the goods that one needs oneself. Another option would be to ask one's family (spouse, parents, grandparents, children, grandchildren, brothers, sisters …) to provide the money. Or to ask them for the direct provision of the goods that one needs. You may fall back on begging and charity or mobilize your friends to help you (mobilize your social network).[2] Finally, there is the option to steal either the money or the goods. The latter option, though clearly chosen by some, will be largely disregarded in this context. This means that we will exclude actions implying the use of violence or force by individuals.

Summarizing: in absence of a benevolent public authority, individuals wanting to satisfy their basic needs can rely on some form of activity on the

Figure 16.2
The Baseline Triangle

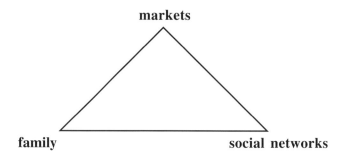

market (either the labor market or a product market) or rely on their family or mobilize socially available networks. We call this the *Baseline Triangle.*

The Welfare Pentagon

Public authorities are missing from the Baseline Triangle and should be added to it to complete the analytical framework. Very few societies, if any, function without some form of centralized legitimate authority taking up some responsibilities in the production and distribution of social welfare. There is, however, a fifth element that should be added: membership institutions. These are institutions of which individuals can become members and from which they can resign. The basic institutions we think of in this context are firms, labor unions, mutual insurance companies, co-operatives and the like. Although one could try to incorporate these institutions partly among social networks and partly among market institutions, it makes more sense to separate them into a specific category. There are two main reasons for doing so. Firstly, in contrast with social networks, individuals have more freedom and more discretionary power in seeking access to and exit from these institutions. Secondly, in contrast with markets, these institutions rely less purely on market (say price) mechanisms to regulate individual supply- and demand-behavior; they require a minimum form of solidarity. This is true for social networks also, but in the case of membership institutions this solidarity is organized in a formal way. It will be argued below that this holds also for firms or corporations.

This brings us to the *Welfare Pentagon* as the basic framework for social welfare analysis. When individuals have to address the basic needs problem, they really can rely on the five corners of the Welfare Pentagon or a combination of the five elements. The Welfare Pentagon is no more than the stylized representation of the institutional setting wherein welfare production and welfare distribution take place. In practice, solutions within the pentagon rather than on a single corner will be sought and accepted. The two purest forms of corner solutions to the basic needs problem is most probably found when children are considered or when an individual relies on the market only to guarantee the satisfaction of (basic) needs. Children rely mostly on the intergenerational solidarity provided within families, while individual market behavior seems to rely on the market corner only. However, even in these cases some other elements enter the picture. It is hard, for example, to imagine any market to function well without some public intervention in the form of regulation and protection of property rights; and even in the case of children some needs are often satisfied with the help of government or membership institutions (for example education). Concluding it can be said that individuals solve their welfare problem stated in terms of the satisfaction of basic needs by seeking the solution within the context of corners of the Welfare Pentagon or a combination within the Welfare Pentagon.

It is important to remark that the entire space of the Welfare Pentagon is necessarily "social" in nature. All corners of the pentagon require a social dimension in the sense that at least one other person is needed to make the solution viable. That is pretty clear if we talk about social networks, membership institutions, and public authorities. Even adopting a market solution or a family solution, however, requires that there is another party, another individual on the market or in the family. If an individual decides to offer his/her labor in exchange for payment, it is implied that on the labor market there is

Figure 16.3
The Welfare Pentagon

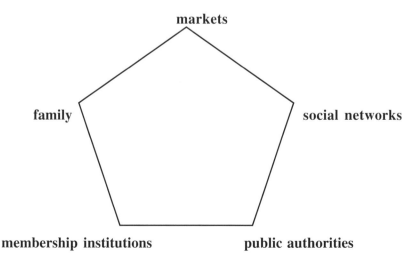

another individual who is prepared to hire the first person and pay out the agreed wage. If an individual decides to grow vegetables and sell them on a market, it is implied that there is another individual willing and able to buy these vegetables (or exchange them for something else). If an individual decides to ask a family member to provide food and shelter it is necessary for the option to be viable, that there is at least one other family member who is prepared and able to provide the goods. Inherently market solutions and family solutions are "social" and require reciprocity between individuals. The reciprocity on a market is direct (something is exchanged immediately for something else); the reciprocity within a family is indirect (in the simplest case, something is received under the implicit promise to return a similar service to other members of the family).

Risk Management

So far it was argued that the satisfaction of basic needs was a relatively simple problem defining the problem in a static one-period framework. Not being able to satisfy the basic needs at a certain moment in time, is the only risk that has been considered. As a consequence social protection policy is then defined as a coping problem: how an individual copes with the situation where he/she has to satisfy his/her needs in a specific moment in time.

However important, this is evidently a very restrictive way to define the "basic risk" from a policy perspective. The subsequent and equally important problem is how individuals secure the fulfillment of their basic needs in the future. The "basic risk" is then redefined as a multi-period dynamic problem wherein individuals manage the risk of the satisfaction of their basic needs now and in the future.

The simplest solution would be saving: persons wanting to secure the fulfillment of their basic needs in the future should save. This means, postponing consumption or, more technically, substituting immediate consumption for consumption in the future. Individuals may do that either by just putting money (or in some cases goods) aside or by using the capital market to make sure the level of their future income is satisfactory to meet their basic needs.

Within the Welfare Pentagon, however, there are other options as well.

Individuals can either rely on some market activity or they can rely on their social network or on their family or on membership institutions or on the public interventions. That is to say, they can make sure that either income from (self-)employment will be generated in the future. They can also secure that they will be able to rely on their family, on their social network, on membership institutions or on "the state." The family/social network options are easy to understand, but the other options require some explanation. Making sure that you will be able to sell products in the future or that you will be employed against a certain wage is only possible if some form of contract is used. On a product market it means to sign a contract that guarantees that someone will buy your goods in the future. On the capital market it means a contract with, for example, an insurance company guaranteeing a future income under certain conditions. On the market for labor it implies a contract that guarantees effort against a wage in the future as well. On the "membership institution corner" of the pentagon, the individual can make a contract with an employer to make sure that the latter will keep him/her employed whatever happens to him/her (for example, when he/she gets ill) or he/she can make sure that his/her membership of a mutual co-operation or a labor union will provide an income that guarantees that he/she will be able to satisfy basic needs. Finally, the individual can make sure (by voting or other forms of political pressure) that the government organizes an income when he/she would not be able to rely on his/her own market activities (get a pension, a unemployment benefit, a social assistance benefit...). Remark that signing a contract is by no means ruling out uncertainty completely: the buyer of your goods may die, your employer may suspend operations or your insurance company may go bankrupt, your government may not honor its promises.

We may rephrase the problem of satisfying basic needs in the future in an interesting way. If we consider needs to be satisfied by an income stream ("income" referring to much more than money) over the life of individuals, the problem of guaranteeing satisfaction of needs in the future can be reformulated as the problem of synchronizing the income stream of individuals with their consumption stream. My income stream may be enough to satisfy my basic needs now, but will it also be satisfactory in the future, which is inherently uncertain in many different ways. The basic welfare problem when the future enters the analysis then becomes a storage problem: how can I store income (or goods and services) in order to be sure that I will be able to satisfy my needs in the future? Of course my possibilities for storage depend on how much I can store after having satisfied my basic needs in the present. My needs for "storage" will depend on my assessment of the likelihood that I will not have enough income, goods or services stemming from my income stream in the future to satisfy my needs in the future. This "storage" problem can be solved in many different ways within the Welfare Pentagon including the simple storage of goods or money (saving), making (implicit) contracts with parties in the product or labor markets or within my family (social networks, membership institutions) or by using instruments of the capital market including insurance and investment.

Restating the basic risk problem in a dynamic multi-period framework implies that we have to analyze individual behavior (and policy options) in a more complicated framework of behavior under uncertainty, that is, a framework wherein choices and transactions are made without knowing for sure what will be the exact outcome. In that framework individuals need to make decisions and choices that stretch out over a longer period. Secondly, individuals have to regard the satisfaction of their needs in the future as a problem they have to deal with: this introduces the plausible assumption of risk-aversion among individuals. Thirdly, individuals have to have an idea of the likeliness (the probability) that a certain unfortunate event (contingency) may happen; and fourthly they will need a counterpart either on a market or within the family (social network …) who is willing to share his/her views on the need to make decisions over at least two periods and on the definition of the probabilities of the contingency (no agreement on the probabilities themselves is needed).

It is important to note that within the Welfare Pentagon not all corner solutions are always possible. This is applicable to all corners of the Welfare Pentagon, but especially important for the market-, family- and social network- corners. There may be situations where no market- or family- (social network-, membership institution-) solution is available, simply because there is no counterpart on the market or within the family (social network). That is to say, situations wherein individuals may have opted for a specific corner-solution for the satisfaction of their basic needs but are unsuccessful in real-izing the option. These situations are called market failure, family failure or network failure. Under these situations the call for public intervention will be apparent. This does not always imply that public intervention is possible or successful because government failure is just as possible as market failure (see also note 1).

Basic Needs or Main Needs?

The argument so far has referred to the satisfaction of basic needs only. This has reduced the analysis to something we thought was understood simi-larly by all. In fact, this was an (temporary useful) illusion. Although all agree that some food and some physical protection in the forms of clothing and a shelter are needed to survive, we would start to disagree when we would try to define what exactly this would mean. How much food? Which food? How much clothing and which clothing? And what kind of roof above our head? It is easy to understand that the actual definition of the content or even the level of basic needs that need to be fulfilled highly depend on physical and geo-graphical location. The need for shelter in Alaska is different from that in the Caribbean; the cloths providing adequate protection against the wind and the sun in the Central African deserts are different from what is basically needed in French Polynesia or in Paris. Attempts to retract to the very basics and talking about minimum calorie-intake when talking about food, may give you the illusion of getting near a universal definition of basic needs. It is, however, defective as well. Even if it would be possible to define the absolute minimum to avoid starvation, the composition of the intake in terms of minerals, proteins, and other substances would matter. And the issue would start to be complicated further if the question arises "avoid starvation to do what?" To sit down in the shadow of a tree, to work on farmland, to deliver (healthy) babies, to attend school or to work in the metal industry?

But yet the complication is not complete: needs also differ across time. Certainly the definition of the basic assets and goods that you need to survive in New York City or Brussels in the twenty-first century differ from those needed in the same places just after the Second World War. And we could go on. It comes down to the observation that it is nearly impossible and perhaps not very useful to try to define what basic needs exactly are. We better talk about needs that individuals want to be fulfilled. They differ across time and location and they are relative to the prevailing standards of a given society.[3] It has an important implication: it de-links the notion of social policy and the idea of securing the fulfillment of basic needs. Social policy is definitely not limited to public interventions aimed at providing means to everybody to satisfy basic needs only. Some parts of social policy are related to that specific aim, but many other parts are not. The link between basic needs and social protection policy is sometimes brought to the footlight in the political rhetoric surrounding the reform of social policy or the welfare state (the minimalist views on social policy), but it is far from actual reality in most of the economies that we consider.

However, does this imply that from now on all needs should be considered as potentially being linked to social policy? Theoretically, this would defendable, but this is as far from actual policy practice as the myopic view that links social policy to basic needs only. Some demarcation of the area is useful and inevitable if we do not want to get lost. The criterion to use for deciding what needs shall be envisaged when talking about the social management of risks, cannot be found in theoretical decisions; we have not much more than common sense and policy practices.

The needs that can be considered as prominently belonging to the realm of the social management of risks are:

- access to housing and utilities
- access to food
- access to health and healthy sexual reproduction
- access to security, civil and human rights
- access to social participation.

The first three are easy to understand ("healthy reproduction" referring to the physical and social circumstances that allow human beings to procreation). Access to security reflects the need to be protected from criminal activities and the access to human rights; access to social participation refers to the need for individuals to be truly embedded in the social and economic life of the community they live in; when this access is not secured we can speak of "social exclusion."

Starting from this list it can be seen that much of what we would define as social policy, is difficult to assess as directly related to one of these needs except for those policies that would define benefits in kind only, such as health care, food distribution, housing. The reality, however, is that much of what we would regard as the social management of risks or social policy is not directly related with providing goods and services that would satisfy these needs, but is focused on the *means* to get access to the fulfillment of these needs. In many situations and in most of the countries, this implies in the first place to secure income for all individuals in order to guarantee that they can buy access to all these things. And besides on income directly, much of social policy is related to mechanisms that allow individuals to generate the income themselves now and in the future, namely to labor and to education. On the other hand, while very important if absent, the access to security in terms of physical protection and human rights is usually not defined as part of social policy. For advanced capitalist economies we could assume that these rights are secured but that does not mean it can be left out of the analysis completely and certainly not when less developed economies are considered. Individual political—and economic—freedom, equal (legal) treatment regardless of gender, ethnicity or religion and institutions guaranteeing democracy are important prerequisites for successful social policy (and economic growth as argued by Amartya Sen).

Defining the scope to the Social Management of Risks, we then can say that it covers the *main needs*:

- access to housing and utilities
- access to food
- access to health and sexual reproduction
- access to social participation,

and *the basic mechanism* that guarantees the fulfillment of these needs:
- access to income.

Access to income has to be understood in its most broad meaning referring not only to income (or stocked wealth) in monetary terms, but also encompassing all means of existence provided in kind.

In advanced capitalist societies social policy cannot be understood if we refer to direct "income" provision only; a big part of social policy is linked to instruments that guarantee or improve the access to income for all members of a society, namely labor and education. Therefore, we explicitly add these two mechanisms to describe the scope of social policy:

- access to labor (as the main income-generating mechanism)
- access to education (as the main source for future income).[4]

Although the problem setting seems to have shifted considerably compared with the simple case we started with in the beginning, it is theoretically only a minor change. Talking about main needs and the mechanisms applied to fulfill them does not change the options for the individuals fundamentally: individuals can still use all the corners of the Welfare Pentagon and their combinations to satisfy their needs. Markets will often be used, but families, social networks and membership institutions stay important as well, even outside the realm of the basic needs. In many more cases than believed at first sight, the production and distribution of wealth within families, social networks, and membership institutions is an important substitute for the production of wealth on markets. Where markets fail, families, etc. can provide an obvious substitute in many cases. But even without failing markets, families, social networks, and institutions will produce a significant part of welfare, although its actual amount depends on many variables (history, tradition, economic development, etc.). The state or public policy comes in where actually the other corners of the Welfare Pentagon fail or where it is understood that the solutions produced by markets, families, etc. are either not efficient or not acceptable (not effective); hence when individuals are not believed, rightly or wrongly, to be able to manage the risks related to these needs and their mechanisms independently and that thus some social management from public authorities is requested.

Risks

What type of risks exactly are we considering? Basically, only one risk, although it comes in many different forms, namely the risk of not or no longer being able to rely on either markets or the family, social networks, membership institutions to secure the satisfaction of the main needs.

Under the assumption that different types of risks require different types of reactions (within the Welfare Pentagon), it is useful for the analysis to distinguish different types of risks and different types of effects. We need these distinctions to analyze the efficiency and effectiveness of different welfare solutions provided by markets, families, social networks, membership institutions, and the state now and in the past.

The first criterion to distinguish risks is by the population that is potentially affected. We then distinguish three basic forms: universal risks, life-cycle risks, and categorical risks.

Universal risks are in principle shared by all regardless of age, gender or position in society. An easy example is the risk of getting involved in an accident that limits or prevents further activities on labor or product markets. It is tempting to believe that universal risks are randomly distributed among the population, but this is, in fact, not true and theoretically unnecessary. Universal risks, theoretically, can strike everybody in a society, but that does not imply that everybody is exposed to the same degree of risk. In our example, everybody can be involved in an accident, but some groups in society are more "accident-prone" than others. This is an important remark and we need this as an element to explain insurance and government interventions in insurance markets.

Life-cycles risks are also in principle shared by all but are specific to a certain age or to specific stages in the course of life for everybody. Old-age infirmity caused by Alzheimer's disease, for example, is an obvious example.

Categorical risks (sometimes called class- or group-risks) are risks that are peculiar to certain groups in the society, for example, miners, women or men. The risk to develop mining-related lung diseases or to develop cervical or prostate cancer is not shared by everybody. It can be immediately remarked that there is an element of choice involved in the example of the miner: nobody is strictly born a miner. It makes, however, clear that belonging to a category and, therefore, being sensitive to certain types of risk can be conditional on other variables, for example, geographical location, professional choices or others.[5]

Trying to distinguish risks by their effects, three categories stand out: incident effects, lifetime effects, and intergenerational effects.

Incident effects refer to the effects that are directly related to the event and disappear after a relatively short period of time. Temporary unemployment and short-term illnesses usually have only incident effects.

Lifetime effects are related to risks that usually have a long-lasting effect on a person's life. Long-term unemployment and disability usually can be seen as having lifetime effects.

Intergenerational effects are seen when the effects of an unfortunate event are passed on to the next generation and reproduced over generations. Disability leading to welfare benefit dependency may affect the earning capacity of a breadwinner in a way that it jeopardizes the chances of his/her children to invest in education and to enter the labor market.

Remark that risks can have various effects simultaneously; an event can first lead to incident effects, but later lifetime and/or intergenerational effects may result.

Risks and their effects can be classified according to these criteria and further refining in the classifications can be made (see, for example, Holzmann and Jørgensen 1999). These distinctions will be important in order to analyze how much of the risk management is left to markets, social networks, membership institutions and families and how much is (or could be) taken up by public interventions (the state). Table 16.1 summarizes the typology as explained above and intuitively it can already be understood that markets, families, and social networks have more difficulties in coping with the risks if we go from left to right and from top to bottom in the table.

Table 16.1
Risks and Their Effects

	Incident Effects	Life-time Effects	Intergenerational Effects
Universal risks			
Life-cycle risks			
Categorical risks			

Summarizing the theoretical framework so far:

Individuals face the risk of not being able to satisfy their main needs at a given moment in time or at a given moment in the future. In order to manage this risk, people operate within the Welfare Pentagon using markets, families, social networks, membership institutions, and public authorities. Each of the corners of the pentagon provides specific mechanisms to address the risks and their outcomes. Labor markets, product markets, and capital markets allow the individual to trade and exchange in order to secure resources to satisfy the main needs at a certain moment. On the labor market effort is traded against a (future) wage; on product markets effort is traded against a (future) profit; on the capital market income is traded against future income by savings, insurances, borrowings, and the like. Families, social networks, and membership institutions provide various (and different) basic mechanisms of solidarity between their members providing transfers of resources to satisfy main needs at any given moment in time.

Due to uncertainty about the probabilities of contingencies and their outcomes, individuals make choices intended to minimize the impact of risks by combining different options within the Welfare Pentagon, that is, combining all elements within the Welfare Pentagon in order to secure current and future welfare.

Within the framework of a given economy, some options are not always available or (temporarily) unsuccessful. Under certain conditions, individuals may require public authorities to play a role in order to minimize the impact of contingencies or in order to prevent certain risks from materializing. Social (protection) policy is defined as the social management of risks in the sense that public policy takes over some aspects of the risk management. The aim is to provide individuals a less uncertain or a better-covered environment.

There are various types of risks potentially affecting different parts of the population and having potentially incidental, lifetime or even intergenerational effects. Social protection policy, or the social management of risks, intends to reduce the risks and their effects.

The Social Management of Risks

The definition of social policy as the social management of risks, allows a new and more interesting analysis of policy options. It starts the analysis from a different angle. Traditionally, social protection policy would react on a problem and find the rationale for public intervention in markets in either efficiency or equity arguments. Unemployment, for example, can be viewed as a temporary difficulty in finding a job and the obvious policy reaction is to bridge the income gap for those being affected by unemployment (unemployment benefits) and to assist them in finding a job (labor exchange efforts). Unemployment, however, can also be regarded as a risk shared by all who depend on the labor market for income generation and thus for the satisfaction of their main needs. The real risk is then an income loss due to unemployment and the policy options within the social risk management framework may be manifold. Policy can have a *preventive* nature, aimed at avoiding the risk for persons to become unemployed; policy action may be *mitigating* aimed may be *coping* aimed at relieving the impact of unemployment. Unemployment benefits (whether provided as an insurance benefit, a social assistance benefit or a basic income) are tools belonging to the coping strategy. Investment in human capital formation, organizing labor clearing houses, employment protection regulation, investment in social capital formation (networks), (extended) family formation, stimulating savings and other policy instruments that reduce the impact of unemployment by spreading the income-sources or social and economic resources of an individual, all are examples of mitigating strategies. Securing economic growth, public investments, and fiscal and monetary policy are all examples of instruments belonging to a preventive strategy. It is also clear that a risk analysis does not necessarily lead to a single strategy, let alone a single instrument. Moreover, taking the institutional framework of the Welfare Pentagon into consideration, public authorities may seek solutions that are not entirely under their direct control, but may "use" the other corners of the pentagon in designing and implementing policy options. It is important to note that public intervention does not require that public authorities organize, finance and produce the policy-goods or -services all by its own (see following).

Designing social protection policy within the social risk management framework implies a *risk analysis*. That means that the risks related to the main needs and their satisfaction at any point in time are mapped and that the *probabilities of contingencies* are estimated. Not all risks are of the same direct relevance in all situations; it is for example clear that the lack of food and/or shelter in certain areas or during specific periods/events is more important than anything else. Consequently, a *hierarchy of risks* have to be constructed; this hierarchy is historic specific. Because not all risks are universal, this also means that for every risk an analysis is made of the *poten-*

tially affected population. Relaxing the implicit assumption made so far that all individuals are equal except for biological or geographical differences, it is also clear that unequal individuals are not only faced with different risks but also with different resources in terms of the institutions within the Welfare Pentagon. Some individuals are better endowed within their families and their social networks and do have more resources to face certain contingencies. Even within the market, individuals are faced with different possibilities leaving some individuals more vulnerable when confronted with certain risk than others. Therefore, an empirically based *vulnerability analysis* is necessary in order to map risks and their impact seriously. This vulnerability analysis has to be based on the relevant differences between individuals. However, since the relevance of certain differences may shift over time and events, this is not an easy exercise. The definition of the main needs and the endowments of individuals in terms of their access to the corners of the Welfare Pentagon (and their combinations) provide the guidelines in this respect. The degree of access of individuals to the resources provided by families, social networks, membership institutions, markets and public authorities, for the satisfaction of their main needs *and* to the mechanisms that guarantee the fulfillment of these needs (income, education, and labor), is the crucial variable in the analysis.

Once the vulnerability analysis is available, policy can be designed.

Following Holzmann and Jørgensen (2000) we distinguish preventive strategies, mitigation strategies, and coping strategies.

Preventive strategies are aimed at avoiding the risk by organizing economic and social life in a way that the probability of a contingency is reduced. Good governance of the physical environment, for example, macroeconomic stabilization policy, sufficient regulation of markets, effective law enforcement are all instances of instruments that can be used in this respect. Special attention should be given to effective employment protection and regulation of labor contracts, since they protect at least the main income source for many individuals in an economy. Many more policy actions can be referred to in this context. All the initiatives have in common that they intend to produce a less risky environment for the members of a society.

Mitigation strategies are aimed at reducing the potential impact of a contingency once the risk materializes. Public stimulation of saving accounts and mandated or public pension systems are examples of instruments in this respect. Largely mitigation strategies can consist of portfolio diversification strategies and insurance mechanisms. Portfolio diversification strategies aim at reducing the impact of a contingency by spreading the income or social and economic resources of an individual. Investment in human capital, investment in social capital (networks), extended family formation and savings in cash and kind belong to this category. Insurance mechanisms pool the risks of many individuals and spread the impact of a contingency over many persons.

Coping strategies relieve the impact of a contingency that is not covered by a mitigation strategy-instrument. Direct social assistance in cash and kind and other direct income transfers are examples of public interventions that belong to this category.

Strategies can be used exclusively or combined and within each strategy many different instruments and tools can be used. Cataloguing all these instruments and tools would be an impossible task but we can distinguish two major subdivisions:

a. policy instruments can aim at *correcting* the functioning of markets, families, etc., at *complementing* the functioning of markets, families, etc., and at *substituting* markets, families, social networks, and membership institutions;

b. policy instruments can merely focus on the organization of markets (information, regulation, enhancing transparency, prohibition of production), on financing some activities that produce welfare or (re-)distribute welfare (income transfers, taxes, subsidies) and/or on the production of welfare (public production). It should be noted in this context that public policy could do the three things together or separately. Although in some cases the three elements are apparent in public policy, there is no need why these elements should be always part of public intervention. It is perfectly possible that public interventions are confined to regulating markets; it is also perfectly possible that public interventions finance certain activities while the actual production is left to markets or families or networks or membership organizations; it is equally possible that public authorities simultaneously regulate, finance, and produce certain provisions. There is, however, no reason why the latter solution would be preferable in the case of social (protection) policy.

The endless possibilities in designing social policy as the social management of risks, are summarized by combining the options available in Table 16.2 with the basic idea presented in the former sections; that is, all combinations within the Welfare Pentagon are theoretically feasible (excluding the points where no public intervention is incorporated, by definition). In practice the theoretically available options will be drastically reduced when confronted with the risk analysis (as mapped in Table 16.1) and the vulnerability analysis as explained above.

Although the number of policy options is limited in practice, it still provides an enormous catalogue of public interventions that may be considered when confronted with a certain problem/risk structure. In fact, many of these options can be seen implemented when international comparisons of social policy are being made (see Table 16.2).

Table 16.2
Policy Options

		Organization	Financing	Production
Preventive strategies	Correcting			
	Complementing			
	Substituting			
Mitigating strategies	Correcting			
	Complementing			
	Substituting			
Coping strategies	Correcting			
	Complementing			
	Substituting			

Conclusion

The chapter introduces a conceptual framework that redefines social policy in a way that facilitates the analysis of actual policy practices and allows a more comprehensive way of *assessing and comparing the impact, effectiveness, and efficiency of social risk management arrangements* across societies. The conceptual framework starts with the notion of main needs and defines and subdivides the risks threatening the satisfaction of these main needs. An important feature of the framework is that social policy is not only linked to the satisfaction of the main needs at a certain moment, but to the risk that, at a certain moment in the life-course of an individual, the needs cannot not be satisfied. Social policy is then no longer solely focused on the guaranteeing that all individuals in an economy can fulfill their main needs in a static framework. Quite the contrary, social policy is focused on preventing contingencies to materialize, on mitigating the effects before they materialize, and on coping with the unfortunate moment bad luck, shocks or unfortunate events strike. The social risk management framework rests on the observation that the satisfaction of main needs and the management of risks is not the sole responsibility of public authorities. Social welfare is produced by five institutions symbolically summarized as the social Welfare Pentagon of which markets, families, social networks, membership organizations, and public authorities form the corner-points.

It may sound as if the Social Risk framework provides us with the ultimate yardstick to judge the efficiency and effectiveness of social policy and to compare its results across countries and time. This is, however, not true. What it does is provide a framework that widens our scope of policy instruments and strategies when it comes to designing social policy. It also enhances our understanding of the interdependencies between what public authorities do and what markets, families, social networks, and membership institutions contribute to the optimisation of social welfare and it even provides a unified scheme for mapping policy initiatives and their impact. It is a major progress compared to the practice where social policy or welfare states are compared on the basis of Continental European or Anglo-Saxon social security institutions, but it does not solve the problem that judgments have to be made. Societies and governments make choices and these choices are not purely technical. They encompass visions on what is desirable in terms of outcomes and on what would be acceptable in terms of costs. It still makes a great deal of difference whether a society aims at relieving extreme poverty or whether a society wants the welfare of individuals to become independent from the welfare of their parents. Trying to judge the first policy objective with the yardstick of the latter, or vice versa, is uninteresting and misleading. The introduction of the social risk management framework does not change that. It does change, however, our view on the toolkits we may use in order to reach the policy objectives set and it provides us with a comprehensive and powerful conceptual instrument to understand the outcomes and impact of social policy as well as its costs.

Notes

1. Elsewhere we argue that even when there are efficiency reasons for state intervention, this does not automatically mean that public interventions are technically possible nor that public interventions yield more efficient outcomes than market processes. There the classical arguments of government failure referring to the fact that public authorities are themselves subject to utility maximizing behavior by decision makers and to the possibility that social welfare is not necessarily the "utility" that is maximized by public authorities. There are also arguments linked to the fact that the origin of some market failures does not necessarily disappear when public authorities are taking action. Informational problems and related asymmetric information, for example, can sometimes not be reduced by public intervention (see Esping-Andersen and de Neubourg, forthcoming).
2. Mobilizing your network or relying on family can also take the form of establishing a new family or a new social unit either within or outside marriage.
3. This does not mean we that we can dismiss the question of minimum standards all together; it comes up when problems of poverty and the actual social policy practices are addressed.
4. For a discussion of the human right issue, see de Neubourg and Weigand (2000).
5. Please note that all types of conditions can be considered in this context except age. In the latter case the risk is defined as a life-cycle risk.

References

Esping-Andersen, G., and de Neubourg, C. (forthcoming). *Social Welfare: Theories and International Practices* (working title). Oxford: Oxford University Press.

Gassmann, F., and de Neubourg, C. (2000). *Coping with Little Means in Latvia*. New York/Riga: UNDP.

Holzmann, R., and Jørgensen, S. (2000). *Social Risk Management: A New Conceptual Framework for Social Protection and Beyond*, Social Protection Discussion Paper No. 0006, Washington, D. C.: World Bank.

de Neubourg, C., and Weigand, C. (1999). "Social Security as Social Risk Management." *Innovation—European Journal of Social Sciences*, 13 (4), 401-412.

17

Holes in the Safety Net? Social Security and the Alleviation of Poverty in a Comparative Perspective

Christina Behrendt

Although most industrialized welfare states devote a large part of their national income to social protection, income poverty has not been eradicated in these countries. The expansion of the welfare state during the twentieth century and the economic boom after World War II led many people to believe that poverty would disappear or would at last be reduced to an insignificant minimum affecting only marginal groups of the population. Yet a sizeable proportion of the population live in economic poverty in all industrial welfare states. According to one of the most common standards used in international poverty research, on average roughly one in ten households live in relative poverty in Organization for Economic Co-operation and Development (OECD) countries (Atkinson et al., 1995).

The persistence of poverty in industrial welfare states calls for an explanation. If these welfare states offer elaborate systems of income maintenance, why is there still a considerable amount of poverty? Although welfare states differ in terms of aspiration, institutional design, and policies, this objective of poverty alleviation is in principle embraced in all welfare states (Goodin et al., 1999: 21-36). In this vein, Stein Ringen has proposed to use the issue of poverty alleviation as a yardstick for the general effectiveness of the welfare state:

> It is important to raise the issue of poverty, because of the historical significance of the problem, because its elimination has been the first priority of the welfare state, and because it offers an opportunity for discussing social policy on a basis of consensus. While there is a disagreement about the responsibility of government with regard to overall inequality, its responsibility in relation to poverty has been

accepted for generations and is not seriously contested today. *If poverty prevails, the welfare state is a failure.* (Ringen, 1987: 141; emphasis added)

If modern welfare states are not effective in alleviating poverty, their very purpose is fundamentally challenged, irrespectively of whether they are effective in achieving other goals or not. However, the persistence of poverty in highly developed welfare states casts doubt on the fundamental operating procedures of income distribution and redistribution. What are the reasons for this apparent failure of the welfare state in alleviating poverty? Why are some countries more effective than others in this respect? What can explain these variations in effectiveness?

This chapter explores the effectiveness of welfare states in alleviating poverty in a comparative perspective on the basis of household micro-data from the Luxembourg Income Study (LIS). After a short descriptive overview over poverty rates in highly developed welfare states, the available evidence on the effectiveness of the welfare state in terms of poverty alleviation and the relationship between social spending and poverty rates is briefly summarized. While this stream of research focuses on the relationship between the level of expenditure and the alleviation of poverty, this chapter emphasizes the question of *how* the money is spent. Especially minimum income schemes play a critical role in the alleviation of poverty and may be responsible for apparent "holes" in the social safety net. Drawing on the results of a larger research project (Behrendt, 2002),[1] the following analysis of minimum income schemes in three countries—Germany, Sweden, and the United Kingdom—sheds some light on the mechanisms of an effective alleviation of poverty.

What Do We Know about Poverty and Poverty Alleviation in Industrialized Welfare States?

Poverty in Industrialized Welfare States

Poverty still constitutes a widespread phenomenon in highly developed welfare states. The empirical picture of relative income poverty in industrial welfare states suggests that a sizeable proportion of the population find themselves below the poverty line, yet poverty rates and the structure of poverty vary. Figure 17.1 reports poverty profiles for a number of industrialized countries for the early 1990s.[2] As in most comparative analyses, households are considered to live in poverty if their disposable equivalent income is lower than 50 percent of the national median income.[3] In order to account for different intensities of poverty, three additional poverty lines are applied. Households are deemed to live in "extreme poverty" if their income remains below a poverty line of 30 percent of median equivalent income; a poverty line of

40 percent demarcates "severe poverty," whereas households with an income between 40 percent and 50 percent of median equivalent income are considered as living in "moderate poverty." Households whose income exceeds the poverty line of 50 percent, but remain below 60 percent of median equivalent income are considered as living "near poverty." In Figure 17.1, countries are ranked according to their poverty rate at the 50 percent level, while the shading of the columns show different intensities of poverty or low income.[4]

Figure 17.1 shows that a considerable share of the population live in relative income poverty in all industrialized welfare states, yet with a large variation across countries in terms of incidence and structure of poverty. The lowest poverty rate of 3.4 percent is found in Luxembourg, followed by Belgium, Denmark, Finland, Germany, the Netherlands, and France. The middle ranks are taken by Sweden, the United Kingdom, Norway, and Canada, where roughly one in ten private households live in poverty. Australia and Italy display poverty rates of some 12-13 percent, but at the very bottom of this ranking, we find the United States with a poverty rate of almost a fifth of the household population.

The Redistributional Impact of the Welfare State

The first glance on poverty rates in industrialized countries above has shown that a substantial proportion of the population live in income poverty despite elaborate systems of income redistribution. At face value, the presence of poverty in these countries suggests that the welfare state thus is not effective in alleviating poverty, but this issue deserves more attention.

International variations in poverty profiles are driven not only by variations in the effectiveness of welfare state redistribution, but also by variations in socio-demographic and socioeconomic structures, as theses factors put different strains on income transfer schemes (Kangas and Ritakallio, 1998b). An alternative approach allows some control on external effects on poverty, thus allowing a more refined analysis of the redistributional impact of the welfare state. The rationale of this approach (sometimes dubbed budget incidence approach or Beckerman ratios) is a comparison of pre- and post-redistribution poverty rates, that is, market income and disposable income (Beckermann, 1979; Mitchell, 1991).

Table 17.1 shows more recent empirical results on the redistributional impact of the welfare state, based on the most recent LIS data available for selected industrial countries. Whereas the first two columns show poverty rates before and after transfers and taxes (that is, for market income and for disposable income), the last two columns present the reduction of poverty in two ways, the absolute reduction of poverty rates in percentage points, and the relative reduction in percent. Countries are ranked according to their poverty rate after taxes and transfers. As the overall redistributional impact of

Figure 17.1
Relative Poverty in Industrialized Countries

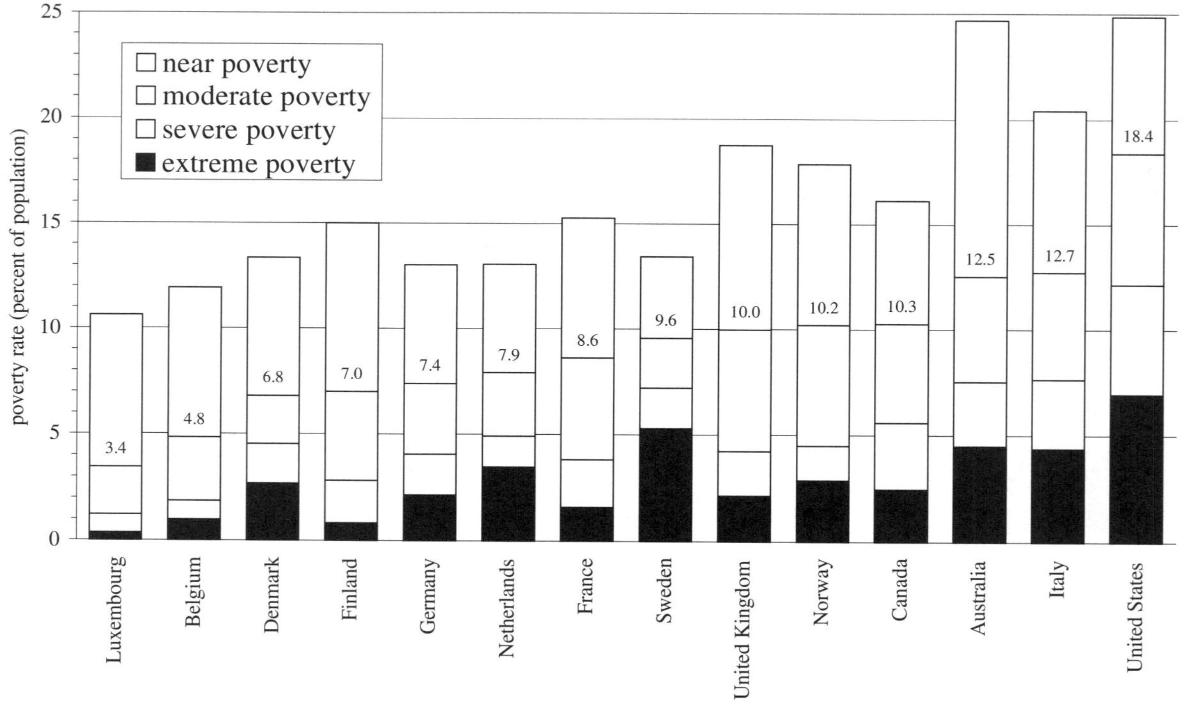

the welfare state is strongly dependent on the public-private mix in the pension system, this table and Figures 17.2 and 17.3 are confined to the prime-age population, defined as households whose head is no older than 55 years.[5]

The empirical evidence suggests that welfare state redistribution indeed has a strong impact on poverty rates among prime-age households, yet there are marked variations across countries. Some clusters of countries can be identified: a high effectiveness of the welfare state in terms of poverty reduction is found in Belgium, Finland, Denmark, and the United Kingdom. Whereas the first three of these countries also end up with low poverty rates for disposable incomes, the United Kingdom somewhat deviates from this pattern with medium poverty rates. An astonishing pattern of poverty reduction is also found in Sweden. Sweden achieves the highest reduction in absolute terms, but only a mediocre performance in relative terms, and ends up with fairly high poverty rates for disposable incomes. These startling results can partly be accounted for by a differing household definition.[6]

At the other end of the spectrum, a group of countries reduces poverty to a much smaller degree. The United States clearly stands out with a meager reduction of poverty through transfers and taxes. With some distance, the

Table 17.1

The Effectiveness of Welfare State Redistribution for Prime-Age Households, Early 1990s (household head under 55)

Country (sorted by poverty rate after redistribution)	Poverty rate (rank order)				Poverty rate reduction (rank order)			
	before taxes and transfers		after taxes and transfers		absolute (percentage points)		relative (percent)	
Belgium 1992	13.0	(1)	2.9	(1)	-10.1	(8)	-78%	(1)
Finland 1995	25.7	(10)	7.9	(2)	-17.8	(2)	-69%	(2)
Germany 1994	14.7	(2)	7.9	(2)	-6.8	(11)	-46%	(10)
Denmark 1992	22.6	(9)	8.1	(4)	-14.5	(4)	-64%	(3)
France 1994	22.3	(8)	8.5	(5)	-13.8	(5)	-62%	(5)
Netherlands 1994	19.5	(3)	9.1	(6)	-10.5	(7)	-54%	(7)
Norway 1995	20.7	(5)	9.5	(7)	-11.2	(6)	-54%	(7)
United Kingdom 1995	26.2	(11)	9.8	(8)	-16.4	(3)	-63%	(4)
Australia 1994	20.2	(4)	10.4	(9)	-9.8	(9)	-49%	(9)
Canada 1994	21.0	(6)	11.7	(10)	-9.3	(10)	-44%	(11)
Sweden 1995	31.4	(12)	13.1	(11)	-18.3	(1)	-58%	(6)
United States 1994	21.6	(7)	18.2	(12)	-3.4	(12)	-16%	(12)

Note: Poverty rates are based on a poverty line of 50% of national median income, adjusted for household size according to the modified OECD scale (weights of 1.0 for head of household, 0.5 for each additional adult and 0.3 for each child). Italy and Luxembourg could not be considered because LIS includes only data on net incomes for these two countries.

Source: LIS; own calculations.

Canadian, German, and Australian welfare states also reduce poverty rates to a relatively small degree. Nevertheless, poverty rates after transfers and taxes are rather low in the German case, but must be attributed less to the redistributional impact of the welfare state rather than to relatively good protection from poverty in the primary income distribution. In contrast, Canada and Australia show high poverty rates of more than one-tenth of the prime-age population.[7]

What can explain different degrees of effectiveness of poverty alleviation? Are specific features of welfare states typically related to certain outcomes? In particular, is there a connection between welfare state effort and outcomes? In other words, are extensive welfare states more effective in alleviating poverty than the tighter ones?

Welfare State Effort and the Incidence of Poverty

Using social expenditure as a proxy for welfare effort, the relationship between welfare state effort and outcomes in terms of poverty has been described in a fairly succinct way: "The bigger the welfare state the smaller is the poverty rate" (Gustafsson and Uusitalo, 1990: 255). More recent data confirm these results in principle for the prime-age population, although the correlation is less strong than in the earlier studies (see Figure 17.2).[8]

Figure 17.2 illustrates that there is, in fact, some correlation between social expenditure ratios and poverty rates. Countries with large social expenditure ratios tend to have lower poverty rates than countries with lower social expenditure ratios. Yet social expenditure ratios explain only somewhat more than one-third of the variance in poverty rates. Some countries display much higher or lower poverty rates than what would have been expected on the basis of their level of social expenditure. Notably, Belgium is very effective in this respect, to a lesser extent also Australia, France, Germany, and the United Kingdom. In contrast, the United States and—with some methodological reservations—Sweden, as well as Norway are much less efficient.

However, this simple cross-sectional regression fails to fully elucidate the complex relationship between welfare state effort and the alleviation of poverty. The variation of poverty levels may also be determined by the primary income distribution, reflecting variations in socio-demographic and socioeconomic structures. We would therefore expect that the size of the welfare effort would have a stronger impact on the *reduction* of poverty through welfare state redistribution rather than on the *level* of poverty as such.

Welfare State Effort and the Redistributional Impact of the Welfare State

The redistributional impact of the welfare state should also be exemplified by a clear correlation between welfare state effort and the reduction of pov-

Figure 17.2
Welfare State Effort and the Alleviation of Poverty: Social Expenditure and Relative Poverty Rates for Prime-Age Households in OECD Countries (household head younger than 55 years)

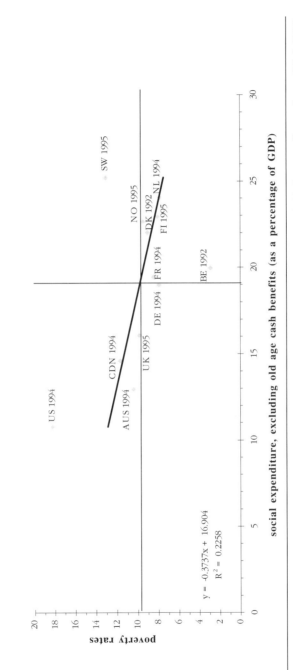

Poverty rates are calculated on the basis of 50% of median household disposable income adjusted for household size according to the modified OECD equivalence scale (weight of 1.0 for head of household, 0.5 for additional adults and 0.3 for children). Data reported refer to the most recent available data for each country. Social expenditure includes public and private mandatory expenditure, but excludes old age cash benefits.

Source: Luxembourg Income Study; OECD Social Expenditure Database; own calculations.

erty rates. Figure 17.3 depicts the relationship between social expenditure and the reduction of poverty rates by welfare state redistribution for the prime-age population.

Indeed, Figure 17.3 indicates that countries with high social spending tend to reduce poverty more effectively than countries with a lower social expenditure ratio. Welfare effort is more closely correlated with the reduction of poverty rates than to the level of poverty as such (see Figure 17.2). This evidence suggests that the persistence of poverty in industrialized welfare states can partly be explained by the fact that countries do not spend enough on social transfers. Consequently, according to this logic, a further reduction of poverty rates could be best achieved by more extensive social expenditure.

Nevertheless, countries scatter widely and display specific patterns of poverty alleviation. Relative to their level of social expenditure, the United Kingdom, and to a lesser extent also Australia, Finland, France, and Sweden were overproportionally effective in alleviating poverty. In contrast, the United States, Germany, Norway, and the Netherlands achieve lower levels of poverty alleviation than what would have been expected on the basis of their social expenditure.

However, these simple regressions do not tell the whole story. There is large variation in the relationship between input (social expenditure) and output (reduction of poverty rates), hence, in the efficiency dimension. Countries with similar levels of social expenditure reach divergent levels of poverty reduction. For example, Germany, France, and Belgium spend a comparable share of their Gross Domestic Product (GDP) on social security for the prime-age population, yet their effectiveness in poverty reduction varies. Whereas France and Belgium are relatively successful in bringing down poverty rates, Germany is relatively inefficient in this respect and finds itself far below the regression line. In contrast, the United Kingdom reaches a similar reduction of poverty rates as Finland or even Sweden, but on a markedly lower level of social expenditure. What can explain these large variations? Which factors can explain why some countries are more efficient than others in reducing poverty rates? Basically, these variations may be due to a number of substantial factors, including variations in policies, as well as different socioeconomic and sociodemographic contexts.

Assessing the Effectiveness of Social Policies:
Unsolved Puzzles and a Possible Solution

Limitations of the Existing Studies

The review of the existing evidence on the redistributional impact of the welfare state has uncovered some interesting patterns, but has sketched a fairly crude picture of poverty alleviation. Welfare states face different de-

Figure 17.3

Welfare State Effort and the Alleviation of Poverty: Social Expenditure and the Reduction of Poverty Rates through Transfers and Taxes for Prime-Age Households in OECD Countries (household head younger than 55 years)

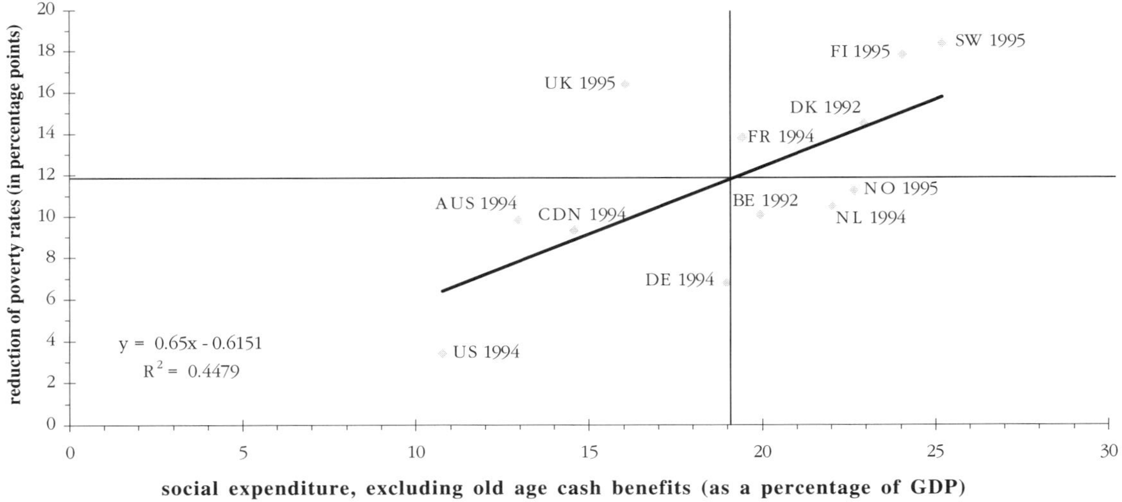

Poverty rates are calculated on the basis of 50% of median household disposable income adjusted for household size according to the modified OECD equivalence scale (weight of 1.0 for head of household, 0.5 for additional adults and 0.3 for children). Data reported refer to the most recent available data for each country. Social expenditure includes public and private mandatory expenditure, but excludes old age cash benefits.

Source: Luxembourg Income Study; OECD Social Expenditure Database; own calculations.

grees of external pressure, so the redistributional impact of the welfare state is dependent on socioeconomic and sociodemographic conditions. In particular, variations in public-private mix may bias the measured effectiveness of the welfare state. Welfare states may achieve the same objectives in different ways, by regulative, distributive or redistributive policies associated with different levels of public involvement and levels of public spending. Although outcomes of these policies do not necessarily differ, this method will produce different results for the measured effectiveness in poverty alleviation.[9]

In addition, the measured effectiveness of social transfers fails to tell anything about the causes and the conditions of an effective alleviation of poverty. In particular, do institutional settings have an impact on an effective alleviation of poverty? Our knowledge on the institutional conditions of effectiveness still is astonishingly sparse. This opinion is shared by Deborah Mitchell who concludes that most of the studies analyzing outcomes of redistribution "arrive at a set of observations which observe what has happened in each country's transfer process without making clear *how* it had happened." (Mitchell, 1991: 158; emphasis original). Esping-Andersen takes the same line by stating that "why welfare state structures have such different distributional consequences is left largely unexplained." (Esping-Andersen, 1990: 56).

While the analyses presented above provide a very straightforward and efficient tool for evaluating the distributive effects of public policies and allow a relatively easy comparison of redistributional effectiveness over time and across countries, the evaluation of the causes of a certain outcome in terms of income distribution or poverty requires a detailed assessment of a country's institutional framework that structures redistribution. In particular, a closer evaluation of the bottom safety net of the welfare state promises useful insights. In modern welfare states, the ultimate responsibility for the alleviation of poverty is given to social assistance schemes and other minimum income schemes. These schemes form the basic net of the welfare state and are ultimately responsible for the alleviation of poverty. If this net does not hold, the effectiveness of the welfare state as a whole is fundamentally challenged.

Focusing on the Basic Safety Net of the Welfare State

As the basic safety net of the welfare state, minimum income schemes play a decisive role for the alleviation of poverty.[10] We would expect that minimum income benefits form an income ceiling below which no individual or household should fall (Veit-Wilson, 1998). These schemes step in if the primary income distribution and social insurance schemes fail to provide a decent income level. However, the persistence of poverty in industrial welfare states suggests that this basic safety net of the welfare state fails to achieve this goal, as a sizeable proportion of the population appears to fall through this safety net and find themselves in poverty. By this token, the persistence of poverty in industrial welfare states may eventually be explained by a failure of minimum income schemes.

If minimum income schemes play a decisive role for the alleviation of poverty in industrial welfare states, our focus of analysis should shift from the welfare state as a whole to its basic safety net. A thorough analysis of these schemes can offer some further insights into the causal patterns of poverty alleviation in industrial welfare states, and can help to solve some of the puzzles that are still present in poverty research. In particular, this approach can shed more light on the mechanisms that are responsible for the persistence of income poverty. Variations in the effectiveness of poverty alleviation may be explained by the performance of the basic safety net of the welfare state.

In spite of their importance for the alleviation of poverty, social assistance schemes have rarely ever stood in the focus of the mainstream of comparative welfare state analysis. Most major studies have addressed social insurance schemes while social assistance was considered a relic of the old, poor law tradition that would subsequently be eliminated with the maturing of social insurance schemes (Atkinson, 1999: 3). Nevertheless, these expectations have not been fulfilled; social assistance schemes still make up—and always have made up—a considerable portion of social expenditure in Western European welfare states. Only in recent years, rising expenditure on social assistance in a time of persistent mass unemployment in many Western European welfare states appears to have attracted the interest of comparative welfare state research towards social assistance schemes and other minimum income schemes. A number of large-scale reports have sought to systematically compare the institutional design of minimum income schemes in industrialized countries (Eardley et al., 1996a, 1996b; OECD, 1998a, 1998b, 1999).

Not only has comparative welfare state research underestimated the role of minimum income schemes, but poverty research also has shown little interest in these schemes. Although social assistance schemes are explicitly aimed at alleviating poverty, poverty research has seldom thoroughly assessed the relationship between minimum income schemes and poverty. When assessing the causes of poverty, poverty research largely has scrutinized factors to be found in the distribution of earnings, the labor market, in the social structure, and also social transfers for specific groups of the population, yet often neglected the basic safety net of the welfare state. The incidence of poverty in advanced welfare states seems to have been attributed to a general mismatch of concepts of poverty and societal minimum income standards embodied in these schemes. While some observers appear to have tacitly assumed that social assistance benefits are too stingy as to provide a sufficient protection from poverty, others have rather sought the causes of this discrepancy in the measurement of poverty. Especially the widely used relative poverty line of 50 percent of median equivalent disposable income has been criticized as reflecting income inequality rather than a standard of subsistence, thus overstating poverty in rich countries (Krämer, 1997; Blackburn, 1998).

Indeed, a large proportion of private households are poor even if they have received social assistance benefits or other means-tested benefits. The suspiciously small overlapping of social assistance receipt and poverty has often been interpreted as an indicator for flaws of income as an indicator for poverty (Halleröd, 1991; Kangas and Ritakallio, 1998a). Possible reasons for a flawed measurement of income poverty could be that low-income strata are not adequately represented in income surveys, that they tend to have higher non-response rates than other groups of the population, and that many households do not properly report their income, especially income from means-tested benefits that are of particular relevance here (Atkinson et al., 1995).

The lack of knowledge about the relationship between minimum income schemes and poverty is only one example of a more general deficit. Whereas comparative social policy research has extensively analyzed the genesis and institutional similarities and differences of social security schemes, research into the outcome dimension is still underdeveloped. In particular, only a small number of studies have systematically evaluated the quality of social security schemes in a comparative perspective. In the following, the focus of analysis will be shifted from the welfare state as a whole to its basic safety net.

The Basic Safety Net of the Welfare State and Its Effects on the Alleviation of Poverty: Evidence from Britain, Germany, and Sweden

An alternative approach can help to contribute to the explanation of the incidence and the causes of poverty in industrialized welfare states. This approach confronts the evidence from survey data with the institutional regulations in each country in order to cross-check the quality of the data, and to come up with some institutional explanations for the apparent ineffectiveness of the welfare state.

What can explain this apparent failure of the basic safety net of the welfare state? Let us assume that a household is in need because of an insufficient market income and/or insufficient social transfers. Need is defined as an inadequate level of resources that does not allow a decent standard of living. At this stage, the redistributional impact of the welfare state depends exclusively on the social assistance scheme since all other potential income sources are exhausted. Once the social assistance scheme comes into play, a three-stage process determines whether this household can be effectively protected from poverty or not. First, effectiveness depends on the question of whether the person or household is actually entitled to receive social assistance (eligibility). If this is true, the second dimension of effectiveness becomes relevant: benefits must be generous enough to cover the needs of the household (adequacy) and to push it over the poverty line. Finally, households can be effectively protected from poverty only if benefits are actually claimed by the household in need (take-up). If this is not the case, the household will stay poor even if the first two conditions are met. The sequence of these three conditions is shown in Figure 17.4.

The following sections will scrutinize these three conditions of effectiveness for three West European countries—Britain, Germany, Sweden—chiefly drawing on the results of a larger research project (Behrendt, 2002). These three countries have often been considered as "paradigmatic" cases for three distinct "welfare state regimes." Comparative welfare state research has often used typologies as a shortcut to describe institutional similarities and differences of modern welfare states (Titmuss, 1974; Esping-Andersen, 1990, 1999). Attempts to establish typologies of minimum income schemes on the basis of their institutional characteristics have also positioned these countries in different clusters (Eardley et al., 1996a; Leibfried, 1992; Lødemel and Schulte, 1992).[11] The Swedish *socialbidrag* scheme is characterized by a marked division of social assistance and social insurance, as social assistance is administrated at the communal level with a high level of administrative discretion and a strong emphasis on social work treatment. In contrast, the British *income support* is closely integrated with non-means-tested social insurance benefits, administrated at the central government level, with strong entitle-

Figure 17.4
Social Assistance Schemes and an Effective Alleviation of Poverty:
A Simplified Model

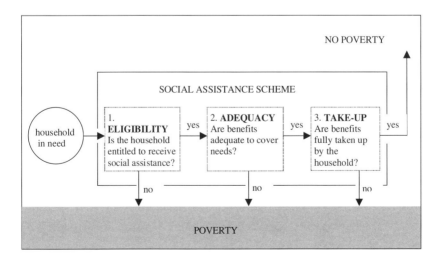

ments and a high degree of standardization. The German *Sozialhilfe* operates with a medium degree of division between social insurance and social assistance. Rights positions and administrative discretion are balanced, as is the involvement of central and local units in the regulation and administration of social assistance.

These three countries are also characterized by a specific profiles of poverty and poverty alleviation. Sweden and the United Kingdom display similar poverty rates at the 50 percent level, yet their poverty profiles are very different. Sweden exhibits a markedly higher proportion of extreme poverty, whereas the poor in Britain are dominated by households living in moderate poverty. The German welfare state surprises with relatively low poverty rates, although being notorious for a weak intensity of vertical income redistribution and lacking minimum income elements outside of social assistance.

Eligibility

The first condition of effectiveness, eligibility, cannot contribute much to the explanation of poverty in these three countries. Social assistance schemes are virtually universal in each of the three countries considered while only small groups of the population are excluded from general social assistance schemes. This applies in particular to some categories of recent migrants, but as these groups are unlikely to be included in the samples that are used for the calculation of poverty rates, their exclusion cannot explain the incidence of poverty.[12]

Adequacy

The second condition of an effective alleviation of poverty, the adequacy of social assistance benefits, offers further guidance on this question. Are benefit levels high enough to guarantee an effective protection from poverty?

Social assistance entitlement levels are evaluated on the basis of model calculations that keep the need level of the household constant and thus permit an informed comparison of social assistance entitlements across countries. Basically, this approach defines a number of model households with different structure, largely following Eardley et al. (1996a).[13] We can then assess the entitlements to social assistance the families would have in each of the countries considered. However, the choice of household types to be assessed invariably involves a certain degree of arbitrariness and is far from satisfactory reflecting the actual variation of household types in the real world. The circumstances of these model households have to be specified in detail in order to enhance the precision of the comparison across countries. However, the more specific the characteristics of model households, the less representative these are for the whole population.

For each of these model families, social assistance entitlements have been calculated on the basis of institutional regulations, including the standard benefit rate, premiums for special needs, one-off benefits and housing allowances. This benefit package constitutes a minimum income standard for the majority of the population (Veit-Wilson, 1998).

In order to evaluate the adequacy of social assistance benefits for the alleviation of poverty, the level of social assistance entitlements of these model households can be easily compared to the minimum income level as defined by a relative poverty line. If poverty is defined as 50 percent of median equivalence income, do minimum income benefits bring people out of poverty?[14] Which income level do recipients of social assistance reach relative to the general income level in the society in which they live?

Figure 17.5 displays the level of social assistance entitlements after housing cost as a proportion of median income for the United Kingdom in 1995, and illustrates the relationship of social assistance benefits after housing cost to the poverty line. This allows the evaluation of the question whether social assistance entitlements would bring the model households above the poverty line. Since the actual entitlement of households may vary depending upon individual circumstances and divergent rent levels, the figure includes an error indicator that allows for a scope of 10 percent in each direction.

For the model households specified above, British social assistance provides an income level of between 44 percent and 58 percent of median income. Only the households of the elderly and single parents are brought above a poverty line of 50 percent of median income, whereas childless working-age households and two-adult families with children have an income lower than the 50 percent income standard, with only the exception of a two-parent family with two children exactly matching the 50 percent level. None of these model households falls below the 40 percent poverty line, though. Interestingly, the preferential treatment of the elderly and single parents mirrors exactly the liberal idea that the welfare state should comfort people whose earnings capacity is limited (by old age or caring responsibilities), while only providing a basic minimum income for less vulnerable groups.

For Germany, 1994, social assistance entitlements provide an effective protection from poverty for each of the model households (Figure 17.6). The level of social assistance varies from 51 percent of median income to 67 percent of median income, or even to 90 percent for families with infants receiving parent allowance.[15] Even families who do not receive any parent allowance (see corresponding household types with older children) still reach an income level above the 50 percent poverty line. Relatively well-off are elderly couples, families with several children and single parents, whereas especially prime-age singles and couples have to live on a rather low-benefit level. Nevertheless, none of the model families used in this comparison can be considered as poor at the 50 percent level.

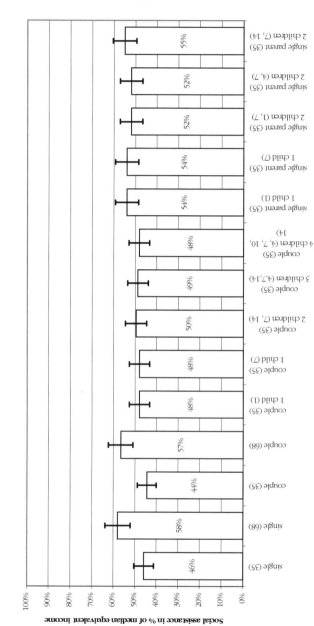

Figure 17.5
Level of Social Assistance Entitlements in Percent of
Median Income, Britain 1995

Median income calculated from LIS. Equivalence scale: head of household 1.0, other adults 0.5, children 0.3 ("modified OECD scale").

The lines at the top of the columns account for an error of 10% in each direction.

Figure 17.6
Level of Social Assistance Entitlements in Percent of Median Income, Germany, 1994

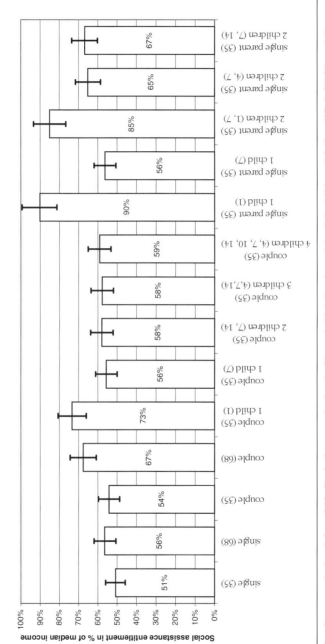

Median income calculated from LIS. Equivalence scale: head of household 1.0, other adults 0.5, children 0.3 ("modified OECD scale").

The lines at the top of the columns account for an error of 10% in each direction.

Figure 17.7
Level of Social Assistance Entitlements in Percent of Median Income, Sweden, 1995

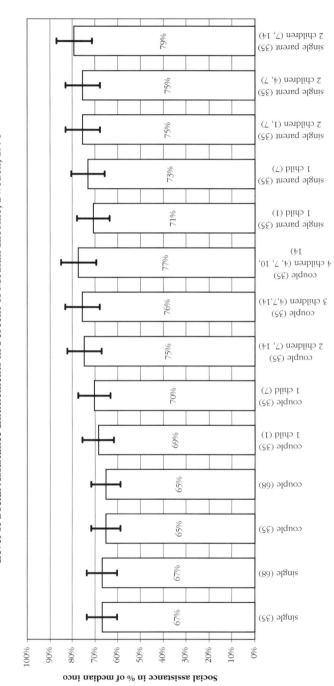

Median income calculated from LIS. Equivalence scale: head of household 1.0, other adults 0.5, children 0.3 ("modified OECD scale").

The lines at the top of the columns account for an error of 10% in each direction.

Overall, the German social assistance scheme appears to provide for a fairly generous benefit level that would allow model households to find their way out of poverty. Benefit levels are not particularly generous, so most model households reach an income level of shortly above 50 percent of median equivalent income. Similarly to the British case, the elderly and single parents enjoy a more generous benefit level than prime-age households, and parents with small children receiving parent allowance will reach an even more comfortable income level well above the 60 percent poverty line.

The Swedish social assistance offers a more uniform pattern that appears to provide for a decent standard of living. Figure 17.7 shows that each of the model families is brought above the 60 percent poverty line; some even enjoy an income position of more than 70 percent of median income. Moreover, there seems to be a strong relationship between the size of the household and the level of provision, the larger the family, the more generous are the benefits. Benefit rates may, however, be slightly overstated since the rent level used in the calculations refers to the capital of Stockholm, whereas the average rent level is somewhat lower. In addition, claimants are required to pay a higher share of housing costs other than the rent out of their standard benefit rate than in the other two countries (Eardley et al., 1996a: 109-139). However, even if the rent level was markedly reduced, the Swedish social assistance scheme would still bring households over the 50 percent poverty line.

It should be remembered, however, that the relationship between the level of social assistance and the alleviation of poverty is very complex. Even a sophisticated calculation of benefit packages cannot fully reflect the complexity of social assistance payments, especially in the Swedish case where the recommended benefit rates as used here can only give some guidance on real benefit rates. Yet we can identify some patterns of benefit structure in the three countries on the basis of the model household approach. Sweden provides for the most generous level of social assistance benefits which not only lifts the model households out of poverty, but offers a comfortable income position even above the near poverty bracket (60 percent poverty line). The second rank is taken by Germany, which is characterized by a strong variation of benefit rates depending on household circumstances, yet all model households are brought over the poverty line. Britain is the only country of the three for which the model household approach testifies inadequate for some working-age households. Only the elderly, and to some degree also single parent households, can expect adequate social assistance benefits.

However, these conclusions have to be qualified, again considering the underlying methodological assumptions of this study. The above analysis was based on the assumption that every household is eligible for social assistance benefits, and actually realizes its entitlement. Whereas the first assumption supposedly has only a negligible impact on measured poverty rates, the second one is more problematic. Empirical studies show that a marked proportion of households do not claim their social assistance benefits for a number of reasons. At this stage, the last condition of take-up comes into play.

Take-up

Even if social assistance schemes cover the entire population and guarantee an adequate benefit, poverty may still occur if benefits are not claimed by those who are eligible to receive them. Unlike the first two conditions, eligibility and adequacy, public policies have only a limited influence on the question of take-up, as the process of claiming cannot entirely be controlled by the state. Ultimately, the question of take-up is largely governed by individual actions on the part of potential claimants, but individual perceptions and behavior are strongly influenced by public policies. There is a broad array of possible causes of non-take-up that relate to the direct or indirect impact of public policies on non-take-up (Corden, 1995). Basically, three factors can hamper take-up, each closely associated with public policies. First, people may not be aware of benefits available and their entitlement to these benefits (ignorance). Second, claimants may fear stigmatization when claiming benefits (stigma). Finally, social assistance regulations and the claiming process may be fashioned in a way that impedes the full take-up of benefits (complexity).

Although there is hardly any comparable evidence on the extent of non-take-up in the three countries considered, we can quite safely conclude from a comparison of national studies that 15-20 percent of private households do not realize their claim in the United Kingdom, compared to some 40-50 percent in Germany, and possibly as many in Sweden where there is hardly any empirical evidence (van Oorschot, 1995, 1998).

Britain is not only the country with the strongest concern about non-take-up and the best empirical evidence on this issue, but also seems to have the least problem of non-take-up. What does account for this large difference? Can institutional settings, such as the general program structure and the administration of social assistance, account for this fact? The following factors have been found to be particularly relevant.

First, the British social assistance scheme is organized in a more standardized way than in Germany and Sweden, with several implications for the take-up of benefits. As the program structure is rather simple, based on national regulations without regional variations in benefit rates and administered at the national level, information on the availability of benefits and eligibility conditions is more easily disseminated than in the fragmented and more complex benefit schemes in Germany and Sweden. As leaflets and claiming forms for social assistance are accessible at every post office and at every branch of the Benefit Agency, potential claimants can easily obtain the necessary information about their entitlement. In addition, the administrative integration of income support with other social security benefits possibly leads to a higher familiarity with eligibility conditions on the part of social security officers, and makes it easier to complement insufficient incomes by income support.

Second, take-up is expected to be high where social assistance is considered an individual right rather than something to be granted on a discretionary or charity basis. Entitlements are very strong in Britain; social assistance is highly regulated and the administration of social assistance largely parallels the administration of non-means-tested social security benefits. In terms of administrative procedures, it does not make much of a difference to claim a pension or income support in Britain while the gap between non-means-tested and means-tested benefits is much larger in Germany and Sweden. In terms of administrative routines, notably the scope of administrative discretion is assumed to have a negative effect on take-up rates since it often involves time-consuming application procedures and intensive checks of the claimant's situation that may be perceived as stigmatizing. In addition, discretionary decisions of social assistance officers may be more strongly subject to flawed results than more standardized routines. In Britain, only the social fund provides a discretionary element, yet the significance of this scheme is relatively small. Discretion at the local level is much stronger in Sweden, where municipalities have a say in benefit rates, yet limited by jurisdiction. The German social assistance scheme is governed by national framework legislation, and benefit rates hardly vary across federal states. Yet, there is some scope of administrative discretion in granting one-off benefits.

Third, the rights-based character of British social assistance is also supported by the relatively generous exemptions for earned income and assets, whereas income and assets usually are fully taken into account in Sweden. In a way, the design of the Swedish social assistance requires claimants to be "poorer" than in Britain before granting any benefits. The Swedish social assistance is much more strongly grounded in a poor law tradition than the British scheme, and the internal division of the welfare state into social insurance and social assistance is much more pronounced. Germany appears to be situated once again in a middle position, with relatively strong institutionalization of individual rights, yet with some degree of administrative discretion.

Fourth, the rules about liability of the extended family in the German social assistance schemes are assumed to have a detrimental effect on take-up. There is strong evidence that many people abstain from claiming social assistance because they fear that their relatives will be made liable for any social assistance payment. Although this rule is hardly ever applied because of generous income disregards and the general suspension of this rule in some federal states, many people seem to refrain from claiming because they are not aware of these exemptions or because they do not want the test of their relatives' income situation to reveal their own financial situation to their relatives, even if those relatives would not have to pay. Only the German social assistance scheme entails such a regulation of family liability, whereas the British and the Swedish schemes do not require contributions by members of the extended family.

By and large, the institutional structure of the British social assistance schemes seems to be arranged in a way that incorporates relatively few obstacles to claiming benefits in comparison to Germany and Sweden. The markedly higher non-take-up rates in the latter two countries suggest that potential claimants face more serious impediments, possibly to be found in the less readily accessible information on the availability of benefits and entitlement rules. In addition, the very strict means-tests in Sweden and the liability of the wider family in Germany may also contribute to higher non-take-up rates in these countries.

Conclusion

The evidence presented for the three countries of Britain, Germany, and Sweden has shown that an assessment of the institutional framework can help to explain the incidence and the causes of poverty in highly developed welfare states. Minimum income schemes especially play a decisive role for the alleviation of poverty. The evaluation of their effectiveness in the dimensions of eligibility, adequacy, and take-up has uncovered specific national patterns of poverty alleviation.

For the United Kingdom, there is some evidence that the incidence of poverty is closely associated with a relatively low benefit level that does not bring poor households over the 50 percent poverty line. However, in relation to a lower poverty line of 40 percent, the alleviation of poverty is very effective, as the small amount of extreme and severe poverty shows (see Figure 17.1). This finding can be related to the fact that take-up rates are relatively high. In contrast, the Swedish social assistance scheme offers a very high benefit level (yet with large local variation) that guarantees an effective alleviation of poverty for all household types considered. However, only a small proportion of the eligible population seems to claim benefits. One reason for the supposedly low take-up rates is the very strict means-tests in the Swedish social assistance scheme. This illustrates two opposing strategies of poverty alleviation in Sweden and the United Kingdom. Whereas Sweden offers a very generous benefit level but operates with a number of hurdles that are supposed to be overcome only by the "truly needy," the United Kingdom has established a scheme that is more easily accessible, but guarantees a rather low standard of living for some family types below the poverty line. Germany once more finds itself between these two extremes: benefits almost exactly match the poverty line, so most households should be brought out of poverty. However, as the calculations operate with some assumptions that make the calculation of benefit levels not very robust, it may well be that some house-holds actually will remain slightly below the poverty line. A low take-up rate also contributes to the explanation of poverty, partly spurred by the family liability regulations. These results may also contribute to the explanation of different patterns in the reduction of poverty rates found in Figure 17.1, where the United Kingdom stands out with an extraordinarily high degree of effec-tiveness in relation to its level of spending, while Germany was much less successful in reducing poverty, yet ends up with lower poverty rates.

The patterns of poverty alleviation identified in the three case studies illustrate that different stories hide behind seemingly similar poverty rates. A closer analysis of the basic safety net of the welfare state can help to uncover the mechanisms of poverty alleviation and can provide some guidance for future reforms. In order to mend the "holes" in the safety nets, the United Kingdom would have to increase benefit levels, while Germany and Sweden should rather inspect the organization and administration of social assistance and remove barriers to take-up, possibly through a closer integration of mini-mum income benefits with other social security schemes and more transpar-ent administrative procedures. By this token, welfare states could have a much more successful record in poverty alleviation, provided that problems in the measurement of poverty can also be solved (but this is another story).

Notes

1. Please refer to this book for a more detailed discussion and documentation of the issues mentioned here.
2. The choice of countries is informed by the availability of recent data in LIS. For an overview of the construction of this database, cf. Smeeding et al. (1990), Atkinson et al. (1995), and http://www.lisproject.org.
3. In order to account for variations in needs according to household size, equivalence scales are used to adjust household income according to the size and composition of the household (Atkinson et al., 1995: 18-21; Buhmann et al., 1988). The "modi-fied OECD equivalence scale" that is applied here attaches a weight of 1.0 to the head of household, 0.5 for each additional member of the household, and 0.3 for each child under the age of 18.
4. The LIS data referring to the United Kingdom is subject to Crown Copyright; has been made available by the Office for National Statistics through the ESRC Data Archive; and has been used by permission. Neither the Office for National Statis-tics nor the ESRC Data Archive bear any responsibility for the analysis or the interpretation of the data reported here. This disclaimer also applies to all following tables and figures based on LIS data.
5. Please note that the poverty rates stated here deviate from those in Figure 17.1 because they refer only to the prime-age population while excluding the elderly. As a large part of the total reduction of poverty rates is concentrated on the elderly, cross-national comparisons including the elderly are very dependent on variations in the sociodemographic structure and differences in the public-private mix. Focusing on the prime-age population only can avoid at least some of these effects.

6. However, the Swedish household definition leads to an overestimation of poverty among young adults and obviously has a strong impact on poverty rates of prime-age households. Deviating from the household definition of most other countries, the Swedish data consider all young adults from the age of 18 as separate households, even if they continue to live with their parents and are still economically dependent on them. Consequently, poverty rates tend to be higher than if a household definition more similar to that of other countries had been applied, but the size of this bias is not clear.

7. The Australian position in this rank order stands in a certain tension to Castles' and Mitchell's characterization of the Ozeanian welfare states as belonging to a cluster of "radical welfare states" that are portrayed as countries that spend a relatively low share of national income on social transfers and services, but, nevertheless, achieve a high degree of income redistribution (Mitchell, 1991; Castles and Mitchell, 1993). The results for the early 1990s put Australia closer to the bottom ranks than in Mitchell's (1991) earlier analysis, yet the distance to the United States is still apparent.

8. As Figure 17.2 only considers poverty rates for the prime-age population, pensions and other cash expenditure for the elderly have been excluded from the social expenditure ratios. To be sure, it would have been more accurate to exclude *all* social expenditure on the non-prime-age household population from this analysis, yet aggregate data do not allow a detailed break-down of this kind, social expenditure ratios excluding old-age cash benefits are taken as a proxy.

9. One example for similar outcomes of different welfare state strategies can be found in pension systems. Although some countries have chosen to organize a large part of their system of old-age income security in terms of occupational pensions provided by private bodies, redistributional effects are hardly distinguishable from public pension schemes, largely because of a strict regulation and supervision of private pension schemes in some countries (Pedersen, 1999; Behrendt, 2000). It is therefore questionable whether the focus on public redistribution leads to adequate results for an evaluation of the impact of the welfare state.

10. The Commission of the European Communities recently has again emphasized the role of minimum income benefit schemes. One of the goals of a reform of social protection in the European Union is to "ensure effective safety nets, consisting of minimum income benefits and accompanying provisions, with a view to efficiently combat poverty and exclusion of individuals and families" (CEC, 1999: 14).

11. However, Eardley et al. group Germany together with "Beveridgean" welfare states such as the United Kingdom and Ireland in the category of "welfare states with integrated safety nets," yet they concede that the classification of Germany poses some problems and propose to regard Germany as a "bridge" to the "dual social assistance" type (Eardley et al., 1996a: 169, footnote 13).

12. These groups may be eligible for some specialized social assistance benefits for migrants or urgent payments, but as benefit levels are lower than in the general scheme, these programs do not guarantee the same level of protection from poverty.

13. As social assistance benefits may vary markedly with the age of household members, different ages of adults and children are assumed. In order to keep the household need level constant across countries, this method requires the definition of model households. The more detailed the definition of model households, the less representative are the chosen model households for the recipient population. Thus, the definition of model households inevitably has to balance precision and representativity.

14. As for the poverty rates presented above, a poverty line of 50 percent of median equivalent household income has been computed on the basis of LIS data. The calculations of the poverty line and the equivalent income of model household are also based on the modified OECD equivalence scale.
15. The family types with an infant are chosen to account for a peculiarity of the German social assistance scheme which permits a full income disregard of parent allowance (*Erziehungsgeld*) and thus considerably improves the income situation for many parents with young children under three years.
16. This effect must be accounted to the fact that the institutional equivalence scales that are embodied in the social assistance scheme attach a larger weight to children than does the modified OECD equivalence scale that has been used in Figure 17.7.

References

Atkinson, A. B. (1999). *The Economic Consequences of Rolling Back the Welfare State*. Cambridge, Mass.: MIT Press.

Atkinson, A. B., Rainwater, L., and Smeeding, T. M. (1995). *Income Distribution in OECD Countries: Evidence from the Luxembourg Income Study*. Paris: OECD.

Beckerman, W. (1979). "The Impact of Income Maintenance Programmes on Poverty in Britain." *Economic Journal*, 89, 261-279.

Behrendt, C. (2000). "Private Pensions—a Viable Alternative? Their Distributive Effects in a Comparative Perspective." *International Social Security Review*, 53 (3), 3-26.

____. (2002). *At the Margins of the Welfare State: Social Assistance and the Alleviation of Poverty in Germany, Sweden and the United Kingdom*. Aldershot: Ashgate (forthcoming).

Blackburn, M. L. (1998). "The Sensitivity of International Poverty Line Comparisons." *Review of Income and Wealth*, 44 (4), 449-472.

Buhmann, B., Rainwater, L., Schmaus, G., and Smeeding, T. M. (1988). "Equivalence Scales, Well-being, Inequality and Poverty: Sensitivity Estimates across Ten Countries Using the Luxembourg Income Study (LIS) Database." *Review of Income and Wealth*, 34, 114-142.

Castles, F. G., and Mitchell, D. (1993). "Worlds of Welfare and Families of Nations." In Castles, F. G. (ed.), *Families of Nations: Patterns of Public Policy in Western Democracies*. Aldershot: Dartmouth.

Corden, A. (1995). *Changing Perspectives on Benefit Take-Up*. London: HMSO.

Eardley, T., Bradshaw, J., Ditch, J., Gough, I., and Whiteford, P. (1996a). *Social Assistance in OECD Countries*, Volume I: Synthesis Report. Department of Social Security Research Report, No. 46. London: HMSO.

____. (1996b). *Social Assistance in OECD Countries*, Volume II: Country Reports. London: HMSO.

Esping-Andersen, G. (1990). *The Three Worlds of Welfare Capitalism*. Cambridge, Mass.: Polity.

____. (1999). *Social Foundations of Postindustrial Economies*. Oxford: Oxford University Press.

CEC (Commission of the European Community). (1999). *A Concerted Strategy for Modernising Social Protection*. Brussels: CEC.

Goodin, R. E., Headey, B., Muffels, R. A., and Dirven, H.-J. (1999). *The Real Worlds of Welfare Capitalism*. Cambridge: Cambridge University Press.

Gustafsson, B. A., and Uusitalo, H. (1990). "The Welfare State and Poverty in Finland and Sweden from the Mid-1960s to the Mid-1980s." *Review of Income and Wealth*, 36 (3), 249-266.

Halleröd, B. (1991). *Den svenska fattigdomen: En studie av fattigdom och socialbidrags-tagande.* Lund: Arkiv förlag.

Kangas, O. E., and Ritakallio, V.-M. (1998a). "Different Methods—Different Results? Approaches to Multidimensional Poverty." In Andreß, H.-J. (ed.), *Empirical Poverty Research in a Comparative Perspective.* Aldershot: Ashgate.

____. (1998b). Social Policy or Structure? Income Transfers, Socio-demographic Factors and Poverty in the Nordic Countries and in France. Luxembourg Income Study Working Paper Series No. 190. Luxembourg: LIS.

Krämer, W. (1997). *Statistische Probleme bei der Armutsmessung, Gutachten im Auftrag des Bundesministeriums für Gesundheit.* Baden-Baden: Nomos.

Leibfried, S. (1992). "Towards an European Welfare State? On Integrating Poverty Regimes into the European Community." In Ferge, Z., and Kolberg, J. E. (eds.), *Social Policy in a Changing Europe.* New York/Frankfurt (Main): Campus/Westview.

Lødemel, I., and Schulte, B. (1992). "Social Assistance: A Part of Social Security or the Poor Law in New Disguise?" In European Institute of Social Security (ed.), *Reforms in Eastern and Central Europe: Beveridge 50 Years After.* Leuven: Acco.

Mitchell, D. (1991). *Income Transfers in Ten Welfare States.* Aldershot: Avebury.

OECD. (1998a). *The Battle Against Exclusion: Social Assistance in Australia, Finland, Sweden and the United Kingdom.* Paris: OECD.

____. (1998b). *The Battle Against Exclusion: Social Assistance in Belgium, the Czech Republic, the Netherlands and Norway.* Paris: OECD.

____. (1999). *The Battle Against Exclusion: Social Assistance in Canada and Switzerland.* Paris: OECD.

Pedersen, A. W. (1999). *The Taming of Inequality in Retirement: A Comparative Study of Pension Policy Outcomes.* Oslo: FAFO.

Ringen, S. (1987). *The Possibility of Politics: A Study in the Political Economy of the Welfare State.* Oxford: Clarendon.

Smeeding, T. M., O'Higgins, M., and Rainwater, L. (eds.). (1990). *Poverty, Inequality and Income Distribution in Comparative Perspective.* Hemel Hempstead: Harvester Wheatsheaf.

Titmuss, R. (1974). *Social Policy.* London: Allen and Unwin.

van Oorschot, W. (1995). *Realizing Rights: A Multi-level Approach to Non-Take-Up of Social Security Benefits.* Aldershot: Avebury.

____. (1998). "Failing Selectivity: On Extent and Causes of Non-take-up of Social Security Benefits." In Andreß, H.-J. (ed.), *Empirical Poverty Research in a Comparative Perspective.* Aldershot: Ashgate.

Veit-Wilson, J. (1998). *Setting Adequacy Standards: How Governments Define Minimum Incomes.* Bristol: Policy Press.

18

Back to Basics: Safeguarding an Adequate Minimum Income in the Active Welfare State

Bea Cantillon and Karel Van den Bosch

It has been clear for some time that social policy must be aimed at reducing levels of benefit dependency by creating more jobs, by guiding long-term benefit dependants to the labor market, and by increasing the productive capacity of the long-term unemployed through training. These are the basic ingredients which, partly as a result of European guidelines, have been incorporated into the national policies of most member states of the European Union.

The new emphasis can be found very clearly in statements by the European Commission (CEC 1999: 3). In 1999 it set out four new "key objectives" for social protection which are now presented as essential for the "modernization of the European social model." These new "broad objectives to which social protection systems should respond" are:

1. to make work pay and provide secure income;
2. to make pensions safe and pension systems sustainable;
3. to promote social inclusion; and
4. to ensure high quality and sustainable health care.

One might argue that the first two objectives on this list are good examples of secondary objectives of the type, "while boiling an egg, do not let the water boil over." They are much like the "very first requirements" that Florence Nightingale set out in 1859 in her *Notes on Hospitals*: "It may seem a strange principle to enunciate as the very first requirement in a hospital that it should do the sick no harm" (quoted in Titmuss 1969 [1958]: 131). However, just as people go to a hospital in order to get better, so one might expect of income protection systems not only that they are sustainable and work-friendly, but also that they achieve some positive result.

The central point of this chapter is that if one wants to guarantee an adequate standard of living to every European citizen, minimum income protection must be put back on the list of central objectives. There is a danger of regarding active labor market policies as a kind of panacea, producing less poverty and less social exclusion, with lower levels of social expenditure. However, research suggests that more jobs will not automatically lead to less poverty and that a properly conceived activation policy presupposes *other* rather than *lower* social expenditure.

The next section looks at empirical evidence about the link between employment rates and poverty, reviewing historical trends in Belgium and the Netherlands, as well as cross-country comparative results. The third section spells out the policy implications of these findings for national welfare states. In the fourth section we indicate in what way the European Union might play a useful role here.

"More Jobs, Less Poverty?" Empirical Evidence

A comparison between households within a particular country at a point in time suggests that employment significantly reduces the poverty risk. In Belgium the poverty rate among work-poor families (i.e., households where no one has paid work) is around 16 percent, while it is only 1 percent among work-rich households (where at least two adults are working) (Cantillon et al. 1999). Therefore, poverty might be expected to drop, as more jobs become available. Yet, the relationship between work and poverty is not as linear as it seems, as one can infer from historical trends and from international comparative research. We will now look at this evidence in some detail.

Historical Trends in Belgium and the Netherlands

For the period 1976-1988, studies in Belgium have shown neither a surge in inequality nor an increase in poverty (Deleeck et al. 1986, 1991). At the time they were first published, these findings contradicted the prevailing discourse on new poverty, growing inequity, and the dualisation of society. It was generally accepted that the "economic crisis," and growing unemployment in particular, could not but have had negative consequences for the distribution of income and welfare. Yet the dramatic increase in unemployment and the declining employment rate, from 58 percent in 1976 to barely 54 percent in 1985, seemed to coincide with a considerable drop in the prevalence of poverty in Flanders, from 10 to 6 percent.

The principal reason for the enormous drop in poverty was an increase in the relative welfare of the elderly (Cantillon and Lesthaeghe 1987). But poverty levels also declined among people of working age, from 4.5 percent in 1976 to 2.4 percent in 1988. Yet during that same period, the proportion of households receiving unemployment benefits increased from 15 to 23 percent (see Figure 18.1).

There was a double explanation for this paradoxical development. On the one hand, rising unemployment was mostly affecting dual-income households, who usually received an income from labor besides benefits. This situation does usually not result in poverty. On the other hand, the prevailing social security system, with relatively generous benefits for single-income households, in many cases provided adequate protection against the risk of non-employment. On might therefore say that it was partly thanks to a greater

Figure 18.1
Poverty and Benefit Dependency among Households with Heads
under the Age of 50, Flanders, 1976-1997

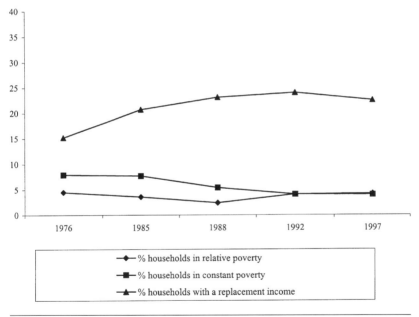

Notes: Relative poverty: below 50 percent of average equivalent income in each year, using modified OECD scale (with weights 1.0 for the first adult, 0.5 for other adults and 0.3 for children).

Constant poverty: below relative poverty line for 1992, adjusted to other years using the index of consumer prices.

Households with a replacement income: households where a person receives unemployent benefits, sickness or invalidity benefits, pensions or social assistance.

Source: Calculations using the Belgian Socio-Economic Panel (BSEP).

degree of income redistribution that the Belgian welfare state got through this period of economic and social transition without experiencing greater social insecurity in the lowest income classes (Cantillon, 1990).

After 1988, both these trends reversed. Although the 1990s saw the labor market recover and benefit dependency drop, inequality rose again and the poverty rate increased somewhat to 4 percent. Importantly, poverty measured with a constant poverty line was no longer declining. (Cantillon et al., 1999).

These observations for Flanders lead us to the significant conclusion that an increase in benefit dependency need not necessarily coincide with a rise in poverty and, conversely, that a drop in benefit dependency through job creation will not automatically reduce poverty levels. Similar observations have been made in other welfare states. In many countries on the European continent, growing benefit dependency in the 1970s and 1980s did not coincide with growing poverty (see Cantillon et al., 1997; Atkinson, 1999).

Recent studies have shown that (quite dramatic) job growth in the Netherlands has not resulted in a reduction of poverty, including long-term poverty, but, on the contrary, suggests that there has been an increase since the beginning of the 1990s (de Beer, 1999; De Lathouwer, 2000). It seems that the increase in labor participation was predominantly to the benefit of women (re)entering the labor market, as a result of which the number of dual-income households has increased considerably. Conversely, the number of households *without* an income from work has not declined.

These trends appear to be universal. The OECD reports that between a third and half of all unemployed persons in the OECD belong to workless households (OECD, 1995a). In the 1980s and 1990s, many OECD countries saw this proportion increase. In Belgium, the proportion of households with two (or more) income earners grew from 42 percent in 1983 to 52 percent in 1994 (Figure 18.2). At the same time, the proportion of households with no income from work increased from 16 to 20 percent. By comparison, over that same period in the United Kingdom, the proportion of multiple-income households increased from 54 to 62 percent, while the number of zero-earners rose from 6 to 19 percent. A similar polarization has been observed in France, Germany, and Luxembourg.

We conclude that, in many countries, rapidly growing unemployment did *not* lead to more poverty, because much of the unemployment occurred in financially more resilient dual-income households. Conversely, the more recently observed job growth appears not always to coincide with a drop in poverty, as relatively few of the new jobs are supplied to work-poor households.

Cross-country Comparative Evidence

Although unemployment is generally regarded to be one of the principal causes of poverty, comparative international research has shown that there is

Figure 18.2
Proportion of Work-Poor and Work-Rich Households in Germany, France,
Belgium, and the UK, 1983-1994

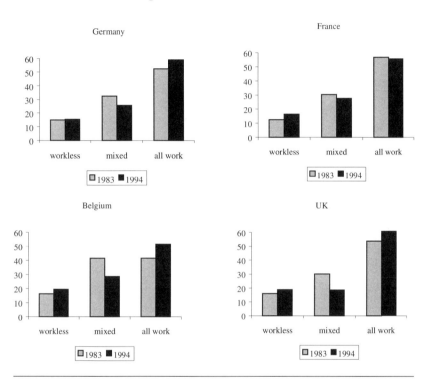

Source: Gregg & Wadsworth (1996).

not at all a linear relation between unemployment (including long-term un-employment) and poverty (Figure 18.3a). One can distinguish between four different clusters of countries. The first encompasses such countries as Norway, Sweden, and Switzerland, which in the mid-1980s had relatively low unemployment as well as a low financial poverty rate for the active population. A second cluster consists of the United States, Canada, and Australia, where low unemployment coincides with a high poverty level. And a third cluster includes most continental European countries, all of which have relatively high unemployment levels combined with comparatively low poverty rates. Only in Ireland does a high unemployment rate coincide with a high poverty rate. Nor is there a linear connection between the overall level of long-term unemployment and poverty at active age. In fact, the above-mentioned clusters are even more clearly defined.

Figure 18.3a
Poverty and Unemployment in OECD Countries

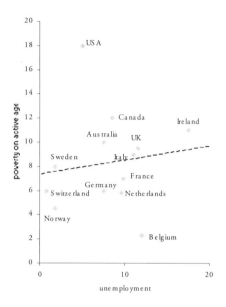

Figure 18.3b
Poverty and Employment in OECD Countires

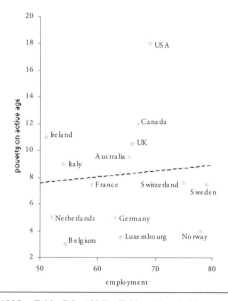

Source: OECD (1995a: Table 7.2, 1995b: Tables 14 and 15).

It is often suggested that more employment is the surest road to reducing poverty. But clearly high employment rates do not necessarily imply lower poverty levels (Figure 18.3b). Only Switzerland, Sweden, and Norway combine a very high employment rate (over 75 percent) with a low poverty level. Sweden and Norway have in the past pursued very active employment policies, unlike the United States, Canada, and Australia, where one tries to boost employment by keeping benefit levels low and through local wage formation. However, the latter countries are confronted with the highest poverty rates in the OECD. At the other extreme we find the continental European states, such as Belgium, the Netherlands, and Germany, which have relatively low poverty rates despite a relatively elevated level of non-employment.

A seemingly obvious explanation for this finding is the potential trade-off between employment and low wages. Countries with the highest non-subsidized employment levels, i.e., the United States, Canada, and Australia, also have the most substantial wage differences and largest low-wage sector (Figure 18.4).

The strong cross-national correlation between the distribution of low-wage labor and poverty suggests that "poverty among the employed" is more widespread in countries where low wages are most common. This is indeed the case, but only to a certain extent. The high proportion of so-called working

Figure 18.4
Poverty and Low Wages in OECD Countries

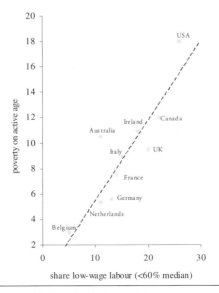

Source: OECD (1995a: Table 7.2, 1994: Tables 1.11).

poor explains only very partially the high poverty level in countries with high (non-subsidized) employment. The extent of poverty among the employed should not be exaggerated, even in countries where low-wage labor is relatively widespread. *What is much more striking is that poverty levels among the non-employed are very high in the Anglo-Saxon world.* The poverty rate among non-employed Americans of active age is 40 percent (Figure 18.5). That is about twice as high as the corresponding rate in any European country (with the exception of the United Kingdom), and about four times the level found in Belgium, Denmark, Finland or Norway. The cross-national differences are equally striking if one compares poverty rates among "workless" households, which appear to be particularly high in such countries as the United States, Canada, and the United Kingdom. Moreover, poverty at an active age is concentrated mostly in this category. In contrast to what one would expect given the low wages in the United Kingdom, 75 percent of the poor live in workless households.

We conclude that the high poverty level in countries with high (non-subsidized) employment is connected with an inadequate minimum protection for the employed (e.g., minimum wage) and—especially—for those who

Figure 18.5
Poverty among the Low-Paid and Non-Working
Population in OECD Countries

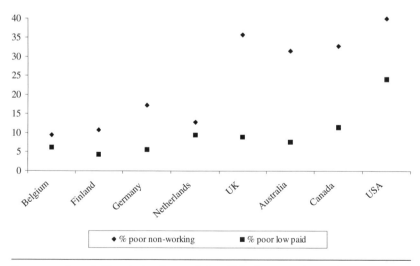

Notes: poor: household equivalent income below 50% of mean equivalent income, modified OECD scale.
low paid: earnings below 67% of median gross earnings of full-time workers.

Source: Calculations by Marx and Verbist (1998), using the LIS database.

are out of work despite the high employment rate (e.g., unemployment benefits and social assistance).

Policy Implications

The empirical findings reviewed in the previous section point to two obstacles in the course from more work to less poverty. The first lies in the fact that additional jobs will not automatically be filled in by members of vulnerable work-poor families. The second obstacle has to do with the extent to which an "activation policy" can be coupled with adequate social protection for those who, in spite of all investment strategies, remain jobless. From this follows two important policy conclusions. Of strategic importance on the road from "more work to less poverty" is, *firstly*, the extent to which new jobs are filled in by members of work-poor household. In the OECD-region this does not appear to occur automatically. This represents a first obstacle for a policy that strives to be employment generating and poverty reducing at the same time. The *second* strategic policy factor is the extent to which the social security system continues to provide adequate protection for those who, despite all investment strategies, are left without a job. Indeed, experience in work-rich countries has shown that we must take due consideration of the—as yet unresolved—issue of unemployment among the low skilled.

Ingredients of a Win-Work Strategy

How can an activation and job-creation policy assure that newly created jobs are directed maximally to these work-poor, that is, unskilled, households? Naturally, the suppression of the low skilled on the job market will be reduced if enough additional jobs are created. But both the Dutch and the Anglo-Saxon examples show that this does not suffice. Even in so-called "work-rich countries" the low skilled make up a large proportion of the unemployed. Moreover, experience in countries with high wage flexibility has shown that this simple market mechanism (i.e., declining level of low wages) does not lead automatically to more jobs for the low skilled. The hypothesis that cutting low wages will lead to a substantial increase in employment for the low skilled has been refuted in various empirical studies (see, among others, Glyn and Salverda, 2000; Nickell and Bell, 1995; Card et al., 1996; Krueger and Pischke, 1997). Even in countries where the lowest wages have been cut considerably, unemployment among the low skilled remains an unresolved problem.

In other words, it would be simplistic to believe that job creation and wage cost reduction will inevitably lead to substantially more employment for work-poor households, for there are very fundamental factors at work here. The *technological revolution* is not neutral vis-à-vis schooling levels, but rather knowledge intensive. It leads to a relative drop in demand for low-skilled labor and a relative increase in demand for high-skilled workers. On top of that, there is the phenomenon of *globalization*, which is affecting the worldwide scarcity of low-skilled labor to a greater degree than it is influencing the scarcity of high-skilled labor. Furthermore, all forms of *social regulation* (minimum wage, increase of labor costs through social security contributions, and the like) are most important to the lower incomes. And benefit dependency itself leads to the *erosion of skills and talents*. For all these reasons low-skilled persons, individuals with limited skills and experience, people with social handicaps, and long-term benefit dependents have great difficulty finding their way to the labor market. They need help to get there.

The key question is: how should the gap be bridged between the perspectives of the employer and the worker, that is, the gap between the excessive cost of simple, low-productive work in care or services and the inadequate earnings of the worker involved. Three possibilities present themselves. *Firstly*, one could substantially reduce the fiscal burden on low-productivity labor, both for the employer and for the employee. *Secondly*, benefits could be recycled. Passive benefits must be transformed into service labor that is meaningful to society. *Thirdly* (and in conjunction with the previous item), through direct, subsidized job creation for the low skilled, especially in the growing field of carework (for example, childcare outside of schools). All these possibilities boil down to the *subsidizing of low-skilled labor*.

In addition, one should take notice of the fact that educational systems are still inadequate in developing the talents that are required in today's new economic and social environment. Despite a strong increase in levels of schooling, the democratization of the educational system has stagnated in most countries (Shavit and Blossfeld, 1993). Children from the lower classes still attain significantly lower levels of education than children from better-off families. This implies that many potentialities may remain untapped. Especially in technical and vocational training, where children often end up as a last resort after dropping out of mainstream education, the time seems right for a reassessment. In addition, substantial investments need to be made in the (re)activation of the potentialities of the large stock of long-term unemployed.

Therefore, the "active welfare state" (in the sense of a welfare state that takes positive measures to bring people back onto the labor market) is not a cheap option (Vandenbroucke, 1999). An activation policy that also aspires to reduce poverty requires a reorientation (not a reduction!) of social expenditure, from merely passive transfers to a service-rendering care model that not only guarantees social security, but also uses and valorizes talents maximally.

More generally, it appears that from a macro-economic perspective there is a positive relationship between the volume of public social expenditure (social security and collective goods and services) and poverty. Poverty levels are the lowest in countries that spend the most, and they increase (albeit not in a linear fashion) as the expenditure level drops (see Figure 18.6). The more passive transfer-oriented appropriation of means in the Benelux countries generates the same results in terms of financial poverty as the more activating service-oriented public spending in the Scandinavian countries: the two regions realize a similar (low) poverty level. If anything, international comparative research has demonstrated that combating poverty requires high social expenditure. There is no reason to believe that this will not be so in the active welfare state.

Back to Basics: The Necessity of Adequate Minimum Income Protection

The second strategic element in poverty policy—even in the active welfare state—is minimum protection for those who remain without a job in spite

Figure 18.6
Poverty and Social Expenditure in OECD Countries

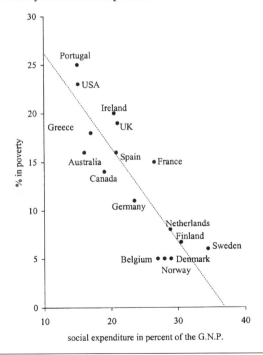

Notes: Poverty: household equivalent income below 50% of mean equivalent income, modified OECD scale.

Source: Van den Bosch (1998), and OECD Social Expenditure Statistics.

of all social investment strategies. As experience has shown that, even in very work-rich countries, the problem of underemployment among the low skilled is quite persistent, an activation policy should be conceived as a complement rather than an alternative to a broad and comprehensive system of social protection. Freezing minimum benefits in order to combat unemployment traps, for example, will inevitably result in a widening gap between those holding a job and those who remain unemployed.

It is important to be aware of the serious consequences if social security is allowed to deviate from its objective of assuring adequate (minimum) income protection to those affected by a social risk. There has been an (albeit slow) erosion of minimum benefits in Belgium, relative to the average standard of living. The increase in poverty among work-poor households who are entirely dependent on social security is a direct consequence of this trend (see Cantillon et al., 1999). These developments have occurred at the same time when many politicians and policy-makers have expressed their adherence to the activation logic and an often unreflective belief in a positive linear relationship between job creation and poverty reduction.

Achieving a correct balance between rights and duties in the active welfare state presupposes that, besides an activation discourse, there should also be a discourse on adequacy. Although social security needs to aim at preventing risks, its single most important purpose is to assure subsistence in case of a social risk.

Towards a European Poverty Line

The European Union could play an important role in this regard, through the process of "benchmarking," both in terms of poverty, and in terms of effective minimum income protection. In this way the European Union could help in guiding the discourse and setting the agenda in the member states. A very useful step in this context would be the introduction of a European poverty line. Such a move would establish an institution at the European level (such as the official poverty line in the United States) that consolidates the goal of poverty reduction and stimulates the development of social policies to tackle this problem (cf. Atkinson, 1997; see also Atkinson et al., 2001). This implies that a consensus on four points should be reached among policymakers at EU level.

First of all, there should be agreement on the method of measurement: that is, the approach used to develop a poverty line and the technical details of its empirical application. At present, there is within academia no consensus about the best method to measure poverty. Therefore, it can be said that every poverty line is a convention, that is, established on the basis of consensus between experts and policy-makers. Three criteria should guide the choice of a European poverty standard. Of course, the norm must be proven to be statistically reliable and feasible. Furthermore, the chosen norm must be acceptable for the general public. This means that the method should be understandable, at least in its general principles, and also that, to a certain extent, the measurement of poverty should refer to an absolute definition of poverty, that is, the inability to satisfy one's basic needs. Finally, the norm must be relevant for policy-making; that is, reducing poverty as measured by this norm must be a reachable goal.

None of the methods currently in use satisfies all these requirements. In the short term, a relative standard, where the poverty line is set at a certain percentage (e.g., 60 percent) of median equivalent family-income in each member state, seems to be the only feasible method. In the long term, the budget method appears to be the best option. The budget method uses a basket of goods and services that are identified as essential consumer goods (Bradshaw, 1993). The same basket may not be appropriate for each country; rather, on the basis of common principles and guidelines, separate baskets should be defined for each country.

The second element on which an agreement should be reached at EU-level is the poverty rate that should be set as an aim for policy: that is, the goal that can and must be set for the medium term. Although it remains a political decision which level of poverty should be aimed at, all decisions should take into consideration that the goal must be reachable by using available social and economical policies, and also that the goal should not exclude certain policies which might be used to fight poverty. It should do justice to the consequences of economic growth, which results in the same percentage income increase for everyone; it should do justice to the consequences of income redistribution as well as to the consequences of specific income transfers to target groups (this can be shown through mapping the relative poverty level per group).

A relative poverty line (percentage of median equivalent income) will by definition move in tandem with the average standard of living. This means it is not well suited to show the poverty alleviating effects of economic growth. Therefore, in addition to relative poverty lines, we should also apply poverty lines that remain fixed (in each country) in terms of purchasing power. In practical terms this could mean that the relative poverty line in a particular base year is updated using the index of consumer prices. Given sufficient economic growth, poverty measured with such poverty lines should decrease rather rapidly. This is illustrated in Table 18.1, which shows simulated poverty rates in the European Union in 2005 and 2010 under the assumptions that the incomes of all households grow with 1, 2 or 3 percent per year. At the optimistic assumption of 3 percent growth, poverty in 2005 would be more than halved relative to 1995, and in 2010 it would be reduced by more than two-thirds. At the more moderate assumption of 2 percent growth, poverty would be still more than halved in 2010. This is equally true for non-aged adults, children, and aged persons.

An additional policy target could be that relative poverty in the EU decreases through reducing relative poverty in countries where the level is above average, and relative poverty among risk-groups in each country (i.e., categories within the population with a percentage of poor above average, e.g., children, single-parent families, low-skilled, elderly) should also be reduced. (See CBS [1999] for useful results on the distribution of poverty risk across population categories in the member states of the EU.)

The third element on which a consensus among policy-makers within the EU should be reached is an instrument that evaluates the performance of the social security and social assistance systems in the EU member states. After all, the development of poverty rates is to a large extent the result of circumstances and developments beyond the reach of social policies. Therefore, a more direct evaluation of policies is required. A methodology can be developed that allows annual updating and international comparison of policy efforts, that is, the input of policy, both on the macro- and the micro-level. On the macro-level such input indicators measure the evolution of the total volume of social security and social assistance outlays, as a proportion of GDP (general, per branch, per system, and per function). Input indicators on the micro-level focus on the evaluation of individual reference benefit amounts (e.g., minimum and maximum unemployment benefits, minimum and maximum pensions). Trends in these indicators can be compared with indices of purchasing power, indices of average welfare, and poverty standards. The importance of social benefits is illustrated in Table 18.2, which is similar to Table 18.1, except that the assumption is made that social benefits do not

Table 18.1
Simulated Poverty Rates in the European Union in 2005 and 2010 under Various Assumptions of Income Growth, Using a Constant Poverty Line

Year	1995	2005			2010		
Income growth per year		1%	2%	3%	1%	2%	3%
All households	17.2	13.0	10.1	7.9	11.5	7.9	5.9
All individuals	16.0	12.0	9.4	7.4	10.6	7.4	5.4
Children	17.7	13.4	10.3	8.0	11.9	8.0	5.9
Non-aged adults	15.1	11.5	9.2	7.3	10.3	7.3	5.4
Aged persons	19.5	13.9	10.2	7.7	12.0	7.7	5.3

Note: Poverty line is 60 percent of median equivalent income in each Member State in the base year (1995), which remains constant across the simulations. The assumption is that the incomes of all households grow in real terms at the rates indicated. Results for 1995 are measured poverty rates.
Source: Calculations on the European Community Household Panel.

grow in real terms, but only follow price increases. Unsurprisingly, poverty among aged persons hardly decreases under this assumption. But even among children and non-aged adults, the reduction in poverty is only half of what it is when all incomes, including social benefits, grow in real terms.

A limited set of non-financial indicators is the final element on which an agreement needs to be reached. Such indicators give a general insight in the non-income-related aspects of poverty as well as the policies that are useful in the fight against poverty. Poverty in its broad definition is a multiple-dimensional concept that covers many areas of life (UNDP, 1997). It is too simple to approach poverty only from a financial point of view, the more because poverty policies are part of a wider general social policy. Indeed, the importance of "non-cash benefits" that people receive within universal programs (free education, National Health Service, etc.) must be stressed. In order to be useful, these indicators should be limited in number, related to policy areas, and based on indisputable statistics.

Conclusion

The link between unemployment and poverty is not clear-cut. In many countries rapidly growing unemployment in the seventies and early eighties did not lead to more poverty, because much of the unemployment occurred in financially resilient dual-income households. Conversely, the more recent job growth appears not always to coincide with a drop in poverty, as relatively few of those new jobs are supplied to work-poor households. Some

Table 18.2

Simulated Poverty Rates in the European Union in 2005 and 2010 under the Assumption That Transfer Incomes Do Not Grow, Using a Constant Poverty Line

Year	1995	2005	2010				
Market income growth		**1%**	**2%**	**3%**	**1%**	**2%**	**3%**
Transfer income growth		**0%**	**0%**	**0%**	**0%**	**0%**	**0%**
All households	17.2	15.7	14.6	13.6	15.1	13.6	12.6
All individuals	16.0	14.2	12.9	11.9	13.6	11.9	10.9
Children	17.7	15.0	13.3	11.7	14.3	11.7	10.2
Non-aged adults	15.1	13.0	11.5	10.3	12.3	10.3	9.2
Aged persons	19.5	19.1	18.7	18.0	18.8	18.3	18.0

Note: Poverty line is 60 percent of median equivalent income in each Member State in the base year (1995), which remains constant across the simulations. The assumption is that the incomes of all households grow in real terms at the rates indicated, except social transfer incomes, which are kept unchanged. Results for 1995 are measured poverty rates.

Source: Calculations on the European Community Household Panel.

countries experience high poverty rates at the same time as high (non-subsidized) employment, partly due to low wages, but especially due to inadequate minimum income protection for those who are out of work despite the high employment.

These empirical findings lead us to three important policy conclusions. Of strategic importance on the road from "more work to less poverty" is, firstly, the extent to which new jobs are filled in by members of work-poor households. Social policy must be aimed at reducing levels of benefit dependency not just by creating more jobs, but in particular by guiding long-term benefit dependents to the labor market, and by increasing the productivity capacity of the long-term unemployed through training. The second strategic policy factor is the extent to which the social security system continues to provide protection for those who, despite all social activation strategies, are left without a job. An adequate safety net of minimum income protection in social security and social assistance remains of crucial importance to prevent poverty. Thirdly, the European Union could play an important role in this regard, through the process of "benchmarking," both in terms of poverty, and in terms of effective minimum income protection.

References

Atkinson, A. B. (1997). *Poverty in Europe*. Oxford: Blackwell.

___. (1999). "The Distribution of Income in the UK and OECD Countries in the Twentieth Century." *Oxford Review of Economic Policy*, 15 (4), 56-75.

Atkinson, A. B., Cantillon, B., Marlier E., and Nolan, B. (2001). *Indicators for Social Inclusion in the European Union*. Oxford: Oxford University Press.

Bradshaw, J. (ed.). (1993). *Budget Standards for the United Kingdom*. Aldershot: Avebury.

Cantillon, B. (1990). *Nieuwe behoeften naar zekerheid. Vrouw, gezin en inkomensverdeling*. Leuven, Acco.

___. (1999). *De welvaartsstaat in de kering*. Kapellen: Pelckmans.

Cantillon, B., and Lesthaeghe, R. (1987). "Generatie, gezinsvorm en inkomen: ontwikkelingen in Vlaanderen 1976-1985." *Tijdschrift voor Sociologie*. 8 (2-3), 201-238.

Cantillon, B., Marx, I., and Van den Bosch, K. (1997) "The Challenge of Poverty and Social Exclusion." In OECD (ed.), *Towards 2000: The New Social Policy Agenda*. Paris: OECD.

Cantillon, B., De Lathouwer, L., Marx, I., Van Dam, R., and Van den Bosch, K. (1999). "Sociale indicatoren 1976-1997." *Belgisch Tijdschrift voor Sociale Zekerheid*, 41 (4), 747-800.

Card, D., Kramarz, F., and Lernieux, T. (1996). *Changes in the Relative Structure of Wages and Employment*. NBER Working Paper, No. 5487. Washington, D. C.: National Bureau of Economic Research.

CBS. (1999). *Social Reporting: Reconciliation of Sources and Dissemination of Data: Recommendations on the Measurement of Social Exclusion and Poverty and a Blueprint for a Periodic Publication*. Heerlen: Centraal Bureau voor de Statistiek.

CEC. (1999). *A Concerted Strategy for Modernising Social Protection*. Brussels: Commission of the European Communities.

de Beer, P. (1999). "Werk en armoede." *Armoedemonitor,* 3, 111-138.

De Lathouwer, L. (2000). "Meer werk is geen garantie voor minder armoede en minder ongelijkheid. Kritische reflecties bij het Nederlandse poldermodel vanuit België." In Salverda, W. (ed.), *De houdbaarheid van het Nederlandse "model": verder met loonmatiging en deeltijdarbeid.* 's Gravenhage: Elsevier bedrijfsinformatie bv.

Deleeck, H., Cantillon, B., De Lathouwer, L., Van den Bosch, K., and Wyns, M. (1986). *Indicators of Social Security (general results) 1976-1985.* Antwerp: Centre of Social Policy, University of Antwerp.

Deleeck, H., Cantillon, B., Meulemans, B., and Van den Bosch, K. (1991). "Indicateurs sociaux de la sécurité sociale 1985-1988." *Revue Belge de Sécurité Sociale,* 33 (10-11-12), 689-756.

Glyn, A., and Salverda, W. (2000). "Does Wage Flexibility Really Create Jobs?" *Challenge,* 43, 32-43.

Gregg, P., and Wadsworth, J. (1996). *It Takes Two: Employment Polarisation in the OECD.* London: Centre for Economic Performance, London School of Economics.

Krueger, A., and Pischke, J.-S. (1997). *Observations and Conjectures on the U.S. Employment Miracle.* NBER Working Paper No. 6146. Washington, D. C.: National Bureau of Economic Research.

Marx, I., and Verbist, G. (1998). "Low-paid Work and Poverty: A Cross-country Perspective." In Bazen, S., Gregory, M., and Salverda, W. (eds.), *Low-wage employment in Europe.* Cheltenham: Edward Elgar.

Nickell, S., and Bell, B. (1995). "The Collapse in the Demand for the Unskilled across the OECD." *Oxford Review of Economic Policy* 11 (1), 40-62.

OECD. (1994). *The OECD Jobs Study.* Paris: OECD.

____. (1995a). *Employment Outlook.* Paris: OECD.

____. (1995b). *Historical Statistics, 1960-1993.* Paris: OECD.

Shavit, Y., and Blossfeld, H. P. (1993). *Persistent Inequality. Changing Educational Attainment in Thirteen Countries.* Boulder, Col.: Westview Press.

Titmuss, R. (1969 [1958]). *Essays on "the Welfare State."* London: Unwin University Books.

UNDP. (1997). *Human Development Report.* New York, Oxford: Oxford University Press.

Van den Bosch, K. (1998). "The Evolution of Financial Poverty in Western Europe." In Rhodes, M., and Mény, Y. (eds.), *The Future of European Welfare: A New Social Contract?* Houndmills: Macmillan.

Vandenbroucke, F. (1999). "De Europese sociaal-democratie en Labours Derde Weg." *Samenleving en Politiek,* 6 (3), 3-18.

List of Contributors

Santiago Álvarez is Associate Professor of Public Finance at the University of Oviedo (Spain). His research interests focus on taxation theory, public spending on social policy and fiscal federalism. He has developed several research projects for the Fundación Banco Herrero and the Fundación BBV. He has authored two monographs and published various articles in specialized journals. He is currently working as Director of Research Studies on Public Budget and Expenditure at the National Institute of Fiscal Studies of the Ministry of Finance (Madrid).

Christina Behrendt works as a freelance researcher and consultant for the International Social Security Association in Geneva. Previously, she served as research fellow and lecturer at the University of Konstanz (Germany). Her research focuses on social policy and income distribution in a comparative perspective, especially in the field of minimum income schemes and income maintenance in old age.

Helen Bolderson was formerly Reader in Social Policy in the Department of Government at Brunel University (United Kingdom). Since her retirement she has worked as a researcher at Brunel where she currently holds the European Union project on disability policy and a study funded by the Nuffield Foundation on the history of the concept of disability in the UK. Dr Bolderson is a sociologist and social policy analyst by training. Her research and publications include theoretical work on the developments of policy and historical, institutional, and cross-national comparative analyses.

Koen Caminada is Assistant Professor of Economics at Public Finance Section, Law School, Leiden University, the Netherlands. His main research areas are social security, fiscal policy, and taxation.

Bea Cantillon is Professor of Social Policy at the University of Antwerp (Belgium) and Director of the Centre for Social Policy at the same university.

Eero Carroll is Senior Research Fellow at the Swedish Institute for Social Research, Stockholm, Sweden.

Bob Deacon is Director of the Globalism and Social Policy Programme (GASPP), an Anglo-Finnish program examining the relationship between globalization and social policy (www.stakes.fi/gaspp). He is Professor of Social Policy at the University of Sheffield and author of several books including

377

Global Social Policy, published by SAGE. He is founding editor of the new journal, *Global Social Policy*, also published by SAGE. He has advised several international agencies including UNDESA, UNDP, ILO, WHO, UNRISD, EU, and the Council of Europe on aspects of the internationalization of social policy.

Chris de Neubourg is Jean Monnet Professor of Economics and Director of the Masters Programme in Social Protection Financing at the University of Maastricht in the Netherlands.

Alain Euzéby is Professor of Economics at the Institute for Political Science (l'Institut d'études politiques) in Grenoble, France.

Katja Forssén is Professor of Social Work at the Department of Social Policy, University of Turku, Finland. Her current research interests are child poverty, social exclusion, and family policy in a comparative perspective.

Kees P. Goudswaard is Professor of Economics and Professor of Social Security at Public Finance Section, Law School, Leiden University, the Netherlands, and Crown-member of the Social and Economic Council (the main government advisory body on social and economic policy in the Netherlands). Research areas: social security, fiscal policy, and taxation.

Ian Gough is Professor of Social Policy at the University of Bath, UK, where he was co-director of "Social Policy in Development Contexts," a research program funded by the Department for International Development. He is a member of the Advisory Board of the InFocus Programme on Socio-Economic Security at the ILO. His latest books are *Capitalism and Social Cohesion* and *Global Capital, Human Needs and Social Policies: Selected Essays 1994-99*.

Ana M. Guillén is Associate Professor of Sociology at the University of Oviedo (Spain), where she teaches Comparative Social Policy. She has written extensively on welfare state development, health policy, and comparative social policy. In addition, she has done consulting work for the European Commission and the ILO. In 1998-99, she was a Jean Monnet Fellow and participant in the European University Institute's European Forum "Recasting the European Welfare State."

Mia Hakovirta is a Research Fellow at the Department of Social Policy, University of Turku, Finland. She is writing a Ph.D. thesis about employment and work incentives in single-parent families. Her current research interests also include social exclusion in early childhood.

Karl Hinrichs is Senior Research Associate at the University of Bremen's Center for Social Policy Research and, during the academic year 2001/02, Visiting Professor at Humboldt University in Berlin, Germany. As a political scientist, his main area of research is the German welfare state and its development in a comparative perspective.

Audrey Koulinsky is a research scholar studying for her doctorate at the Centre d'Economie et de Finances Internationales (CEFI), Aix-en-Provence,

France. After obtaining a advanced studies degree (DEA) from CEFI on inter-
regional insurance mechanisms in economic and currency unions, she is now
focusing her research on the transformation and convergence of European
models of social protection.

Jon Kvist is Senior Researcher at The Danish National Institute of Social
Research (SFI), Copenhagen, Denmark, and affiliated with Copenhagen Business School and Copenhagen University. He is Deputy Head of a research
unit at SFI and chair of a working group under the COST A15 program "Reforming Social Protection Systems in Europe." His main research interests are
social and labor market policy, both in Denmark and cross-nationally, and
comparative methodology.

Deborah Mabbett is Lecturer in the Department of Government at Brunel
University, where she specializes in the comparative analysis of social security policies. Currently she is managing a European Union project on disability policy. Dr Mabbett is an economist by training and has worked as a
consultant and advisor on social policy in several countries, including countries in the former Soviet Union.

François-Xavier Merrien is Professor of Social Sciences at the University
of Lausanne, Switzerland. He is a member of the National Committee of the
National Centre for Scientific Research (CNRS), France. His teaching relates
to comparative sociology of welfare states and evaluation in the social field
while his research focused on the analysis of changes in public action, state
structures and welfare systems in a comparative perspective. Among his most
recent publications are *L'Etat providence* (The Welfare State) (2000), *Towards a New Governance for Universities?* (1999, with D. Braun), and *Face
à la pauvreté* (Facing up to Poverty (ed., 1994).

Nadine Richez-Battesti is Senior Lecturer in Economics at the University
of Aix-Marseille II, France, and a researcher at the Centre d'Economie et de
Finances Internationales (CEFI), Aix-en-Provence. She is Director of Studies
for the advanced specialized degree (DESS) in "Social Economy Organization Engineering" and a member of the Euro Group, and combines her expertise in European economic and monetary integration with her specialist
knowledge of social economics.

Simon Roberts is Researcher at the Centre for Research in Social Policy
(CRSP) at Loughborough University in the UK. Dr Roberts' research experience includes UK, European, and international social security; migration and
social security; international comparisons of public management reforms;
the application of Business Process Re-engineering to the UK National Health
Service; and performance audit. Dr Roberts is the Project Leader of the ISSA
study "Assessing the coverage gap." He is the UK expert on the European
Commission's "Observatory on Social Security for Migrant Workers" and a
member of the European Commission's Working Group looking at the impact
of globalization on European social security systems.

Fritz W. Scharpf is Director of the Max Planck Institute for the Study of Societies (MPIfG) in Cologne (Germany) and a member of numerous professional committees and editorial boards. He has published extensively on questions of multilevel governance, applications of game theory and the role of institutions, the political economy of inflation and unemployment in Western Europe, and the comparative political economy of the welfare state.

Roland Sigg is Head of Research at the International Social Security Association in Geneva, Switzerland, and Lecturer at the University of Geneva. He served as research fellow at the University of California, Berkeley, and at McGill University, Montreal. He currently co-ordinates comparative research projects in the field of the development of the welfare state, pension, work incapacity and reintegration, and the administration of social security. He has edited several books on various social security issues and has published papers in national and international periodicals.

Karel Van den Bosch is Senior Researcher at the Centre for Social Policy at the University of Antwerp, Belgium.

Index

Accessibility
    significance of, 232
    unemployment benefits and, 229-230
Activation policies, 8-9
"Active welfare state"
    defined, 368
    win-work strategy, 368
Adequacy
    assistance benefits evaluation, 347
    calculations of, 347
    country levels of, 347-351
    poverty alleviation and, 351
    social assistance entitlements and, 345, 347-350
    social assistance schemes and, 345-346
Adjustments with a Human Face, 24
Álvarez, Santiago, 4
Amsterdam Treaty, 206, 278
Asian Development Bank, 62
Asylum-seekers
    competition over, 205-206
    European Commission initiative, 206-207
    European discrimination prohibition, 204
    exclusionary measures and, 205
    exclusionary policy adoptions, 206
    externality significance, 207
    Geneva Convention interpretations, 204-205
    government application deterring, 205
    policy harmonization obstacles, 207
    reception center residency, 213-214
    social security and, 213

Baseline triangle
    example problem, 315-316
    See also Welfare pentagon

Basic needs
    advanced capitalist societies, 322
    income access for, 322
    need determining, 320-321
    problem setting shifts, 323
    social policy linking, 321-322
    social risk management, 321-322
    time differences, 321
Behrendt, Christina, 10
Belgium employment
    benefit dependency increasing, 362
    conclusions on, 362
    elderly welfare and, 360-361
    explanations for, 361-362
    head of household dependency, 361
    job growth in, 362
    labor market recovery, 362
    poverty static in, 360
Benefit entitlement conditions
    "habitual resident" status, 213
    nationality and, 212-213
    residency and, 213
Bilateral agreements
    goals of, 214
    insurance-based schemes, 218
    international social security agreements, 214
    "national" defined in, 217
    new agreement characteristics, 217-218
    protection under, 217
    purpose of, 218
Blair, Tony, 227
Bolderson, Helen, 6
Borrowing
    EMU member impact, 94
    global financial volatility, 94

Caminada, Koen, 6
Cantilon, Bea, 10
Capital market integration

competition areas of, 89
economic constraints types, 89
"embedded liberalism" period, 87-88
interest rate impacts, 86
international regulatory consequences, 86
legal vs economic pressures, 89
policy option alternatives, 87-88
policy outcomes differing, 87
Carroll, Eero, 5
Council of Europe Instruments, 220

Deacon, Bob, 3

East Asia case
  conclusions on, 62-63
  countries in, 52
  crisis in, 59-62
  economic globalization impact, 62-
    63
  globalization undermining, 47-50
  North and South regimes, 50-52
  welfare regimes, 53-59
East Asia welfare regimes
  characteristics of, 58-59
  country variations in, 59
  welfare mix institutional programs,
    53-57
  welfare outcomes, 58
East Asian crisis
  causes of, 60
  Korea and, 60-61
  Malaysia and, 61
  social effects of, 59
  social impact of, 60
  Thailand, 61-62
Economic globalization, 62-63
Economism
  defined, 39-40
  international competition and, 39-40
Elderly
  mother's employment and, 301-304
  welfare for, 360-361
Eligibility, social assistance schemes
  and, 345-346
Employment
  dimensions missing in, 280-281
  European building models, 279
  initiatives for, 282
  progress significance on, 277-278
  reform basics, 281-282
  social protection and, 278-279

as social right, 8
social security system interrelationships, 280
"Triad" changes in, 278
unemployment scale and, 277
vs flexibility tenets, 281
vs income distribution, 282-283
vs U.S. model, 282
white paper on, 280
Employment cross-country evidence
  OECD poverty, 364
  poverty reduction from, 365
  protection inadequate for, 366-367
  vs low wages, 365-366
  vs unemployment, 362-363
  work-poor vs work-rich proportions,
    363
Employment effects
  country differences, 92
  exposed sector employment rates,
    90-91
  industry employment losses, 91
  sheltered sectors and, 91
  stabilization reasons, 89-90
Employment empirical evidence
  cross-country comparative evidence,
    362-367
  historical trends in, 360-362
"Employment miracle"
  annual hours worked increases, 256
  "Dutch patient," recovery, 259
  employment growth reasons, 257-258
  employment redistribution, 258-259
  Europe's small economies and, 256-
    257
  labor market recovery, 255-256
  See also Labor markets; Unemploy-
    ment combating
Employment obstacles
  contribution as unemployment
    sources, 37-39
  tax contribution levels, 36-37
Employment performance
  employment potential utilization,
    253
  employment and population ratio,
    252
  performance criteria, 255
  quantitative success vs normal jobs,
    254-255
  unemployment rate changes as, 250-
    251

unemployment rate questioning, 251-252
vs unemployment-related features, 253-254
Employment policy implications
European poverty line, 370-373
minimum income protection, 369-370
win-work strategy elements, 367
Employment vs social protection
conclusions on, 291-292
existence of, 283-291
globalization trends and, 273
incompatibility triangle, 274-283
variables defined in, 292-293
See also Social protection
Equity threats
global initiative re-establishing, 27-28
middle class social security, 25-26
re-establishing focus of, 26-27
tendencies undermining, 25
vs global social agenda, 24-25
vs globalization, 26
"Europe Agreement," Lomé IV Convention and, 219-220
European Economic Community (EEC)
benefits exportability, 195-196
European integration and, 196-197
exportability and, 193-194
exposed sector employment in, 97
insurance-assistance distinctions, 194-195
nationalism themes, 197
non-contributory benefits, 196
social benefits access, 193
social security allocations, 194
state social security responsibilities, 197
welfare policy reality, 197
worker's rights expanding, 195
European Monetary Union (EMU), 73, 123-124
incompatibility triangle and, 276-277
European poverty
"benchmarking" process and, 370
measurement methods, 370-371
non-financial indicator identifying, 373
poverty rate goal setting, 371-372
social assistance system evaluations, 372-373

European Refugee Fund, 206
European Union Economic Transfers, 75
Euzéby, Alain, 3, 17
Exposed sectors employment
EMU impact, 97
tax burden relationships, 96-97

Family policy
benefit disincentives, 297-298
discussions on, 306-308
family formation transforming, 297
mother's employment, 301-304
Nordic welfare state model, 307
poverty risking, 304-306
responsibility divisions differing, 298-301
social policy importance, 306-307
vs labor force participation, 307-308
work incentives complexity, 308
Family policy responsibilities
aims of, 299
country approaches to, 299-301
economic support systems for, 299
government's role in, 298-299
types of, 299
Farnsworth, Kevin, 47
Financing structures evolution
fiscal pressure growth, 74
growth periods, 72
indirect tax reliance, 73-74
tax receipts of, 73
tax structure reforms, 72
unemployment and inflation periods, 72
Fiscal effects
fiscal constraints tightening, 92
1990's recession, 92-93
oil price crisis, 92
Forssén, Katja, 9
Free movement
conclusions on, 204
EU non-discrimination provisions, 202
financial benefit access, 202
U.S. treatments, 203-204
welfare magnet theory, 201-202

General Agreement on Tariffs and Trade (GATT), 31, 124
Generosity
significance of, 232
unemployment benefits and, 230-231

Germany
  employment problem origins, 260
  labor market rigidities, 263
  low-wage sector subsidizing, 262
  1990's labor market and, 259-260
  political reform inability, 264
  reforms abstaining, 263-264
  "service gap" determining, 261
  social insurance schemes and, 261-
    262
  unification and, 260
  wage inequality levels, 263
  wage policy responsiveness, 262-263
  "welfare without work" cycle, 261
Global policy challenges
  labor markets and, 7-9
  migrants social rights, 6-7
  social cohesion, 9-11
Global social responsibility
  equity rethinking, 28-29
  equity threats, 24-28
  initiative re-thinking for, 27-28
  procedural disagreements, 24
  social concern politics, 23-24
  steps shifting to, 23
Global village issues
  challenges dual in, 2
  challenges past, 1
  globalization and, 2-6
  globalization process effects, 1
  policy challenges for, 6-11
  social security future and, 11-12
Globalization
  alternative conceptualization of, 122-
    123
  as created phenomenon, 32
  East Asia impact from, 4
  economic globalization definitions,
    47
  environment influences, 49
  equity rethinking, 28-29
  equity threats, 24-28
  global social security system, 3-4
  as ideology, 123
  import/export dependence, 120
  incompatibility triangle and, 276
  indicator classes, 120
  international financial regulations,
    122
  labor markets and, 7
  national welfare undermining, 47
  openness levels, 122

pressure mediating in, 50
  regulation uses, 122
  social policy and, 17, 22-24, 48, 120-
    124
  social protection and, 32
  social security and, 1, 3, 28-29
  socially responsible globalization, 18
  stages for, 18
  structural power of, 47-48
  studies findings, 2-3
  trade exposures, 120-122
  vs global economic governance, 48
  welfare state and, 4, 49, 123-124,
    141
  See also International environment;
    Neo-liberal globalization
Globalization cross-national analysis
  analysis results, 128
  financial market openness, 126-127
  globalization indicator testing, 130
  negative hypothesis and, 125
  policy governance issues, 129
  pooled time series analysis, 129
  social transfer expenditures, 125
  trade dependence, 126-127
  unemployment insurance coverage,
    130
  vs welfare state development, 124
Goudswaard, Kees P., 6
Gough, Ian, 4
Guillén, Ana, 4

Habitual residents
  resident rights exclusions, 199
  status as, 213
  test for, 201
  See also immigration policy
Hakovirta, Mia, 9
Hinrichs, Karl, 8
Host state responsibilities
  French pension exporting, 198
  "habitual residence test," 201
  migrants rights, 198
  non-national non-workers depen-
    dence, 200-201
  non-workers and, 199-200
  residence rights exclusions, 199
  social policy perspectives, 197-198
  Veil approach to, 199
  "worker" concept limits, 198-199
  See also Welfare state

Immigration policy
  EU countries and, 212
  social security arrangement, 212
  spouse benefit restrictions, 212
Immobile tax bases
  tax competition and, 95
  See also Mobile tax bases
Income distribution empirical evidence
  income inequality data, 164
  income inequality differences, 164-165
Income distributions
  empirical evidence on, 164-165
  empirical research on, 163
  inequality investigations, 163
  introduction to, 163-164
  Netherlands budget analysis, 177-185
  1980s inequity trends, 165-167
  1990s inequities, 165
  1979-1995 inequity trends, 167-169
  replacement rates, 173-177
  social policy roles, 169-170
  social security transfers, 170-173
  time-series data for, 164
Income inequalities
  approaches to, 165
  aspects of, 166-167
  country rankings in, 165-166
  cross national comparisons, 165-166
  increases in, 169
  inequality ranges, 169
  long-run trends in, 167-169
Income minimums
  conclusions on, 373-374
  empirical evidence on, 360-367
  goals of, 360
  policy implications, 367-373
  social protection objectives and, 359
Income protection
  adequacy needs and, 370
  social security objective deviating, 370
  as strategic poverty element, 369-370
Incompatibility triangle
  approach to, 283
  collective choice types, 276
  data on, 284
  diagram of, 275
  element sacrificing, 275
  EMU integration and, 276
  EMU monetary policy and, 276-277

European social protection and, 274
  globalization effects and, 276
  ideal models using, 275
  incompatibility within, 283
  industrial sector decline, 274-275
  results, 287-291
  single currency enduring, 277
  statistical description of, 284-287
Incompatibility triangle research
  data, 284
  employment vs social spending, 283
  explanatory variables and, 284-285
  first hypotheses, 285-286
  government funding correlation, 286
  regression analysis of, 286
  results on, 287-291
  second hypothesis, 286
  social expenditures correlation, 285
  social transfer correlation, 285
  total employment dependent variable, 283
Indonesia, 61-62
Institutional responsibility matrix, 52
Internal adjustments
  external pressures in, 5
  income inequality increasing, 5-6
  national responses to, 4-5
  OECD constraints, 5
  social transfer programs, 6
International competition tyranny
  Economism and, 39-40
  international social fund needs, 42-43
  social financing values, 40-41
  world social governance needs, 41
International Conference on Social Security Research, 2
International environment
  advanced welfare state actions, 103
  employment protection legislation ranks, 102
  employment rate declining, 101
  fiscal constraints impacts, 103
  wage differentiation, 102
  welfare state changes from, 101
  See also Globalization
International Labour Organization (ILO), 217
  International Social Fund management, 42
  social justice ideal, 40
  social policy development and, 22

world social justice and, 41
International Monetary Fund (IMF), 3,
    22, 62, 123
    developing nature inability, 35
    economic importance of, 48
    global social responsibility concerns,
        23
    social policy development and, 22
    vs Keynesian analyses, 32
International Social Fund
    management of, 42
    purpose of, 42
International social security agreements
    benefits covered, 217-218
    bilateral agreements, 214
    Council of Europe instruments, 220
    countries covered by, 215-216
    history of, 214-215
    multilateral agreements, 218-220
    See also Bilateral agreements

Jamsostek Fund, 55

Korea, East Asia crisis and, 60-61
Koulinsky, Audrey, 8
Kvist, Jon, 9

Labor markets
    de-industrialization links, 8
    "employment miracles" and, 8
    employment as social security right,
        8
    globalization and, 7
    social policy impacts, 9
    structural changes in, 7
    "workfare" and, 8-9
Labor unit costs
    analysis of, 74-75
    social protection vs competitiveness,
        74
Labour Standard Law, 61
Luxembourg Income Study, 163-165

Maastricht Treaty, 73
Mabbett, Deborah, 6
Malaysia, East Asia crisis and, 60-61
Malaysian Employee Provident Fund
    (EPE), 55
Merrien, François-Xavier, 5
Migrant Workers and Overseas Filipi-
    nos Act, 61
Migrants social rights, 198

demographic aging and, 7
    European Union and, 6
    third-country nationals and, 7
Migration
    conclusions on, 220-222
    economic effects of, 191-192
    EEC and, 193-197
    international social security agree-
        ments, 214-228
    migrant rights sources, 211
    state's domestic arrangements, 212-
        214
    See also State's domestic migration
Mobile tax bases
    cross pressures for, 95
    international tax effectiveness, 95
    tax revenue flattening, 94
    See also Immobile tax bases
Mother's employment
    country categories for, 302-303
    decisions with, 301
    employment rates vs employment
        forms, 303
    intensity of, 303
    single vs mother's with partners, 302
    as social phenomenon, 301
    working patterns varieties, 303-304
Multilateral agreements
    EEC regulations, 218
    EU Association and Cooperation
        Agreements, 218-219
    EU-Turkey Agreement, 219

Neo-liberal globalization
    developing countries outcomes, 20-
        21
    "global social responsibilities," 23-
        24
    international organizations ap-
        proaches, 22-23
    outcomes from, 18-19
    scholarly consensus on, 21
    Social policy development, ap-
        proaches to, 22
    vs European welfare states, 19-20
Netherlands
    employment in, 360-362
    unemployment explosion, 266-267
Netherlands budget analysis
    methodology for, 178-180
    results, 180-185
    social security reform, 177-178

de Neubourg, Chris, 10
New Zealand
    economic competitiveness, 149
    pension system privatization, 150
    social policy transfers in, 149
    welfare state foundation changes,
        149-150
Non-tax influences
    regulation impediments, 101
    service employment expansion, 101
    See also Taxes

Obligations
    significance of, 232
    unemployment benefits and, 231
Organization for Economic Co-opera-
    tion and Development (OECD), 123,
    163
    economic importance of, 48
    global social progress undermining,
        25
    internal adjustments within, 5
    poverty in, 364
    social policy development and, 22
    vs Keynesian analyses, 32
    welfare regimes features, 50
    welfare regimes types, 50-51

Philippine Overseas Employment Ad-
    ministration, 61
Policy reform evolutions
    Catholic ideology and, 79-80
    civil society, 79
    EU recommendations and influence,
        79
    expansionary tendencies reasons, 78-
        79
    external pressures origins, 80
Policy transferring
    Dutch unions and, 266
    "miracle" process, 265
    Netherlands "unemployment explo-
        sion," 266-267
    one-to-one basis for, 264-265
    regional differences, 267
    turnaround elements, 265-266
    unemployment feasibility, 265
Poverty
    social expenditures ratios, 338-339
    See also European poverty; Family
    policy; Welfare state poverty
Poverty alleviation

industrial welfare states poverty and,
    334-335
    redistribution impact of, 338-340
    social cohesion and, 10-11
    social policy and, 340-342
    vs poverty incidence, 338
    welfare state efforts, 338
    welfare state impact and, 335-338
Poverty risks
    single-parent families and, 305
    two-parent families and, 306
    vs work incentives, 304-305
Private pension plans, 76-77

Rate replacement
    data relationships, 174-177
    hypothesis supporting, 177
    limitation of, 174
    purpose of, 174
Resource reducing
    enterprise competitive demands, 34
    fiscal and social competition, 33-34
    inflation combating, 34
Richez-Battesti, Nadine, 8
Risk management
    "basic risk" defined, 318
    as coping problem, 318
    market solution non-availability, 320
    solution approaches, 318
    welfare pentagon options, 318-320
    See also Social management of risks
Risks
    criteria of, 323-324
    effect categories, 324
    as main need unsatisfying, 323
    option availability, 325
    social cohesion and, 10
    theoretical framework summarizing,
        325
    types of, 325
Roberts, Simon, 7

Safety net
    minimum income and poverty rela-
        tionships, 344
    minimum income schemes, 343
    poverty alleviation schemes, 342-
        343
    research limits, 343-344
    social assistance overlapping, 344
    social assistance schemes, 343
    See also Welfare state

Safety net effects
    adequacy, 346-352
    eligibility, 346
    take-up, 352-354
Safety net holes
    conclusions on, 354-355
    modern welfare states and, 334
    poverty alleviation, 334-340
    poverty persistence, 333-334
    safety net effects, 344-354
    social problem assessing, 340-344
    welfare state effectiveness, 334
Safety net poverty alleviation
    countries characterized by, 346
    effectiveness conditions, 345-346
    failure reasons, 344-345
    social assistance schemes, 345
Sala, Martinez, case decision, 200-201
Scharpf, Fritz W., 5, 17
Sheltered sectors employment
    private price rises, 97-99
    tax type differences, 99-101
    taxation levels effects, 97
Simplistic Dyad
    analytical framework problems, 314
    individual behavior modeling, 315-316
    non-market wealth production, 314-315
    social protection policies, 315
    welfare production and, 314
Social adjustments
    conclusions on, 155-157
    country comparisons, 141-142, 153-155
    country differences, 143-146
    globalization vs welfare state declining, 141
    hypotheses evaluation, 143
    ideology influence, 155-156
    international economic variables, 142-143
    policy recommendations, 142, 149-151
    social philosophy destruction, 155
    theoretical questions in, 146-149
    trade internationalization impact, 155
Social adjustments conclusions
    change influences, 154
    external factors, 153
    radical reforms, 153

reforms nature variables, 154-155
Social citizenship
    asylum-seekers, 193, 204-207
    conclusions on, 207-209
    Europe's legal position on, 193
    free movement implications, 201-204
    host state responsibilities, 197-201
    migration in EEC, 193-197
    migration economic effects, 191-192
    non-nationals and, 192-193
    welfare sovereignty, 192
Social cohesion
    goals in, 9-10
    momentum in, 10
    poverty alleviation, 10-11
    risk protection, 10
Social dumping
    age of, 68
    competitiveness factors, 69-70
    conclusions on, 78
    defined, 67
    economic integration vs social protection, 69
    income guarantee policies, 77
    labor market policies, 77-78
    national competitiveness and, 67
    private pension plans, 76-77
    social policies harmonization, 69
    social policy reform results, 76
    as social protection diminishing, 70
    Southern European model, 75-76
    spending level increases, 75
    "upward harmonization" principle, 68
    vs catching up concept, 68
Social financing
    social justice and, 40-41
    social protection inadequacies, 40
Social management of risks, 322
    coping strategies, 328
    mitigating strategies, 327-328
    policy option analysis, 326
    policy options and, 328-329
    preventive strategies, 327
    social protection policy designing, 326-327
    See also Risk management social policy
Social policy
    causal issues, 134
    empirical issues in, 133-134

existing studies limitations, 340-342
family policy importance, 306-307
future research and, 134-136
globalization and, 17, 22-24, 48
host state responsibilities, 197-198
ILO and, 22
income distributions, 169-170
need linking with, 321
poverty alleviation and, 340-342
safety net focusing, 342-344
social dumping and, 69, 76
social management of risks and, 322
social transfer effectiveness, 342
Social policy impacts
conclusions on, 133-136
cross-national analysis methods, 124-133
data appendix for, 136
globalization measures, 120-124
labor market and, 9
prior investigations on, 118-120
welfare state future, 117
Social policy investigations
benefit level changes, 119
future income uncertainty, 119
institutionalize theory on, 119-120
research disagreements on, 120
second-order hypotheses, 118-119
world polity integration trends, 118
Social policy roles
change causes, 169-170
country-ordering dissimilarity, 170
social policy, income inequality coinciding, 169
straightforward approach in, 170-173
Social protection
free trade trends, 32-33
globalization and, 32
income minimums and, 359
incompatibility triangle and, 274
international trade liberalization, 33
needs increasing in, 35-36
neo-liberal thinking, 32
resource reducing, 33-34
social dumping, 69-70
social management of risks, 326-327
See also Employment vs social protection
Social protection downsizing
international context and, 147-148
national dimension disappearing,
148

policy reorientation factors, 148-149
preferences transformations, 146-
147
short-term capital movement vulnerabilities, 147
Social protection expenditures
country wealth and, 70-72
growth of, 70
Social protection financing
difficulties in, 32-36
as employment obstacles, 31, 36-39
international competition tyranny,
39-43
problem types, 31-32
Social protection needs
economic insecurity vulnerabilities,
35-36
globalization effects, 35
globalization effects on, 36
unskilled labor and, 35
Social protection policy
defined, 313, 325
See also Social management of risks
Social rights. See Migrant social rights
Social risk management
basic vs main needs, 320-323
conclusions on, 329-330
risk and, 323-325
risk management, 318-320
risk social management, 326-329
simplistic dyad, 314-316
social protection and, 313
social welfare and, 313
society institutions for, 313
welfare pentagon, 316-318
Social security
EEC allocations for, 194
financing of, 3
future of, 11-12
globalization interlocking with, 1
private pension plans and, 76-77
state responsibilities for, 197
Social security contributions
capital for labor substitutions, 38
international competition impact, 39
labor costs and, 38
manpower-based enterprises, 38-39
problems in, 37
unemployment and, 37-39
unskilled workers unemployment, 39
Social security equity
administrators challenges, 29

challenges to, 28
globalization's challenges, 28-29
Social security future
coverage improving, 11
determining of, 12
"global village" and, 11
labor market performance, 11
welfare state recalibration, 11-12
Social security transfers
expenditure role changes, 171
income inequality vs safety net expansions, 171
OECD programs and, 6
plotting of, 171-172
system comparing, 170-171
Social welfare, defined, 313
Southern European welfare states
attention on, 67
policy patterns in, 75-78
policy reform interpreting, 78-80
social dumping in, 67-70
welfare effort assessing, 70-75
State's domestic migration
asylum-seekers and, 213-214
benefit entitlement effects, 212-213
immigration policies effects, 212
Sweden
economic competitiveness in, 150
1980's economic crisis, 150-151
reforms in, 151
Switzerland
policy transformation reasons, 152
unemployment reforms, 152

Take-up
factors relevant, 352-354
as governing element, 352
public policies and, 352
Taxes
compulsory contribution exaggerations, 36-37
contribution vulnerability of, 105
as employment obstacle, 36-37
exposed sector employment and, 96-97
immobile bases of, 94-95
psychological and political effects of, 37
See also Financial structure evolving; Non-tax influencing; Sheltered sector employment; Social financing; Social protection financing

Thailand, East Asia crisis and, 60-61
Triangle of Incompatibility. See Incompatibility triangle

Unemployment combating
conclusions on, 267-268
"economic miracle" growth, 247
"employment miracle" learning, 248-250
"employment miracle" routes, 255-259
employment performances successes, 250-255
Germany and, 259-167
policy sharing approaches, 248
small states open economies, 248
social security and, 37-39
See also Employment performance; Obligations
Unemployment insurance
conclusions on, 242
European policy making and, 227-228
methods and materials, 228-232
models emerging for, 237-242
political rhetoric effects, 228
role changes in, 232-237
social rights vs obligations, 228
Unemployment insurance methods
concepts related to, 229-231
investigation scope in, 229
social rights citizenship, 228-229
verbal label for, 231-232
Unemployment insurance models
dominant political ideologies and, 239
Liberal welfare state model, 238-239
membership scores in, 241
model examples of, 239
Old Social Democratic model, 240
Social Democratic state model, 238, 240-242
understanding of, 237-238
Unemployment insurance rights
countries actions in, 233-237
membership scores, 232-233
United Nations Children's Fund (UNICEF), social policy development and, 22
United States
free movement in, 203-204
vs European employment approaches, 282

United States Federal Reserve, economic importance of, 48
United States Treasury, economic importance of, 48
Universal Declaration of Human Rights, 40
"Upward harmonization," concept, 68

Van den Bosch, Karel, 10
Vulnerabilities
    Anglo-Saxon countries, 110-111
    continental countries, 111-113
    country distinction types, 103
    employment level differences, 106-108
    means testing approaches, 104
    resources claimed differences, 106
    Scandinavian countries, 108-109
    taxes contributions, 105
    welfare function distinctions, 103
    welfare state performance indicators, 107

Welfare effort assessing
    EU economic transfers, 75
    financial structures evaluation, 72-72
    social protecting expenditures, 70-72
    unit labor costs, 74-75
Welfare Magnet Theory, 201-204
Welfare mix
    community, 56
    components of extending, 52
    components of, 50
    educational role in, 54
    family and, 56-57
    health expenditures, 54-55
    international components of, 57
    market and, 55-56
    South policy analysis, 51-52
    state social policies, 53-54
    summary of, 57
Welfare outcomes, 58
Welfare pentagon
    diagram of, 317
    membership institutions, 316
    public authorities role, 316
    social welfare analysis framework, 316-317
    space as social in, 317-318
Welfare regimes
    countries in, 52
    features of, 50

    regimes types, 50-51
    South social policy analysis, 51-52
Welfare sovereignty, 192
Welfare state
    advanced capitalist characteristics, 85
    borrowing, 94
    challenges to, 89-93
    conclusions on, 114-115
    constraints on, 86-89
    economic viability defenses, 114
    EEC policy realities, 197
    EMU vulnerabilities, 114-115
    exposed sectors employment impact, 96-97
    future of, 117
    globalization and, 4, 49, 123-124, 141
    immobile tax bases, 95
    influences on, 101-103
    international environment and, 101
    international market integration, 86
    mobile tax bases, 94-95
    poverty alleviation efforts, 335-338
    shelter sectors employment impact, 97-101
    stagflation crisis, 85-86
    vulnerability differences, 103-113
    welfare adjustment ability, 114
    See also Host state responsibilities; Safety net
Welfare state challenges
    employment effects, 89-92
    fiscal effects, 92-93
Welfare state poverty
    alternative approaches to, 335-337
    effectiveness of, 337
    effort and reduction of, 338-340
    high social spending countries, 340
    industrialized states and, 334-335
    international variations in, 335
    populations living in, 335-336
    poverty alleviation patterns, 340
    poverty rate impacts, 337
    transfer approaches, 337-338
Win-work strategy
    "active welfare state" alternatives, 368
    educational systems inadequacies, 368
    employer vs worker perspectives, 368

low skilled job market and, 367
public social expenditure relationships, 368-369
simplistic approaches to, 367-368
Women
poverty risks, 306
See also Family policy; Mother's employment
Worker's rights
ECJ expansion of, 195
social security and, 8
Workfare, 8-9
World Bank, 3, 62
developing nature inability, 35
economic importance of, 48
global social progress undermining,
25

global social responsibility concerns,
23
social policy development and, 22
vs Keynesian analyses, 32
vs social rights, 23
World social governance
concept of, 41
ILO vs WTO on, 41
World Trade Organization (WTO), 23,
124
economic importance of, 48
global social progress undermining,
25
vs Keynesian analyses, 32
world social justice and, 41